YOU DECIDE!

Current Debates in Introductory Philosophy

BRUCE N. WALLER

Youngstown State University

PEARSON
Longman

New York   Boston   San Francisco
London   Toronto   Sydney   Tokyo   Singapore   Madrid
Mexico City   Munich   Paris   Cape Town   Hong Kong   Montreal

Editor-in-Chief: Eric Stano
Senior Marketing Manager: Ann Stypuloski
Production Cordinator: Scarlett Lindsay
Project Coordination and Electronic Page Makeup: Lorraine Patsco
Cover Designer/Manager: John Callahan
Manufacturing Manager: Mary Fischer
Cover Image: © Stock Illustration Source/Getty Images, Inc.
Printer and Binder: Courier/Stoughton
Cover Printer: Courier/Stoughton

Library of Congress Cataloging-in-Publication Data

Current debates in introductory philosophy / [edited by] Bruce N. Waller.
    p. cm. -- (You decide!)
  ISBN 0-321-43956-2
  1. Philosophy--Introductions. I. Waller, Bruce N., 1946-
  BD21.C88 2007
  100--dc22

                    2006038397

Visit us at www.ablongman.com

ISBN 0-321-43956-2

1 2 3 4 5 6 7 8 9 10–CRS–09 08 07 06

CONTENTS

5. ARE ALL MY HOPES AND THOUGHTS ULTIMATELY JUST ELECTROCHEMICAL BRAIN IMPULSES? 68

6. WHO AM I? 88

10. ARE THERE OBJECTIVE ETHICAL TRUTHS?   172

11. IS ETHICS BASED ON A SOCIAL CONTRACT?   196

Ethical Life (New York: HarperCollins, 2000) is a very readable and engaging collection of his essays.

SOURCE: "Ethics Beyond Species and Beyond Instincts: A Response to Richard Posner," from Cass R. Sunstein and Martha C. Nussbaum, Editors, *Animal Rights* (New York: Oxford University Press, 2004): 78–92 (copyright by Cambridge University Press).

PREFACE

This book is designed to introduce issues and debates in contemporary philosophy. Though the topics have been arranged in a standard order for an introductory philosophy course of the undergraduate level, readers could start anywhere and take the topics in any preferred order. Each pair of essays is presented as a stand alone topic, and the introduction to each topic should provide adequate background for exploring that issue through the readings. The book could be used as the primary text in an introduction to contemporary issues in philosophy course, or as the primary text for an introduction to philosophy focusing on key issues and major figures in contemporary philosophical thought. The book could also serve as a supplementary introductory text, giving students an opportunity to explore important current ideas on standard philosophical questions. For example, students might study Descartes' writings on skepticism, followed by an examination of how contemporary philosophers attempt to deal with some of the same issues; or Hobbes' version of social contract theory together with the contemporary debate on social contract ethics; or Kant's account of rationalist ethics, compared with the contemporary perspectives of Williams and Nagel.

Many people have been very generous with their help in completing this book. My colleagues at the Department of Philosophy and Religious Studies at Youngstown State University are at the top of that list, as well as many friends from other departments at YSU. Our departmental secretary, Joan Bevan, solves every problem that arises, prevents even more problems than she solves, and makes it all look easy. Our student assistants, Justina Rachella and Hannah Detec, are invariably helpful and unfailingly cheerful. The many superb librarians at YSU have been amazingly efficient in finding material—books, articles, Web sites—and also wonderfully forgiving when I forget to return material. And my students at YSU—with their genuine curiosity, challenging questions, and interesting perspectives—make my teaching experiences a profound pleasure and a constant source of new ideas.

Many other friends have helped in a wide variety of ways; thanks to Fred Alexander, Nawal Ammar, Allen Belsheim, Richard Double, Bryan Hilliard, Jerry Lanier, Luke Lucas, Phil Pendleton, Steve Peck, Chris and Jack Raver, Robyn Repko, and Lia Ruttan.

Special thanks for advice, encouragement, and gentle prodding supplied by my editor at Longman, Eric Stano; and to the editors of this series, Ted Knight and Jeff Hahn.

My greatest debt is to my family for their constant love, support, and encouragement: to my wife, Mary; to my sons, Russell and Adam; and to Bruno, the wonder dog.

Finally, thanks to the following reviewers who gave valuable recommendations after reading earlier drafts:

Kent Baldner, Western Michigan University; Laurence Carlin, University of Wisconsin—Oshkosh; Claudia Close, Cabrillo College; Richard Greene, Weber State University; Christina Huggins, Florida State University; William Jamison, University of Alaska—Anchorage; Hye-Kyung Kim, University of Wisconsin—Green Bay; John Messerly, Austin Community College; Walter Ott, Virginia Tech; James Rovira, Rollins College; Charles Wrenn, University of Alabama; David Yount, Mesa Community College

Bruce N. Waller
November 15, 2006

INTRODUCTION

This book designed to introduce the reader to some of the central topics and issues of contemporary philosophical dispute; but it does much more than merely introduce. The debates are lively, and the essays have been chosen both for the quality and inventiveness of their arguments as well as for the engaging style of their authors. These debates take on serious issues and represent carefully developed positions, tested and tried against vigorous opposing arguments. Philosophy lives in the give and take of tough argument, rather than in static finished conclusions; and contemporary philosophy is better understood by examining serious philosophical arguments than by merely noting conclusions.

The debates start with a recent exchange on an ancient philosophical question: the existence of God. The next debate concerns the relation between science and religion. Debates 3 and 4 focus on epistemological issues, examining questions about the nature, justification, and limits of knowledge. The next two debates concern mind, consciousness, and personal identity, followed by debates over free will and moral responsibility. Debates concerning the nature of ethics make up the next section, and the book ends with debates on some specific ethical issues and examination of questions in political philosophy. The issues have important connections, and conclusions about one question may well influence the position taken on another. However, each debate is self-contained, and readers could easily start at any point, and arrange the order to suit themselves.

Philosophy at its best has always responded to new developments in the sciences and in other areas of research, and endeavored to understand the further implications of recent discoveries: Descartes taking stock of the Copernican Revolution in astronomy; Hume considering the implications of Newtonian physics; James and Dewey examining the impact of Darwinian natural selection. The contemporary philosophical issues debated here have been influenced by a variety of contemporary scientific findings, including research in situationist psychology, neuropsychology, artificial intelligence, quantum mechanics, genetics, and anthropology. Although many of the debates examine issues with a long history, they are all made fresh and original by consideration of new research and ongoing changes. Some of the questions debated by contemporary philosophers—the existence of God, the challenge of skepticism, the role of reason in ethics, the nature of free will—may be old, but the perspectives and arguments are strikingly original.

The essays in this book contain strong *arguments*. In many debates the arguments pit one writer directly against the other, and in every case the writers hold strong views and have deep disagreements. The authors of the essays *argue* for the views they favor, presenting the best reasons they can develop in favor of their own views and in criticism of opposing positions. But although the debates are vigorous and intense, the writers scrupulously avoid argumentative *fallacies*. A *fallacy* is simply a common argument error or deception. Fallacies come in a wide variety. For example, the *irrelevant reason* fallacy (also known as the *red herring* fallacy) is a common ploy. Suppose you are serving on a jury, and the defendant in the case has been charged with a brutal murder. In this case, the defendant is claiming he is not guilty because he had absolutely nothing to do with the crime: the defense claims that this is a case of mistaken identity, the police have charged the wrong man with the crime, and the defendant was nowhere around the crime scene and had no connection to this brutal murder. In this case, the *question* is whether the prosecutor can offer strong and convincing evidence that the defendant really is the person who committed the crime. But suppose the prosecution attorney makes this closing argument: "Ladies and gentlemen of the jury, this was a brutal, cruel, vicious murder; the victim died from a savage beating, and was shown no mercy. And so I am asking that you find the defendant *guilty* of murder in the first degree." The prosecutor has just paraded an irrelevant reason—a "red herring"—before the jury box. True, this *was* a brutal, cruel murder; but that's not the relevant issue. The question is not whether the murder was vicious, but whether the defendant did it. It's a terrible and deeply disturbing fact that a vicious murder was committed; but the question the jury must settle is whether there is solid proof that the vicious murder was committed by *this defendant*, and the fact that the murder was vicious is *irrelevant* to that question. But if the jury is not very careful, they will become so incensed by the viciousness of the murder that they will forget that the real question is something else altogether.

The fallacy of irrelevant reason is tricky, and it is important not to be fooled by it. But among the many fallacies, there are two that cause special problems when dealing with intense debates (such as those found in this book). First is the *ad hominem* fallacy. The ad hominem fallacy is the fallacy of trying to refute an argument by attacking the *source* of that argument. When you are examining an *argument*, the *source* of the argument is irrelevant. The argument has to stand or fall on its own merits, and it doesn't matter whether the *arguer* is wicked or virtuous, sincere or hypocritical, drunk or sober. Suppose I give you an *argument* for why you should *always* wear your seat belt when driving. My argument may be good or bad, but you must evaluate the quality of the argument by looking at the argument itself, *not* at the *source* of the argument. You have evaluated my argument for always wearing a seatbelt, and you conclude that it's a strong argument. Now you see me driving home, and I'm *not* wearing my seatbelt. That might well change your opinion of *me*: you might conclude that I'm a sleazy hypocrite. But it should not change your evaluation of my *argument*: my argument is still exactly the same argument, whether I live up to the position I advocate or not. Suppose you discover that the person you thought was me was actually my twin brother, who *never* wears his seat belt, though I *always* wear my seat belt. That won't suddenly *redeem* my argument: my argument never changed. Or suppose you discover that I'm being paid megabucks by the insurance industry for giving this argument in favor of wearing seat belts, in hopes that they will save money on insurance payments to accident victims. Again, that might change your evaluation of *me*: I'm not a pure generous spirit offering an argument simply out of my concern for potential victims of automobile injury; instead I'm a paid gun, offering arguments for hire to the highest bidder. But whether my motives in giving the argument are pure and altruistic or selfish and mercenary, the *argument* remains exactly the same argument. If you assert that my *argument* must be bad because I'm bad—I'm a hypocrite, or greedy, or stupid, or selfish—then you are committing the *ad hominem fallacy*. And that sort of personal attack on an arguer not only has nothing to do with the real quality of the argument; it also undercuts any attempt at serious debate and discussion. Personal attacks against your argument opponent may be fun, but they are also fallacious, and the shrill tone of ad hominem attacks soon drowns out rational discussion.

Along with the ad hominem fallacy, there is a second nasty fallacy that undercuts rational debate: the *strawman* fallacy. The strawman fallacy occurs when someone *distorts* or *misrepresents* an opposing position or argument, and then claims a cheap "victory" by refuting that *strawman* position rather than the real position. It's easier to knock over a strawman than a real man, and it's easier to refute a strawman distortion than a genuine position; but sadly, such strawman distortions are common practice. Consider the debate over prayer in school. *Opponents* of school prayer sometimes claim that those who *favor* school prayer want to require every child to join in a Christian prayer every morning at school. That's a *strawman* distortion. Most who favor school prayer favor a nondenominational prayer, or perhaps a moment of silence when students could pray if they wish; and they would not *require* that any students participate. The advocates of school prayer may be right or may be wrong, but you cannot *refute* their position by attacking a more extreme position (every child should be required to recite a Christian prayer) that they do not hold; and you will never convince people that their views are wrong by critiquing distortions of their views. Of course the strawman fallacy cuts both ways: those who advocate school prayer sometimes claim that *opponents* of school prayer want to ban all mention of religion in school and ban all prayers by school children. That's also a strawman fallacy: those who oppose prayer in school oppose the formal institutional use of prayer in public schools (such as a prayer led by a teacher before class, or a prayer broadcast throughout the school over the intercom). If a student wishes to whisper a quiet prayer during a geometry exam, that's fine; and if two or three students want to hold hands and briefly pray as they move between classes or at their lunch table, that's their own business. And if a history teacher wants to describe the religious views of the Iroquois Confederation or the New England Puritans or the Protestant Reformation, that is obviously a legitimate and important part of history. But—say the opponents of school prayer—neither public schools nor public school teachers should abuse their positions of authority by attempting to promote a particular religious view. The question of school prayer is an important issue, and it deserves serious rational discussion. But if both sides insist on misrepresenting the views of their opponents, then genuine rational discussion can't even get started.

It's always tempting to take cheap ad hominem shots at those who champion opposing views, and it's also tempting to try to win a hollow strawman victory by distorting opposing positions. Both fallacies are standard practice in political debate, and will probably remain so until citizens demand that our politicians behave rationally. But if you are interested in genuine exploration of controversial questions—that is, if you are willing to subject your *own* views to rational criticism, and you want a real chance of convincing your opponent— then strawman and ad hominem fallacies are an indulgence you can't afford.

LINKING CONTEMPORARY DEBATES WITH
THE PHILOSOPHICAL TRADITION

Though these debates can be used in many combinations, the following are some suggestions for linking the material with standard topics examined in many introductions to philosophy.

Existence of God: Debates 1 and 2 are both relevant, with debate 1 taking a contemporary look at some traditional arguments for and against the existence of God, including the design argument, the cosmological argument, and the problem of evil.

Theory of Knowledge: The issue of skepticism is examined in debates 3 and 4; the nature of genuine knowledge is examined in 3 and 4; foundationalism is debated in 3; debate 4 is particularly relevant on the relation between the knower and what is known; and debate 2 concerns claims of special religious knowledge.

Philosophy of Mind: Debates 5 and 6 focus on issues in the philosophy of mind, with debate 6 examining the question of personal identity, and debate 5 taking a contemporary look at the question of mind/body relation.

Free Will: Debates 7 and 8 examine determinism; debates 7, 8, and 9 cover various accounts of free will, particularly the compatibilist and the libertarian views, but also the hard determinism position; and debate 9 focuses on moral responsibility, an issue also discussed in debate 8.

Ethical Theory: The basic question of ethical objectivity is debated in 10; Kantian ethics is examined in debate 10, and also discussed in debate 7; social contract ethics is covered in debate 11, and debate 13 is also relevant for that issue; virtue ethics is considered in debates 12 and 15; utilitarianism is discussed in debate 13, and briefly in 14; feminist/care ethics is examined in debate 12; moral responsibility is debated in 9.

Ethical Issues: Debate 13 focuses on animal rights; the issue of state/community promotion of values is examined in debate 14; patriotism is debated in 15; the obligation to aid those outside our own country is debated in 16; moral responsibility and just deserts (including the problem of punishment) is examined in debate 9.

Political Philosophy: Social contract theory is examined in debate 11; the relation of citizens to the state is explored in debates 15 and 16; debate 14 focuses on the conflicts among liberal, conservative, and communitarian political philosophies.

1   DOES GOD EXIST?

There Are Good Reasons to Believe That God Exists

ADVOCATE: William Lane Craig, Research Professor of Philosophy, Talbot School of Theology; author of *God, Time, and Eternity* (Kluwer, 2001).

SOURCE: *Does God Exist? The Craig-Flew Debate* (Burlington, Vt.: Ashgate, 2003), pp. 19–24; from a debate held at the University of Wisconsin, February 18, 1998.

There Are No Good Reasons to Believe in the Existence of God

ADVOCATE: Antony Flew, Emeritus Professor of Philosophy, University of Reading, England. Flew has taught at many universities, including University of Keele, University of Aberdeen, and York University; he is the author of *God and Philosophy* (London: Hutchinson, 1966), *The Logic of Mortality* (Blackwell, 1987), and *Atheistic Humanism* (Buffalo: Prometheus, 1993). A prominent and long-term advocate of atheism, more recently Flew has favored something closer to deism (still rejecting any sort of personal God who intervenes in the workings of the world).

SOURCE: *Does God Exist? The Craig-Flew Debate* (Burlington, Vt.: Ashgate, 2003), pp. 24–27; from a debate held at the University of Wisconsin, February 18, 1998.

Perhaps the first philosophical question that crossed your mind was: Is there a God? And that may well have been the first philosophical question posed by humankind. Actually, the earliest philosophical questions probably had a different form: Are there any gods? And that brings up a question prior to the question of whether God exists: the question of what *concept* of God we are considering. The Judeo-Christian-Muslim conception of God draws on a common heritage, and so it is hardly surprising that Jews, Muslims, and Christians share the view of God as a powerful Creator Who actively intervenes in His creation. Aristotle had a very different idea of God. Though the Christian church has long struggled to marry the Hebraic and the Aristotelian views, it has never been a very happy marriage. The Hebraic God is not only the creator of the world, but also intervenes on a regular basis: sending plagues on the Egyptians, parting the Red Sea, halting the Sun in the sky (so that Joshua could have more daylight to smite his enemies), dictating commandments to Moses, destroying cities with fire. The Aristotelian God, in stark contrast, is not a creator God, much less an intervener. Aristotle's God is absolutely and eternally perfect, and therefore cannot change: if God changed, that would imply that God was once imperfect and improved to perfection, or was perfect but has now become less than perfect. Nor can God create anything, for that would imply God is lacking something. And certainly Aristotle's perfect God cannot change His mind, nor become angry. But the Hebrew God becomes so enraged at the children of Israel after they worship the golden calf that He resolves to kill them all; but then, under Moses' persuasion, changes His mind and decides to kill only a few thousand. Spinoza, the great Dutch philosopher of the 17th Century, focused on the *infinite* attributes of God and concluded that there could be *nothing* outside of God: everything in the cosmos must be a part of the one God. The American philosopher, William James, was so troubled by the problem of evil that he concluded God must not be infinitely powerful but is instead a *strong* but not omnipotent force for good, and that human efforts may therefore be a deciding factor in whether good or evil ultimately triumphs. Thus before plunging headlong into debates over the existence of God, it is important to be clear on what concept of God is under discussion.

As the debate is usually framed in philosophy, the question is really one of whether there is any supernatural power or force beyond the natural world; or another way of asking the question: if we had a *complete* science of the natural world (including biology and astronomy and physics and psychology) would there be anything left that is not covered? In the debate between Craig and Flew, that question is examined, and then the debate gets more specific: is there good reason to believe in a very specific God, namely the Judeo-Christian God as described in the Bible. If you answer yes to that question, you will also believe in God; but obviously you might believe in God without believing in that specific account of God.

Thomas Aquinas, the 13th Century Catholic theologian, is the classic source for arguments for the existence of God, including this early version of the perennially popular design argument:

> We see that things which lack knowledge, such as natural bodies, act for an end, and this is evident from their acting always, or nearly always, in the same way, so as to obtain the best result. Hence it is plain that they achieve their end, not fortuitously, but designedly. Now whatever lacks knowledge cannot move toward an end, unless it be directed by some being endowed with knowledge and intelligence; as the arrow is directed by the archer. Therefore some intelligent being exists by whom all natural things are directed to their end; and this being we call God.

Craig's first two arguments are traditional arguments for the existence of God: the *cosmological* argument, that God must exist in order to explain the origins of the universe; and second, the *design* (or *teleological*) argument, that God must exist to account for the complex order we observe in the world. His third argument concerning the existence of objective values, and the fourth argument based on Biblical testimony regarding the resurrection of Jesus, are less common.

The most prominent argument against the existence of God is the problem of evil. It is a tough argument for traditional monotheistic views to handle—God is omniscient, and knows there is massive suffering and evil; God is omnipotent, and has the means to stop it; and God is omnibenevolent and loving, so why doesn't God do something about it?—but other views of God are not so severely challenged by the problem of evil. As noted earlier, William James favored a "meliorist" religion, in which God does His best, and struggles on the side of good, but the forces of evil are powerful and God is not *all* powerful, so evil sometimes wins; and since the contest is a close one, James insists that human efforts can tip the scales toward the triumph of righteousness or the victory for evil.

Flew brings up the problem of hell—of eternal torture of the damned—as an argument against belief. This issue is rarely discussed in such debates, since the philosophical debate concerning the existence of God is usually framed in more abstract terms: the question is not whether God as depicted by Muslim or Jewish or Christian theology exists, but whether some all-powerful Being or "Godly force" exists. But if the question concerns the existence of some specific God—a God Who inflicts eternal torture on nonbelievers—then the problem of how to square this view with our basic sense of fairness and justice becomes an important issue. Indeed, the issue becomes even more problematic if we add "predestination" to the mix; and as Martin Luther makes clear, the Bible certainly seems to favor the predestination of souls: some are chosen by God, and others are damned, and there is nothing whatsoever we can do about it, and God's reasons for this are far beyond our puny understanding: "It is not of man that chooseth, but of God that calleth." Even if one rejects predestination (as Craig does) the problem of *eternal* punishment still looms large: it seems out of all proportion to the offenses of even the worst humans. John Hick, a Christian theologian, finds the problem so intractable that he argues for the redemption of souls after death: souls are not eternally damned, but continue to develop until they reach a state of grace.

POINTS TO PONDER

➤ In a criminal trial, the prosecution bears the burden of proof; that is, the prosecution must prove that the defendant is guilty, rather than the defendant having to prove innocence. In the debate over the existence of God, which side has the burden of proof?

➤ *Suppose* that we could *reason* our way to objective moral values (as Kant believed we could), *or* that we know objective moral values through basic *intuition* of their truth (as W. D. Ross claimed). Would either or both of those results undermine Craig's third argument?

➤ In *God's Trombones*, the poet James Weldon Johnson offers a poetic account of the Hebraic creation story; and in the opening scene, God says: "I'm lonely; I'll make me a world." It's charming poetry, but it raises thorny theological quandaries. If God is perfect and complete, then God could hardly be *lonely*; but even if we reject the description of God as lonely, there remains the question of *why* a perfect and perfectly self-sufficient God would create anything. Craig's first argument for the existence of God is that God is the most plausible answer to the question of how the universe came into existence. Could an infinite and self-sufficient God be a plausible candidate for Creator of the universe?

➤ One of the most famous arguments for *belief* in God was developed by the 17th Century French philosopher and mathematician, Blaise Pascal. Called *Pascal's Wager*, the argument goes like this: You must choose whether to believe or not to believe in God (refusing to make a decision means that you can never believe, so the choice is forced upon you). If you *believe* and you're right, you gain eternal reward; if you believe and you're wrong, your life ends with death, and you've lost nothing by believing, and perhaps you lived a more hopeful and happier life by believing. If you do *not* believe, and you're right, then you die and your life ends, and your belief hasn't gained you any great advantage. But if you do *not* believe and you're *wrong*, you suffer eternal punishment. Therefore, you get much better odds by believing: belief is a much better wager than nonbelief. So it makes sense to believe in God: belief is your best bet. That's not really an argument that God exists; rather, it's an argument for why it is better to *believe* that God exists. Is that a good argument for belief in God?

There Are Good Reasons to Believe That God Exists

WILLIAM LANE CRAIG

Are there good reasons to think that God exists? I am going to present five reasons why I think theism is more plausibly true than atheism....These reasons are independent of one another, and, taken together, they constitute a powerful cumulative case for the existence of God.

I. THE ORIGIN OF THE UNIVERSE

Have you ever asked yourself where the universe came from? Why anything at all exists instead of just nothing? Typically, atheists have said that the universe is just eternal and uncaused. As Russell remarked to Copleston: "The universe is just there and that's all." But is that really all? If the universe never began to exist, then that means that the number of events in the past history of the universe is infinite. But mathematicians recognize that the existence of an actually infinite number of things leads to self-contradictions. For example, what is infinity minus infinity? Well, mathematically you get self-contradictory answers. This shows that infinity is just an idea in your mind, not something that exists in reality. David Hilbert, perhaps the greatest mathematician of this century, states, "The infinite is nowhere to be found in reality. It neither exists in nature nor provides a legitimate basis for rational thought....The role that remains

for the infinite to play is solely that of an idea." But that entails that since past events are not just ideas but are real, the number of past events must be finite. Therefore, the series of past events can't go back forever. Rather, the universe must have begun to exist.

This conclusion has been confirmed by remarkable discoveries in astronomy and astrophysics. The astrophysical evidence indicates that the universe began to exist in a great explosion called the "Big Bang" 15 billion years ago. Physical space and time were created in that event, as well as all the matter and energy in the universe. Therefore, as the Cambridge astronomer Fred Hoyle points out, the Big Bang theory requires the creation of the universe from nothing. This is because as you go back in time, you reach a point at which, in Hoyle's words, "The universe was shrunk down to nothing at all." Thus the Big Bang model requires that the universe began to exist and was created out of nothing.

Now, this tends to be very awkward for the atheist for, as Anthony Kenny of Oxford University urges, "A proponent of the [Big Bang] theory, at least if he is an atheist, must believe that...the universe came from nothing and by nothing." But surely that doesn't make sense? Out of nothing,

nothing comes. So why does the universe exist instead of just nothing? Where did it come from? There must have been a cause which brought the universe into being.

We can summarize our argument thus far as follows:

1 Whatever begins to exist has a cause.
2 The universe began to exist.
3 Therefore, the universe has a cause.

Now from the very nature of the case, as the cause of space and time, this cause must be an uncaused, timeless, changeless and immaterial being of unimaginable power which created the universe. Moreover, I would argue, it must also be personal. For how else could a timeless cause give rise to a temporal effect like the universe? If the cause were an impersonal set of necessary and sufficient conditions, then the cause could never exist without the effect. If the cause were timelessly present, then the effect would be timelessly present as well. The only way for the cause to be timeless and for the effect to begin to exist in time is for the cause to be a personal agent who freely chooses to create an effect in time without any prior determining conditions. Thus, we are brought, not merely to a transcendent cause of the universe, but to its personal creator.

Isn't it incredible that the Big Bang theory thus confirms what the Christian theist has always believed—that "In the beginning God created the heavens and the earth"? Now I simply put it to you: which do you think makes more sense— that the theist is right, or that the universe just "popped" into being, uncaused, out of nothing? I, at least, don't have any trouble assessing these alternatives.

II. THE COMPLEX ORDER IN THE UNIVERSE

During the last 30 years scientists have discovered that the existence of intelligent life depends on a delicate and complex balance of initial conditions simply given in the Big Bang itself. We now know that life-*prohibiting* universes are vastly more probable than any life-*permitting* universe like ours. How much more probably? Well, the answer is that the chances that the universe should be life-permitting are so infinitesimal as to be incomprehensible and incalculable. For example, Stephen Hawking has estimated that if the rate of the universe's expansion one second after the Big Bang had been smaller by even one part in a hundred thousand million million, the universe would have recollapsed into a hot fireball. P.C.W. Davies has calculated that the odds against the initial conditions being suitable for later star formation (without which planets could not exist) is one followed by a thousand billion billion zeros, at least. Davies also estimates that a change in the strength of gravity or of the weak force by only one part in 10^{100} would have prevented a life-permitting universe. There are around 50 such quantities and constants present in the Big Bang which must be fine-tuned in this way if the universe is to permit life. And it's not just each quantity which must be finely tuned. Their ratios to one another must also be exquisitely fine-tuned. So improbability is multiplied by improbability by improbability, until our minds are reeling with incomprehensible numbers.

There is no physical reason why these constants and quantities possess the values they do. The one-time agnostic physicist Paul Davies comments, "Through my scientific work, I have come to believe more and more strongly that the physical universe is put together with an ingenuity so astonishing that I cannot accept it merely as a brute fact." Similarly, Fred Hoyle remarks, "A common sense interpretation of the facts suggests that a super-intellect has monkeyed with physics." Robert Jastrow, the head of NASA's Goddard Institute for Space Studies, calls this the most powerful evidence for the existence of God "ever to come out of science."

So, once again, the view that Christian theists have always held—that there is a designer of the cosmos—seems to make much more sense than the atheistic view that the universe, when it "popped" into being uncaused out of nothing, just happened to be, by chance, fine-tuned to an incomprehensible precision for the existence of intelligent life.

We can summarize our reasoning as follows:

1 The fine-tuning of the initial conditions of the universe is due to either law, chance or design.

2 It is not due to either law or chance.

3 Therefore, it is due to design.

III. OBJECTIVE MORAL VALUES IN THE WORLD

If God does not exist, then objective moral values do not exist. Many theists and atheists alike concur on this point. For example, Russell observed:

> Ethics arises from the pressure of the community on the individual. Man...does not always instinctively feel the desires which are useful to his herd. The herd, being anxious that the individual should act in its interests, has invented various devices for causing the individual's interest to be in harmony with that of the herd. One of these...is morality.

Michael Ruse, a philosopher of science at the University of Guelph, agrees. He explains:

> Morality is a biological adaptation, no less than are hands and feet and teeth...considered as a rationally justifiable set of claims about an

objective something, [ethics] is illusory. I appreciate that when somebody says "Love thy neighbour as thyself," they think they are referring above and beyond themselves....Nevertheless,...such reference is truly without foundation. Morality is just an aid to survival and reproduction,...and any deeper meaning is illusory....

Friedrich Nietzshe, the great nineteenth-century atheist who proclaimed the death of God, understood that the death of God meant the destruction of all meaning and value in life. I think that Friedrich Nietzsche was right.

But we've got to be very careful here. The question here is *not*: "Must we believe in God in order to live moral lives?" I'm not claiming that we must. Nor is it the question "Can we recognize moral values without believing in God?". I think that we can. Rather, the question is: "If God does not exist, do objective moral values exist?"

Like Russell and Ruse, I don't see any reason to think that, in the absence of God, the herd morality evolved by *Homo sapiens* is objective. After all, if there is no God, then what's so special about human beings? They're just accidental by-products of nature which have evolved relatively recently on an infinitesimal speck of dust lost somewhere in a hostile and mindless universe and which are doomed to perish individually and collectively in a relatively short time. On the atheistic view, some action—say, rape—may not be socially advantageous and so in the course of human development has become taboo. But that does absolutely nothing to prove that rape is really wrong. On the atheistic view there is nothing really wrong with raping someone. Thus, without God there is no absolute right and wrong which imposes itself on our conscience.

But the problem is that objective values *do* exist and, deep down, I think we all know it. There's no more reason to deny the objective reality of moral values than the objective reality of the physical world. Actions like rape, cruelty and child abuse aren't just socially unacceptable behaviour. They are moral abominations. Some things are really wrong. Similarly, love, equality and self-sacrifice are really good.

Thus we can summarize this third consideration as follows:

1 If God does not exist, objective moral values do not exist.

2 Objective values do exist.

3 Therefore, God exists.

IV. THE HISTORICAL FACTS CONCERNING THE LIFE, DEATH AND RESURRECTION OF JESUS

The historical person Jesus of Nazareth was a remarkable individual. New Testament critics have reached something of a consensus that the historical Jesus came on the scene with an unprecedented sense of divine authority—the authority to stand and speak in God's place. He claimed that in himself the Kingdom of God had come, and as visible demonstrations of this fact he carried out a ministry of miracles and exorcisms. But the supreme confirmation of his claim was his Resurrection from the dead. If Jesus did rise from the dead, then it would seem that we have a divine miracle on our hands and, thus, evidence for the existence of God.

Now, most people would probably think that the Resurrection of Jesus is something you just either believe in by faith or not. But there are actually three established facts, recognized by the majority of New Testament historians today,

which I believe are best explained by the Resurrection of Jesus.

- Fact 1. *On the Sunday following his crucifixion Jesus' tomb was found empty by a group of his women followers.* According to Jacob Kremer, an Austrian scholar who has specialized in the study of the Resurrection, "By far most scholars hold firmly to the reliability of the biblical statements about the empty tomb."

- Fact 2. *On separate occasions different individuals and groups saw appearances of Jesus alive after his death.* According to the prominent German New Testament critic Gerd Lüdemann, "It may be taken as historically certain that...the disciples had experiences after Jesus' death in which Jesus appeared to them as the Risen Christ." These appearances were witnessed not only by believers, but also by unbelievers, skeptics and even enemies.

- Fact 3. *The original disciples suddenly came to believe in the Resurrection of Jesus despite their having every predisposition to the contrary.* Jews had no belief in a dying, much less a rising, Messiah. And Jewish beliefs about the afterlife precluded anyone's rising from the dead before the end of the world. Nevertheless, the original disciples suddenly came to believe in the Resurrection of Jesus so strongly that they were willing to die for the truth of that belief. Luke Johnson, a New Testament scholar from Emory University, muses, "Some sort of powerful, transformative experience is required to generate the sort of movement earliest Christianity was." N.T. Wright, an eminent British scholar, concludes, "That is why, as a historian, I cannot explain the rise of early Christianity unless Jesus rose again, leaving an empty tomb behind him."

Attempts to explain away these three great facts—like the disciples stole the body or Jesus wasn't really dead—have been universally rejected by contemporary scholarship. The simple fact is that there is just no plausible, naturalistic explanation of these three facts. And therefore, it seems to me, the Christian is amply justified in believing that Jesus rose from the dead and was who he claimed to be. But that entails that God exists.

V. THE IMMEDIATE EXPERIENCE OF GOD

This isn't really an *argument* for God's existence. Rather, it's the claim that you can know that God exists wholly apart from arguments, simply my immediately experiencing Him. This was the way in which people in the Bible knew God. As Professor John Hick explains:

> God was known to them as a dynamic will interacting with their own wills, a sheer given reality as inescapably to be reckoned with as

destructive storm and life-giving sunshine....To them, God was not...an idea adopted by the mind but an experiential reality which gave significance to their lives.

Now, if this is the case, then there is a danger that proofs for God could actually distract your attention from God Himself. If you are sincerely seeking God, then God will make His existence evident to you. The Bible promises: "Draw near to God and He will draw near to you." We mustn't so concentrate on the external proofs that we fail to hear the voice of God speaking to our own hearts. For those who listen, God becomes an immediate reality in their lives.

In conclusion, then, we have yet to see any arguments to show that God does not exist, and we have seen five reasons to think that God does exist. Together these constitute a powerful, cumulative case for the existence of God, and therefore I think that theism is the more plausible world-view....

Intimate
Experience
change of
heart moment.

There Are No Good Reasons to Believe in the Existence of God

Antony Flew

I thought I was going to have to begin as Socrates ended, with an apology, because I thought I was going to have to explain that I wasn't going to try to show that there is no God. I was going to try to show that there are no sufficient reasons for believing that there is. And Dr. Craig apparently was wanting to maintain the exact opposite: that I wouldn't be able to establish that there is no God, but he thinks he's provided sufficient reasons for thinking that there is.

He has offered so many arguments that it will be impossible for me in any reasonable amount of time to answer them all. But what I am going to say, if it's correct, will provide a sufficient reason for thinking that he and others are altogether too bold in thinking that they know what caused the universe or even that they *could* know what caused the universe. My fundamental point is that we are, all of us, creatures whose entire knowledge and experience has been of the universe. It is, after all, the only one there is and certainly the only one we have experience of. So why should anyone think that they are able to provide an answer to the question that Dr. Craig posed: *"Where did the universe come from?"*

Take this business about whether God caused the Big Bang or whether the universe just "popped" into existence. Why are we offered only two possibilities here? Why does anyone think that these are the only two possibilities?

I think there are two things one needs to say about this. One concerns the ultimates of explanation. Every explanation of why anything is the case is given an answer in terms of something else, some general or more general law, which at that stage is taken as a brute fact—the fact that explains other things. This is surely the nature of the case: you cannot have an end to all explanations that is anything other than a brute fact. Of course, some people find some sort of brute fact satisfactory and think: "That's a good place to stop." And one can't say it's absolutely *wrong* to stop at that point. So it seems to me that you can't rule out the possibility that our knowledge of the universe or all knowledge must stop with the Big Bang; that this itself is the ultimate fact; that, if there's any first cause, it's the beginning or something some microseconds away from the beginning (because after all, everything else in the universe is being explained now).

Of course, the whole cosmology may be different next year, but we're debating in Wisconsin tonight. So one has at least to entertain the possibility that it's not ridiculous for the universe to pop into existence out of nothing. If someone was there beforehand, watching, they'd say, "Gosh! It's started out of nothing." But we're just not in a position to answer the question. And concerning the fact that one is unable to suggest a cause for the Big Bang, why should you think that anyone but a physicist is going to explain that? And if physics stops there, isn't that the end of human knowledge?

Now let's consider the alternative. Let us actually produce a definition of "God," the supposed explanation of everything.

This is the definition offered by a Richard Swinburne, which is generally accepted as the standard definition within the English-speaking countries:

> ...a person without a body, (i.e., a spirit), present everywhere, the creator and sustainer of the universe, a free agent, able to do everything, (i.e., omnipotent), knowing all things, perfectly good, a source of moral obligation, immutable, eternal, a necessary being, holy, and worthy of worship.

Well, that's a lot of characteristics for this cause, and some of the audience clearly think, "Got it! That's what must have caused the whole universe." Well, it would be perfectly possible that there should be a being that was omnipotent and omniscient and created the universe, but it wasn't particularly interested in human conduct. Of course, everyone thinking of creation is thinking of the first two chapters of Genesis. This God created the whole universe in order to have some human beings created in His image. But why should we assume, in this definition of God as first cause, that He has this interest in human behaviour—in morality and so on? And if this God was omnipotent and omniscient and wanted people to behave in a certain way, why couldn't he accomplish this? If you were omnipotent wouldn't you expect results and expect people to do exactly what you wanted? And shouldn't our presumption be, looking at human behaviour, that as far as omnipotence is concerned, He is not interested in human behaviour? You might as well have an argument that might show there was an existing being possessing some of these characteristics but not others, but not an argument for a being with all these characteristics.

The second thing I want to say is that these characteristics are at least compati-ble, but the God that I understand Dr. Craig to believe in is one who is described as good and benevolent Himself but is also described as a being who expects that He is going to torture forever the majority of creatures He has created. Well, if you think these characteristics are compatible with benevolence, if your absolute values hold that torturing anyone at all, apart from forever, is OK, then we have different ideas of benevolence. I regard it as morally compulsory not to torture anyone at all.

I'm not saying that this is a reason for not believing there is a torturer who runs the universe. I am saying that these two characteristics are incompatible. I think actually that Dr. Craig is sometimes a little anxious about these things. He says:

> If we take Scripture seriously, we must admit that the vast majority of persons in the world are condemned and will be forever lost, even if in some relatively rare cases a person might be saved through his response to the light that he has apart from special revelation.

He then goes on to indicate that "No orthodox Christian *likes* the doctrine of hell or delights in anyone's condemnation. I truly wish that universalism were true, but it is not." Well, I regard that as a sign of grace, that he says that, but I still have to say that these two things are simply incompatible—it's a nightmare. As for the idea that such a punishment could be just, don't you know what justice is? Of course, the right ones are getting the punishment. But justice isn't a matter of simply getting the right ones punished for the crime. The punishment needs to be to some extent proportionate to the seriousness of the crime. And how can there be any offense committed by a human being in a short life that deserves a literally infinite punishment?

So what I am basically trying to show is that there aren't good reasons for believing in God, and my very fundamental contention is that one shouldn't expect to be able to know things outside the universe. And, if you like, the burden of proof lies on the person who says that one can know such things. So, no number of arguments from Dr. Craig which I leave unanswered will be sufficient grounds to ignore my argument by saying, "Well, that's no use— I've produced all these arguments he hasn't answered." No one could answer in the available time all the great, long lists of arguments he has produced. But this is the answer that I think couldn't be answered— the argument, if you like, against the presumption of thinking that we're in a position to say what was going on (if anything was going on) outside the universe.

But let's look at what I believe is called the *kalam* argument, which is a great favorite of Dr. Craig's: "The universe must have had a beginning because nothing could exist without beginning and without end." Fair enough, I think this is a good argument. But this is supposed to be an argument for a creation by a bodiless person (a notion I find very difficult to understand anyway, as all the people I know are creatures of flesh and blood) who apparently was himself uncreated and eternal. Now I don't doubt that the universe had a beginning because this is the present view of physical science. It looks as if at least this part of the Big Bang theory is likely to be with us permanently (although some further things may be added). But surely, if time had to have a beginning, how do we explain that beginning by saying "Oh well, the beginning was started off, the whole universe was created by a being that existed eternally"? Well, if this argument assumes that time must have had a beginning, then how is it that the same is not true of God? Of course, one may respond that God never had a beginning and will never have an end. But this simply won't do: the argument that gets us to the creation is inconsistent with the desired explanation of it.

So, I think we come back again to a decent ignorance. I'm often thought to be a rather arrogant chap (how wrong people can be!), but I've never believed that I could give you a sort of guidebook outside the universe. I've been a bit hard-pressed to give you a guidebook to a fairly small area inside the universe. But this idea that we could gather a group of rational chaps and expect that they could all recognize an argument showing that this is how the universe began, that we know something about what must exist behind the universe, is absurd. I don't think this argument will work at all.

What about my contention that an omnipotent being, if he wanted people to behave in a certain way (as devoted and obedient children), could perfectly well make them that way? Ordinary human parents would love their children to be obedient and virtuous and so on. Wouldn't we all, being parents? And we have all, I suspect, been rather unsuccessful. But granted the resources of omnipotence, I think I could manage to have such perfectly obedient children.

But apparently the God whom Dr. Craig is asking us to believe is the creator very much wants people to believe in a certain way and He wants this so much that He's prepared to torture them forever to punish them for not obeying "Me." Well, it seems to me that anyone who knew that this was what this cosmic "Saddam Hussein" wanted would behave like the sensible subjects of Saddam Hussein. They would say anything about His merits and goodness. Wouldn't you if you were going to fall into the hands of his torturers? But omnipotence could avoid all this by simply making them such that they would choose to obey Him. This is an argument which I think may give Dr. Craig a little pause.

About design: Everyone has heard of the argument to design—about how if we found a watch in the bush, we'd infer that this was a product of design, and so on. But surely the reason why we infer that something was made by an intelligent being is not its complexity. It's simply that it is obviously an artifact and not a natural phenomenon. The most complicated, sophisticated entities in the whole universe are entities of a sort of which I see about 3000 around here. They were not, at least within the universe itself, designed. They (we) were, at least within the universe itself, products of unconscious physical and mechanical forces.

As this argument from design concerns design within the universe, the argument from design concerning design outside the universe is another one of like kind.

depends on how god was presented

Some ppl have problems with how God is presented

not if god is.

depends on how God is defined

is he Nature or did he design Nature - automatic now)

or does he run Nature

depends on how you see why we are

created - company/friends competition

"Let's see what humans do w/

free will"

if we choose God - what is

that to him? were

nothing until

we bow down)

THE CONTINUING DEBATE:
Does God Exist?

What Is New

The argument from design never quite goes away. Centuries ago William Paley suggested the image of God as a "divine watchmaker" Who must have designed the complex world we see around us—including the marvelous human hand—because such intricate results could not have occurred without a designer. Though the design argument has been subjected to severe criticism from both scientists and philosophers (David Hume argued that if we observe our world and then attempt to guess the nature of its "designer" on the basis of those observations, it would be more plausible to suggest that the world was created by a fumbling apprentice god than by a perfect and omnipotent God), it continues to find adherents as it evolves into ever new forms in response to its critics. "Creationism" was the design argument in favor a few years ago; more recently "intelligent design" has come into prominence, with its champions promoting it as an alternative "scientific theory" that should be taught in our science classes. Though U.S. courts have generally ruled that "creationism" and "intelligent design" are supported more by faith than by scientific reasoning, the controversy shows no sign of abating.

Where to Find More

The debate between Craig and Flew continues well beyond the short excerpts reprinted here, and in Stan W. Wallace, editor, *Does God Exist? The Craig-Flew Debate* (Burlington, Vt.: Ashgate, 2003) their debate is supplemented by the essays of a number of critics and commentators, followed by the responses of Craig and Flew.

J. J. C. Smart and J. J. Haldane conduct an extensive argument concerning the existence of God, in *Atheism and Theism*, second edition (London: Blackwell, 2003). An excellent anthology on philosophy of religion is John Hick, *Classical and Contemporary Readings in the Philosophy of Religion*, 2nd Edition (Englewood Cliffs, N.J.: Prentice-Hall, 1970). Philip L. Quinn and Charles Taliaferro, editors, *A Companion to Philosophy of Religion* (Oxford: Blackwell, 1997) is a collection of specially commissioned essays by leading scholars. *Philosophy of Religion: Selected Readings*, 2nd Edition, edited by Michael Peterson, William Hasker, Bruce Reichenbach, and David Basinger (Oxford: Oxford University Press, 2001) brings together key essays on almost every major issue. *Philosophy of Religion: A Guide and Anthology*, edited by Brian Davies (Oxford: Oxford University Press, 2000) contains excellent sections on arguments for the existence of God. A very good collection of essays by contemporary writers is offered by Steven M. Cahn and David Shatz, editors, *Contemporary Philosophy of Religion* (Oxford: Oxford University Press, 1982). Another excellent and more recent collection is William J. Wainwright, editor, *The Oxford Handbook of Philosophy of Religion* (Oxford: Oxford University Press, 2005). *Readings in the Philosophy of Religion: An Analytic Approach*, 2nd Edition, edited by Baruch A. Brody (Englewood Cliffs, N.J.: Prentice-Hall, 1992) contains important writings ranging from Plato through Aquinas to Locke and Hume, and including good contemporary essays as well. For serious examination of contemporary arguments in philosophy of religion, a superb source is the debates collected by Michael L. Peterson and Raymond J. Vanarragon in *Contemporary Debates in the Philosophy of Religion* (Oxford: Blackwell, 2004). A good brief introduction to some of the key issues in philosophy of religion is presented by Brian Davies in *An Introduction to the Philosophy of Religion* (Oxford: Oxford University Press, 1982). All of the above books discuss arguments for the existence of God. A good collection that deals exclusively with that issue is edited by Richard M. Gale and Alexander R. Pruss, *The Existence of God* (Burlington, Vt.: Ashgate, 2003).

While arguments for the existence of God go back at least to Plato (*The Laws*, Book X) and Aristotle (*Metaphysics*), the best-known early systematic source of arguments for the existence of God is St. Thomas Aquinas, in his "Five Ways," in the *Summa Theologica*, Part I. Criticism of those arguments can be found in Hume's *Dialogues Concerning Natural Religion*, as well as in Section XI of Hume's *Inquiry Concerning Human Understanding*. One of the best-known 20th Century critics of religious belief was Bertrand Russell, whose views are found in his *Religion and Science* (London: Oxford University Press, 1935, paperback) and *Why I Am Not a Christian and Other Essays* (London: Allen & Unwin, 1957).

The design argument is critiqued by Richard Dawkins in *The Blind Watchmaker* (London: Longman, 1986). For a debate on intelligent design, based on a set of articles in *Natural History* Magazine (April 2002), go to http://www.actionbioscience.org/evolution/nhmag.html. The site contains papers favoring intelligent design as well as critiquing the view, and each author lists favorite web links to other resources. Kenneth R. Miller is a professor of biology at Brown University who follows the Christian religion; he explains his own reconciliation of his scientific and religious views in *Finding Darwin's God: A Scientist's Search for Common Ground Between God and Evolution* (New York: HarperCollins, 1999). Neil A. Manson has edited a superb collection of essays on the design argument, both pro and con: *God and Design: The Teleological Argument and Modern Science* (London: Routledge, 2003).

The "problem of evil" is one of the most intractable in the philosophy of religion. There is a fascinating debate on the subject among three distinguished British philosophers: Antony Flew, R. M. Hare, and Basil Mitchell. It was first published in 1955, in *New Ideas in Philosophical Theology*, edited by Antony Flew and Alasdair MacIntyre (New York: Macmillan), and has been widely anthologized. A Christian response to the problem of evil is offered by Richard Swinburne, *Providence and the Problem of Evil* (Oxford: Oxford University Press, 1998). An interesting answer to the problem, proposed from the perspective of process theology, is offered by John B. Cobb and David Ray Griffin in *Process Theology: An Introductory Exposition* (Philadelphia: Wesminster Press, 1976), pp. 69–75. Marilyn McCord Adams, *Horrendous Evils and the Goodness of God* (Ithaca: Cornell University Press, 1999), offers a new slant on this ancient debate; and the anthology she edited with Robert Merrihew Adams—*The Problem of Evil* (Oxford: Oxford University Press, 1990)—is a good collection of contemporary essays on the issue. Another good collection of contemporary essays is *The Evidential Argument from Evil*, edited by Daniel Howard-Snyder (Bloomington: Indiana University Press, 1996).

2   ARE RELIGION AND SCIENCE IN CONFLICT?

There Is No Basic Conflict Between Religion and Science

ADVOCATE: Stephen Jay Gould was the Alexander Agassiz Professor of Zoology at Harvard University until his recent death. He was the author of many books, including his great work on evolutionary theory, *The Structure of Evolutionary Theory* (Cambridge, Mass.: Harvard University Press, 2002); and wonderfully entertaining collections of scientific essays, such as *The Hedgehog, the Fox, and the Magister's Pox* (New York: Three Rivers Press, 2003).

SOURCE: "Non-Overlapping Magisteria," *Skeptical Inquirer*, (July/August 1999): 55–61. Originally published in *Leonardo's Mountain of Clams and the Diet of Worms* (New York: Harmony Books, 1998).

Religion and Science Cannot Be Reconciled

ADVOCATE: Richard Dawkins is the Charles Simonyi Professor of the Public Understanding of Science at Oxford University, author of *A Devil's Chaplain* (Boston: Houghton Mifflin, 2003), *Unweaving the Rainbow* (London: Penguin Books, 1998), *The Blind Watchmaker* (New York: Norton, 1986), and *The Selfish Gene*, 2nd Ed. (Oxford: Oxford University Press, 1989).

SOURCE: "You Can't Have it Both Ways: Irreconcilable Differences?" *Skeptical Inquirer*, (July/August 1999): 62–64. Originally published in *Quarterly Review of Biology*, volume 72 (1997): 397–399.

God created the world in six days, shaping each type of creature into a distinctive form, and molding humankind as a special being—made in God's own image—on the final day. The Big Bang occurred billions of years ago, and eventually a small rocky planet fell into orbit around the Sun, and over tens of millions of years complex life forms evolved by natural selection from single cell organisms. Those certainly appear to be very different and conflicting accounts of the same thing. The former account you hear in religious services, the latter in your biology and geology and astronomy classes. Are religion and science on a collision course?

The tension between religion and science has a long and turbulent history. Perhaps the most famous chapter of the conflict was the battle over the Copernican Theory. When Copernicus proposed his account of planetary motion—with the Sun at the center of the universe, and all the planets (including Earth) moving in orbits around the Sun—it was in conflict with the Ptolemaic-Aristotelian model of the universe that was favored by Christianity. Under the Christian interpretation of the Ptolemaic model, the Earth was the stationary center stage, which of course was the appropriate place for the great drama of human creation and salvation. At the greatest distance from the corruptible Earth was the almost perfect realm of the fixed stars, with the angelic hosts and God Himself dwelling in the perfect spheres beyond the stars. Both Catholics and Protestants condemned the Copernican theory as heretical. Giordano Bruno—a champion of Copernican astronomy—was burned at the stake in 1600, and a few years later Galileo was threatened with torture if he refused to renounce his allegiance to the Copernican theory. The 20th Century witnessed the epic battle between Clarence Darrow and William Jennings Bryan in Scopes, Tennessee, over the teaching of the Darwinian account of biological evolution. Only recently—and rather reluctantly—has the Catholic Church withdrawn its condemnation of evolution; and in parts of the United States, the battle still rages over whether evolution should be taught in public schools.

In the current debate, Stephen Jay Gould champions the position that religion and science occupy different spheres and play different roles, and so avoid any basic conflict; that is, religion and science have "Nonoverlapping magisteria," which Gould designates the NOMA principle. He believes the NOMA principle prevents religion from interfering in the realm of scientific inquiry, and reminds scientists that their factual discoveries about the empirical world do not give them special knowledge of moral truth. Thus religion cannot claim knowledge of how humans evolved, but neither can science interfere in religious beliefs concerning souls and deep moral truths. While scientists may or may not find the religious perspective appealing, Gould believes that recognizing their distinctive areas of focus can enhance respectful exchanges between religion and science.

Richard Dawkins, on the other hand, is in no mood for reconciliation. In his view, religion inevitably makes claims that have important empirical implications, and scientists must not shrink from examining and rejecting those claims. In particular, there is no reason for scientists to suppose that religious claims belong to a different sphere that is off limits to scientific scrutiny. Even religious claims about souls have important scientific implications, and Dawkins maintains that those implications are fundamentally contrary to what is shown by scientific research. Ironically, on this issue Dawkins finds himself on the side of some fundamentalist Christians who would agree with him that religion and science are antithetical. But then their views diverge dramatically, with Dawkins opting for science while fundamentalists follow faith. Still, at the conclusion of his essay, Dawkins states that he prefers "honest-to-goodness fundamentalism" to any "obscurantist" effort to deny conflict between science and religion.

POINTS TO PONDER

➢ Gould maintains that religion and science occupy different spheres, different "Magisteria," though their borders are sometimes perilously close. If both religion and science staked a claim over some area of inquiry, how would Gould propose settling the question of which sphere legitimately controls that area?

➢ If scientists could give *scientific proof* of some moral principle, would that refute Gould's view?

➢ Dawkins maintains that "A universe with a supernatural presence would be a fundamentally and qualitatively different kind of universe from one without. The difference is, inescapably, a scientific difference." Do you agree with Dawkins?

What sort of "fundamental and qualitative" *scientific* difference might one find between a world with a supernatural presence and one without?

➤ Dawkins insists that the claim of "the survival of our own souls after death" is a claim that is "of a clearly scientific nature." What does he mean by that? Is that claim correct?

There Is No Basic Conflict Between Religion and Science

STEPHEN JAY GOULD

Incongruous places often inspire anomalous stories. In early 1984, I spent several nights at the Vatican housed in a hotel built for itinerant priests....One day at lunch, the priests called me over to their table to pose a problem that had been troubling them. What, they wanted to know, was going on in America with all this talk about "scientific creationism"? One of the priests asked me: "Is evolution really in some kind of trouble; and, if so, what could such trouble be? I have always been taught that no doctrinal conflict exists between evolution and Catholic faith, and the evidence for evolution seems both utterly satisfying and entirely overwhelming. Have I missed something?"

A lively pastiche of French, Italian, and English conversation then ensued for half an hour or so, but the priests all seemed reassured by my general answer—"Evolution has encountered no intellectual trouble; no new arguments have been offered. Creationism is a home-grown phenomenon of American sociocultural history—a splinter movement (unfortunately rather more of a beam these days) of Protestant fundamentalists who believe that every word of the Bible must be literally true, whatever such a claim might mean." We all left satisfied, but I certainly felt bemused by the anomaly of my role as a Jewish agnostic, trying to reassure a group of priests that evolution re-

mained both true and entirely consistent with religious belief....

This story illustrates a cardinal point, frequently unrecognized but absolutely central to any understanding of the status and impact of the politically potent, fundamentalist doctrine known by its self-proclaimed oxymoron as "scientific creationism"—the claim that the Bible is literally true, that all organisms were created during six days of twenty-four hours, that the earth is only a few thousand years old, and that evolution must therefore be false. Creationism does not pit science against religion (as my opening stories indicate), for no such conflict exists. Creationism does not raise any unsettled intellectual issues about the nature of biology or the history of life. Creationism is a local and parochial movement, powerful only in the United States among Western nations, and prevalent only among the few sectors of American Protestantism that choose to read the Bible as an inerrant document, literally true in every jot and tittle.

I do not doubt that one could find an occasional nun who would prefer to teach creationism in her parochial school biology class, or an occasional rabbi who does the same in his yeshiva, but creationism based on biblical literalism makes little sense either to Catholics or Jews, for neither religion maintains any extensive tradition for reading the Bible as literal truth, other than illuminating literature based partly on metaphor and allegory (essential components of all good writing), and demanding interpretation for proper understanding. Most Protestant groups, of course, take the same position—the fundamentalist fringe notwithstanding.

The argument that I have just outlined …represents the standard of all major Western religions (and of Western science) today. (I cannot, through ignorance, speak of Eastern religions, though I suspect that the same position would prevail in most cases.) The *lack of conflict* between science and religion arises from a *lack of overlap* between their respective domains of professional expertise—science in the empirical constitution of the universe, and religion in the search for proper ethical values and the spiritual meaning of our lives. The attainment of wisdom in a full life requires extensive attention to both domains—for a great book tells us both that the truth can make us free, and that we will live in optimal harmony with our fellows when we learn to do justly, love mercy, and walk humbly.

In the context of this "standard" position, I was enormously puzzled by a statement issued by Pope John Paul II on October 22, 1996, to the Pontifical Academy of Sciences, the same body that had sponsored my earlier trip to the Vatican. In this document, titled "Truth Cannot Contradict Truth," the Pope defended both the evidence for evolution and the consistency of the theory with Catholic religious doctrine. Newspapers throughout the world responded with front-page headlines, as in *The New York Times* for October 25: "Pope Bolsters Church's Support for Scientific View of Evolution."

Now I know about "slow news days," and I do allow that nothing else was strongly competing for headlines at that particular moment. Still, I couldn't help feeling immensely puzzled by all the atten-

tion paid to the Pope's statement.... The Catholic Church does not oppose evolution, and has no reason to do so. Why had the Pope issued such a statement at all? And why had the press responded with an orgy of worldwide front-page coverage?...

Clearly, I was out to lunch; something novel or surprising must lurk within the papal statement, but what could be causing all the fuss?—especially given…that the Catholic Church values scientific study, views science as no threat to religion in general or Catholic doctrine in particular, and has long accepted both the legitimacy of evolution as a field of study and the potential harmony of evolutionary conclusions with Catholic faith.

As a former constituent of Tip O'Neill, I certainly know that "all politics is local"—and that the Vatican undoubtedly had its own internal reasons, quite opaque to me, for announcing papal support of evolution in a major statement. Still, I reasoned that I must be missing some important key, and I felt quite frustrated. I then remembered the primary rule of intellectual life: When puzzled, it never hurts to read the primary documents—a rather simple and self-evident principle that has, nonetheless, completely disappeared from large sectors of the American experience.

I knew that Pope Pius XII (not one of my favorite figures in twentieth-century history, to say the least) had made the primary statement in a 1950 encyclical entitled *Humani Generis*. I knew the main thrust of his message: Catholics could believe whatever science determined about the evolution of the human body, so long as they accepted that, at some time of his choosing, God had infused the soul into such a creature. I also knew that I had no problem with this argument—for, whatever my private beliefs about souls, science cannot touch such a subject and therefore cannot be threatened by any theological position on such a legitimately and intrinsically religious issue. Pope

Pius XII, in other words, had properly acknowledged and respected the separate domains of science and theology. Thus, I found myself in total agreement with *Humani Generis*—but I had never read the document in full (not much of an impediment to stating an opinion these days).

I quickly got the relevant writings from, of all places, the Internet....Having now read in full both Pope Pius's *Humani Generis* of 1950 and Pope John Paul's proclamation of October 1996, I finally understand why the recent statement seems so new, revealing, and worthy of all those headlines. And the message could not be more welcome for evolutionists, and friends of both science and religion.

The text of *Humani Generis* focuses on the *Magisterium* (or Teaching Authority) of the Church—a word derived not from any concept of majesty or unquestionable awe, but from the different notion of teaching, for *magister* means "teacher" in Latin. We may, I think, adopt this word and concept to express the central point of this essay and the principled resolution of supposed "conflict" or "warfare" between science and religion. No such conflict should exist because each subject has a legitimate magisterium, or domain of teaching authority—and these magisteria do not overlap (the principle that I would like to designate as NOMA, or "nonoverlapping magisteria"). The net of science covers the empirical realm: what is the universe made of (fact) and why does it work this way (theory). The net of religion extends over questions of moral meaning and value. These two magisteria do not overlap, nor do they encompass all inquiry (consider, for starters, the magisterium of art and the meaning of beauty). To cite the usual clichés, we get the age of rocks, and religion retains the rock of ages; we study how the heavens go, and they determine how to go to heaven.

This resolution might remain entirely neat and clean if the non-overlapping magisteria of science and religion stood far apart, separated by an extensive no-man's-land. But, in fact, the two magisteria bump right up against each other, inter-digitating in wondrously complex ways along their joint border. Many of our deepest questions call upon aspects of both magisteria for different parts of a full answer—and the sorting of legitimate domains can become quite complex and difficult. To cite just two broad questions involving both evolutionary facts and moral arguments: Since evolution made us the only earthly creatures with advanced consciousness, what responsibilities are so entailed for our relations with other species? What do our genealogical ties with other organisms imply about the meaning of human life?

Pius XII's *Humani Generis* (1950), a highly traditionalist document written by a deeply conservative man, faces all the "isms" and cynicisms that rode the wake of World War II and informed the struggle to rebuild human decency from the ashes of the Holocaust. The encyclical bears the subtitle "concerning some false opinions which threaten to undermine the foundation of Catholic doctrine," and begins with a statement of embattlement:

> Disagreement and error among men on moral and religious matters have always been a cause of profound sorrow to all good men, but above all to the true and loyal sons of the Church, especially today, when we see the principles of Christian culture being attacked on all sides.

...Pius presents his major statement on evolution near the end of the encyclical, in paragraphs 35 through 37. He accepts the standard model of non-overlapping magisteria (NOMA) and begins by acknowledging that evolution lies in a difficult area where the domains press hard against each other. "It remains for Us now to speak about those questions which, although they pertain to the positive sciences, are nevertheless more or less connected with the truths of the Christian faith."

Pius then writes the well-known words that permit Catholics to entertain the evolution of the human body (a factual issue under the magisterium of science), so long as they accept the divine creation and infusion of the soul (a theological notion under the magisterium of religion).

> The Teaching Authority of the Church does not forbid that, in conformity with the present state of human sciences and sacred theology, research and discussions, on the part of men experienced in both fields, take place with regard to the doctrine of evolution, in as far as it inquires into the origin of the human body as coming from pre-existent and living matter—for the Catholic faith obliges us to hold that souls are immediately created by God.

I had, up to here, found nothing surprising in *Humani Generis*, and nothing to relieve my puzzlement about the novelty of Pope John's recent statement. But I read further and realized that Pius had said more about evolution, something I had never seen quoted, and something that made John Paul's statement most interesting indeed. In short, Pius forcefully proclaimed that while evolution may be legitimate in principle, the theory, in fact, had not been proven and might well be entirely wrong. One gets the strong impression, moreover, that Pius was rooting pretty hard for a verdict of falsity.

Continuing directly from the last quotation, Pius advises us about the proper study of evolution:

> However, this must be done in such a way that the reasons for both opinions, that is, those favorable and those unfavorable to evolution, be weighed and judged with the necessary seriousness, moderation and measure....Some, however, rashly transgress this liberty of discussion, when they act as if the origin of the human body from preexisting and living matter were already completely certain and proved by the facts which have been discovered up to now and by reasoning on those facts, and as if there were nothing in the sources of divine revelation which demands the greatest moderation and caution in this question.

To summarize, Pius generally accepts the NOMA principle of nonoverlapping magisteria in permitting Catholics to entertain the hypothesis of evolution for the human body so long as they accept the divine infusion of the soul. But he then offers some (holy) fatherly advice to scientists about the status of evolution as a scientific concept: the idea is not yet proven, and you all need to be especially cautious because evolution raises many troubling issues right on the border of my magisterium. One may read this second theme in two rather different ways: either as a gratuitous incursion into a different magisterium, or as a helpful perspective from an intelligent and concerned outsider. As a man of goodwill, and in the interest of conciliation, I am content to embrace the latter reading.

In any case, this rarely quoted second claim (that evolution remains both unproven and a bit dangerous)—and not the familiar first argument for the NOMA principle (that Catholics may accept the evolution of the body so long as they embrace the creation of the soul)—defines the novelty and the interest of John Paul's recent statement.

John Paul begins by summarizing Pius's older encyclical of 1950, and particularly by reaffirming the NOMA principle—nothing new here, and no cause for extended publicity:

> In his encyclical "Humani Generis" (1950) my predecessor Pius XII had already stated that there was no opposition between evolution and the doctrine of the faith about man and his vocation.

To emphasize the power of NOMA, John Paul poses a potential problem and a sound resolution: How can we possibly reconcile science's claim for physical continuity in human evolution with Catholicism's insistence that the soul must enter at a moment of divine infusion?

> With man, then, we find ourselves in the presence of an ontological difference, an ontological leap, one could say. However, does not the posing of such ontological discontinuity run counter to that physical continuity which seems to be the main thread of research into evolution in the field of physics and chemistry? Consideration of the method used in the various branches of knowledge makes it possible to reconcile two points of view which would seem irreconcilable. The sciences of observation describe and measure the multiple manifestations of life with increasing precision and correlate them with the time line. The moment of transition to the spiritual cannot be the object of this kind of observation.

The novelty and news value of John Paul's statement lies, rather, in his profound revision of Pius's second and rarely quoted claim that evolution, while conceivable in principle and reconcilable with religion, can cite little persuasive evidence in support, and may well be false. John Paul states—and I can only say amen, and thanks for noticing—that the half century between Pius surveying the ruins of World War II and his own pontificate heralding the dawn of a new millennium has witnessed such a growth of data, and such a refinement of theory, that evolution can no longer be doubted by people of goodwill and keen intellect:

> Pius XII added…that this opinion (evolution) should not be adopted as though it were a certain, proven doctrine.…Today, almost half a century after the publication of the encyclical, new knowledge has led to the recognition of the theory of evolution as more than a hypothesis. It is indeed remarkable that this theory has been progressively accepted by researchers, following a series of discoveries in various fields of knowledge. The convergence, neither sought nor fabricated, of the results of work that was conducted independently is in itself a significant argument in favor of the theory.

In conclusion, Pius had grudgingly admitted evolution as a legitimate hypothesis that he regarded as only tentatively supported and potentially (as he clearly hoped) untrue. John Paul, nearly fifty years later, reaffirms the legitimacy of evolution under the NOMA principle—no news here—but then adds that additional data and theory have placed the factuality of evolution beyond reasonable doubt. Sincere Christians must now accept evolution not merely as a plausible possibility, but also as an effectively proven fact. In other words, official Catholic opinion on evolution has moved from "say it ain't so, but we can deal with it if we have to" (Pius's grudging view of 1950) to John Paul's entirely welcoming "it has been proven true; we always celebrate nature's factuality, and we look forward to interesting discussions of theological implications." I happily endorse this turn of events as gospel—literally good news. I may represent the magisterium of science, but I welcome the support of a primary leader from the other major magisterium of our complex lives. And I recall the wisdom of King Solomon: "As cold waters to a thirsty soul, so is good news from a far country" (Proverbs 25:25).

Just as religion must bear the cross of its hardliners, I have some scientific colleagues, including a few in prominent enough positions to wield influence by their writings, who view this rapprochement of the separate magisteria with dismay. To colleagues like me—agnostic scientists who welcome and celebrate the rapprochement, especially the Pope's latest statement—they say, "C'mon, be honest; you know that religion is addlepated, superstitious, old-fashioned BS. You're only making those welcoming noises because religion is so powerful, and we need to be diplomatic in order to buy public support for science." I do not thing that many scientists hold this view, but such a position fills me with dismay—and I therefore end this essay with a personal statement about religion, as a testimony to what I regard as a virtual consensus among thoughtful scientists (who support the NOMA principle as firmly as the Pope does).

I am not, personally, a believer or a religious man in any sense of institutional commitment or practice. But I have great respect for religion, and the subject has always fascinated me, beyond almost all others (with a few exceptions, like evolution and paleontology). Much of this fascination lies in the stunning historical paradox that organized religion has fostered, throughout Western history, both the most unspeakable horrors and the most heartrending examples of human goodness in the face of personal danger. (The evil, I believe, lies in an occasional confluence of religion with secular power. The Catholic Church has sponsored its share of horrors, from Inquisition to liquidations—but only because this institution held great secular power during so much of Western history. When my folks held such sway, more briefly and in Old Testament times, we committed similar atrocities with the same rationales.)

I believe, with all my heart, in a respectful, even loving, concordant between our magisteria—the NOMA concept. NOMA represents a principled position on moral and intellectual grounds, not a merely diplomatic solution. NOMA also cuts both ways. If religion can no longer dictate the nature of factual conclusions residing properly within the magisterium of science, then scientists cannot claim higher insight into moral truth from any superior knowledge of the world's empirical constitution. This mutual humility leads to important practical consequences in a world of such diverse passions.

Religion is too important for too many people to permit any dismissal or denigration of the comfort still sought by many folks from theology. I may, for example, privately suspect that papal insistence on divine infusion of the soul represents a sop to our fears, a device for maintaining a belief in human superiority within an evolutionary world offering no privileged position to any creature. But I also know that the subject of souls lies outside the magisterium of science. My world cannot prove or disprove such a notion, and the concept of souls cannot threaten or impact my domain. Moreover, while I cannot personally accept the Catholic view of souls, I surely honor the metaphorical value of such a concept both for grounding moral discussion, and for expressing what we most value about human potentiality: our decency, our care, and all the ethical and intellectual struggles that the evolution of consciousness imposed upon us.

As a moral position (and therefore not as a deduction from my knowledge of nature's factuality), I prefer the "cold bath" theory that nature can be truly "cruel" and "indifferent" in the utterly inappropriate terms of our ethical discourse—because nature does not exist for us, didn't know we were coming (we are, after all, interlopers of the latest geological moment), and doesn't give a damn about us (speaking metaphorically). I regard such a position as liberating, not depressing, because we then gain the capacity to conduct moral discourse—and nothing could be more important—in our own terms, free from the delusion that we might read moral truth passively from nature's factuality.

But I recognize that such a position frightens many people, and that a more spiritual view of nature retains broad appeal (acknowledging the factuality of evolution, but still seeking some intrinsic meaning in human terms, and from the magisterium of religion). I do appreciate, for example, the struggles of a man who wrote to *The New York Times* on November 3, 1996, to declare both his pain and his endorsement of John Paul's statement:

> Pope John Paul II's acceptance of evolution touches the doubt in my heart. The problem of pain and suffering in a world created by a God who is all love and light is hard enough to bear, even if one is a creationist. But at least a creationist can say that the original creation, coming from the hand of God, was good, harmonious, innocent and gentle. What can one say about evolution, even a spiritual theory of evolution? Pain and suffering, mindless cruelty and terror are its means of creation. Evolution's engine is the grinding of predatory teeth upon the screaming, living flesh and bones of prey....If evolution be true, my faith has rougher seas to sail.

I don't agree with this man, but we could have a terrific argument. I would push the "cold bath" theory; he would (presumably) advocate the theme of inherent spiritual meaning in nature, however opaque the signal. But we would both be enlightened and filled with better understanding of these deep and ultimately unanswerable issues. Here, I believe, lies the greatest strength and necessity of NOMA, the non-overlapping magisteria of science and religion. NOMA permits—indeed enjoins—the prospect of respectful discourse, of constant input from both magisteria toward the common goal of wisdom. If human beings can lay claim to anything special, we evolved as the only creatures that must ponder and talk. Pope John Paul II would surely point out to me that his magisterium has always recognized this uniqueness, for John's gospel begins by stating *in principio erat verbum*—in the beginning was the word.

Religion and Science Cannot Be Reconciled

RICHARD DAWKINS

A cowardly flabbiness of the intellect afflicts otherwise rational people confronted with long-established religions (though, significantly, not in the face of younger traditions such as Scientology or the Moonies). S. J. Gould, commenting in his *Natural History* column on the Pope's attitude to evolution, is representative of a dominant strain of conciliatory thought, among believers and nonbelievers alike:

> Science and religion are not in conflict, for their teachings occupy distinctly different domains…I believe, with all my heart, in a respectful, even *loving* concordat [my emphasis]….

Well, what are these two distinctly different domains, these "Non-overlapping Magisteria" which should snuggle up together in a respectful and loving concordat? Gould again:

> The net of science covers the empirical universe: what is it made of (fact) and why does it work this way (theory). The net of religion extends over questions of moral meaning and value.

Would that it were that tidy. In a moment I'll look at what the Pope actually says about evolution, and then at other claims of his church, to see if they really are so neatly distinct from the domain of science. First though, a brief aside on the claim that religion has some special expertise to offer us on moral questions. This is often blithely accepted even by the nonreligious, presumably in the course of a civilized "bending over backwards" to concede the best point your opponent has to offer—however weak that best point may be.

The question, "What is right and what is wrong?" is a genuinely difficult question which science certainly cannot answer. Given a moral premise or a priori moral belief, the important and rigorous discipline of secular moral philosophy can pursue scientific or logical modes of reasoning to point up hidden implications of such beliefs, and hidden inconsistencies between them. But the absolute moral premises themselves must come from elsewhere, presumably from unargued conviction. Or, it might be hoped, from religion—meaning some combination of authority, revelation, tradition and scripture.

Unfortunately, the hope that religion might provide a bedrock, from which our otherwise sand-based morals can be derived, is a forlorn one. In practice no civilized person uses scripture as ultimate authority for moral reasoning. Instead, we pick and choose the nice bits of scripture (like the Sermon on the Mount) and blithely ignore the nasty bits (like the obligation to stone adulteresses, execute apostates, and punish the grandchildren of offenders). The God of the Old Testament himself, with his pitilessly vengeful jealousy, his racism, sexism, and terrifying bloodlust, will not be adopted as a literal role model by anybody you or I would wish to know. Yes, *of course* it is unfair to judge the customs of an earlier era by the enlightened standards of our own. But that is precisely my *point!* Evidently, we have some alternative source of ultimate moral conviction which overrides scripture when it suits us.

That alternative source seems to be some kind of liberal consensus of decency and natural justice which changes over historical time, frequently under the influence of secular reformists. Admittedly, that doesn't sound like bedrock. But in practice we, including the religious among us, give it higher priority than scripture. In practice we more or less ignore scripture, quoting it when it supports our liberal consensus, quietly forgetting it when it doesn't. And, wherever that liberal consensus comes from, it is available to all of us, whether we are religious or not.

Similarly, great religious teachers like Jesus or Gautama Buddha may inspire us, by their good example, to adopt their personal moral convictions. But again we pick and choose among religious leaders, avoiding the bad examples of Jim Jones or Charles Manson, and we may choose good secular role models such as Jawaharlal Nehru or Nelson Mandela. Traditions too, however anciently followed, may be good or bad, and we use our secular judgment of decency and natural justice to decide which ones to follow, which to give up.

But that discussion of moral values was a digression. I now turn to my main topic of evolution, and whether the Pope lives up to the ideal of keeping off the scientific grass. His Message on Evolution to the Pontifical Academy of Sciences begins with some casuistical doubletalk designed to reconcile what John Paul is about to say with the previous, more equivocal pronouncements of Pius XII whose acceptance of evolution was comparatively grudging and reluctant. Then the Pope comes to the harder task of reconciling scientific evidence with "revelation."

Revelation teaches us that [man] was created in the image and likeness of God…if the human body takes its origin from preexistent living matter, the spiritual soul is immediately created by God…Consequently, theories of evolution which, in accordance with the philosophies inspiring them, consider the mind as emerging from the forces of living matter, or as a mere epiphenomenon of this matter, are incompatible with the truth about man…With man, then, we find ourselves in the presence of an ontological difference, an ontological leap, one could say.

To do the Pope credit, at this point he recognizes the essential contradiction between the two positions he is attempting to reconcile:

However, does not the posing of such ontological discontinuity run counter to that physical continuity which seems to be the main thread of research into evolution in the field of physics and chemistry?

Never fear. As so often in the past, obscurantism comes to the rescue:

Consideration of the method used in the various branches of knowledge makes it possible to reconcile two points of view which would seem irreconcilable. The sciences of observation describe and measure the multiple manifestations of life with increasing precision and correlate them with the time line. The moment of transition to the spiritual cannot be the object of this kind of observation, which nevertheless can discover at the experimental level a series of very valuable signs indicating what is specific to the human being.

In plain language, there came a moment in the evolution of hominids when God intervened and injected a human soul into a previously animal lineage (When? A million years ago? Two million years ago? Between *Home erectus* and *Homo sapiens?* Between "archaic" *Homo sapiens* and *H. sapiens sapiens?*). The sudden injection is necessary, of course, otherwise there would be no distinction upon which to base Catholic morality, which is speciesist to the core. You can kill adult animals for meat, but abortion and euthanasia are murder because *human* life is involved.

Catholicism's "net" is not limited to moral considerations, if only because Catholic morals have scientific implications. Catholic morality demands the presence of a great gulf between *Homo sapiens* and the rest of the animal kingdom. Such a gulf is fundamentally anti-evolutionary. The sudden injection of an immortal soul in the time-line is an anti-evolutionary intrusion into the domain of science.

More generally it is completely unrealistic to claim, as Gould and many others do, that religion keeps itself away from science's turf, restricting itself to morals and values. A universe with a supernatural presence would be a fundamentally and qualitatively different kind of universe from one without. The difference is, inescapably, a scientific difference. Religions make existence claims, and this means scientific claims.

The same is true of many of the major doctrines of the Roman Catholic Church. The Virgin Birth, the bodily Assumption of the Blessed Virgin Mary, the Resurrection of Jesus, the survival of our own souls after death: these are all claims of a clearly scientific nature. Either Jesus had a corporeal father or he didn't. This is not a question of "values" or "morals," it is a question of sober fact. We may not have the

evidence to answer it, but it is a scientific question, nevertheless. You may be sure that, if any evidence supporting the claim were discovered, the Vatican would not be reticent in promoting it.

Either Mary's body decayed when she died, or it was physically removed from this planet to Heaven. The official Roman Catholic doctrine of Assumption, promulgated as recently as 1950, implies that Heaven has a physical location and exists in the domain of physical reality—how else could the physical body of a woman go there? I am not, here, saying that the doctrine of the Assumption of the Virgin is necessarily false (although of course I think it is). I am simply rebutting the claim that it is outside the domain of science. On the contrary, the Assumption of the Virgin is transparently a scientific theory. So is the theory that our souls survive bodily death and so are all stories of angelic visitations, Marian manifestations, and miracles of all types.

There is something dishonestly self-serving in the tactic of claiming that all religious beliefs are outside the domain of science. On the one hand miracle stories and the promise of life after death are used to impress simple people, win converts, and swell congregations. It is precisely their scientific power that gives these stories their popular appeal. But at the same time it is considered below the belt to subject the same stories to the ordinary rigors of scientific criticism: these are religious matters and therefore outside the domain of science. But you cannot have it both ways. At least, religious theorists and apologists should not be allowed to get away with having it both ways. Unfortunately all too many of us, including nonreligious people, are unaccountably ready to let them get away with it.

I suppose it is gratifying to have the Pope as an ally in the struggle against fundamentalist creationism. It is certainly amusing to see the rug pulled out from under the feet of Catholic creationists such as Michael Behe. Even so, given a choice between honest-to-goodness fundamentalism on the one hand, and the obscurantist, disingenuous doublethink of the Roman Catholic Church on the other, I know which I prefer.

THE CONTINUING DEBATE:
Are Religion and Science in Conflict?

What Is New

The contemporary debate in the U.S. adds a twist to the issue, with claims that "Creationism" and "Intelligent Design" are alternative scientific hypotheses that therefore should be taught as science. While almost all scientists disagree—they note that the "intelligent design" hypothesis is not one that makes interesting predictions or generates testable hypotheses or leads to new discoveries, and thus that it fails to meet the basic criteria of genuine scientific theory—the movement continues its efforts to have intelligent design taught in high schools as an "alternative scientific theory." In 2004 in Dover, Pennsylvania, members of the school board voted to require the teaching of intelligent design as an alternative to evolution. Teachers and parents sued to reverse the policy, and after a lengthy trial U.S. District Judge John F. Jones ruled that intelligent design is "a religious view, a mere re-labeling of creationism, and not a scientific theory," and that the real purpose the school board had in promoting intelligent design was to "promote religion in the public school classroom." In the next election, all eight school board members who were candidates for re-election were defeated by the Dover voters.

Where to Find More

Stephen Gould develops his position further and in more detail in *Rocks of Ages: Science and Religions in the Fullness of Life* (New York: Ballantine Books, 1999). Richard Dawkins' views are elaborated in *The Blind Watchmaker* (London: Longman, 1986) and in *A Devil's Chaplain: Reflections on Hope, Lies, Science, and Love* (Boston: Houghton Mifflin, 2003). Two writers who share many of Gould's views on this subject are Kenneth R. Miller, *Finding Darwin's God* (New York: HarperCollins, 1999), and Chet Raymo, in *Skeptics and True Believers: The Exhilarating Connection Between Science and Religion* (New York: Walker and Company, 1998). Richard P. Feynman, a Nobel Prize-winning physicist, takes a position very similar to the view of Dawkins in "What Is and What Should Be the Role of Scientific Culture in Modern Society," in Richard P. Feynman, *The Pleasure of Finding Things Out* (Cambridge, Mass.: Perseus Publishing, 1999). E. O. Wilson is another scientist who seems to hold that view; see his *Consilience* (New York: Alfred A. Knopf, 1998), especially the last two chapters.

Thomas Kuhn's *The Copernican Revolution: Planetary Astronomy in the Development of Western Thought* (Cambridge, Mass.: Harvard University Press, 1957) is a fascinating examination of the development and impact of the Copernican theory. There are many excellent books on Galileo's conflict with the Catholic Church over Copernican theory; two of the best recent works are Pietro Redondi, *Galileo: Heretic* (Princeton, N.J.: Princeton University Press, 1987), and Mario Biagioli, *Galileo, Courtier: The Practice of Science in the Culture of Absolutism* (Chicago: University of Chicago Press, 1993).

Edward J. Larson, *Summer for the Gods: The Scopes Trial and America's Continuing Debate Over Science and Religion* (Cambridge, Mass.: Harvard University Press, 1997), is a remarkably good study of the Scopes Trial, and of the larger cultural setting in which it occurred. Larson's *Evolution: The Remarkable History of a Scientific*

Theory (New York: Modern Library, 2004), is a very readable brief survey of the development of evolutionary theory and the controversy it generated. An interesting perspective on the contemporary evolution-creation controversy is Michael Ruse, *The Evolution-Creation Struggle* (Cambridge, Mass.: Harvard University Press, 2005).

3 HOW DO I KNOW THAT JUPITER IS THE LARGEST PLANET IN OUR SOLAR SYSTEM?

The Coherence of Our Beliefs Provides Sufficient Justification

ADVOCATE: Catherine Z. Elgin, Professor of Philosophy of Education at Harvard Graduate School of Education; author of *Considered Judgment* (1996) and *Between the Absolute and the Arbitrary* (1997).

SOURCE: "Non-foundationalist Epistemology: Holism, Coherence, and Tenability," from *Contemporary Debates in Epistemology*, edited by Matthias Steup and Ernest Sosa (Oxford: Blackwell Publishing, 2005): 156–167.

The Justification of Our Beliefs Requires a Foundation

ADVOCATE: James van Cleve, Professor of Philosophy at Brown University, author of *Problems from Kant* (New York: Oxford University Press, 2003).

SOURCE: "Why Coherence Is Not Enough: A Defense of Moderate Foundationalism," from *Contemporary Debates in Epistemology*, edited by Matthias Steup and Ernest Sosa (Oxford: Blackwell Publishing, 2005): 168–180.

Do you know which planet in our solar system is the largest? Of course you do. It's Jupiter, and you would not hesitate to give that answer. That's something you *know*. But suppose some obnoxious person questions your knowledge: *How* do you know that Jupiter is the largest planet? Have you measured it? You would refer to an astronomy text, or an encyclopedia. But how do you know that information is true? If you continued to push this inquiry, where would it end? Would you find some solid fixed *foundation* for your knowledge, some foundation that might involve observations and measurements by astronomers? Or would you instead find that your belief does not ultimately rest on a fixed foundation, but instead *coheres* with a system of beliefs that taken together seems plausible (but without containing any stopping point of final justification).

Think for a moment of your system of beliefs, particularly the beliefs you regard as *justified*. Your justified beliefs cover a wide range: you believe that what you are holding is a book, you believe that broccoli is good for you, that snow is cold, that 2 plus 2 is 4, that Jupiter is the largest planet in our Solar System. Some of these beliefs may be more strongly justified than others; but ask yourself, how is the *system* of your justified beliefs constructed? The traditional answer is that the system—if it is *really* justified—must be built up, step by step and level by level, from a *solid foundation*. Most of your justified beliefs are inferred from other beliefs; but the buck has to stop somewhere. Coherence theorists—who deny that knowledge must be based on foundations—emphasize the "epistemic regress problem": what nonarbitrary point could serve to halt the continuing pattern of inferences? And if no such point exists, foundationalism falls prey to a vicious regress.

The exact nature of the knowledge foundation is a vexed question for foundationalists. For some the foundation must be reason, and truths—such as mathematical truths—known purely by reason. But if that is the foundation, it is difficult to see how we can go from there to knowledge of the empirical world. Direct sensory experience is also a popular candidate; but (as Wilfrid Sellars argued) if we examine carefully what our *direct* sensory experiences are (red blob against dark background experience, *not* I see an apple resting on the table) then it is doubtful that such experiences could serve as the foundation for knowledge; and by the time those immediate experiences are transformed into more substantial reports (there is an apple on the table) they involve a great deal more than direct sensory experience. Whatever the candidate for foundational knowledge, it must deal with the question of exactly how *it* is known and justified: is it known intuitively, is its truth indubitable, is it a self-justifying truth?

There are three possible reactions to this *foundationalist* approach to knowledge. First, of course, you may agree that a solid bedrock foundation is an essential base for a system of knowledge, *and* conclude that we do have such a foundation. Second, you may agree that a solid foundation is essential for knowledge, *but* deny that such a foundation is possible: the result is profound skepticism. Or third, you might deny that any such foundation exists, but also deny that a foundation is essential for knowledge: our system of knowledge is justified by its *coherence*, how the entire system hangs together and works effectively; not by its relation to some fixed foundation. (Actually, Peter Klein has recently suggested a fourth alternative: *infinitism*, which claims that all justification is inferential, and that there is no end to the infinite range of inferences; but he believes that even finite beings may have the *capacity* to advance an infinite number of justifications, though they could never *complete* the infinite line of justification.)

Foundationalism has been the dominant view in the history of philosophy. The 18th Century French philosopher, René Descartes, used his famous method of doubt to find one *indubitable* fact that could serve as the fixed foundation on which all his other knowledge could be constructed. Even if Descartes imagines some powerful deceiver that constantly tried to mislead him, Descartes believes it would still be possible to discover a bedrock certainty that could form the essential solid foundation for our knowledge:

> But there is some deceiver or other, very powerful and very cunning, who ever employs his ingenuity in deceiving me. Then without doubt I exist also if he deceives me, and let him deceive me as much as he will, he can never cause me to be nothing so long as I think that I am something. So that after having reflected well and carefully examined all things, we must come to the definite conclusion that this proposition: I am, I exist, is necessarily true each time that I pronounce it, or that I mentally conceive it. Descartes, Meditation II, from *Meditations on First Philosophy*, trans. Elizabeth Haldane and G. R. T. Ross (London: Cambridge University Press, 1931); originally published in Latin, 1641.

The coherence view has many contemporary advocates. Otto Neurath, a social scientist and philosopher of the early 20th Century, rejected the idea that we could ever get outside our system of belief to establish some foundation for the entire system. Neurath held that our beliefs must be tested as a system or network, and none of them has the status of foundational certainties. Instead, we must rebuild our system of knowledge on the go, piece by piece; we cannot build it up, story by story, from a set foundation. In his famous metaphor, Neurath compared revising our system of knowledge to making repairs on a ship at sea: "Like sailors we are, who must rebuild their ship upon the open sea, never able to dismantle it in drydock or to reconstruct it there from the best materials." That does not show that we never have genuine knowledge, but rather that genuine knowledge does not require a fixed foundation.

In contrast to both foundationalists and coherence theorists, skeptics deny that knowledge is possible. Skepticism has always found champions, from the ancient Greeks to the present. One of its most eloquent advocates was the 16th Century skeptic, Michel de Montaigne, who lived during the height of the controversy that pitted those who favored the old Ptolemaic planetary system (the Earth is the center of the universe, and immobile) and the champions of the Copernican Revolution who claimed that our Earth is not stationary (as our senses teach us) but instead spins as it orbits the Sun:

> Let us leave aside that infinite confusion of opinions that is seen among the philosophers themselves, and that perpetual and universal debate over the knowledge of things. For this is a very true presupposition: that men are in agreement about nothing, I mean even the most gifted and ablest scholars, not even that the sky is over our head....Besides this infinite diversity and division, it is easy to see by the confusion that our judgment gives to our own selves, and the uncertainty that each man feels within himself, that it has a very insecure seat. How diversely we judge things! How many times we change our notions! What I hold today and what I believe, I hold and believe it with all my belief....I belong to it entirely, I belong to it truly. But has it not happened to me, not once but a hundred times, a thousand times, and every day, to have embraced...something else that I have since judged false? *Apology for Raymond Sebond*, from *The Complete Works of Montaigne*, trans. by Donald M. Frame (Stanford, Cal.: Stanford University Press, 1948), p. 423.

While coherence theorists avoid the problems of foundations, they face obvious challenges of their own. Perhaps the most obvious challenge is that a system can be quite coherent while also being quite false (the elaborate worlds created by science fiction writers are examples of coherent systems that are fantasies rather than fact).

Catherine Elgin's coherence theory focuses on *justification* for beliefs, emphasizing that a coherent system of beliefs may be justified when its being true is the "best explanation" for the coherence of that belief set; and she emphasizes that such coherence requires careful adjustment and deliberation. James van Cleve maintains that we need not start from a foundation of fixed certainties, but we do require inputs having "high intrinsic credibility," and thus require at least a *moderate* foundationalism.

➤ Works of fiction or fantasy may be wonderfully *coherent* though we do not regard them as *true*. Catherine Elgin proposes a solution to that problem; is it successful?

➤ Elgin states that her view "might be classified as a very weak foundationalism or as a coherence theory"; if you were placing it in one category or the other, where would you classify it?

➤ While Elgin maintains that our basic belief contents need only a very slight presumption of being true, James van Cleve insists that they must have "high initial credibility." Is this an irreconcilable difference between their views, or is some compromise possible?

The Coherence of Our Beliefs Provides Sufficient Justification

CATHERINE Z. ELGIN

Much epistemology assumes that cognitive success consists in knowledge, where knowledge is justified or reliable true belief. On this conception, since propositions are the contents of beliefs and the bearers of truth values, they are what is known. If this is right, the sort of justification of interest to epistemology seems to be the justification of individual propositions. A linear model of justification is almost inevitable. To justify a given proposition is either to infer it from already justified propositions or to show how belief in it emerges from reliable belief forming mechanisms. S is justified in believing p on the basis of q, and q on the basis of r, and so on. Holists contend that this picture is misleading. They maintain that epistemic acceptability is, in the first instance, acceptability of a fairly comprehensive system of thought, comprised of mutually supportive commitments. The priority in question is epistemological, not historical. There is no contention that

people come to believe a theory before coming to believe the various claims that comprise it. The point is that regardless of the order in which they are acquired, claims are justified only when they coalesce to constitute a tenable system of thought. The acceptability of individual sentences, as well as methods and standards, is derivative, stemming from their role in a tenable system.

The challenge for such an epistemology is to explain how systematic interconnections give rise to justification, how the fact that deliverances dovetail affords reason to believe they are true. Some philosophers hold that the coherence of a sufficiently comprehensive constellation of claims makes them true. This strikes me as implausible, but I will not argue against it here. The position I want to investigate is that coherence is the source of epistemic justification, not the ground of truth. But if truth is independent of what we believe, why should mutual accord among our beliefs be indicative of truth? What is the connection? To avoid begging questions, it is perhaps better to begin by focusing not on the justification of beliefs, but on the justification of deliverances, these being representations that present themselves as candidates for belief. If we are concerned with justification, we should not limit ourselves to assessing the status of what we actually believe, but ask which of the things that could in given circumstances be believed should in those circumstances be believed. Deliverances, as I use the term, include perceptual inputs, fixed or transient beliefs, passing thoughts, and so forth.

Perhaps things will become clearer if we consider a case. Yesterday Meg's Latin book was stolen from her locker. Three students may have witnessed the theft. None of them is very reliable. Anne is given to proving theorems in her head, and tends to be oblivious to her surroundings when preoccupied with a tricky proof. To compensate for her habitual distractedness, she draws plausible inferences about mundane events, and often does not notice whether her opinion is due to observation or to such an inference. Ben frequently forgets to wear his glasses. Like Anne, he draws plausible inferences about events around him, and tends not to remember having done so. Chauncy is simply a liar. Presumably he knows when he is speaking sincerely, but given the fluency and frequency of his lies, nothing he says is trustworthy. Not surprisingly, the social circles of the three students do not intersect; none would deign to speak to the others. When questioned about the theft, Anne and Ben report what they think they saw, but confess that they are not sure what they actually witnessed and what they inferred. Chauncy insists that his report is accurate, but in view of his record, his claim is suspect.

Individually, none of the reports would count for much. Had only one of the witnesses been present, the most we could reasonably conclude would be that the thief might fit the description. But all three reports agree, and agree in alleging that the thief had an unusual appearance: he had spiked green hair. This makes a difference. Even though individually each report is dubious, and the probability of a green haired textbook thief is low, the fact that the three reports provide the same antecedently improbable description inclines us to believe it. Their accord evidently enhances the epistemic standing of the individual reports. We seem to have more reason to believe each of them in light of the others than we have to believe them separately. The question is: why? How can multiple statements, none of which is tenable, conjoin to yield a tenable conclusion? How can their relation to other less than tenable claims enhance their tenability?

Given the unreliability of the witnesses, we might expect them to be wrong about the thief. But we would not expect them to all be wrong in the same way. The fact that they agree needs an explanation. If they were in cahoots, the explanation would be straightforward: they conspired to tell the same tale. But not being on speaking terms, they are probably not co-conspirators. If the description they provided fit a relevant stereotype, then a penchant for plausibility could explain their accord. But green spiked hair is far from any stereotype one might harbor for a textbook thief. So despite Anne's and Ben's propensity to draw inferences based on plausibility, their descriptions of the thief do not seem to result from such an inference. Evidently the best explanation of the agreement is that the reports are true.

It is not just our ability to exclude obvious alternatives that leads us to credit the allegation. A variety of collateral considerations support it. Some bear directly on the content of the claim. Dan dimly recalls seeing an odd looking stranger lurking in the hallway. The custodian thinks he saw a container of hair dye in the trash. Although the tentativeness of these reports makes them less than wholly credible, they are suggestive enough to buttress the eyewitness testimony. Other collateral considerations concern the witnesses and their circumstances. Book thefts are observable events, so there is nothing inherently dubious about a claim to have seen someone steal a book. The light and the sight lines were such that the witnesses could have seen what they report. The witnesses are adept at recognizing furtive adolescent behavior. None was subject to psychological experiments with implanted memories. None was on drugs. And so on. Separately, these factors count for little. Either their credibility is low or their bearing is slight. But they weave together to make a solid case. This suggests that the epistemic tenability of the several reports and the conclusion they sanction derives from their mutual supportiveness.

Although our focus is on the status of the allegation, it is the account as a whole that is or is not acceptable. Many of the relations of justification are reciprocal. The allegation is acceptable only if (at least most of) the rest of the constellation of supporting considerations is. But since the eyewitnesses are unreliable and the contentions of the collateral witnesses are tenuous, the acceptability of the testimony likewise depends on the acceptability of the allegation. The epistemic status of the allegation is inseparable from the status of the rest of the story. Some of the background information may be separately secured, but to a considerable extent, the various components of the story stand or fall together.

The thesis of the sort of epistemological holism that I want to consider is that epistemic justification is primarily a property of a suitably comprehensive, coherent account, when the best explanation of coherence is that the account is at least roughly true. The epistemic justification of individual claims derives from their membership in a justified account. There is no universally accepted criterion of coherence. But at least this is required: the components of a coherent account must be mutually consistent, cotenable and supportive. That is, the components must be reasonable in light of one another. Since both cotenability and supportiveness are matters of degree, coherence is too. So if it can be shown that epistemic justification is a matter of coherence, there remains the question of how coherent an account must be in order for it to be epistemically justified. Before facing that worry, though, other challenges need to be met. At least two worries immediately arise. The first is that coherence is too demanding an epistemic requirement. The second is that it is not demanding enough.

Even where we take ourselves to be on solid ground, contravening considerations are not uncommon. Mrs. Abercrombie, the aging geometry teacher, says that during the relevant period she saw a young man sporting a green hat. A green hat is not green hair, so her report conflicts with the reports of the other witnesses. Ms. Mintz, the hall monitor, insists no one was in the corridor at the time of the alleged theft. Mr. Miller, the classics teacher, disputes the allegation on the grounds that students do not want Latin books enough to steal them. These reports are clearly relevant to and at odds with the account I gave. If we incorporate them into my account, we render it incoherent. But we seem to have no legitimate reason to exclude them. The problem is this: the discussion so far suggests that the credibility of the various claims comprising an account depends on how well they hang together. If so, the failure of other, equally relevant information to cohere threatens to discredit the account.

Although true, this is not so daunting as it appears. The immediate threat of incoherence comes from assuming that we must take seemingly contravening considerations at face value and incorporate them into an account as they stand. But we need do no such thing. Rather, we assess contravening considerations just as we do the rest of our evidence. Recall that we did not take the eyewitness reports at face value. We initially deemed them suspect because our background information indicated that the informants are unreliable. The credibility of the reports increased because of their agreement with one another and the support provided by collateral information. That agreement gave us reason to think that the general unreliability of the witnesses did not affect the standing of these particular reports. Contravening considerations are subject to similar assessments. Mrs. Abercrombie, being nearsighted and woefully out of date, cannot even imagine that a green thatch on someone's head might be his hair. That being so, her characterization of the suspect as wearing a green hat seems close enough to count as supporting rather than undermining the original allegation. Although Ms. Mintz flatly disputes what others have said, there are reasons to doubt that her claim is true. Since the three eyewitnesses saw each other in the corridor during the period when Ms. Mintz denies that anyone was there, her contention is dubious on independent grounds. Since she occasionally goes AWOL to smoke a cigarette, there is reason to suspect that she was absent when the theft occurred. Mr. Miller's argument cannot be so easily discredited. But the book is gone. Meg put it in her locker when she arrived at school. It was not there when she returned. Even if Latin

books are not attractive targets for teenage thieves, the book's having been stolen may better explain its absence than any available alternative would. Just as other considerations compensate for the improbability of a green haired thief, other considerations compensate for the improbability of a Latin book thief. In determining the acceptability of a claim, we assess the considerations that afford evidence pertaining to its tenability. This is not always a simple yes/no matter. We may find that although an evidence statement is unacceptable or unsupportive as it stands, with suitable modifications, it would be. And we may find that the modifications themselves are acceptable. Coherence remains crucial. Sometimes it is achieved directly, sometimes by discrediting or disarming threats.

The coherence that affords epistemic justification is not just coherence among object-level deliverances. We have higher-order commitments about what sorts of object-level deliverances are trustworthy, about how much credibility to accord them, about how they ought to mesh, and about what to do when commitments clash. These higher-order commitments supply reasons to revise or reject some deliverances but not others when conflicts occur. The coherence that constitutes epistemic justification is something we achieve, not something that simply falls out of the relations in which our object-level deliverances happen to stand to one another.

The second worry is that coherence can readily be achieved through epistemically illicit means. A good nineteenth-century novel is highly coherent, but not credible on that account. Even though *Middlemarch* is far more coherent than our regrettably fragmentary and disjointed views about the book theft, the best explanation of its coherence lies in the novelist's craft, not in the truth (or approximate truth) of the story. The coherence of the story affords virtually no reason to think it is true. This is surely right. But rather than taking this objection to completely discredit the contention that coherence conduces to epistemic acceptability, I suggest that it indicates something different: coherence conduces to epistemic acceptability only when the best explanation of the coherence of a constellation of claims is that they are (at least roughly) true....

One might argue that even the best nineteenth-century novel does not pose as great a threat as we sometimes suppose. No matter how deeply immersed I am in the story, a single glance up from the page is enough to convince me that I am not in a drawing room in nineteenth-century England. The story, though internally coherent, manifestly fails to mesh with the rest of my experience. This is true, but the question is what to make of it. On the one hand, too restricted a cluster of mutually supportive claims seems inadequate to engender credibility. We can't make the story credible simply by ignoring everything else we believe. On the other hand, insisting that all our commitments need to cohere seems unduly demanding. If acceptability requires coherence with everything we accept (or with everything we accept for cognitive purposes), it is but a short step to skepticism. One wayward belief, however remote from current concerns, could discredit an entire constellation of beliefs. Theories that ground justification in coherence then face a problem of scope.

Worries about scope, however, seem not to do justice to the problem that confronts us here. Faced with a clash between the deliverances of the novel and those of my glance, it is obvious which I should accept. There is no temptation to resolve the tension by dismissing perceptual deliverances or taking *them* to be the fiction. They seem to possess an epistemic privi-

lege that prevents considerations of coherence from overriding them. The capacity of perceptual differences to trump the claims of a tightly knit novel may seem conclusively to demonstrate that epistemological justification cannot consist in coherence.

The matter deserves further consideration though. Until the source of perception's epistemic privilege is clear, it is premature to rule coherence out....

If we think about our situation when we glance away from the novel, we recognize that we draw on more than the sentences comprising the novel and our current perceptual deliverances. We tacitly rely on a fairly extensive and epistemologically informed understanding of novels and perception. We know enough about underlying mechanisms to have reason to credit some perceptual deliverances. We know enough about literature to realize that novels are typically literally false. That constitutes sufficient reason for even casual perceptual deliverances to override the claims of the novel.

Juxtaposing the novel with perception might seem to make the problem too easy, though. Regardless of what we think about perception, if we recognize that a novel is a work of fiction, we have reason to discount any direct claims it may seem to make on our epistemic allegiance. (I say direct claims because I believe that novels play a significant, albeit indirect, role in the advancement of understanding. But how they do so is not germane to this discussion.) The serious challenge comes from a coherent factual account that conflicts with perceptual deliverances. If holism holds that such an account always overrides perceptual deliverances, it seems plainly unacceptable. However tightly woven an empirical account may be, we would be epistemically irresponsible to ignore recalcitrant evidence. Foundationalists take this latter point to be decisive: if observation can show a theory to be unjustified, then coherence cannot be the locus of justification.

This would be so, if observation worked in isolation. For then, owing to its epistemic privilege, one perceptual deliverance would have the capacity to discredit an entire system of thought. But this is a myth. Only observations we have reason to trust have the power to unseat theories. So it is not an observation in isolation, but an observation backed by reasons that actually discredits the theory.

The holist response to the challenge presented by observation is this: *a priori*, perceptual deliverances have no special weight. They are just deliverances jockeying for inclusion in coherent bodies of thought. But over time, as we attend to the fates of our various deliverances, we learn that the incorporation of some, but not others, yields accounts which are borne out by further experience, hence which retain their coherence over time. This gives us grounds for discrimination. We realize that the deliverances we take to be perceptual are more likely to be confirmed than spontaneous deliverances that just leap to mind. So we assign greater weight to perceptual deliverances than to passing thoughts. Moreover, we learn that not all perceptual deliverances are on a par. Those that are credible tend to come in mutually reinforcing streams, so isolated perceptual deliverances count for little. We begin to draw distinctions among perceptual deliverances. For example, we discover that peripheral vision is less trustworthy than central vision. So we have reason to discount what we see out of the corner of the eye. This is not to say that we dismiss the deliverances of peripheral vision out of hand, but that we demand more in the way of corroboration. Some of us discover that we are color blind or

tone deaf or myopic. That is, we learn that our perceptions of colors, tones, or the dimensions of distant objects are not to be trusted. And so on. We come to assign different weights to perceptual deliverances depending on how well they accord with other things we take ourselves to have reason to credit—other appearances of the same object, the reports of other observers, the implications of our best theories about the visible properties of items of the kind in question, and so forth.

The issue is not simply how well a given content meshes with other things we believe, but how well a given content from a given source in given circumstances does. The weight we attach to perceptual deliverances derives from our understanding of the world and our access to it. Initially, perhaps, this is just a matter of track records. Some perceptual deliverances seem to integrate better into acceptable systems of thought than spontaneous thoughts that just leap to mind. Later, as we develop physiological and psychological accounts of ourselves, which explain our perceptual mechanisms, we gain additional reasons to take some perceptual deliverances to be credible. The epistemic privilege that some perceptual deliverances enjoy then derives from an understanding of ourselves as perceiving organisms. That is, the reason for assigning those deliverances significant epistemic weight derives from the coherent account of perception that backs the assignment....the justification for privileging perception derives from the relation of perceptual judgments to the rest of our theory of ourselves as cognitive agents interacting with a mind-independent world....

This argument explains both why some perceptual deliverances have the capacity to unsettle theory, and why those deliverances are not intrinsically privileged. They owe their epistemic status to their place in our evolving understanding of the world and our modes of access to it.…

Achieving coherence is not just a matter of excluding untoward deliverances. In the interests of systematicity, we may incorporate considerations we have no antecedent reason to believe. For example, although there is no direct evidence of positrons, symmetry considerations show that a physical theory that eschewed them would be significantly less coherent than one that acknowledged them. So physics' commitment to positrons is epistemically appropriate. Considerations we have no independent reason to believe can acquire tenability then because they strengthen the coherence of the systems they belong to.…

Epistemological positions that construe knowledge as justified true belief generally treat being justified, being true, and being believed as three separate features of a propositional content. The standard objection to coherentism is that coherence among propositional contents is so easily achieved that it affords no reason to believe that the contents are true, hence no justification for them. This overlooks the fact that the contents in question are not just any propositional contents, they are belief contents or deliverance contents. That is, they are contents that present themselves as true. This makes a difference. For the fact that they present themselves as true gives us some slight reason to think that they are true. The word "slight" is crucial. I do not contend that we have sufficient reason to credit such contents. But at least two considerations speak in favor of granting them a slight measure of credibility. Beliefs form the basis for action, so the success of our actions affords evidence of the truth of the corresponding beliefs. Moreover, we learn from experience. Once we come to recognize that premonitions tend not to be borne out, we cease to credit them. We may continue to experience feelings of foreboding, for example, but they cease to qualify as deliverances.

Manifestly these considerations are far too weak to demonstrate that beliefs or deliverances are epistemically justified. They do, however, give us reason to think that beliefs and deliverances have some claim on our epistemic allegiance. They have an epistemic edge. We have better reason to incorporate them into our systems of thought than to incorporate contents we are neutral about. Beliefs and deliverances are, I suggest, initially tenable. But initial tenability is a weak and precarious epistemic status. Considerations of overall coherence often require revision or rejection of initially tenable commitments. Initially tenable commitments can conflict. They may be mutually incompatible or non-cotenable. Or they may be sufficiently isolated that they are incapable of giving support to or gaining support from other things we believe. Then they cannot be incorporated into an epistemically acceptable system.

Epistemical acceptability, I contend, requires reflective equilibrium. A system of thought is in equilibrium if its elements are reasonable in light of one another. This is a matter of coherence. An equilibrium is reflective if the system is as reasonable as any available alternative in light of our initially tenable commitments. Such a system is not required to incorporate as many initially tenable commitments as possible. As we have seen, there are weighting factors that favor some incorporations over others. Moreover, rather than incorporating commitments, a system may show why we were misled into accepting them, or may include modifications of them.

The standards of reasonableness are second-order commitments, and are subject to the same sorts of considerations as our first-order deliverances. The fact that we accept them indicates that they are prima facie acceptable. But they can conflict, or fail to yield verdicts in cases where they should, or yield verdicts that we find unacceptable. Then they too are subject to revision or rejection in order to yield a comprehensive system of first- and second-order commitments that is on reflection something we can endorse.

Whether the sort of holism that results is a coherence theory is not clear. Using BonJour's categories, it might be classified as a very weak foundationalism or as a coherence theory. Deliverances derive their initial tenability from their status as deliverances. That suggests that something other than coherence is involved. But initially tenable commitments display at least two features that are not characteristic of standard foundational beliefs. First, there are no intrinsically privileged kinds of deliverances. The account does not insist that there is something epistemically special about perception or introspection or analyticity. It simply says that the fact that a consideration presents itself as true gives it a modest measure of tenability. Second, even that small measure of tenability is easily lost. Tenable theories are justified in part by reference to initially tenable deliverances, but they need not incorporate the deliverances by reference to which they are justified.

Whether we call such an epistemology a coherence theory does not in the end matter. The virtues of the theory are as follows. (1) It does not privilege any sorts of beliefs or representations *a priori*. What beliefs and representations are worthy of acceptance is something we learn by developing increasingly comprehensive, coherent accounts of the world and our access to it. (2) It enables us to start from whatever deliverances we happen to have. But because it insists that we subject those deliverances to rigorous assessment, such a starting point is not question begging. (3) The standards of assessment are themselves the fruits of epistemic activity, and can change in response to feedback. (4) Hence, everything is subject to revision. A system of thought that we can on reflection accept today may be one that we cannot on reflection accept tomorrow. But so long as a system is in reflective equilibrium and the best explanation of its being so is that it is at least roughly true, it and its components are justified. What results is neither certainty nor skepticism but a fallible, provisional, but reasonable epistemological stance.

The Justification of Our Beliefs Requires a Foundation

JAMES VAN CLEVE

I

Foundationalism has been characterized as the view that "the knowledge which a person has at any time is a structure or edifice, many parts and stages of which help to support each other, but which as a whole is supported by its own foundation." To unpack the metaphor, we may say that the foundation consists of *basic beliefs*—beliefs that a subject is justified in holding even in the absence of any justifying reason for them—and all other justified beliefs derive their justification at least in part from such basic beliefs.

The classical argument for foundationalism is an infinite regress argument going back to Aristotle: unless there were basic beliefs, every justified belief would rest on further justified beliefs, and so on without end. An infinite regress is not in fact the only alternative to basic beliefs, but the other alternatives are equally problematic, or so foundationalists maintain. To canvass all the options, let us set down four propositions that jointly imply the existence of an infinite regress of justified beliefs:

1 Some beliefs are justified.

2 No belief is justified unless some other belief serves as a reason for it.

3 One belief cannot serve as a reason justifying another unless the first is itself justified.

4 If A serves as a reason justifying B, then B cannot serve (directly or indirectly) as a reason justifying B.

These four propositions jointly entail the existence of an infinite regress of justified propositions. We are therefore faced with five alternatives: accept the infinite regress or reject one of the four assumptions.

Skeptics (of the universal ilk) deny 1, maintaining that no beliefs whatever are justified. *Foundationalists* deny 2, maintaining that some beliefs are justified in the absence of reasons. *Positists* (not to be confused with positivists) deny 3, maintaining that chains of justifying reasons can terminate in reasons that are not justified themselves, but are simply individual or societal posits. *Coherentists* deny 4, maintaining that beliefs can be justified in virtue of relations of mutual support. *Infinitists* accept all four assumptions and the resulting infinite regress.

All five options have their takers....But I think it is fair to say that the leading contenders among the five options are foundationalism and coherentism.

Coherentism is sometimes characterized as a view that sanctions circular reasoning, but that is an oversimplified construal of it. Coherentists do not typically endorse simple loops in which A justifies B, B justifies C, and C justifies A; rather, they envision vast webs of belief in which everything is supported by some significant portion of the remaining beliefs: A by B and C, B by A, D, J, and K, and so on.

For their part, foundationalists do not typically deny the power of coherence to contribute to the overall epistemic status of a body of belief. They simply insist that coherence cannot do all the work on its own—there must be at least a modicum of intrinsic credibility or non-inferential warrant possessed by basic beliefs before coherence can have its amplifying effect.

Laurence BonJour distinguishes three grades of foundationalism. According to *strong* foundationalism, basic beliefs are "not just adequately justified, but also *infallible, certain, indubitable,* or *incorrigible.*" According to *moderate* foundationalism, the non-inferential warrant possessed by basic beliefs need not amount to absolute certainty or any of the other privileged statuses just mentioned, but it must be "sufficient by itself to satisfy the adequate-justification condition for knowledge." Finally, according to *weak* foundationalism,

> basic beliefs possess only a very low degree of epistemic justification on their own, a degree of justification insufficient by itself either to satisfy the adequate-justification condition for knowledge or to qualify them as acceptable justifying premises for further beliefs. Such beliefs are only "initially credible," rather than fully justified.

We must rely on coherence among such initially credible beliefs to amplify their level of warrant up to the point where it is adequate for knowledge.

As BonJour notes, weak foundationalism could be regarded as a hybrid view, mixing together foundational and coherentist elements....

But if coherence can elevate the epistemic status of a set of beliefs in this way, what prevents it from generating warrant entirely on its own, without any need for basic beliefs? This is a question that has been asked by several authors, including BonJour:

> The basic idea is that an initially low degree of justification can somehow be magnified or amplified by coherence, to a degree adequate for

knowledge. But how is this magnification or amplification supposed to work? How can coherence, not itself an independent source of justification on a foundationalist view, justify the rejection of some initially credible beliefs and enhance the justification of others?

The implied suggestion is that if coherence can do what the weak foundationalist allows, it can also do what the thoroughgoing coherentist says it can do....

II

...Can coherence alone be a source of warrant without need of inputs with initial credibility?...If several individually unreliable reporters agree with collusion, then the fact to which they bear common witness may have high probability in the end. But in attaching a high final probability to the fact attested, we are of course taking for granted that the various witnesses *do* testify to it. If we had reason to think that the courtroom and all its proceedings were happening only in a dream or a novel, the fact that the ostensible reports hang together would count for little. And so it is with the reports of memory, the senses, and cognitive systems more generally: coherence among them lends high final credibility only on the assumption that the reports genuinely occur.

How, then, do we know *these* things: that witness A does say X, that I do ostensibly remember Y, that I do seem to see Z? Many foundationalists would say that these are the grounds on which the rest of our knowledge rests, and that they must themselves be matters of basic knowledge. Lewis himself famously maintained that nothing can be probable unless something is certain, and among the certainties he placed the facts that I do have this or that presentation of sense or memory. His insistence on certainty is controversial, but it seems to me that a good case can be made that there must at least be high intrinsic credibility—perhaps high enough to constitute knowledge—attaching to the facts that such-and-such cognitive states (be they experiences, ostensible memories, or beliefs at large) are actually taking place. If this is right, we must not only abjure pure coherentism: we must also adopt a moderate rather than a weak foundationalism.

I see only one plausible alternative to an assumption of high initial credibility or knowledge-sufficient warrant at the foundational level, and that is the view that the promptings of sense or memory function as *external* conditions of knowledge. An external condition of knowledge is a condition that makes knowledge possible regardless of whether it is itself known to obtain. For example, in Goldman's reliability theory, if a subject comes to believe p as the result of a reliable process, his belief is knowledge regardless of whether the subject knows anything about the reliability of the process. Perhaps the facts that I have such-and-such ostensible perceptions or memories could function in this external way, contributing to my knowledge even if not themselves known. The idea would be that my ostensible perceivings and rememberings are not pieces of evidence on which I conditionalize when their epistemic status is high enough; instead, they are facts whose mere obtaining confers credibility on their contents.

I turn now to another point at which I think a theory of knowledge that invokes coherence must make a concession to either foundationalism or externalism.

The example of the witnesses who agree is in one respect a drastically oversimplified case of coherence. The agreement of the witnesses is literal identity, or at least logical equivalence, of content: witness 1 says X and so does witness 2. But the coherence that figures in episte-mology is typically a much looser sort of hanging together. The coherence of ostensible memories is not their all being memories that p, for the same p or something logically equivalent. Nor is the coherence of beliefs or cognitions generally like that. Rather, it is a type of coherence that is exemplified by the following items:

I seem to remember seeing a skunk last night;

I seem to remember smelling a skunk last night;

I seem to remember that the lid was on the garbage can when I went to bed;

I now see that the can has been knocked over and trash strewn about;

There was a skunk here last night;

and so on. In other words, it is not identity or even equivalence of content, but rather something like the relation Lewis calls congruence: a matter of each item being more probable given the rest than it is on its own.

What are these coherence-constituting relations of probability founded upon, and how do we know that they obtain?

One answer has been given by Russell: "It is only by assuming laws that one fact can make another probable or improbable." Perhaps Russell goes too far in requiring strict laws in order for one fact to make another probable, but it is plausible that we at least require rough empirical generalizations. Where do these generalizations come from? Presumably, they are inferred inductively from particular facts gathered by memory. And now the following difficulty emerges: ostensible memories give rise to knowledge only with the help of coherence; coherence depends on laws or empirical generalizations; and such generalizations can be known only with the help of memory. In short, we cannot get coherence without the help of laws, and if memory does not suffice on its own to give knowledge of particular facts from which the laws are inferred, we cannot get laws without the help of coherence. It appears to follow that we cannot have any knowledge from memory unless the occurrence of ostensible memories is prima facie sufficient for knowledge. Such was Russell's own conclusion:

> memory is a premise of knowledge....When I say memory is a premise, I mean that among the facts upon which scientific laws are based, some are admitted solely because they are remembered.

Note the word "solely." Russell is saying that individual memories must be capable of giving rise to knowledge on their own, without benefit of coherence. This is compatible, of course, with allowing that the warrant provided by memory is defeasible, as Russell did allow. But the resulting view is nonetheless a foundationalism of memory knowledge stronger than that of Lewis, who required only an initial "slight" presumption in favor of the truth of any ostensible memory. Russell's view accords to memory greater epistemic powers than that: ostensibly remembering that p is a source of prima facie warrant that, if undefeated (and if p is true) is strong enough for knowing that p. In BonJour's terms, we have again advanced from weak to moderate foundationalism, this time as regards the contents of ostensible memories rather than the occurrences of them as mental events.

Russell's argument assumes that coherence and the laws that underlie it contribute to our knowledge only if they are themselves known. As in the case of the occurrences of our ostensible memories,

one could challenge this assumption by going external, holding that coherence does its work regardless of whether the subject knows it obtains....I believe coherentism can avoid a concession to foundationalism only by making a concession to externalism. The fact that p, q, and r do cohere with one another, as well as the facts that they are deliverances of our cognitive systems to begin with, are facts that must either function externally or be known foundationally.

III

As the debate between foundationalists and coherentists has progressed, each side has moved in the direction of the other. Contemporary foundationalists are seldom foundationalists of the strong Cartesian variety: they do not insist that basic beliefs be absolutely certain. They also typically allow that the elements in a system of belief can acquire enhanced justification through their coherence. On the other side, many coherentists admit that coherence alone is not the sole source of justification—there must be some initially credible inputs before coherence can work its wonders. Is there anything more to disagree about, or do foundationalists and coherentists now meet in the middle?

There are indeed still points of difference. To highlight several of them, I shall discuss the broadly coherentist views of Catherine Elgin....

Elgin characterizes herself as a proponent of reflective equilibrium. As she conceives of it, reflective equilibrium has two chief requirements: "The components of a system in reflective equilibrium must be reasonable in light of one another, and the system as a whole reasonable in light of our initially tenable commitments." It is by the second requirement that Elgin distinguishes her view from a pure coherentism: the components of a system in equilibrium must be answerable not just to one another, but also to our initially tenable commitments.

The second requirement puts a "tether" on permissible systems, thereby enabling Elgin to avoid some of the objections to pure coherentism. For example, one of the standard objections to coherentism is that the contents of a consistent fairy tale would be a body of warranted propositions. Not so for Elgin, since the propositions in the story may be reasonable in light of each other without being reasonable in light of our initially tenable commitments.

Of the various things we believe, which have initial tenability? In Elgin's view, they *all* do, if we genuinely believe them: anything actually held has some initial tenability or presumption in its favor. The presumption may only be slight and it may be lost in the end, but it is there in the beginning.

What about the various principles of logic, evidence, and method whereby some things are reasonable in light of others? In Elgin's view, these have the same status as everything else: they are initially tenable if held, and they may gain or lose in tendability depending on how they fit in with everything else.

Why is Elgin's view as so far set forth not simply a form of weak foundationalism, in which initially tenable claims function as basic beliefs? She cites two differences: unlike the justification that attaches to foundationalism's basic claims, initial tenability can be lost; it can also be augmented through coherence.

It is not clear to me, however, that either of these features should be regarded as a prerogative of coherentists alone. In a typology of possible foundationalisms, Roderick Firth has suggested that the minimal tenet of foundationalism is simply this: basic beliefs have some measure of initial warrant that is not derived from

coherence. This level of warrant may be increased by coherence with other statements or diminished, even to the vanishing point, by lack of coherence with other statements. Firth's minimal view thus incorporates both of the features Elgin sees as antithetical to foundationalism.

Nonetheless, I see two other questions on which foundationalists are apt to disagree with Elgin. First, are all commitments initially tenable, or only those in some specially marked out class? Second, are all commitments likewise revisable, or are some immune from subsequent rejection? On each question, Elgin takes the more egalitarian stand....

...Are all commitments on a par as regards the possibility of revision? Elgin holds, with Quine, that in the quest for reflective equilibrium, anything may be revised. There is no commitment that may not be sacrificed in order to maximize the tenability of the entire system. Here I would like to protest that there are certain principles of logic, at least, that cannot be given up, because they are framework principles without which coherence could scarcely be defined. What would happen if we gave up the law of non-contradiction? It is not clear that there could any longer be such a thing as what Quine calls a recalcitrant experience, forcing changes elsewhere in the system. If a new deliverance stood in contradiction to things we already accepted, we could simply accept it with a "What—me worry?" shrug.

Here is another difficulty for a coherentism that holds everything revisable, at least if we understand this as "anything could be justifiably rejected," symbolized as "(p)possibly J ~ p." Suppose there is some proposition q (the law of noncontradiction, perhaps?) whose truth is necessary for anything to belong to a coherent system and therefore necessary for anything to be justified. Since ~q entails that nothing is justified, we now have *possibly J (nothing is justified)*, which is absurd.

A related question about the status of the rules and principles of logic and evidence is whether they have force only because a subject is committed to them. I gather Elgin would say yes, but I say no. Consider a system of beliefs containing the elements p, q, and p → ~q. Suppose it is not a sheer fact of logic, independent of anything the subject believes, that the system is inconsistent and in need of revision. Could we make the system intolerably inconsistent by adding the principle: if any two of {p, q, and p → ~q} are true, then the third must be false? No, for anyone who could live comfortably with the original system could live comfortably with the expanded system....

I wish to raise one more question about the role of logical and evidential relations in Elgin's coherentism. Elgin defines both coherence and equilibrium in terms of the relation "p is reasonable in light of q, r, and s." What is the required epistemic status of this relation (or of the logical and other relations on which it supervenes)? Must such relations be known to hold among the propositions in a system before the propositions are warranted for the subject? And if so, how does such knowledge arise?

I see three possibilities to consider in answer to these questions. First, the holding of coherence-constituting relations might be regarded as an external condition of knowledge, making knowledge possible regardless of whether the subject knows that such relations hold. Although this seems to me a good way for a coherentist to go, I gather that Elgin would not find it congenial. On more than one occasion, she expresses her dissatisfaction with externalist stratagems in epistemology. Second, it might be held that logical relations and other relations of support are known to hold because they are necessary relations,

apprehendable *a priori*. But this, too, is an option Elgin would reject. In the first place, it would be a concession to foundationalism; in the second place, she has Quinean qualms about there being any propositions at all that are true necessarily and known *a priori*. Third, it might be held that coherence-constituting relations are known to hold because the propositions saying that they hold are part of the best overall coherent system that is reasonable in light of our antecedent commitments. But that way lies an infinite regress. A proposition p affirming a relation of coherence would be justified only because the subject is justified in believing that p belongs to a coherent system. That belief in turn would be justified only because the subject is justified in believing that *p belongs to a coherent system* belongs to a coherent system, and so on. Even if it is the same system every step of the way, we still get a regress in which ever more complicated propositions must be believed with justification to belong to the system. The untenability of such a regress suggests to me that we should go instead with one of the first two options, agreeing with the externalist that coherence propositions need not be known at all or with the foundationalist that they are known because they are either basic propositions or propositions inferrable from basic propositions.

IV

I have not lived up to the title of this essay, for I have not offered a complete defense of moderate foundationalism. I hope nonetheless to have shown that an internalist coherentism cannot be a satisfactory theory of justification. We must be either externalists or foundationalists, and if we are foundationalists, our foundationalism must be of the moderate rather than the weak variety.

THE CONTINUING DEBATE:
How Do I Know That Jupiter Is the Largest Planet in Our Solar System?

What Is New

Foundationalism seemed an obvious and almost trivial truth for thousands of years: *if* there is knowledge, then it must rest on some solid foundation of certainty. The nature of that foundation was of course a subject of dispute; but for Plato, up through Descartes, all the way to the 20th Century logical positivists—who endeavored to build a knowledge system by combining logical operations with a foundation of immediate sensory experiences—there was consensus that knowledge must rest on a foundation. So the entire debate over coherence vs. foundationalism might be regarded as new: almost its entire history has occurred in the last half century, which is the blink of an eye in philosophical time. Perhaps one of the most interesting recent developments is the conversion of Laurence BonJour—formerly a leading coherentist critic of foundationalism—to a form of foundationalism.

Where to Find More

Knowledge: Readings in Contemporary Epistemology (Oxford: Oxford University Press, 2000), edited by Sven Bernecker and Fred Dretske, contains key contemporary essays by foundationalists and their critics. An excellent collection of important papers on foundationalism and coherence from the last several decades is *Epistemology: An Anthology,* edited by Ernest Sosa and Jaegwon Kim (Oxford: Blackwell, 2000). Laurence BonJour, "The Dialectic of Foundationalism and Coherentism," in John Greco and Ernest Sosa, editors, *The Blackwell Guide to Epistemology* (Oxford: Blackwell Publishers, 1999), is a good survey of the foundationalist/coherentist controversy, though BonJour ultimately sides with the foundationalists. Another good survey article is "Theories of Justification," by Richard Fumerton, which is Chapter 6 in *The Oxford Handbook of Epistemology*, edited by Paul K. Moser (Oxford: Oxford University Press, 2002).

Basic challenges to the foundationalist tradition occurred in the second half of the 20th Century, particularly in the work of Willard van Orman Quine and Wilfred Sellars. See particularly Quine's essays collected in *Ontological Relativity and Other Essays* (New York: Columbia University Press, 1969), and in *The Ways of Paradox and Other Essays* (New York: Random House, 1966); and Sellars' *Science, Perception and Reality* (London: Routledge and Kegan Paul, 1963).

Peter Klein's arguments for infinitism can be found in his "Human Knowledge and the Infinite Regress of Reasons," in *Philosophical Perspectives*, volume 13 (1999), edited by James Tomberlin: 51–69; and "Why Not Infinitism?" in *Epistemology: Proceedings of the Twentieth World Congress in Philosophy*, edited by Richard Cobb-Stevens, volume 5 (2000): 199–208.

A sustained attack on foundationalism is offered by Michael Williams, in *Groundless Belief: An Essay on the Possibility of Epistemology*, 2nd edition (Princeton, N.J.: Princeton University Press, 1999).

Several writers have advanced mixed theories, which involve some combination of foundationalism and coherentism. One of the most interesting such theories is developed by Susan Haack, in *Evidence and Inquiry* (Oxford: Blackwell Publishers, 1993).

Laurence BonJour's earlier coherence view, and his criticisms of foundationalism, can be found in *The Structure of Empirical Knowledge* (Cambridge, Mass.: Harvard University Press, 1985); his more recent foundationalist views are presented in *In Defense of Pure Reason* (London: Cambridge University Press, 1997).

Online, the Stanford Encyclopedia of Philosophy—http://plato.stanford.edu—is an excellent resource; see the articles on epistemology, as well as several articles under the heading "justification, epistemic." Keith DeRose maintains "The Epistemology Page," at http://pantheon.yale.edu/~kd47/e-page.htm. It is an interesting mix of recent articles in several areas of epistemology and good bibliographical resources, as well as a collection of course syllabi, ratings of graduate programs in epistemology, and even a few pictures of contemporary epistemologists.

4   CAN WE EVER HAVE GENUINE KNOWLEDGE?

Contextualism Can Resolve the Paradox of Skepticism

ADVOCATE: Stewart Cohen, Professor of Philosophy at Arizona State University, has written many influential articles in the area of epistemology, including "Knowledge and Context," *Journal of Philosophy*, volume 83 (1986): 574–583; "Knowledge, Context, and Social Standards," *Synthese*, volume 73 (1987): 3–26; "Contextualist Solutions to Epistemological Problems: Scepticism, Gettier, and the Lottery," *Australasian Journal of Philosophy*, volume 76 (1998): 289–306; and "Two Kinds of Skeptical Argument," *Philosophy and Phenomenological Research*, volume 58 (1998): 143–159.

SOURCE: "Contextualism, Skepticism, and the Structure of Reasons," *Philosophical Perspectives*, volume 13: Epistemology, 1999; pages 57–69.

Contextualism Is Not the Solution to Skepticism

ADVOCATE: Anthony Brueckner, Professor of Philosophy at University of California, Santa Barbara; his research has focused primarily on the question of skepticism, and his writings include "Knowledge of Content and Knowledge of the World," *Philosophical Review* (January 1994), "Semantic Answers to Skepticism," *Pacific Philosophical Quarterly* (September 1992), and "Brains in a Vat," *Journal of Philosophy* (March 1986).

SOURCE: "The Elusive Virtues of Contextualism," *Philosophical Studies,* volume 118; pages 401–405.

You're at a college assembly, seated next to a friend who grew up in extreme poverty in Bangladesh, without access to television or newspapers. The featured speaker strides across the stage, flashes a big smile, and launches into his speech. "Who is that?" your friend whispers. "That's Bill Clinton, the former President," you confidently reply. And you have no doubt of the truth of your answer: you have often seen photographs of Clinton, you heard him give a speech at a campaign rally, you have often seen him on television, you recognize his face and his voice and his mannerisms. Besides, the President of the College introduced the speaker as former President Bill Clinton. You *know* the person at the podium is Bill Clinton. But suppose that the situation is somewhat altered: you have recently read newspaper accounts that Bill Clinton was getting tired of all these speaking engagements, but he liked the money he was being paid; so he had hired a very clever impersonator, made up to look and sound remarkably like the former President, to give some of his speeches while Clinton himself relaxed at home. You seem to have the same evidence that this is Bill Clinton (the evidence of your eyes and ears, and the statement of the college president); but in this altered context, you might be more reluctant to assert that you *know* the speaker is Bill Clinton. If that is so, do you still want to say that in the original context—minus the reports of the Clinton impersonator—you actually *knew* the speaker was Bill Clinton?

G. E. Moore, an influential early 20th Century British philosopher, proposed this straightforward refutation of skepticism: Holding out a hand, Moore confidently asserted: "I know that this is a hand," *and* Moore insisted that he knew the existence of his hand much better than he could possibly know any skeptical reason for doubting it. Therefore, since Moore knows that he does in fact have a physical hand it follows that he is not a brain-in-a-vat, and thus he knows that skepticism is false:

> We *know* that there are and have been in the Universe the two kinds of things—material objects and acts of consciousness. We *know* that there are and have been in the Universe huge numbers of both. We *know* that the vast majority of material objects are unconscious. We *know* that things of both kinds *have* existed in the past, which do not exist now, and things of both kinds do exist now, which did *not* exist in the past. All these things we should, I think, certainly say that we *know*. G. E. Moore, *Some Main Problems of Philosophy* (New York: The Macmillan Company, 1953).

In *On Certainty*, Ludwig Wittgenstein lodges an objection against Moore's argument: in everyday contexts, it might make perfectly good sense to affirm that I know I have a hand; but the skeptic's challenge operates in a very different *context*. Moore is using the context of common sense in everyday life, while the skeptic is exploring questions of what certainties could be relied upon under the most severe challenge. It is one thing to say "that is my hand" in ordinary circumstances; something quite different when the context is one in which I am under the effect of some mind-altering drug, or when the mirrors in an arcade have left me confused and disoriented, or when I awaken—still groggy from anesthesia—having undergone an arm transplant after a severe accident and am not quite sure that I am in control of the five-fingered object I see down at the end of my arm. What is obviously true in one context may not be true in all contexts. As Wittgenstein states:

> When Moore says he *knows* such and such, he is really enumerating a lot of empirical propositions which we affirm without special testing; propositions, that is, which have a peculiar logical role in the system of our empirical propositions....It is not single axioms that strike me as obvious, it is a system in which consequences and premises give one another *mutual* support....I should like to say: Moore does not *know* what he asserts he knows, but it stands fast for him, as also for me; regarding it as absolutely solid is part of our *method* of doubt and certainty....For when Moore says "I know that that's..." I want to reply "you don't *know* anything!"—and yet I would not say that to anyone who was speaking without philosophical intention. That is, I feel (rightly?) that these two mean to say something different. Ludwig Wittgenstein, *On Certainty*, edited by G. E. M. Anscombe and G. H. von Wright (New York: Harper & Row, 1969/1972).

Thus Wittgenstein objects to Moore using what is *known* in one context to justify larger claims of knowledge in response to the challenge of skepticism. But contemporary contextualists tend to draw a rather different conclusion from this contextualist point. They insist that the radical skeptical hypothesis is *not* part of the context of ordinary life, and thus in the ordinary context it *is* legitimate to assert that we know the truth of our ordinary beliefs. Skepticism may not be totally defeated, but at least it is pushed far enough back so that it should not trouble us in our ordinary pursuits and our common claims of genuine knowledge.

In his argument, Stewart Cohen makes use of the *closure principle*; basically, the principle that if it is true that I know X, and I also know that X guarantees (entails) Y, then I must also know Y. For example, if I know that the Steelers scored more points than the Browns, and I also know that scoring more points entails winning the game, then I must know that the Steelers won. Cohen finds the principle useful in his argument for contextualism. In the course of that argument, Cohen uses a common valid argument form you have used all your life; logicians call it *modus tollens*. The form of that argument is simple: If A then B, not B, therefore not A. Any argument of that form is the valid argument *modus tollens*: for example, if State scored three touchdowns, then State won; but State did not win; therefore, State did not score three touchdowns. If I flunked the final exam, then I flunked the course; but I did not flunk the course; therefore, I did not flunk the final exam. Suppose that we reword the argument just a bit, without really changing the *structure* of the argument: If State scored three touchdowns, then State did *not* lose. But State *did* lose. Therefore, State did not score three touchdowns. In this case, the second part of the conditional statement is a negation, and the second premise of the argument *denies* that negation (by making a *positive* statement: State did lose). Or we might have stated it like this: If State scored three touchdowns, then State did not lose. But it is *not* the case that State did not lose. That's still just *modus tollens*, and that's the argument form Cohen uses in discussing the closure argument.

In his critique of contextualism, Anthony Brueckner challenges the contextualist solution to skepticism, arguing that the contextualist boundaries cannot exclude skeptical concerns.

POINTS TO PONDER

➤ You have a seminar today, but you won't be penalized for missing the class; and you *know* that your seminar meets in Greenlaw Hall, Room 254, at 3 p.m. Next week, you have the same seminar, but this time you must give a major presentation: if you are late your professor will flunk you and you will not graduate. On Stewart Cohen's contextualist view, you *know* the time and place for today's less important seminar; but next week, with *precisely the same evidence*, you might *not* know when and where the critically important seminar meeting will occur (because its greater importance changes the context). Does that seem plausible?

➤ Cohen maintains that in everyday, ordinary contexts, we can legitimately affirm that our ordinary beliefs are true. Is that contextualist answer a sufficient reply to skepticism? Is it the best we can do?

➤ Brueckner finds the "good news" of contextualism to be cold comfort in response to skeptical worries. How might Cohen respond?

Contextualism Can Resolve the Paradox of Skepticism

STEWART COHEN

Suppose one speaker says about a subject *S* and a proposition *P*, "*S* knows *P*." At the very same time, another speaker says of the very same subject and proposition, "*S* does not know *P*." Must one of the two be speaking falsely? According to the view I will call "contextualism," both speakers can be speaking the truth. Contextualism is the view that ascriptions of knowledge are context-sensitive—the truth-values of sentences containing the words "know," and its cognates depend on contextually determined standards. Because of this, sentences of the form "*S* knows *P*" can, at one time, have different truth-values in different contexts. Now when I say "contexts," I mean "contexts of ascription." So the truth-value of a sentence containing the knowledge predicate can vary depending on things like the purposes, intentions, expectations, presuppositions, etc., of the speakers who utter these sentences.

In what follows, I defend the view that ascriptions of knowledge are context-sensitive. I then argue that a contextualist account of knowledge ascriptions, when combined with a particular view about the structure of reasons, can go a long way toward providing a satisfactory response to skepticism....

CONTEXTUALISM

We can begin by considering what I will call "the entailment principle":

> *S* knows *P* on the basis of (reason or evidence) *R* only if *R* entails *P*.

As we know, the entailment principle leads to skepticism. Most philosophers re-ject the entailment principle thereby embracing fallibilism. The motivation for fallibilism stems from the widely held view that what we seek in constructing a theory of knowledge is an account that squares with our strong intuition that we know many things. It is not that skepticism is to be avoided at all costs. But while the entailment principle may look attractive in the abstract, it does not command the kind of assent sufficient to withstand the overwhelming case against it provided by our intuitions concerning what we know.

Let an alternative to *P* be any proposition incompatible with *P*. Then we can define fallibilism as the view that:

> *S* can know *P* on the basis of *R* even if there is some alternative to *P*, compatible with *R*.

Fallibilism allows that we can know on the basis of non-entailing reasons. But how good do the reasons have to be? Reflection on cases shows that this can be a difficult question to answer:

> Mary and John are at the L.A. airport contemplating taking a certain flight to New York. They want to know whether the flight has a lay-over in Chicago. They overhear someone ask a passenger Smith if he knows whether the flight stops in Chicago. Smith looks at the flight itinerary he got from the travel agent and responds, "Yes I know—it does stop in Chicago." It turns out that Mary and John have a very important business contact they have to make at the Chicago airport. Mary

says, "How reliable is that itinerary? It could contain a misprint. They could have changed the schedule at the last minute." Mary and John agree that Smith doesn't really *know* that the plane will stop in Chicago. They decide to check with the airline agent.

What should we say about this case? Smith claims to know that the flight stops in Chicago. Mary and John deny that Smith knows this. Mary and John seem to be using a stricter standard than Smith for how good one's reasons have to be in order to know. Whose standard is correct? Let's consider several answers:

1 Mary and John's stricter standard is too strong, i.e., Smith's standard is correct and so Smith can know the flight stops in Chicago (on the basis of consulting the itinerary).

Is this a good answer? If we say that contrary to what both Mary and John presuppose, the weaker standard is correct, then we would have to say that their use of the word "know" is incorrect. But then it is hard to see how Mary and John should describe their situation. Certainly they are being prudent in refusing to rely on the itinerary. They have a very important meeting in Chicago. Yet if Smith knows on the basis of the itinerary that the flight stops in Chicago, what *should* they have said? "Okay, Smith knows that the flight stops in Chicago, but still, we need to check further." To my ear, it is hard to make sense of that claim. Moreover if what is printed in the itinerary is a good enough reason for Smith to know, then it is a good enough reason for John and Mary to know. Thus John and Mary should have said, "Okay, *we* know the plane stops in Chicago, but still, we need to check further." Again it is hard to make sense of such a claim.

Perhaps then the correct answer is:

2 John and Mary are right and so Smith's standard is too weak. (Smith can not know, but John and Mary can know—after checking further with the agent.)

I think this is a natural response to this case as I have described it. But notice that this contrasts with the standards we typically use for knowledge ascriptions. In everyday contexts, we readily ascribe knowledge to someone on the basis of written information contained in things like flight itineraries. If we deny that Smith knows, then we have to deny that we know in many of the everyday cases in which we claim to know. We would have to say that a considerable amount of the time in our everyday lives, we speak falsely when we say we know things.

And it gets worse. We could describe a case where even Mary and John's standard does not seem strict enough: If someone's life were at stake, we might not even be willing to ascribe knowledge on the basis of the testimony of the airline agent. We might insist on checking with the pilot. So it does not look promising to say that Smith's standard is too weak.

We could, at this point, pursue a third option, viz., all of these standards are too weak. This option leads, of course, to skepticism and presumably, this is a result we want to avoid.

So far we have examined three different answers to the question of whose standard is correct: (1) Smith's is correct and so John and Mary's standard is too strong. (2) John and Mary's standard is correct and so Smith's standard is too weak. (3) Neither Smith's nor John and Mary's standard is correct—both are too weak. None of these answers seems satisfactory. So let me say what I take to be the best answer: Neither standard is simply correct or simply incorrect. Rather, context determines which standard is correct. Since the standards for knowledge ascriptions can vary across contexts, each claim, Smith's as well as Mary and John's, can be correct in the context in which it was made. When Smith says, "I know…," what he says is true given the weaker standard operating in that context. When Mary and John say "Smith does not know…," what they say is true given the stricter standard operating in their context. *And there is no context independent correct standard.*

So I claim that this case, and others like it, strongly suggests that ascriptions of knowledge are context-sensitive. The standards that determine how good one's reasons have to be in order to know are determined by the context of ascription.…

SEMANTICAL CONSIDERATIONS

Many, if not most, predicates in natural language are such that the truth-value of sentences containing them depends on contextually determined standards, e.g., "flat," "bald," "rich," "happy," "sad."… These are all predicates that can be satisfied to varying degrees and that can also be satisfied *simpliciter*. So, e.g., we can talk about one surface being flatter than another and we can talk about a surface being flat *simpliciter*. For predicates of this kind, context will determine the degree to which the predicate must be satisfied in order for the predicate to apply *simpliciter*. So the context will determine how flat a surface must be in order to be flat.

Does knowledge come in degrees? Most people say no. But it doesn't really matter. For, in my view, justification, or having good reasons, is a component of knowledge, and justification certainly comes in degrees. So context will determine how justified a belief must be in order to be justified *simpliciter*.

This suggests a further argument for the truth of the contextualists' claim about knowledge. Since justification is a component of knowledge, an ascription of knowledge involves an ascription of justification. And for the reasons just indicated, ascriptions of justification are context-sensitive.…

How precisely do the standards for these predicates get determined in a particular context of ascription? This is a very difficult question to answer. But we can say this much. The standards are determined by some complicated function of speaker intentions, listener expectations, presuppositions of the conversation, salience relations, etc.—by what David Lewis calls the conversational score.

In the case of knowledge ascriptions, salience relations play a central role in determining the standards. In particular, when the chance of error is salient, it can lead knowledge ascribers to intend, expect, presuppose, etc., stricter standards. In the case of John and Mary, it is the importance of the Chicago meeting that makes the chance of error salient. Of course, since we reject the entailment principle, we allow that we can know a proposition, even when there is a chance of error. But when the chance of error is *salient* in a context, the standards tend to rise to a point that falsifies the knowledge ascription.

Now I certainly have no general theory of how precisely the context determines the standard. But this is no special problem for my claim that ascriptions of knowledge are context-sensitive. Even for (relatively) uncontroversial cases of predicates whose application depends on context-sensitive standards, e.g., "flat," it is very difficult to say exactly how the context determines the standards. I am not proposing a semantic theory for predicates of this kind. I am just proposing that we view the knowledge predicate as a predicate of this kind.

SKEPTICISM

We saw earlier that in order to avoid skepticism, we had to reject the entailment principle. Unfortunately skepticism is not so easily dispatched. For a weaker principle that is very difficult to reject threatens to reinstate skepticism even for fallibilist theories.

The skeptical argument based on the entailment principle simply notes the existence of alternatives consistent with our evidence. The argument based on the weaker principle begins with the very plausible claim that whatever else we say about the significance of skeptical alternatives, we do not know they are false. We might think that we have some reason to believe that we are not deceived in the ways the skeptic suggests, but it is very hard to hold that we *know* we are not so deceived.

Suppose, to use Dreske's example, that you are at the zoo looking at the Zebra exhibit. Consider the possibility that what you see is not a zebra but rather a cleverly-disguised mule. Though you may have some reason to deny you are looking at a cleverly-disguised mule, it seems wrong to say you *know* you are not looking at a cleverly-disguised mule. After all, that's just how it would look if it were a cleverly-disguised mule.

The skeptic then appeals to a deductive closure principle for knowledge:

(C) If *S* knows *P* and *S* knows that *P* entails Q, then *S* knows Q.

This principle has considerable intuitive force. Now, let *P* be some proposition I claim to know and let *H* be a skeptical alternative to *P*. Then from the closure principle, we can derive

(1) If I know *P*, then I know not-*H*

Put this together with

(2) I do not know not-*H*

and it follows that

(3) I know *P*

is false.

RESPONSES TO SKEPTICISM

To respond to the deductive closure argument, a fallibilist must deny either premise (1) or premise (2). The problem, as we have seen, is that both of these premises are intuitively quite appealing....

A CONTEXTUALIST TREATMENT OF THE SKEPTICAL PARADOX

One of the chief virtues of a contextualist account of knowledge ascriptions is that it provides a treatment of the skeptical paradox that meets our criteria. Such an account can preserve the truth of our everyday knowledge ascriptions while still explaining the cogency of skeptical arguments....

As we saw in the case of Mary and John at the LA airport, the context of ascription determines how good one's reasons have to be in order for one to know. So the truth-value of a knowledge ascription will depend on whether the subject of the ascription has strong enough reasons relative to the standard of the context. This means that the truth-value of a knowledge ascription can vary with either the strength of the subject's reasons or the strictness of the standard. On the contextualist view, we explain our confidence in the truth of our everyday knowledge ascriptions (the appeal of (3)) by supposing that our reasons are sufficient for us to know, relative to the standards of everyday contexts. When confronted with skeptical arguments however, the chance of error becomes salient and the standards can shift. Skeptical arguments are forceful precisely because they can have this effect on us. In this new context, the standards are stricter and knowledge ascriptions true in everyday contexts are false. So while the strength of our reasons remains fixed, the strictness of the standards for how strong those reasons have to be varies across contexts. By supposing that knowledge ascriptions are context-sensitive in this way, we can do justice both to our strong inclination to say we know and to the undeniable appeal of skeptical arguments.

So on a contextualist approach, which proposition of the paradox gets denied? As we have seen, some take the apparent truth of both (2) and (3) to show that (1) is false, thereby giving up the closure principle. But most find rejecting the closure principle to be unacceptable. An advantage of contextualism is that it can defend the closure principle while explaining why there is an appearance of closure failure.

We can illustrate this through Dretske's zebra case: My reasons for believing I see a zebra consist of the animal's looking like zebras and being in pens marked "Zebra." My reason for believing I do not see a cleverly disguised mule consists of the inductive evidence I have against the possibility of such a deception. It looks as if I know I see a zebra but I fail to know I do not see a cleverly-disguised mule. We might be tempted to think my reasons for believing I see a zebra are stronger than my reasons for thinking I do not see a cleverly-disguised mule. But surely if we accept the closure principle, we accept that where P entails Q, the strength of my reasons for believing P can be no greater than the strength of my reasons for believing Q. So my reasons for believing *I see a zebra* can be no stronger than my reasons for believing *I do not see a cleverly-disguised mule.* According to contextualism, however, the standards for how strong my reasons have to be in order for me to know can vary across contexts. In contexts where we consider whether I know I do not see a cleverly-disguised mule, the chance of error is salient, unlike in everyday contexts where

we consider whether I know I see a zebra. And when the chance of error is salient in a context, the standards tend to rise. Thus we evaluate whether I know I do not see a cleverly-disguised mule at a stricter standard than that at which we evaluate whether I know I see a zebra. This gives rise to the appearance of closure failure. But if we hold the context, and so the standards, fixed, we see that the closure principle is not threatened.

So in everyday contexts the standards are such that my reasons are good enough for me to know I see a zebra. And since my reasons for denying that I see a cleverly-disguised mule can be no worse, my reasons are sufficient for me to know that proposition as well, given the standards of those contexts. Thus in everyday contexts, I can know that I don't see a cleverly-disguised mule, on the basis of the inductive evidence that I have against such a scenario.

In skeptical contexts where the standards are higher, I fail to know, on the basis of the inductive evidence, that I do not see a cleverly-disguised mule. But since my reasons for believing that I see a zebra can be no better, I fail to know that proposition as well, given the standards of that context. The appearance of closure failure results from the shift in standards that occurs when we move from considering whether I know that I see a zebra to considering whether I know that I do not see a cleverly-disguised mule.

So on a contextualist view, the appearance of closure failure results from our evaluating the antecedent and the consequent of the principle, relative to different standards. This happens in general when we consider instances of the closure principle where the consequent concerns knowing the falsity of a skeptical alternative. Again, this is because thinking about skeptical alternatives can cause the standards to rise. But if we evaluate the closure principle relative to a fixed context, thereby fixing the standards, it comes out true. So the paradox arises because of our failure to be sensitive to contextual shifts.

So which of the three propositions does the contextualist deny? This depends on the context. We have just seen that the closure principle is true in every context. In everyday contexts, (3) is true as well, and (2) is false. And in skeptical contexts, (2) is true and (3) is false.

GLOBAL SKETPICISM VS HIGH-STANDARDS SKEPTICISM

The way I have formulated it so far, contextualism looks to be, at best, a response to what we might call "high-standards skepticism." The contextualist points out that although our evidence does not meet the very high standards of the skeptic, it is nonetheless sufficient for us to know relative to the standards that apply in everyday contexts. But this raises a problem.

We can distinguish between restricted and global skeptical alternatives. Restricted skeptical alternatives are immune to rejection on the basis of a particular kind of evidence. The alternative that I am seeing a cleverly-disguised mule is a restricted alternative to the proposition that I am seeing a zebra. It is immune to rejection on the basis of how things appear to me. In this case, there is the possibility that it can be rejected on the basis of other evidence, e.g., inductive evidence regarding the likelihood of such a deception.

Global skeptical alternatives are immune to rejection on the basis of *any* evidence. The alternative that I am a brain-in-a-vat (being fed experiences as if I were a normally situated, embodied subject) is a global alternative to any empirical proposition. Since this alternative entails that I have all the empirical evidence which I in fact have, it is hard to see how any of that evidence could count against it.

In my discussion so far, I ran the skeptical paradox using restricted alternatives and exploited the fact that we have *some* evidence against them—in the case of the cleverly-disguised mule alternative, we have inductive evidence against the likelihood of such a deception. High-standards skepticism hinges on the claim that this inductive evidence is insufficient for us to know. According to contextualism, the skeptic is correct relative to the high standards of a skeptical context. But this very same evidence is sufficient to know given the standard that operates in everyday contexts. The skeptical paradox arises from inattention to shifts in context.

But there is a problem extending this contextualist approach to the skeptical paradox formulated in terms of global alternatives. Since we appear to have no evidence whatsoever against global alternatives, we cannot hold that the evidence we do have is good enough relative to everyday standards. So it looks as if contextualism is of no use in responding to global skepticism.

We may have been too hasty, however, in deciding that I have no evidence against the alternative that I am not a brain-in-a-vat. Consider the fact that I have no evidence in favor of this alternative. My experience has never been subject to radical unexplained incongruities as might occur if the vat apparatus suffered a power failure or in some way malfunctioned. The vat-meister has never "appeared" to me, etc. Surely the fact that none of this has happened counts against the alternative that I am a brain-in-a-vat. So I do have *some* evidence against this alternative, after all. Now in skeptical contexts (such as the one we are in now as we consider skeptical hypotheses), this evidence will not be sufficient enough for me to know I am not a brain-in-a-vat. Nonetheless, the contextualist can argue that in everyday contexts, this evidence is sufficient for me to know I am not a brain-in-a-vat. In this way, the contextualist can explain why, under skeptical pressure, we are tempted to say we do not know we are brains-in-a-vat, while allowing that in everyday contexts we in fact know we are not.

But this contextualist strategy will go only so far. The absence of radical incongruities in my experience, etc., counts as evidence against my being a brain-in-a-vat only to the extent that the occurrence of such things is probable, conditional on my being a brain-in-a-vat. So consider the alternative that I am a brain-in-a-vat *and I will never have evidence that I am*. Call this the "brain-in-a-vat*" hypothesis. The fact that radical incongruities, etc., have not occurred is no evidence whatsoever against the brain-in-a-vat* hypothesis.

Can the contextualist treatment be extended to apply to the brain-in-a-vat* hypothesis? On the contextualist view we have been considering, context determines how strong one's evidence must be, in order for one to know. But suppose we think of context as determining, more generally, how *rational* one's belief must be in order for one to know. While a belief can be rational in virtue of being supported by evidence, we need not hold that evidence is the only source of rationality for a belief. Consider the belief that I am not a brain-in-a-vat*. Although we may concede that we have no evidence in support of this belief, it still seems intuitively compelling that the belief is rational—at least *to some degree*.

Could this intuition be mistaken? It would be if we were compelled to accept

(R) *P* is rational (to some degree) for *S* only if *S* has evidence for *P*.

By my lights, (R) does not have the kind of axiomatic status that the closure principle (C) has. The belief that I am not a brain-in-a-vat* just looks to be a plausible counterexample. Moreover, many philosophers have held that there are non-evidential (so-called "pragmatic") considerations like simplicity and conservativism relevant to rational acceptance.

In virtue of what precisely is it rational, to some degree, to believe I am not a brain-in-a-vat*? Certainly there is something artificial about a hypothesis that specifies as part of its content that I will never have evidence for it. But I do not have an analysis of rationality in terms of non-evidential criteria that entails that the belief is to some degree rational. I do not have any analysis of rationality. But one does not need an analysis of rationality in order to claim that certain beliefs are rational.

Does this view beg the question against the skeptic? Well perhaps, in some way, it does—but no more than the skeptic begs the question against us. For though the skeptic has an argument that we have no evidence against the brain-in-a-vat* hypothesis, s/he has no argument that it cannot be to some degree rational, without evidence, to deny it.

We have to be clear about the nature of the project. What we are confronting is paradox. We are inclined to assent to each member of an inconsistent set of propositions. What we seek is a way out of paradox, a resolution of our inconsistent inclinations. And it is not a constraint on such a resolution that it appeal to the skeptic. Maybe we are unable to demonstrate to a skeptic that our beliefs are rational. But that does not mean that we cannot satisfy ourselves that they are. If it seems right to say that it is to some degree rational to deny that we are brains-in-a-vat*, then we can appeal to that fact in our attempt to resolve the paradox.

Now, if we accept the closure principle, then surely we will accept that the rationality of believing any empirical proposition, e.g., I have a hand, can be no greater than the rationality of believing I am not a brain-in-a-vat*. So the degree of rationality of denying the brain-in-a-vat* alternative provides an upper bound on the degree of rationality for any empirical belief.

We now have the means to extend the contextualist approach to global skeptical alternatives like the brain-in-a-vat* hypothesis. We can say that the degree of rationality of denying I am a brain-in-a-vat* is sufficient in everyday contexts for me to know that I am not a brain-in-a-vat*. In those same contexts, I can know I have a hand. But under skeptical pressure, the standards rise and the degree of rationality is no longer sufficient for me to know, in those contexts, that I have a hand or that I am not a brain-in-a-vat*. Again the skeptical paradox arises from our insensitivity to contextual shift....

Contextualism Is Not the Solution to Skepticism

ANTHONY BRUECKNER

In this paper, I will discuss the virtues of contextualism about knowledge. In the first place, this view explains why skeptical arguments involving possibilities such as that I am a brain in a vat have intuitive force. In a philosophical conversational context in which skeptical possibilities are being considered, the standards for knowledge attributions are artificially high. (I realize that different contextualists say different things about how the standards get raised, but my points will be unaffected by which version of contextualism is adopted.) From within such contexts, it is false to say that S knows that he is not a brain in a vat (for any S, including myself). By the closure of knowledge under known entailment, it is also false to say, from within such contexts, that S knows that he has hands (for any S, including myself).

But contextualism does more than just explain the dark side of our epistemological position. There is also good news. From within an ordinary, non-philosophical context in which skeptical possibilities are *not* being considered, it is true to say that S knows that he has hands and also knows that he is not a brain in a vat (for many, many S). So there is much ordinarily-attributed knowledge in the world. George W. Bush knows that he has hands, for example.

Wait a minute. The feel-good punchline of the preceding paragraph is not right. *I* am now in the middle of a decidedly philosophical context in which skeptical possibilities are being considered. So what I must say is that George W. Bush does *not* know that he has hands. No one,

including myself, knows that he has hands. No one, including myself, knows anything at all about the external world. Damn!

Well, let me try to save the good news side of contextualism by being a bit more careful in what I write. What I should have said is this. When someone in an ordinary, non-philosophical context says, "George W. Bush knows that he has hands," he utters a truth. Of course, if *I* utter that sentence in the pages of this paper, then a careful grader will write "That's just false!" in the margin. In general, the good news is that many, many knowledge-attributing sentences uttered from within ordinary, non-philosophical contexts express *truths* (ones which my sentences are currently barred from expressing, until I get out of this infernal conversational context).

Wait a minute. How do I know that any speaker is ever in an ordinary conversational context? Sure, in a normal, non-vat-world of the sort I *take* myself to inhabit, there are normal speakers who speak and write (and think) from within ordinary conversational contexts. But I don't know that there are any such contexts in *my* world, which may be a solipsistic vat-world. This might be called the Problem of Knowledge of Other Speakers.

Hold on. I am being too hard on myself. I can state the good news side of contextualism without worrying about the Other. I now remember *being in* various ordinary conversational contexts before getting trapped in the present annoying philosophical context. By that I do *not* mean that memory reveals that I was in a café yesterday with some friends talking about nothing but sports. I cannot presently claim *that* sort of Knowledge of Other Contexts. Rather, I remember being in what was either a real-café-context or a solipsistic hallucinated-café-context, in which I merely *appeared* to say and hear various things. I will count the latter as an ordinary context, much like a soliloquy in inner speech. So if the skeptic grants me memorial knowledge of my past experiences, I can know that there are ordinary contexts.

I'm not out of the woods yet. I must now back up my earlier claim that some knowledge-attributing sentences uttered from within ordinary contexts are *true*. That's my meta-linguistic version of the good news. Let us call the remembered ordinary context C. I remember seeming to hear my friend say, "Can anyone here catch my best knuckleball?". I remember seeming to reply, "Yes, I can; I have good hands." Given that C, whether a real-café-context or vat-context, was an ordinary, non-philosophical context in which skeptical possibilities were not under consideration, I can now say that my knowledge-attributing sentence, uttered in C (in a normal fashion or as in inner speech), is true.

Wait a minute. This will not fly. In order for my knowledge-attributing sentence to have been true as uttered in C, it must have been true that I had hands (and good ones) while uttering the sentence. As things stand, I do not know that anyone has hands. In general, I do not know that there are any true utterances of knowledge-attributing sentences regarding external world circumstances. I am simply not in a position to claim that there are such utterances.

I'm not ready to give up yet. Maybe I can adopt a form of contextualism according to which skeptical possibilities can be ignored in a context even when they have explicitly been raised. For example, imagine that I am talking about sports with a friend who suddenly brings up the possibility that we are both brains in vats. I tell him that I want to stick to the subject, which is sports, and I go on to correctly claim to know various things about sporting matters. I yearn for such a context…

The current season has been tough for the World Champion Los Angeles Lakers. Kobe Bryant's incredible scoring run has been a bright spot for the team, but Kobe knows that the Lakers will not sail through the playoffs this time around.

Stop! I'm just kidding myself. This is a philosophy paper about skepticism, skeptical possibilities, and contextualism, not an article from the sports page. While I'm stuck in this philosophical context, I cannot ignore the skeptical possibilities that I have been discussing at length and then correctly write that Kobe knows things about the playoffs.

Still, this is *my* context. Sure, I'm writing about brains in vats, knowledge, and contextualism. But I hereby declare that in *this* context, which I have created, the standards for knowledge are the *ordinary* ones. Not only can I now correctly say that the sentence "Kobe knows that the playoffs will be grueling" was in fact true when recently uttered by a real sportswriter in an ordinary context, but, further, I can also correctly say that *I* know that the playoffs will be grueling. After all, I have pushed down the standards for *all* knowledge-attributions made in *my* context.

But I don't feel comfortable with this move. However it is that the contextual raising and lowering of standards works, it is not simply up to me to set them where I want them to be. That seems out of keeping with the spirit of contextualism.

Let me try a variation on these last two strategies. I can imagine a context in which my friend, again, suggests that we both may be brains in vats. I say, "Come off it—you know that you're not a brain in a vat. Let's continue talking about the various things I learned from today's sports page." Here, I do *not* pretend that the skeptical possibility has not been raised. Instead, I confront the possibility, and I get my friend to accede to a lowering of the standards for knowing in our context, so that the conversation can go forward in an easy way.

But I'm not sure how to apply this strategy to my current context, in which I am doing some solo thinking about skeptical epistemology. There's no one but me around in this context, no one that I can try to get to accede to a forced lowering of the standards. Except for me. Do *I* accept low standards in this context? If I can pull this off, then I can claim, right here, to know many things in the face of, say, the vat possibility that I have been thinking about (and continue to think about). So I will try to describe the elusive virtues of contextualism from within a low-standards context. This is what I should have been doing all along.

I don't know quite what to say at this point. It seems to me that I am in the middle of the biggest, baddest sort of philo-sophical context there is, and, again, I don't feel comfortable holding that in such a context, I can single-handedly push the standards for knowing down to where I can now correctly claim to know a great many things. Whenever I think about the skeptical possibilities, while in a careful, reflective philosophical context like this, it strikes me that I do *not* know that they do not obtain. That's one of the main motivations for attempting to formulate a successful contextualist theory in the first place.

In the end, the best I can do is to say that knowledge is *possible*. I can say that there are possible worlds in which people have hands and in which speakers in ordinary contexts truly say of such people, "They know that they have hands." I do not know that *this* world is such a world, but contextualism at least enables me to countenance the *possibility* of knowledge.

This falls short of the originally advertised good news, namely that even given the skeptic's problematic possibilities, there is much ordinarily-attributed knowledge in the world. For the contextualist, that "news" cannot be reported here, or anywhere, for that matter.

THE CONTINUING DEBATE:
Can We Ever Have Genuine Knowledge?

What Is New

One interesting effect of the emergence of contextualism is the development of arguments for the contrasting view—now called "invariantism"—which maintains that knowledge is invariant and *not* dependent upon context. This standard view, which went largely unchallenged prior to contextualism, has been refined and elaborated under contextualist pressure.

Where to Find More

Ludwig Wittgenstein developed some key ideas of contextualism in *On Certainty* (Oxford: Basil Blackwell, 1969).

Keith DeRose, "Contextualism: An Explanation and Defense," in John Greco and Ernest Sosa, editors, *The Blackwell Guide to Epistemology* (Oxford: Blackwell Publishers, 1999), is a helpful examination and defense of contextualism, and is particularly good in tracing its origins and history. There is a good survey of contextualist thought in The Internet Encyclopedia of Philosophy; titled "Contextualism in Epistemology," it was written by Tim Black, and can be found at http://www.iep.utm.edu/c/contextu.htm. Several key papers on contextualism are contained in Part 9 of *Epistemology: An Anthology,* edited by Ernest Sosa and Jaegwon Kim (Oxford: Blackwell, 2000).

An excellent debate between Earl Conee (who criticizes contextualism) and Stewart Cohen (who champions contextualism) is contained in chapter two of Matthias Steup and Ernest Sosa, editors, *Contemporary Debates in Epistemology* (Oxford: Blackwell Publishing, 2005).

Influential contextualist writings include Keith DeRose, "Contextualism and Knowledge Attributions," *Philosophy and Phenomenological Research*, volume 52 (1992): 913–929; Keith DeRose, "Solving the Skeptical Puzzle," *Philosophical Review*, volume 104 (1995): 1–52; Stewart Cohen, "Knowledge, Context and Social Standards," *Synthese*, volume 73 (1987): 3–26; and Peter Unger, "The Cone Model of Knowledge," *Philosophical Topics*, volume 14 (1986): 125–178.

One important version of contextualism places great emphasis on eliminating all "relevant alternatives" in order to establish genuine knowledge, a view favored by Fred I. Dretske in "The Pragmatic Dimension of Knowledge," contained in his *Perception, Knowledge and Belief: Selected Essays* (Cambridge: Cambridge University Press, 2000). Stewart Cohen developed an important version of relevant alternatives contexualism in "How to be a Fallibilist," *Philosophical Perspectives 2, Epistemology* (1988): 91–123. Other important papers along relevant alternatives lines are David Lewis, "Elusive Knowledge," *Australasian Journal of Philosophy*, volume 74, number 4 (1996): 549–567; and Gail Stine, "Skepticism, Relevant Alternatives, and Deductive Closure," *Philosophical Studies*, volume 29 (1976): 249–261.

Michael Williams offers a radical version of contextualism which denies that there are any facts at all independent of contexts; see his *Unnatural Doubts: Epistemological Realism and the Basis of Scepticism* (Princeton, N.J.: Princeton University Press, 1996).

Helen E. Longino gives a feminist account of the strengths of contextualism, in her "Feminist Epistemology," which is Chapter 14 in *The Blackwell Guide to Epistemology*, edited by John Greco and Ernest Sosa (Oxford: Blackwell Publishers, 1999).

"Invariantism" is discussed by Peter Unger, in *Philosophical Relativity* (Minneapolis: University of Minnesota Press, 1984).

An interesting critique of contextualism is by Stephen Schiffer, "Contextualist Solutions to Skepticism," *Proceedings of the Aristotelian Society*, volume 96 (1996): 317–333. Another is Hilary Kornblith, "The Contextualist Evasion of Epistemology," *Philosophical Issues 10, Skepticism* (2000): 24–32.

5 ARE MY HOPES AND THOUGHTS ULTIMATELY JUST ELECTROCHEMICAL BRAIN IMPULSES?

Mental Phenomena Are Irreducible to Anything Else

ADVOCATE: John R. Searle, Slusser Professor of Philosophy, University of California, Berkeley; author of *Mind: A Brief Introduction* (2004), *Consciousness and Language* (2002), *Mind, Language, and Society: Philosophy in the Real World* (1998), and *The Mystery of Consciousness* (1997).

SOURCE: "Reductionism and the Irreducibility of Consciousness," from John R. Searle, *The Rediscovery of the Mind* (Cambridge, Mass.: The MIT Press, 1992).

Mental Phenomena Are Reducible to Physical Brain Activities

ADVOCATE: Paul M. Churchland, Professor of Philosophy, University of California at San Diego; author of *Scientific Realism and the Plasticity of Mind* (Cambridge: Cambridge University Press, 1979), *Matter and Consciousness* (Cambridge, Mass.: MIT Press, 1984), and *The Engine of Reason, The Seat of the Soul: A Philosophical Journey into the Brain* (Cambridge, Mass.: MIT Press, 1995)

SOURCE: "Betty Crocker's Theory of Consciousness: A Review of John Searle's *The Rediscovery of the Mind*," *London Review of Books* (1994)

Neuropsychologists have run recent experiments that fascinate some while troubling others. One experiment by Grey Walter involved subjects whose mild seizures had been effectively controlled through the implantation of tiny electrodes in the motor cortex region of the brain. These subjects were invited to watch a slide show, in which they could advance the slides according to their own choice by pressing a button. The button, however, was fake. The slides were actually advanced by a burst of activity in the motor cortex, which the implanted electrodes transmitted directly to the projector. The subjects reported that the projector seemed to not only "read their minds" but actually anticipate their decisions, advancing the slide not only before they pressed the button but slightly before they had actually decided to press the button. Thus the "conscious decision" seems to be almost a byproduct of the real decision process that occurs in the brain *prior* to our conscious sense of willing. Is the conscious mind just a "by-product" of brain activity, as neuropsychologist Daniel Wegner suggests? Is the mind identical with the brain? Is the mind something distinct from the brain?

Descartes championed mental/physical *dualism*: the mind and the body are distinct and different substances, with the body being made of physical stuff and the mind of mental stuff (the mental is nonphysical, nonmaterial, has no weight or electrical charge; and the mind is *not* the brain).

> …Just because I know certainly that I exist, and that meanwhile I do not remark that any other thing necessarily pertains to my nature or essence, excepting that I am a thinking thing, I rightly conclude that my essence consists solely in the fact that I am a thinking thing. And although possibly (or rather certainly, as I shall say in a moment) I possess a body with which I am very intimately conjoined, yet because, on the one side, I have a clear and distinct idea of myself inasmuch as I am only a thinking and unextended thing, and as, on the other, I possess an idea of body, inasmuch as it is only an extended and unthinking thing, it is certain that this I (that is to say, my soul by which I am what I am), is entirely and absolutely distinct from my body, and can exist without it. Descartes, Meditation VI, from *Meditations on First Philosophy*, trans. Elizabeth Haldane and G. R. T. Ross (London: Cambridge University Press, 1931); originally published in Latin, 1641.

This touched off a controversy that continues to this day. Some follow Descartes, and maintain that mind and body are separate substances—though this view runs into the difficult question of how something mental and totally nonphysical could possibly *cause* a physical event: how could my thoughts cause my arm to move? Faced with the problems of mind-body interaction, many favor a single substance view. *Idealists* hold the view that only mental substance is real: the world is really just *ideas* and minds. *Materialists* agree that there is only one substance, but they maintain that the single substance is material: the "mind" is just the brain and central nervous system. The materialist view is probably the dominant contemporary philosophical view (though dualism may still hold the popular majority). Materialism had many advocates among French philosophers of the 18th Century, such as La Mettrie, who offers an early version of the theory:

> Simply open your eyes…and you will see that a labourer whose mind and knowledge extend no further than the edges of his furrow is no different essentially from the greatest genius…; you will be convinced that the imbecile or the idiot are animals in human form, in the same way as the clever ape is a little man in another form; and that, since everything depends absolutely on differences in organisation, a well-constructed animal who has learnt astronomy can predict an eclipse.…Let us then conclude boldly that man is a machine and that there is in the whole universe only one diversely modified substance. Julien Offray de la Mettrie, *Machine Man and Other Writings*, trans. and edited by Ann Thomson (Cambridge: Cambridge University Press, 1996), pp. 38–39.

The conflict between Searle and Churchland is *not* a conflict over mind/body dualism, for both are materialists. But most materialists have maintained that ultimately our ideas and thoughts and consciousness will be *reducible* to explanations in terms of the brain and neurons; and it is that reductionist view that Churchland champions, and that Searle disputes.

John R. Searle insists that consciousness cannot be explained by—and cannot be *reduced* to—characteristics of the brain. Searle is *not* claiming that consciousness comes from some special nonphysical mental substance, as Descartes claims; to the contrary, Searle believes that consciousness comes from the brain, and there is nothing mysterious or nonphysical about it. But according to Searle, consciousness cannot be reductively defined in terms of physical brain events, because in the case of consciousness it is the *appearance* of consciousness—what consciousness "feels like"—that is the key subject of study, and attempts to redefine consciousness in terms of physical events would eliminate the subject of study. As Searle puts it, in the case of consciousness studies, "the appearance is the reality," and thus we cannot reductively define away the appearance in terms of something else. But Searle maintains that this is a trivial point concerning definitions and the nature of the study of consciousness, and it does *not* imply that consciousness "cannot be a subject of scientific investigation or cannot be brought into our overall physical conception of the universe."

Churchland maintains that Searle's arguments for irreducibility are fundamentally flawed, that they beg the question against reductionist views, and that they are not consistent with the basic materialism which Searle claims to favor. According to Churchland, it is true that current reductionist accounts of intentional phenomena (feelings and ideas and thoughts) do not give a fully adequate explanation of these personal experiences; but that is not because intentional phenomena somehow require a different type of explanation, but only because our reductionist neurological accounts are at a very early stage, and we are still ignorant of some of the key elements that produce such phenomena: we do not yet have an adequate account of the brain and its activities. But nothing about the current limits of our theories indicates that subjective experiences will be inexplicable in neurological terms, nor do the current limits show that subjective mental features are not in fact identical with neurological events. Churchland maintains that Searle's insistence to the contrary begs the basic question at issue.

POINTS TO PONDER

➤ At the end of the Searle selection, Searle states that it is *possible* some future intellectual revolution would give us a new (and currently unimaginable) method for reducing consciousness. Is Churchland proposing such a revolution?

➤ Churchland attempts to link Searle's views to Cartesian dualism, a linkage which Searle fiercely denies. *Is* Searle's view a special variety of mind/body dualism?

➤ Searle insists that the irreducibility of consciousness "has only trivial consequences," and no important implications for our scientific world view. Churchland believes that it would have profound and disturbing consequences. Why does Churchland find Searle's proposed irreducibility so disturbing?

➤ At first glance, Searle and Churchland would seem to be almost allies, rather than adversaries; after all, both claim to favor a strictly scientific and materialist view. Is there any way of reconciling their views?

Mental Phenomena Are Irreducible to Anything Else

John R. Searle

I. EMERGENT PROPERTIES

Suppose we have a system, S, made up of elements a, b, c...For example, S might be a stone and the elements might be molecules. In general, there will be features of S that are not, or not necessarily, features of a, b, c...For example, S might weigh ten pounds, but the molecules individually do not weigh ten pounds. Let us call such features "system features." The shape and the weight of the stone are system features. Some system features can be deduced or figured out or calculated from the features of a, b, c...just from the way these are composed and arranged (and sometimes from their relations to the rest of the environment). Examples of these would be shape, weight, and velocity. But some other system features cannot be figured out just from the composition of the elements and environmental relations; they have to be explained in terms of the causal interactions among the elements. Let's call these "causally emergent system features." Solidity, liquidity, and transparency are examples of causally emergent system features.

On these definitions, consciousness is a causally emergent property of systems. It is an emergent feature of certain systems of neurons in the same way that solidity and liquidity are emergent features of systems of molecules. The existence of consciousness can be explained by the causal interactions between elements of the brain at the micro level, but consciousness cannot itself be deduced or calculated from the sheer physical structure of the neurons without some additional account of the causal relations between them.

This conception of causal emergence, call it "emergent1," has to be distinguished from a much more adventurous conception, call it "emergent2." A feature F is emergent2 if F is emergent1 and F has causal powers that cannot be explained by the causal interactions of a, b, c...If consciousness were emergent2, then consciousness could cause things that could not be explained by the causal behavior of the neurons. The naive idea here is that consciousness gets squirted out by the behavior of the neurons in the brain, but once it has been squirted out, it then has a life of its own.

...on my view consciousness is emergent1, but not emergent2. In fact, I cannot think of anything that is emergent2, and it seems unlikely that we will be able to find any features that are emergent2, because the existence of any such features would seem to violate even the weakest principle of the transitivity of causation.

II. REDUCTIONISM

Most discussions of reductionism are extremely confusing....The basic intuition that underlies the concept of reductionism seems to be the idea that certain things might be shown to be *nothing but* certain other sorts of things. Reductionism, then, leads to a peculiar form of the identity relation that we might as well call the "nothing-but" relation: in general, A's can be reduced to B's, if A's are nothing but B's.

However, even within the nothing-but relation, people mean so many different things by the notion of "reduction" that we need to begin by making several distinctions. At the very outset it is important to be clear about what the relata of the relation are. What is its domain supposed to be: objects, properties, theories, or what? I find at least five different senses of "reduction"—or perhaps I should say five different kinds of reduction—in the theoretical literature, and I want to mention each of them so that we can see which are relevant to our discussion of the mind-body problem.

1. Ontological Reduction

The most important form of reduction is ontological reduction. It is the form in which objects of certain types can be shown to consist in nothing but objects of other types. For example, chairs are shown to be nothing but collections of molecules. This form is clearly important in the history of science. For example, material objects in general can be shown to be nothing but collections of molecules, genes can be shown to consist in nothing but DNA molecules. It seems to me this form of reduction is what the other forms are aiming at.

2. Property Ontological Reduction

This is a form of ontological reduction, but it concerns properties. For example, heat (of a gas) is nothing but the mean kinetic energy of molecule movements. Property reductions for properties corresponding to theoretical terms, such as "heat," "light," etc., are often a result of theoretical reductions.

3. Theoretical Reduction

Theoretical reductions are the favorite of theorists in the literature, but they seem to me rather rare in the actual practice of science, and it is perhaps not surprising that the same half dozen examples are given over and over in the standard textbooks. From the point of view of scientific expla-

nation, theoretical reductions are mostly interesting if they enable us to carry out ontological reductions. In any case, theoretical reduction is primarily a relation between theories, where the laws of the reduced theory can (more or less) be deduced from the laws of the reducing theory. This demonstrates that the reduced theory is nothing but a special case of the reducing theory. The classical example that is usually given in textbooks is the reduction of the gas laws to the laws of statistical thermodynamics.

4. Logical or Definitional Reduction

This form of reduction used to be a great favorite among philosophers, but in recent decades it has fallen out of fashion. It is a relation between words and sentences, where words and sentences referring to one type of entity can be translated without any residue into those referring to another type of entity. For example, sentences about the average plumber in Berkeley are reducible to sentences about specific individual plumbers in Berkeley; sentences about numbers, according to one theory, can be translated into, and hence are reducible to, sentences about sets. Since the words and sentences are *logically* or *definitionally* reducible, the corresponding entities referred to by the words and sentences are *ontologically* reducible. For example, numbers are nothing but sets of sets.

5. Causal Reduction

This is a relation between any two types of things that can have causal powers, where the existence and a fortiori the causal powers of the reduced entity are shown to be entirely explainable in terms of the causal powers of the reducing phenomena. Thus, for example, some objects are solid and this has causal consequences: solid objects are impenetrable by other objects, they are resistant to pressure, etc. But these causal powers can be causally explained by the causal powers of vibratory movements of molecules in lattice structures.

Now when the views I have urged are accused of being reductionist—or sometimes insufficiently reductionist—which of these various senses do the accusers have in mind? I think that theoretical reduction and logical reduction are not intended. Apparently the question is whether the causal reductionism of my view leads—or fails to lead—to ontological reduction. I hold a view of mind/brain relations that is a form of causal reduction, as I have defined the notion: Mental features are caused by neurobiological processes. Does this imply ontological reduction?

In general in the history of science, successful causal reductions tend to lead to ontological reductions. Because where we have a successful causal reduction, we simply redefine the expression that denotes the reduced phenomena in such a way that the phenomena in question can now be identified with their causes. Thus, for example, color terms were once (tacitly) defined in terms of the subjective experience of color perceivers; for example, "red" was defined ostensively by pointing to examples, and then real red was defined as whatever seemed red to "normal" observers under "normal" conditions. But once we have a causal reduction of color phenomena to light reflectances, then, according to many thinkers, it becomes possible to redefine color expressions in terms of light reflectances. We thus carve off and eliminate the subjective experience of color from the "real" color. Real color has undergone a property ontological reduction to light reflectances. Similar remarks could be made about the reduction of heat to molecular motion, the reduction of solidity to molecular movements in lattice structures, and the reduction of sound to

air waves. In each case, the causal reduction leads naturally to an ontological reduction by way of a redefinition of the expression that names the reduced phenomenon. Thus, to continue with the example of "red," once we know that the color experiences are caused by a certain sort of photon emission, we then redefine the word in terms of the specific features of the photon emission. "Red," according to some theorists, now refers to photon emission of 600 nanometers. It thus follows trivially that the color red is nothing but photon emissions of 600 nanometers.

The general principle in such cases appears to be this: Once a property is seen to be *emergent1*, we automatically get a causal reduction, and that leads to an ontological reduction, by redefinition if necessary. The general trend in ontological reductions that have a scientific basis is toward greater generality, objectivity, and redefinition in terms of underlying causation.

So far so good. But now we come to an apparently shocking asymmetry. When we come to consciousness, we cannot perform the ontological reduction. Consciousness is a causally emergent property of the behavior of neurons, and so consciousness is causally reducible to the brain processes. But—and this is what seems so shocking—a perfect science of the brain would still not lead to an ontological reduction of consciousness in the way that our present science can reduce heat, solidity, color, or sound. It seems to many people whose opinions I respect that the irreducibility of consciousness is a primary reason why the mind-body problem continues to seem so intractable. Dualists treat the irreducibility of consciousness as incontrovertible proof of the truth of dualism. Materialists insist that consciousness must be reducible to material reality, and that the price of denying the reducibility of consciousness would be the abandonment of our overall scientific world view.

I will briefly discuss two questions: First, I want to show why consciousness is irreducible, and second, I want to show why it does not make any difference at all to our scientific world view that it should be irreducible. It does not force us to property dualism or anything of the sort. It is a trivial consequence of certain more general phenomena.

III. WHY CONSCIOUSNESS IS AN IRREDUCIBLE FEATURE OF PHYSICAL REALITY

There is a standard argument to show that consciousness is not reducible in the way that heat, etc., are....I think the argument is decisive, though it is frequently misunderstood in ways that treat it as merely epistemic and not ontological. It is sometimes treated as an epistemic argument to the effect that, for example, the sort of third-person, objective knowledge we might possibly have of a bat's neurophysiology would still not include the first-person, subjective experience of what it feels like to be a bat. But for our present purposes, the point of the argument is ontological and not epistemic. It is a point about what real features exist in the world and not, except derivatively, about how we know about those features.

Here is how it goes: Consider what facts in the world make it the case that you are now in a certain conscious state such as pain. What fact in the world corresponds to your true statement, "I am now in pain"? Naively, there seem to be at least two sorts of facts. First and most important, there is the fact that you are now having certain unpleasant conscious sensations, and you are experiencing these sensations from your subjective, first-person point of view. It is these sensations that are constitutive of your present pain. But the

pain is also caused by certain underlying neurophysiological processes consisting in large part of patterns of neuron firing in your thalamus and other regions of your brain. Now suppose we tried to reduce the subjective, conscious, first-person sensation of pain to the objective, third-person patterns of neuron firings. Suppose we tried to say the pain is really "nothing but" the patterns of neuron firings. Well, if we tried such an ontological reduction, the essential features of the pain would be left out. No description of the third-person, objective, physiological facts would convey the subjective, first-person character of the pain, simply because the first-person features are different from the third-person features. Nagel states this point by contrasting the objectivity of the third-person features with the what-it-is-like features of the subjective states of consciousness. Jackson states the same point by calling attention to the fact that someone who had a complete knowledge of the neurophysiology of a mental phenomenon such as pain would still not know what a pain was if he or she did not know what it felt like. Kripke makes the same point when he says that pains could not be identical with neurophysiological states such as neuron firings in the thalamus and elsewhere, because any such identity would have to be necessary, because both sides of the identity statement are rigid designators, and yet we know that the identity could not be necessary. This fact has obvious epistemic consequences: my knowledge that I am in pain has a different sort of basis than my knowledge that you are in pain. But the antireductionist point of the argument is ontological and not epistemic.

So much for the antiredutionist argument. It is ludicrously simple and quite decisive. An enormous amount of ink has been shed trying to answer it, but the answers are all so much wasted ink. But to many people it seems that such an argument paints us into a corner. To them it seems that if we accept that argument, we have abandoned our scientific world view and adopted property dualism. Indeed, they would ask, what is property dualism but the view that there are irreducible mental properties? In fact, doesn't Nagel accept property dualism and Jackson reject physicalism precisely because of this argument? And what is the point of scientific reductionism if it stops at the very door of the mind? So I now turn to the main point of this discussion.

IV. WHY THE IRREDUCIBILITY OF CONSCIOUSNESS HAS NO DEEP CONSEQUENCES

To understand fully why consciousness is irreducible, we have to consider in a little more detail the pattern of reduction that we found for perceivable properties such as heat, sound, color, solidity, liquidity, etc., and we have to show how the attempt to reduce consciousness differs from the other cases. In every case the ontological reduction was based on a prior causal reduction. We discovered that a surface feature of a phenomenon was caused by the behavior of the elements of an underlying microstructure. This is true both in the cases in which the reduced phenomenon was a matter of subjective appearances, such as the "secondary qualities" of heat or color; and in the cases of the "primary qualities" such as solidity, in which there was both an element of subjective appearance (solid things feel solid), and also many features independent of subjective appearances (solid things, e.g., are resistant to pressure and impenetrable by other solid objects). But in each case, for both the primary and secondary qualities, the point of the reduction was to carve off the surface features and redefine the original

notion in terms of the causes that produce those surface features.

Thus, where the surface feature is a subjective appearance, we redefine the original notion in such a way as to exclude the appearance from its definition. For example, pretheoretically our notion of heat has something to do with perceived temperatures: Other things being equal, hot is what feels hot to us, cold is what feels cold. Similarly with colors: Red is what looks red to normal observers under normal conditions. But when we have a theory of what causes these and other phenomena, we discover that it is molecular movements causing sensations of heat and cold (as well as other phenomena such as increases in pressure), and light reflectances causing visual experiences of certain sorts (as well as other phenomena such as movements of light meters). We then *redefine* heat and color in terms of the underlying causes of both the subjective experiences and the other surface phenomena. And in the redefinition we eliminate any reference to the subjective appearances and other surface effects of the underlying causes. "Real" heat is now defined in terms of the kinetic energy of the molecular movements, and the subjective feel of heat that we get when we touch a hot object is now treated as just a subjective appearance caused by heat, as an effect of heat. It is no longer part of real heat. A similar distinction is made between real color and the subjective experience of color. The same pattern works for the primary qualities: Solidity is defined in terms of the vibratory movements of molecules in lattice structures, and objective, observer-independent features, such as impenetrability by other objects, are now seen as surface effects of the underlying reality. Such redefinitions are achieved by way of carving off all of the surface features of the phenomenon, whether subjective or objective, and treating them as effects of the real thing.

But now notice: The actual pattern of the facts in the world that correspond to statements about particular forms of heat such as specific temperatures are quite similar to the pattern of facts in the world that correspond to statements about particular forms of consciousness, such as pain. If I now say, "It's hot in this room," what are the facts? Well, first there is a set of "physical" facts involving the movement of molecules, and second there is a set of "mental" facts involving my subjective experience of heat, as caused by the impact of the moving air molecules on my nervous system. But similarly with pain. If I now say, "I am in pain," what are the facts? Well, first there is a set of "physical" facts involving my thalamus and other regions of the brain, and second there is a set of "mental" facts involving my subjective experience of pain. So why do we regard heat as reducible and pain as irreducible? The answer is that what interests us about heat is not the subjective appearance but the underlying physical causes. Once we get a causal reduction, we simply redefine the notion to enable us to get an ontological reduction. Once you know all the facts about heat—facts about molecule movements, impact on sensory nerve endings, subjective feelings, etc.—the reduction of heat to molecule movements involves no new *fact* whatever. It is simply a trivial consequence of the redefinition. We don't first discover all the facts and then discover a new fact, the fact that heat is reducible; rather, we simply redefine heat so that the reduction follows from the definition. But this redefinition does not eliminate, and was not intended to eliminate, the subjective experiences of heat (or color, etc.) from the world. They exist the same as ever.

…it is easy to see why it is rational to make such redefinitions and accept their consequences: To get a greater understanding and control of reality, we want to know how it works causally, and we want our concepts to fit nature at its causal joints. We simply redefine phenomena with surface features in terms of the underlying causes. It then looks like a new discovery that heat is *nothing but* mean kinetic energy of molecule movement, and that if all subjective experiences disappeared from the world, real heat would still remain. But this is not a new discovery, it is a trivial consequence of a new definition. Such reductions do not show that heat, solidity, etc., do not really exist in the way that, for example, new knowledge showed that mermaids and unicorns do not exist.

Couldn't we say the same thing about consciousness? In the case of consciousness, we do have the distinction between the "physical" processes and the subjective "mental" experiences, so why can't consciousness be redefined in terms of the neurophysiological processes in the way that we redefined heat in terms of underlying physical processes? Well, of course, if we insisted on making the redefinition, we could. We could simply define, for example, "pain" as patterns of neuronal activity that cause subjective sensations of pain. And if such a redefinition took place, we would have achieved the same sort of reduction for pain that we have for heat. But of course, the reduction of pain to its physical reality still leaves the subjective experience of pain unreduced, just as the reduction of heat left the subjective experience of heat unreduced. Part of the point of the reductions was to carve off the subjective experiences and exclude them from the definition of the real phenomena, which are now defined in terms of those features that interest us most. But where the phenomena that interest us most are the subjective experiences themselves, there is no way to carve anything off. Part of the point of the reduction in the case of heat was to distinguish between the subjective appearance on the one hand and the underlying physical reality on the other. Indeed, it is a general feature of such reductions that the phenomenon is defined in terms of the "reality" and not in terms of the "appearance." But we can't make that sort of appearance-reality distinction for consciousness because consciousness consists in the appearances themselves. *Where appearance is concerned we cannot make the appearance-reality distinction because the appearance is the reality.*

For our present purposes, we can summarize this point by saying that consciousness is not reducible in the way that other phenomena are reducible, not because the pattern of facts in the real world involves anything special, but because the reduction of other phenomena depended in part on distinguishing between "objective physical reality," on the one hand, and mere "subjective appearance," on the other; and eliminating the appearance from the phenomena that have been reduced. But in the case of consciousness, its reality is the appearance; hence, the point of the reduction would be lost if we tried to carve off the appearance and simply defined consciousness in terms of the underlying physical reality. In general, the pattern of our reductions rests on rejecting the subjective epistemic basis for the presence of a property as part of the ultimate constituent of that property. We find out about heat or light by feeling and seeing, but we then define the phenomenon in a way that is independent of the epistemology. Consciousness is an exception to this pattern for a trivial reason. The reason, to repeat, is that the reductions that leave out the epistemic bases, the appearances, cannot work for the epistemic bases themselves. In such cases, the appearance is the reality.

But this shows that the irreducibility of consciousness is a trivial consequence of the pragmatics of our definitional practices. A trivial result such as this has only trivial consequences. It has no deep metaphysical consequences for the unity of our overall scientific world view. It does not show that consciousness is not part of the ultimate furniture of reality or cannot be a subject of scientific investigation or cannot be brought into our overall physical conception of the universe; it merely shows that in the way that we have decided to carry out reductions, consciousness, by definition, is excluded from a certain pattern of reduction. Consciousness fails to be reducible, not because of some mysterious feature, but simply because by definition it falls outside the pattern of reduction that we have chosen to use for pragmatic reasons. Pretheoretically, consciousness, like solidity, is a surface feature of certain physical systems. But unlike solidity, consciousness cannot be redefined in terms of an underlying microstructure, and the surface features then treated as mere effects of real consciousness, without losing the point of having the concept of consciousness in the first place.

So far, the argument of this chapter has been conducted, so to speak, from the point of view of the materialist. We can summarize the point I have been making as follows: The contrast between the reducibility of heat, color, solidity, etc., on the one hand, and the irreducibility of conscious states, on the other hand, does not reflect any distinction in the structure of reality, but a distinction in our definitional practices. We could put the same point from the point of view of the property dualist as follows: The apparent contrast between the irreducibility of consciousness and the reducibility of color, heat, solidity, etc., really was *only* apparent. We did not really eliminate the subjectivity of red, for example, when we reduced red to light reflectances; we simply stopped calling the subjective part "red." We did not eliminate any subjective phenomena whatever with these "reductions"; we simply stopped calling them by their old names. Whether we treat the irreducibility from the materialist or from the dualist point of view, we are still left with a universe that contains an irreducibly subjective physical component as a component of physical reality.

To conclude this part of the discussion, I want to make clear what I am saying and what I am not saying. I am not saying that consciousness is not a strange and wonderful phenomenon. I think, on the contrary, that we ought to be amazed by the fact that evolutionary processes produced nervous systems capable of causing and sustaining subjective conscious states.... consciousness is as empirically mysterious to us now as electromagnetism was previously, when people thought the universe must operate entirely on Newtonian principles. But I am saying that once the existence of (subjective, qualitative) consciousness is granted (and no sane person can deny its existence, though many pretend to do so), then there is nothing strange, wonderful, or mysterious about its *irreducibility*. Given its existence, its irreducibility is a trivial consequence of our definitional practices. Its irreducibility has no untoward scientific consequences whatever. Furthermore, when I speak of the irreducibility of consciousness, I am speaking of its *irreducibility according to standard patterns of reduction*. No one can rule out a priori the possibility of a major intellectual revolution that would give us a new—and at present unimaginable—conception of reduction, according to which consciousness would be reducible.

V. SUPERVENIENCE

In recent years there has been a lot of heavy going about a relationship between properties called "supervenience." It is frequently said in discussions in the philosophy of mind that the mental is supervenient on the physical. Intuitively, what is meant by this claim is that mental states are totally dependent on corresponding neurophysiological states in the sense that a difference in mental states would necessarily involve a corresponding difference in neurophysiological states. If, for example, I go from a state of being thirsty to a state of no longer being thirsty, then there must have been some change in my brain states corresponding to the change in my mental states.

On the account that I have been proposing, mental states are supervenient on neurophysiological states in the following respect: Type-identical neurophysiological causes would have type-identical mentalistic effects. Thus, to take the famous brain-in-the-vat example, if you had two brains that were type-identical down to the last molecule, then the causal basis of the mental would guarantee that they would have the same mental phenomena. On this characterization of the supervenience relation, the supervenience of the mental on the physical is marked by the fact that physical states are causally sufficient, though not necessarily causally necessary, for the corresponding mental states. That is just another way of saying that as far as this definition of supervenience is concerned, sameness of neurophysiology guarantees sameness of mentality; but sameness of mentality does not guarantee sameness of neurophysiology.

It is worth emphasizing that this sort of supervenience is *causal* supervenience. Discussions of supervenience were originally introduced in connection with ethics, and the notion in question was not a causal notion....the idea was that moral properties are supervienient on natural properties, that two objects cannot differ solely with respect to, for example, their goodness. If one object is better than another, there must be some other feature in virtue of which the former is better than the latter. But this notion of moral supervenience is not a causal notion. That is, the features of an object that make it good do not *cause* it to be good, they rather *constitute* its goodness. But in the case of mind/brain supervenience, the neural phenomena cause the mental phenomena.

So there are at least two notions of supervenience: a constitutive notion and a causal notion. I believe that only the causal notion is important for discussions of the mind-body problem. In this respect my account differs from the usual accounts of the supervenience of the mental on the physical. Thus Kim claims that we should not think of the relation of neural events to their supervening mental events as causal, and indeed he claims that supervening mental events have no causal status apart from their supervenience on neurophysiological events that have "a more direct causal role." "If this be epiphenomenalism, let us make the most of it," he says cheerfully.

I disagree with both of these claims. It seems to me obvious from everything we know about the brain that macro mental phenomena are all caused by lower-level micro phenomena. There is nothing mysterious about such bottom-up causation; it is quite common in the physical world. Furthermore, the fact that the mental features are supervenient on neuronal features in no way diminishes their causal efficacy. The solidity of the piston is causally supervenient on its molecular structure, but this does not make solidity epiphenomenal; and similarly, the causal supervenience of my present back pain on micro events in my brain does not make the pain epiphenomenal.

My conclusion is that once you recognize the existence of bottom-up, micro to macro forms of causation, the notion of supervenience no longer does any work in philosophy. The formal features of the relation are already present in the causal sufficiency of the micro-macro forms of causation. And the analogy with ethics is just a source of confusion. The relation of macro mental features of the brain to its micro neuronal features is totally unlike the relation of goodness to good-making features, and it is confusing to lump them together. As Wittgenstein says somewhere, "If you wrap up different kinds of furniture in enough wrapping paper, you can make them all look the same shape."

Mental Phenomena Are Reducible to Physical Brain Activities

PAUL M. CHURCHLAND

Like Descartes, John Searle is an eloquent and evidently sincere spokesman for what was then loosely called "the mechanical philosophy" and is now loosely called "materialism." Yet Searle, like Descartes, balks "at the very door of the mind" and declares conscious, intentional phenomena to be wholly real, yet distinct from and irreducible to the nonmental physicalistic features of the brain. Like Descartes, Searle has here a profound tension on his hands, and he never entirely succeeds in resolving it.

To be sure, Searle's rejection of all forms of reductive materialism concerning the mind is much more circumspect than was Descartes'. Searle wants no part of any dualism of substances. Rather, Searle makes the bold assertion that mental phenomena are entirely natural phenomena *caused by* the neurophysiological activities of the physical brain. He calls this position "biological naturalism": mental states are natural states of biological organisms.

What distinguishes Searle from other contemporary materialists (identity theorists, functionalists, and eliminative materialists), and what unites him with Descartes, is his firm insistence that mental phenomena form an *ontologically distinct class of natural phenomena*, phenomena that causally arise from and interact with, but cannot be reduced to, any of the familiar classes of physical phenomena—dynamical, electrical, chemical, biological, etc. Here again we may feel the tension that goes unfelt by Searle: how can mental phenomena *fail* to be reducible to physical phenomena within the brain if, as Searle

himself asserts, mental phenomena ultimately arise, evolutionarily and ontogenetically, from nothing other than the complex interaction of those physical phenomena with one another and with the environment?

Searle's position, however, is no oversight. The supposed ontological gulf fixed between mental phenomena and physical phenomena forms the fulcrum of his book-length argument. Here arises both the motive and the systemic basis for his deepest criticisms of various recent orthodoxies in AI, cognitive psychology, semantic theory, transformational grammar, and the philosophy of mind. Searle has a comprehensive critical vision that he wishes to urge on researchers in all of these areas. Let me try to outline what his vision is.

A theme familiar from Searle's earlier writings is his position concerning what philosophers call "intentionality." This is a technical term for what you or I would call the *meaning* or *content* of a thought or sentence. Searle insists on a distinction between the genuine or "intrinsic" intentionality of real mental states, as contrasted with the merely "as if" or "derivative" intentionality of the physical states of various nonmental systems such as thermostats, heliotropic sunflowers, and classical digital computers.

In the present book, this distinction is claimed by Searle to be tightly connected with a second distinction—that between the conscious states (actual or potential) of any individual, as contrasted with the deeply or essentially *non*conscious states of that individual. Intrinsic or genuine intentionality, says Searle, is a property exclusively of states that actually *are* a part of someone's current consciousness (conscious states), and of states that *could be brought* to consciousness by memory, prompting, attention, and so forth ("shallowly unconscious" states). States that do not meet the disjunctive demands of this Connection Principle are denied anything beyond "as if" intentionality. Intrinsic meaning on the one hand, and consciousness on the other, are thus claimed to be essentially connected with one another.

Since thermostats, sunflowers, and computers have no conscious states at all, reasons Searle, their internal states must lack intrinsic intentionality. Accordingly, no form of explanation that presupposes intrinsic intentionality can ever provide more than a metaphorical explanation of their behavior. Literal explanations of their behavior must always be drawn instead from physics, biology, and the other nonmental sciences. The same lesson, urges Searle, applies to the explanation of all aspects of human cognition that fall strictly outside the domain of the actually or potentially conscious.

Searle's demand that nonconscious phenomena receive their literal explanation in appropriate nonmental terms is mirrored in the complementary demand that genuinely conscious intentional phenomena receive their literal explanation in appropriately mental terms. Just as it is wrong to try to explain the lowly sunflower's heliotropic behavior in terms of desires, perceptions, and actions, so is it wrong to try to explain a genuinely conscious creature's perceptions, deliberations, and behavior in terms appropriate solely to the nonmental physical substrate that causes such conscious activity.

This conviction forms the basis of Searle's criticism of all current forms of materialism. They have all of them, he

avers, lost sight of the central importance of the phenomenon of consciousness. Or worse, they deliberately downplay its importance by refocusing our attention on the more obviously formal or structural features of cognition such as grammar, logic, problem solving, and learning. It is high time, insists Searle, that the several cognitive sciences rediscover the importance of consciousness itself, and refocus their explanatory efforts appropriately. Thus the title of his book; it is as much exhortation as description.

It is hard not to resonate with a clarion call to readdress consciousness. Indeed, why ever should we resist? We would all dearly love to understand consciousness better. And yet, Searle's readers are hereby advised to proceed with considerable caution as they follow Searle in pursuit of this worthy goal. Other major positions, materialist to the core but no less interested in consciousness, are summarily dismissed on flimsy grounds. And in the end, Searle himself fails to achieve that goal. Moreover, the interim position he takes is inadequately motivated, doctrinally unstable, and flatly contradicted by every relevant lesson of our scientific history.

Consider first its motivation. The focal issue is Searle's claim that mental phenomena are irreducible to the objective features of the physical brain. The sticking point here, according to Searle, is the *subjective* character of mental states, as opposed to the *objective* character of any and all physical states. In the face of this "rockbottom" divergence of character on each side of the alleged equation, how could mental phenomena possibly be identical with, or somehow constituted from, sheerly physical phenomena? They are as different as chalk from cheese.

The argument, let us admit, is beguiling. That is why it is famous. Searle is not offering us a new argument, but an old one, one made famous in the modern period by Thomas Nagel and Frank Jackson.

There is also a standard and quite devastating reply to this sort of argument, a reply that has been in undergraduate textbooks for a decade. On the most obvious and reasonable interpretation, to say that John's mental states are *subjective* in character is just to say that John's mental states are *known-uniquely-to-John-by-introspection*. And to say that John's physical brain states are objective is just to deny that his physical brain states have the hyphenated property at issue. Stated carefully, the argument thus has the following form:

1. John's mental states are known-uniquely-to-John-by-introspection.

2. John's physical brain states are *not* known-uniquely-to-John-by-introspection.

3. John's mental states cannot be identical with any of John's physical brain states.

Once put in this form, however, the argument is instantly recognizable to any logician as committing a familiar form of fallacy, a fallacy instanced more clearly in the following two examples.

1. Aspirin is known-to-John-as-a-pain-reliever.

2. Acetylsalicylic acid is *not* known-to-John-as-a-pain-reliever.

Therefore, since they have divergent properties,

3. Aspirin cannot be identical with acetylsalicylic acid.

Or,

1. The temperature of an object is known-to-John-by-simple-feeling.

2. The mean molecular kinetic energy of an object is *not* known-to-John-by-simple-feeling.

Therefore, since they have divergent properties,

3. Temperature cannot be identical with mean molecular kinetic energy.

Here the conclusions are known to be false in both cases, despite the presumed truth of all of the premises. The problem here is that the so-called "divergent properties" consist in nothing more than the item's being *recognized, perceived, or known*, by somebody, by a specific means and under a specific description. But no such "epistemic" property is an intrinsic feature of the item itself, one that might determine its possible identity or nonidentity with some candidate thing otherwise apprehended or otherwise described. Indeed, as the two clearly fallacious parallels illustrate, the truth of the argument's premises need reflect nothing more than John's overwhelming *ignorance* of what happens to be identical with what. And as with the parallels, so with the original. Despite its initial appeal, the argument is a non sequitur.

Though he makes no attempt to protect the reader from it, Searle's text indicates that he is aware of this familiar fallacy, for he briefly insists that he does not intend an "epistemic" construal of subjectivity, which is precisely what the above reconstruction of the Subjectivity Argument involves. But beyond this most natural and familiar construal, what other construal is there?

Searle intends an ontological construal. The Subjectivity Argument, he explains, is meant to make "a point about what real features exist in the world and not, except derivatively, about how we know about those features." Fine. Now we need to know which features—beyond the illicit "epistemic features" just discussed—are supposed to discriminate mental states as being forever distinct from physical brain states. Searle answers this question as follows.

"Suppose we tried to say that pain is really 'nothing but' the patterns of neuron firings. Well, if we tried such an ontological reduction, the essential features of the pain would be left out. No description of the third-person, objective, physiological facts would convey the subjective, first-person character of the pain, simply because the first-person features are different from the third-person features." Of this reconstructed version of the Subjectivity Argument, Searle comments, "It is ludicrously simple and quite decisive."

This last remark is an apt characterization of any argument that establishes its conclusion by the simple expedient of assuming as its premise (viz., "the first-person features are different from the third-person features") a thinly disguised restatement of the very conclusion it aims to establish (viz., "a pain and its subjective features are not identical with a brain state and its objective features"). Searle's brief preamble about what certain descriptions can or cannot "convey" is just more "epistemic" smoke screen creeping illegitimately back into the picture. What remains beyond that is a stark example of begging the question. Whether or not the subjective mental features one discriminates in introspection are identical with some objective features of one's brain that might eventually be discriminated in some objective fashion is exactly what is at issue.

What will determine the answer to this question is not whether our subjective properties intuitively *seem* to be different from neural properties, but whether cognitive neuroscience eventually succeeds in discovering suitably systematic neural analogs for all of the intrinsic and causal properties of mental states.

Remember the case of light, to choose one of many historical examples. From the standpoint of uninformed common sense, light and its manifold properties certainly *seem* to be utterly different from anything so esoteric and alien as orthogonal electric and magnetic fields oscillating at a million billion cycles per second. And yet, our strong intuitions of ontological differences notwithstanding, that is exactly what light turns out to be. Who will be so bold as to insist, just as the neuroscientific evidence is starting to pour in, that mental states cannot find a similar fate?

John Searle, apparently. And he cites one final consideration in support of this antireductionist position. Borrowing once again from an earlier argument of Tom Nagel's, Searle points out, as a presumptive final symptom of the alleged ontological distinction enjoyed by mental phenomena, that in historical cases of the scientific reduction of some objective physical property (such as temperature, sound, color, etc.), the reduction always "leaves aside," as something so far unexplained and unreduced, the subjective effects of that objective physical property on the conscious experience of humans.

In fact, this is not entirely true, but it is close enough to the truth to merit being dealt with on that assumption. What Searle sees as a symptom of ontological distinction is a reflection of something much simpler: once again, Our Ignorance. Why is it that statistical mechanics (the nineteenth-century theory that successfully reduced heat and temperature) does not also account for the subjective effects of temperature on human consciousness? Plainly, because such an account would require, in *addition* to Statistical Mechanics, an adequate theory of the human brain and its cognitive activities, something we have only recently begun to construct. Similarly, why is it that wave mechanics (the eighteenth-century theory that successfully reduced acoustic phenomena) does not also account for the subjective effects of sound on human consciousness? Plainly, because such an account would require, in *addition* to wave mechanics, an adequate theory of the human brain and its cognitive activities, something we have only recently begun to construct. And so on.

Note well that all of these theories "leave aside," as unexplained and unreduced, a vast variety of other esoteric properties beyond those found in human consciousness. Statistical Mechanics (SM), for example, also leaves aside the effects of heat and temperature on the GNP of Peru, on bluebirdegg cholesterol levels, on pneumonic infections in infants, on Antarctic anchovy production, on the rotting of forest-floor vegetable matter, and so forth. Each of these phenomena requires some additional theory beyond SM if it is to be successfully addressed. So it is no surprise that each is "left aside" by SM itself. And no one is tempted to insist, on these grounds, that such phenomena must be counted as ontologically distinct, irreducible, nonphysical features of reality. The effects of heat and temperature on human conscious perception are in exactly the same position. Only a man who had *prejudged* the ontological issue would make the mistake of seeing any ontological significance in the historical pattern at issue.

To summarize the motivation behind Searle's antireductionism, it has come apart in our hands. The Subjectivity Argument exploits a familiar fallacy or it falls back on a simple begging of the question. And the "leaves aside" argument is a faulty induction from a misapprehended historical pattern. So far as positive motivation is concerned, I am unable to find further considerations of any significance in Searle's book. My judgment, then, is that his positive position is badly undermotivated.

But the situation is darker than this. For there are independent negative considerations facing a position like Searle's. I mentioned earlier that it is an unstable position. By this I mean the following.

Searle is attempting to embrace both the biologically natural character of mental states, and their physical irreducibility. But one or the other of these has to go. As Searle fits these strange bedfellows together, the relation between the neural and mental is said to be causal. Neural phenomena do not *constitute* mental phenomena, according to Searle, but they do *cause* them.

The difficulty for Searle is that every last one of the many available real scientific examples of what he calls "micro-to-macro forms of causation" are also cases where the macroproperty at issue is *constituted* by some feature of the underlying microreality. For example, the swift compression of the molecules of a gas into a smaller volume will indeed *cause* the temperature of the gas to increase, but temperature is *constituted* by the mean kinetic energy of those molecules. The subtraction of kinetic energy from the molecules of a tray of water will indeed *cause* the water to become solid (to form ice), but the solidity of the ice is *constituted* by the matrix of positionally stable bonds into which the now more quiescent molecules settle. Raising the hydrogen-ion concentration of one's stomach acids will indeed *cause* one's digestion to accelerate, but digestion is *constituted* by the complex chemical decomposition of one's food.

Similarly, while a retinal activation pattern will indeed *cause* a conscious visual image to occur—in the primary visual cortex, perhaps—it will be because the conscious visual image is *constituted* by something like an activation pattern across the cortical neurons, and because the retina is causally connected to those cortical neurons via the optic nerve.

Searle's robust persistence in thinking of mental states as ontologically distinct from, yet causally produced by, physical brain states reminds me of a comparable persistence of thought in a comparable domain. It appears in the introduction to *Betty Crocker's Microwave Cooking*, a book published soon after microwave ovens began to appear in every American kitchen. ("Betty Crocker" is a major American brand name for sundry baking products.) Before turning to the endless recipes, the authors attempt a brief explanation of how such newfangled devices manage to produce heat in the foodstuffs we put inside them. I quote.

> The magnetron tube converts regular electricity into microwaves. …When [the microwaves] encounter any matter containing moisture—specifically food—they are absorbed into it.…The microwaves agitate and vibrate the moisture molecules at such a great rate that friction is created; the friction, in turn, creates heat and the heat causes the food to cook.

The decisive failure of comprehension begins to appear halfway through the last sentence. Instead of asserting that the induced motion of the moisture molecules already *constitutes* heat, and gracefully ending their explanation there, the authors benightedly continue to discuss heat as if it were an ontologically distinct property. They then fall back on their folk understanding of one of the many things that can *cause* heat: friction. The result is massively misleading to the innocent reader, who is left with the impression that rubbing two molecules together causes heat in the same way that rubbing your two hands together causes heat. In this confusion, the real nature of heat—the motion of the molecules themselves—is left entirely out of the account.

I have always treasured this example, since it illustrates the way in which our folk conceptions can blithely persist, even in the face of clean and established scientific reductions. How much firmer their grip, then, when the relevant reduction is still no more than in prospect? What Searle has written, I suggest, is something not too far from *Betty Crocker's Philosophy of Mind*. As a recipe for addressing the true nature of conscious phenomena, it is a bust. What Searle's book resolutely rediscovers is not the mind, but our commonsense, prescientific, folk-psychological conception of the mind. The aim of science, by contrast, is to discover a new and better conception. In this endeavor, Searle's book is not likely to help.

THE CONTINUING DEBATE:
Are My Hopes and Thoughts Ultimately
Just Electrochemical Brain Impulses?

What Is New

Most materialists have held an *identity* view on the mind-body question. That is, they maintain that the mind is *identical* with the brain, and that there is no separate mental substance. On the identity view, our common ideas about mental phenomena—ideas about belief, intention, consciousness, feelings—will ultimately be shown to match with brain processes; in fact, your feeling of elation and your idea of beauty and your sense of conscious willing will be recognized as being specific brain events. But eliminative materialists take a still more radical view: they maintain that advances in neurological psychology may ultimately *eliminate* our common sense "folk psychology," replacing it with more useful and accurate neurological references. Modern science does not give a materialist explanation for demons and spirits, but instead has abandoned that entire framework of thought. Likewise—say the eliminative materialists—advances in neuropsychology might well lead us to abandon our primitive folk psychology notions of how the mind works, in favor of a new perspective.

Where to Find More

John Searle and Paul Churchland are two of the leading figures in contemporary philosophy of mind, and both have had enormous influence. Searle's "Chinese Room Argument" against artificial intelligence is widely anthologized and has provoked an enormous range of response; see John R. Searle, "Minds, Brains, and Programs," *Behavioral and Brain Sciences*, volume 3, number 3 (1980): 417–424, with a number of commentaries following. Among his books are *Minds, Brains, and Science* (Cambridge, Mass.: Harvard University Press, 1983); *The Rediscovery of the Mind* (Cambridge, Mass.: The MIT Press, 1992); *The Mystery of Consciousness* (1997); and *Consciousness and Language* (2002). Searle has also written a very engaging introduction to the philosophy of mind: *Mind: A Brief Introduction* (New York: Oxford University Press, 2004).

Like Searle's, Paul Churchland's writings are always interesting and thought-provoking, and they take strong stands that are championed persuasively. Several of his major books are noted in the introduction to this debate, and others include *A Neurocomputational Perspective: The Nature of Mind and the Structure of Science* (Cambridge, Mass.: MIT Press, 1989), and *Images of Science: Scientific Realism versus Constructive Empiricism* (Chicago: University of Chicago Press, 1985). An excellent collection of essays by Paul M. Churchland and Patricia S. Churchland is *On the Contrary: Critical Essays, 1987–1997* (Cambridge, Mass.: MIT Press, 1998); several of the essays involve critiques of Searle's arguments, and "Betty Crocker's Theory of Consciousness" is reprinted there. In addition to the essays in that volume, Patricia S. Churchland has written some excellent books on the importance of contemporary neurological research for philosophy of mind; see particularly her *Neurophilosophy: Toward a Unified Science of the Mind-Brain* (Cambridge, Mass.: MIT Press, 1986).

Paul Churchland, in *Matter and Consciousness* and in "Eliminative Materialism and the Propositional Attitudes," *Journal of Philosophy*, volume 78 (1981): 67–90, and Patricia Churchland, in *Neurophilosophy*, are leading contemporary advocates of eliminative materialism. Critics of eliminative materialism include Philip S. Kitcher, "In Defense of Folk Psychology," *Journal of Philosophy*, volume 81 (1984): 89–106; Lynne Rudder Baker, *Saving Belief: A Critique of Physicalism* (Princeton: Princeton University Press, 1987); and Jerry Fodor, *Psychosemantics* (Cambridge, Mass.: MIT Press, 1987). A good collection of papers on the issue is edited by S. M. Christensen and D. R. Turner, *Folk Psychology and the Philosophy of Mind* (Hillsdale, N.J.: Lawrence Erlbaum, 1993).

There are many good edited collections on the philosophy of mind and the question of consciousness, including Ned Block, *Readings in the Philosophy of Psychology*, volume 1 (Cambridge, Mass.: Harvard University Press, 1980); Ned Block, Owen Flanagan, and Güven Güzeldere, *The Nature of Consciousness: Philosophical Debates* (Cambridge, Mass.: MIT Press, 1997); David J. Chalmers, *Philosophy of Mind: Classical and Contemporary Readings* (New York: Oxford University Press, 2002), which is particularly good for historical sources; John Heil, *Philosophy of Mind: A Guide and Anthology* (Oxford: Oxford University Press, 2004); William Lycan, *Mind and Cognition: A Reader* (Cambridge, Mass.: Blackwell, 1990); Thomas Metzinger, *Conscious Experience* (Schöningh: Imprint Academic, 1995), which contains an excellent introductory essay by Metzinger and an extensive bibliography; Timothy O'Connor and David Robb, *Philosophy of Mind: Contemporary Readings* (London: Routledge, 2003); David M. Rosenthal, *The Nature of Mind* (New York: Oxford University Press, 1991), with good historical as well as contemporary material and a well-organized bibliography; and Quentin Smith and Aleksandar Jokic, *Consciousness: New Philosophical Perspectives* (New York: Oxford University Press, 2003), an excellent collection of recent essays by leading theorists.

George Graham, *Philosophy of Mind: An Introduction* (Oxford: Blackwell Publishers, 1993) is a superb introduction to the issues, and is particularly good at relating contemporary debates in philosophy of mind to other issues (such as religion, free will, and mental illness), as well as to the history of philosophy. William Seager, *Theories of Consciousness: An Introduction and Assessment* (London: Routledge, 1999) is a very thorough introduction to contemporary theories of consciousness.

Daniel M. Wegner gives an interesting account and interpretation of some fascinating contemporary neuropsychological research in *The Illusion of Conscious Will* (Cambridge, Mass.: MIT Press, 2002); and *The Volitional Brain: Towards a Neuroscience of Free Will*, edited by Benjamin Libet, Anthony Freeman, and Keith Sutherland (Thorverton UK: Imprint Academic, 1999) is a particularly good collection of essays on this area of research.

On the internet, *The Stanford Encyclopedia of Philosophy* is (as always) excellent; see especially the article "Consciousness," Robert Van Gulick, as well as the William Ramsey essay "Eliminative Materialism." The Stanford Encyclopedia can be found at http://plato.stanford.edu/. Another good site for philosophy of mind is *A Field Guide to the Philosophy of Mind*, at http://host/uniroma3.it/progetti/kant/field/.

6

WHO AM I?

Personal Identity Is Not So Important

ADVOCATE: Derek Parfit, Research Fellow of All Souls College, Oxford; has also taught at Harvard University and New York University.

SOURCE: Excerpts from *Reasons and Persons* (Oxford: Clarendon Press, 1984).

Personal Identity Is Essential

ADVOCATE: Christine M. Korsgaard, Arthur Kingsley Porter Professor of Philosophy at Harvard University. Among her books are *The Sources of Normativity* (1996) and *Creating the Kingdom of Ends* (1996).

SOURCE: "Personal Identity and the Unity of Agency: A Kantian Response to Parfit," *Philosophy & Public Affairs*, volume 18, no. 2 (Spring 1989): 101–132.

Laura was a wild kid, who fell in with a bad crowd. When she was 18 she was driving around town with three friends, and all had been drinking heavily. They were out of beer and out of money, and one of Laura's friends, Dave, had the idea of robbing a convenience store. Dave is a couple years older, and exerts enormous influence over the group. Dave has a pistol, and assures everyone that nothing will go wrong: he will wave the pistol at the clerk and grab the money, while two others will grab some cold beer, and they'll all run back to the car. Laura will drive, because she's not quite as drunk as the others. Laura doesn't much like the idea, but she goes along with it. But something goes terribly wrong. The clerk at the store pulls a gun from behind the counter, and Dave kills him. Dave and the other two run out of the store and jump into the car, and Laura drives away: thus becoming the getaway driver for a first degree murder. Laura changes her life dramatically: she quits drinking altogether, moves across country, goes to college and gets a degree in special education, gets married and has three children, and devotes her life to teaching special education students and raising her family. The case remains unsolved for 40 years; but it's a first degree murder, so the case remains open. And one day 40 years later there's a break in the case: Dave is dying of cancer, and he confesses to his part in the murder. Laura is tracked down, and 40 years later—her three children have graduated from college, she has six grandchildren, she has just received an award for 35 years of devoted service to special education students, and she is thinking of retirement—she is charged with first degree murder for her part in the crime; and she faces the prospect of spending the rest of her life in prison. Certainly what the 18-year-old Laura did was terribly wrong; but is it right to punish the 58-year-old Laura for the crime? Is the quiet grandmother who is devoted to her grandchildren and her special education students really the same person as the wild, hard-drinking, 18-year-old girl?

Am I the same person as the child who loved toy trains and jelly beans? Is the woman facing imprisonment the same person as the young woman who participated in a brutal murder 40 years ago? Will *I* have genuine personal immortality if there eternally exists some person (or angel, or disembodied soul) who has no greedy or jealous or lecherous inclinations, no pains nor worries, and seems radically different from the worried, jealous, greedy, lecherous person I now am? Are there—as the famous "split brain" experiments seem to indicate—perhaps two distinct persons occupying each body, corresponding to the two hemispheres of the brain? If "multiple personality" accounts are plausible, is it possible that some single bodies are inhabited by many distinct persons? When we move to science fiction, the problems become even thornier: when there is a complete molecule-by-molecule duplication of my body, are there two identical persons, or one person with two bodies? If my original body is destroyed, but a duplicate survives, then have *I* survived, or is the survivor an imposter?

The dominant philosophical view on personal identity is *psychological*. Though there is great dispute over the details, most—but by no means all—contemporary philosophers hold that the persistence of an individual requires some form of psychological continuity. The most popular candidate to provide that continuity is *memory*: you are identical with some person from the past if you remember her experiences. John Locke, a British philosopher of the 17th Century, is the classic source for this model of personal identity:

> …it is plain [that] consciousness, as far as ever it can be extended—should it be to ages past—unites existences and actions very remote in time into the same *person*, as well as it does the existences and actions of the immediately preceding moment: so that whatever has the consciousness of present and past actions is the same person to whom they both belong. Had I the same consciousness that I saw the ark and Noah's flood as that I saw an overflowing of the Thames last winter, or as that I write now, I could no more doubt that I who write this now, that saw the Thames overflowed last winter, and that viewed the flood at the general deluge, was the same *self*…than that I who write this am the same *myself* now whilst I write…that I was yesterday. *An Essay Concerning Human Understanding* (London: Holt, 1690), Book II, chapter 27.

But there are problems for this view. Joan, who is a college senior, remembers the experiences of Joan the high school senior, and so the college Joan is the high school Joan. Joan the high school senior remembered the experiences of Joan in 3rd grade, so the high school Joan is the elementary school Joan. But Joan the college senior remembers none of the experiences of Joan the 3rd grader, so they seem to be different people. But if college Joan is identical with high school Joan, and high school Joan is identical with elementary school Joan, then college Joan and elementary school Joan must also be identical. Attempting to answer that problem—and others—has led psychological identity theorists into a wide variety of views.

When Derek Parfit speaks of the *reductionist* view, he is referring to the view that the facts of personal identity consist of more particular facts that can be described impersonally; for example, a reductionist might hold that personal identity consists in elements of psychological continuity, or the continued existence of sufficient specific portions of a living brain: personal identity can be *reduced* to such specific impersonal facts. (An example of a *non*reductionist view would be the view that our identity requires the continued existence of a special spiritual or mental substance; however, nonreductionists need not be dualists.) Parfit favors a psychological reductionist view of personal identity, but he goes on to argue that personal identity is not what really matters to us: the important thing is psychological continuity of experiences, *not* that those experiences belong to a particular continuing individual.

Christine M. Korsgaard argues that even if Parfit's arguments were correct, we would still have strong, practical, moral reasons for believing in the continuing personal identity of ourselves as rational agents. First, we require such a unity to be effective actors; and second, unity is "implicit in the *standpoint* from which you deliberate and choose," and having such a standpoint is essential for genuine deliberation. Korsgaard maintains that it is not the metaphysical facts about being a person that establish the nature of your life; rather, *because* you have a life to lead, and life projects in which you are invested, you are one continuing person. As an *agent* who makes deliberative choices, you must have unity and continuity of consciousness. The proof lies in our practical activities, not in metaphysical argument.

POINTS TO PONDER

➤ Parfit concludes that though some might find his view depressing, he himself finds it liberating and consoling. What is your reaction? *If* you were convinced that Parfit's view is correct, would you find that depressing? Liberating?

➤ Suppose that someone draws exactly the opposite of your conclusion about the psychological impact of Parfit's view; that is, if you find it depressing, this person finds it liberating and consoling. *Why* are your reactions so different? Is there some underlying basic difference in beliefs?

➤ Korsgaard distinguishes the *practical* perspective of the free and responsible and deliberative agent from the theoretical perspective that represents us as determined by natural forces. She claims that these perspectives need not be in conflict or contradiction, because they serve different purposes: "When we look at our actions from the theoretical standpoint our concern is with their explanation and prediction. When we view them from the practical standpoint our concern is with their justification and choice." *Is* there a conflict? If one perspective is accurate, must the other be illusory?

Personal Identity Is Not So Important

DEREK PARFIT

DIVIDED MINDS

Some recent medical cases provide striking evidence in favor of the Reductionist View. Human beings have a lower brain and two upper hemispheres, which are connected by a bundle of fibers. In treating a few people with severe epilepsy, surgeons have cut these fibers. The aim was to reduce the severity of epileptic fits, by confining their causes to a single hemisphere. This aim was achieved. But the operations had another unintended consequence. The effect, in the words of one surgeon, was the creation of "two separate spheres of consciousness."

This effect was revealed by various psychological tests. These made use of two facts. We control our right arms with our left hemispheres, and vice versa. And what is in the right halves of our visual fields we see with our left hemispheres, and vice versa. When someone's hemispheres have been disconnected, psychologists can thus present to this person two different written questions in the two halves of his visual field, and can receive two different answers written by this person's two hands.

Here is a simplified version of the kind of evidence that such tests provide. One of these people is shown a wide screen, whose left half is red and right half is blue. On each half in a darker shade are the words, "How many colors can you see?" With both hands the person writes, "Only one." The words are now changed to read: "Which is the only color that you can see?" With one of his hands the person writes "Red," with the other he writes "Blue."

If this is how this person responds, there seems no reason to doubt that he is having visual sensations—that he does, as he claims, see both red and blue. But in seeing red he is not aware of seeing blue, and vice versa. This is why the surgeon writes of "two separate spheres of consciousness." In each of his centers of consciousness the person can see only a single color. In one center, he sees red, in the other, blue.

The many actual tests, though differing in details from the imagined test that I have just described, show the same two essential features. In seeing what is in the left half of his visual field, such a person is quite unaware of what he is now seeing in the right half of his visual field, and vice versa. And in the center of consciousness in which he sees the left half of his visual

field, and is aware of what he is doing with his left hand, this person is quite unaware of what he is doing with his right hand, and vice versa.

…The left hemisphere typically supports or "has" the linguistic and mathematical abilities of an adult, while the right hemisphere "has" these abilities at the level of a young child. But the right hemisphere, though less advanced in these respects, has greater abilities of other kinds, such as those involved in pattern recognition, or musicality.…It is also believed that, in a minority of people, there may be no difference between the abilities of the two hemispheres.

Suppose that I am one of this minority, with two exactly similar hemispheres. And suppose that I have been equipped with some device that can block communication between my hemispheres. Since this device is connected to my eyebrows, it is under my control. By raising an eyebrow I can divide my mind. In each half of my divided mind I can then, by lowering an eyebrow, reunite my mind.

This ability would have many uses. Consider

My Physics Exam. I am taking an exam, and have only fifteen minutes left in which to answer the last question. It occurs to me that there are two ways of tackling this question. I am unsure which is more likely to succeed. I therefore decide to divide my mind for ten minutes, to work in each half of my mind on one of the two calculations, and then to reunite my mind to write a fair copy of the best result. What shall I experience?

When I disconnect my hemispheres, my stream of consciousness divides. But this division is not something that I experience. Each of my two streams of consciousness seems to have been straightforwardly continuous with my one stream of consciousness up to the moment of division. The only changes in each stream are the disappearance of half my visual field and the loss of sensation in, and control over, one of my arms.

Consider my experiences in my "right-handed" stream. I remember deciding that I would use my right hand to do the longer calculation. This I now begin. In working at this calculation I can see, from the movements of my left hand, that I am also working at the other. But I am not aware of working at the other. I might, in my right-handed stream, wonder how, in my left-handed stream, I am getting on. I could look and see. This would be just like looking to see how well my neighbor is doing, at the next desk. In my right-handed stream I would be equally unaware both of what my neighbor is now thinking and of what I am now thinking in my left-handed stream. Similar remarks apply to my experiences in my left-handed stream.

My work is now over. I am about to reunite my mind. What should I, in each stream, expect? Simply that I shall suddenly seem to remember just having worked at two calculations, in working at each of which I was not aware of working at the other. This, I suggest, we can imagine. And, if my mind had been divided, my apparent memories would be correct.

In describing this case, I assumed that there were two separate series of thoughts and sensations. If my two hands visibly wrote out two calculations, and I also claimed later to remember two corresponding series of thoughts, this is what we ought to assume. It would be most im-

plausible to assume that either or both calculations had been done unconsciously.

It might be objected that my description ignores "the necessary unity of consciousness." But I have not ignored this alleged necessity. I have denied it. What is a fact must be possible. And it is a fact that people with disconnected hemispheres have two separate streams of consciousness—two series of thoughts and experiences, in having each of which they are unaware of having the other. Each of these two streams separately displays unity of consciousness. This may be a surprising fact. But we can understand it. We can come to believe that a person's mental history need not be like a canal, with only one channel, but could be like a river, occasionally having separate streams. I suggest that we can also imagine what it would be like to divide and reunite our minds. My description of my experiences in my Physics Exam seems both to be coherent and to describe something that we can imagine.

It might next be claimed that, in my imagined case, I do not have a divided mind. Rather, I have two minds. This objection does not raise a real question. These are two ways of describing one and the same outcome.

A similar objection claims that, in these actual and imagined cases, the result is not a single person with either a divided mind or two minds. The result is two different people, sharing control of most of one body, but each in sole control of one arm. Here too, I believe that this objection does not raise a real question. These are again two ways of describing the same outcome. This is what we believe if we are Reductionists.

If we are not yet Reductionists…we believe that it is a real question whether such cases involve more than a single person. Perhaps we can believe this in the actual cases, where the division is permanent. But this belief is hard to accept when we consider my imagined Physics Exam. In this case there are two streams of consciousness for only ten minutes. And I later seem to remember doing both of the calculations that, during these ten minutes, my two hands could be seen to be writing out. Given the brief and modest nature of this disunity, it is not plausible to claim that this case involves more than a single person. Are we to suppose that, during these ten minutes, I cease to exist, and two new people come into existence, each of whom then works out one of the calculations? On this interpretation, the whole episode involves three people, two of whom have lives that last for only ten minutes. Moreover, each of these two people mistakenly believes that he is me, and has apparent memories that accurately fit my past. And after these ten minutes I have accurate apparent memories of the brief lives of each of these two people, except that I mistakenly believe that I myself had all of the thoughts and sensations that these people had. It is hard to believe that I am mistaken here, and that the episode does involve three quite different people.

It is equally hard to believe that it involves two different people, with me doing one of the calculations, and some other person doing the other. I admit that, when I first divide my mind, I might in doing one of the calculations believe that the other calculation must be being done by someone else. But in doing the other calculation I might have the same belief. When my mind has been reunited, I would then seem to remember believing, while doing each of the calculations, that the other calculation must be being done by someone else. When I seem to remember both these beliefs, I would have no reason to think that one was true and the other false. And after several divisions and

reunions I would cease to have such beliefs. In each of my two streams of consciousness I would believe that I was now, in my other stream, having thoughts and sensations of which, in this stream, I was now unaware.

WHAT EXPLAINS THE UNITY OF CONSCIOUSNESS?

Suppose that, because we are not yet Reductionists, we believe that there must be a true answer to the question, "Who has each stream of consciousness?" And suppose that, for the reasons just given, we believe that this case involves only a single person: me. We believe that for ten minutes I have a divided mind.

Remember next the view that psychological unity is explained by ownership. On this view, we should explain the unity of a person's consciousness, at any time, by ascribing different experiences to this person, or "subject of experiences." What unites these different experiences is that they are being had by the same person. This view is held both by those who believe that a person is a separately existing entity, and by some of those who reject this belief. And this view also applies to the unity of each life.

When we consider my imagined Physics Exam, can we continue to accept this view? We believe that, while my mind is divided, I have two separate series of experiences, in having each of which I am unaware of having the other. At any time in one of my streams of consciousness I am having several different thoughts and sensations. I might be aware of thinking out some part of the calculation, feeling writer's cramp in one hand, and hearing the squeaking of my neighbor's old-fashioned pen. What unites these different experiences?

On the view described above, the answer is that these are the experiences being had by me at this time. This answer is incorrect. I am not just having these experiences at this time. I am also having, in my other stream of consciousness, several other experiences. We need to explain the unity of consciousness within each of my two streams of consciousness, or in each half of my divided mind. We cannot explain these two unities by claiming that all of these experiences are being had by me at this time. This makes the two unities one. It ignores the fact that, in having each of these two sets of experiences, I am unaware of having the other.

Suppose that we continue to believe that unity should be explained by ascribing different experiences to a single subject. We must then believe that this case involves at least two different subjects of experiences. What unites the experiences in my left-handed stream is that they are all being had by one subject of experiences. What unites the experiences in my right-handed stream is that they are all being had by another subject of experiences. We must now abandon the claim that "the subject of experiences" is the person. On our view, I am a subject of experiences. While my mind is divided there are two different subjects of experiences. These are not the same subject of experiences, so they cannot both be me. Since it is unlikely that I am one of the two, given the similarity of my two streams of consciousness, we should probably conclude that I am neither of these two subjects of experiences. The whole episode therefore involves three such entities. And two of these entities cannot be claimed to be the kind of entity with which we are all familiar, a person. I am the only person involved, and two of these subjects of experiences are *not* me. Even if we assume that I *am* one of these two subjects of experiences, *the other* cannot be me, and is therefore not a person.

We may now be skeptical. While the "subject of experiences" was the person, it seemed plausible to claim that what unites a set of experiences is that they are all had by a single subject. If we have to believe in subjects of experiences that are not persons, we may doubt whether there really are such things. There are of course, in the animal world, many subjects of experiences that are not persons. My cat is one example. But other animals are irrelevant to this imagined case. On the view described above, we have to believe that the life of a *person* could involve subjects of experiences that are not persons.

Reconsider my experiences in my right-handed stream of consciousness. In this stream at a certain time I am aware of thinking about part of a calculation, feeling writer's cramp, and hearing the sounds made by my neighbor's pen. Do we explain the unity of these experiences by claiming that they are all being had by the same subject of experiences, this being an entity which is *not* me? This explanation does not seem plausible. If this subject of experiences is *not* a person, what kind of thing is it? It cannot be claimed to be a Cartesian Ego, if I am claimed to be such an Ego. This subject of experiences cannot be claimed to be such an Ego, since it is not me, and this case involves only one person. Can this subject of experiences be a Cartesian Sub-Ego, a persisting purely mental entity which is merely part of a person? We may decide that we have insufficient grounds for believing that there are such things.

I turn next to the other view mentioned above. Some people believe that unity is explained by ownership, even though they deny that we are separately existing entities. These people believe that what unites a person's experiences at any time is the fact that these experiences are being had by this person. Applied to this imagined case, this belief is false. While I am having one set of experiences in my right-handed stream, I am also having another set in my left-handed stream. We cannot explain the unity of either of these two sets of experiences by claiming that these are the experiences that are being had by me. This claim conflates these two sets.

A Reductionist may now intervene. On his view, what unites my experiences in my right-handed stream is that there is, at any time, a single state of awareness of these various experiences. There is a state of awareness of having certain thoughts, feeling writer's cramp, and hearing the sound of a squeaking pen. At the same time, there is another state of awareness of the various experiences in my left-handed stream. My mind is divided because there is no single state of awareness of both of these sets of experiences.

It may be objected that these claims do not explain but only redescribe the unity of consciousness in each stream. In one sense, this is true. This unity does not need a deep explanation. It is simply a fact that several experiences can be *co-conscious*, or be the objects of a single state of awareness. It may help to compare this fact with the fact that there is short-term memory of experiences within the last few moments: short-term memory of what is called "the specious present." Just as there can be a single memory of just having had several experiences, such as hearing a bell strike three times, there can be a single state of awareness both of hearing the fourth striking of this bell, and of seeing ravens fly past the bell-tower. Reductionists claim that nothing more is involved in the unity of consciousness at a single time. Since there can be one state of awareness of several experiences, we need not explain this unity by ascribing these experiences to the same person, or subject of experiences.

It is worth restating other parts of the Reductionist View. I claim:

Because we ascribe thoughts to thinkers, it is true that thinkers exist. But thinkers are not separately existing entities. The existence of a thinker just involves the existence of his brain and body, the doing of his deeds, the thinking of his thoughts, and the occurrence of certain other physical and mental events. We could therefore redescribe any person's life in impersonal terms. In explaining the unity of this life, we need not claim that it is the life of a particular person. We could describe what, at different times, was thought and felt and observed and done, and how these various events were interrelated. Persons would be mentioned here only in the descriptions of the *content* of many thoughts, desires, memories, and so on. Persons need not be claimed to be the thinkers of any of these thoughts.

These claims are supported by the case where I divide my mind. It is not merely true here that the unity of different experiences does not *need* to be explained by ascribing all of these experiences to me. The unity of my experiences, in each stream, *cannot* be explained in this way. There are only two alternatives. We might ascribe the experiences in each stream to a subject of experiences which is *not* me, and, therefore, not a person. Or, if we doubt the existence of such entities, we can accept the Reductionist explanation. At least in this case, this may now seem the best explanation....

It is natural to believe that our identity is what matters. In my division, each half of my brain will be successfully transplanted into the very similar body of one of my two brothers. Both of the resulting people will be fully psychologically continuous with me, as I am now. What happens to me?

...Note that we could not *find out* what happens even if we could actually perform this operation. Suppose, for example, that I do survive as one of the resulting people. I would believe that I have survived. But I would know that the other resulting person falsely believes that he is me, and that he survived. Since I know this, I could not trust my own belief. I might be the resulting person with the false belief. And, since we both claim to be me, other people would have no reason to believe one claim rather than the other. Even if we performed this operation, we would therefore learn nothing.

Whatever happened to me, we could not discover what happened. This suggests a more radical answer to our question. It suggests that the Reductionist View is true. Perhaps there are not here different possibilities, each of which might be what happens, though we could never know which actually happens. Perhaps, when we know that each resulting person would have one half of my brain, and would be psychologically continuous with me, we know everything. What are we supposing when we suggest, for instance, that one of the resulting people might be me? What would make this the true answer?

I believe that there cannot be different possibilities, each of which might be the truth, unless we are separately existing entities, such as Cartesian Egos. If what I really am is one particular Ego, this explains how it could be true that one of the resulting people would be me. It could be true that it is in this person's brain and body that this particular Ego regained consciousness....

The difficult question, for believers in Cartesian Egos, is whether I would survive at all. Since each of the resulting people would be psychologically continuous with me, there would be no evidence supporting either answer to this question. This ar-gument retains its force, even if I am a Cartesian Ego.

As before, a Cartesian might object that I have misdescribed what would happen. He might claim that, if we carried out this operation, it would not in fact be true that *both* of the resulting people would be psychologically continuous with me. It might be true that one or the other of these people was psychologically continuous with me. In either of these cases, this person would be me. It might instead be true that neither person was psychologically continuous with me. In this case, I would not survive. In each of these three cases, we would learn the truth.

Whether this is a good objection depends on what the relation is between our psychological features and the states of our brains. As I have said, we have conclusive evidence that the carrier of psychological continuity is *not* indivisible. In the actual cases in which hemispheres have been disconnected, this produced two series of thoughts and sensations. These two streams of consciousness were both psychologically continuous with the original stream. Psychological continuity has thus, in several actual cases, taken a dividing form. This fact refutes the objection just give. It justifies my claim that, in the imagined case of My Division, both of the resulting people would be psychologically continuous with me. Since this is so, the Cartesian View can be advanced here only in the more dubious version that does not connect the Ego with any observable or introspectable facts. Even if I am such an Ego, I could never know whether or not I had survived. For Cartesians, this case is a problem with no possible solution.

Suppose that, for the reasons given earlier, we reject the claim that each of us is really a Cartesian Ego. And we reject the claim that a person is any other kind of separately existing entity, apart from his brain and body, and various mental and physical events. How then should we answer the question about what happens when I divide?...

On the Reductionist View, the problem disappears....We know what this outcome is. There will be two future people, each of whom will have the body of one of my brothers, and will be fully psychologically continuous with me, because he has half of my brain. Knowing this, we know everything. I may ask, "But shall I be one of these two people, or the other, or neither?" But I should regard this as an empty question. Here is a similar question. In 1881 the French Socialist Party split. What happened? Did the French Socialist Party cease to exist, or did it continue to exist as one or other of the two new Parties? Given certain further details, this would be an empty question. Even if we have no answer to this question, we could know just what happened....

WHAT MATTERS WHEN I DIVIDE?

Some people would regard division as being as bad, or nearly as bad, as ordinary death. This reaction is irrational. We ought to regard division as being about as good as ordinary survival. As I have argued, the two "products" of this operation would be two different people. Consider my relation to each of these people. Does this relation fail to contain some vital element that is contained in ordinary survival? It seems clear that it does not. I would survive if I stood in this very same relation to only one of the resulting people. It is a fact that someone can survive even if half his brain is destroyed. And on reflection it was clear that I would survive if my whole brain was successfully transplanted into my brother's body. It was therefore clear that I would survive if half my brain was destroyed, and the other half was successfully transplanted into my brother's body. In the case that we are now considering, my relation to each of the resulting people thus contains everything that would be needed for me to survive as that person. It cannot be the *nature* of my relation to each of the resulting people that, in this case, causes it to fail to be survival. Nothing is *missing*. What is wrong can only be the duplication.

Suppose that I accept this, but still regard division as being nearly as bad as death. My reaction is now indefensible. I would be like someone who, when told of a drug that could double his years of life, regarded the taking of this drug as death. The only difference in the case of division is that the extra years are to run concurrently. This is an interesting difference. But it cannot mean that there are *no* years to run. We might say: "You will lose your identity. But there are at least two ways of doing this. Dying is one, dividing is another. To regard these as the same is to confuse two with zero. Double survival is not the same as ordinary survival. But this does not make it death. It is further away from death than ordinary survival."...

If it was put forward on its own, it would be difficult to accept the view that personal identity is not what matters. But I believe that, when we consider the case of division, this difficulty disappears. When we see *why* neither resulting person will be me, I believe that, on reflection, we can also see that this does not matter, or matters only a little.

The case of division supports part of the Reductionist View: the claim that our identity is not what matters. But this case does not support another Reductionist claim: that our identity can be indeterminate. If we abandon the view that identity is what matters, we can claim that there *is* an answer here to my question. Neither of the resulting people will be me. I am about to die. While we believed that identity is what matters, this claim implied, implausibly, that I ought to regard My Division as being nearly as bad as ordinary death. But the implausibility disappears if we claim instead that this way of dying is about as good as ordinary survival....

...On the Non-Reductionist View, a person is a separately existing entity, distinct from his brain and body, and his experiences. On the best-known version of this view, a person is a Cartesian Ego. On the Reductionist View that I defend, persons exist. And a person is distinct from his brain and body, and his experiences. But persons are not separately existing entities. The existence of a person, during any period, just consists in the existence of his brain and body, and the thinking of his thoughts, and the doing of his deeds, and the occurrence of many other physical and mental events.

Since these views disagree about the nature of persons, they also disagree about the nature of personal identity over time. On the Reductionist View, personal identity just involves physical and psychological continuity. As I argued, both of these can be described in an impersonal way. These two kinds of continuity can be described without claiming that experiences are had by a person. A Reductionist also claims that personal identity is not what matters. Personal identity just involves certain kinds of connectedness and continuity, when these hold in a one-one form. These relations are what matter.

On the Non-Reductionist View, personal identity is what matters. And it does not just involve physical and psychological continuity. It is a separate further fact, which must, in every case, either hold completely, or not at all. Psychological unity is explained by ownership. The unity of consciousness at any time is explained by the fact that several experiences are being had by a person. And the unity

of a person's life is explained in the same way. These several claims must, I have argued, stand or fall together.

Some of the evidence [against the Non-Reductionist View] is provided by the actual cases of divided minds. Because their hemispheres have been disconnected, several people have two streams of consciousness, in each of which they are unaware of the other. We might claim that, in such a case, there are two different people in the same body. This treats such cases as being like the imagined case where I divide, which I review below. Our alternative is to claim, about these actual cases, that there is a single person with two streams of consciousness.

If we make this claim, how can we explain the unity of consciousness in each stream? We cannot explain this unity by claiming that the various different experiences in each stream are being had by the same person, or subject of experiences. This describes the two streams as if they were one. If we believe that the unity of consciousness must be explained by ascribing different experiences to a particular subject, we must claim that in these cases, though there is only a single person, there are two subjects of experiences. We must therefore claim that there are, in a person's life, subjects of experiences that are *not* persons. It is hard to believe that there really are such things. These cases are better explained by the Reductionist Psychological Criterion. This claims that, at any time, there is one state of awareness of the experiences in one stream of consciousness, and another state of awareness of the experiences in the other stream.

Though they raise this problem for the Non-Reductionist View, these cases of divided minds are only a small part of the evidence against this view. There is no evidence that the carrier of psychological continuity is something whose existence, like that of a Cartesian Ego, must be all-or-nothing. And there is much evidence that the carrier of this continuity is the brain. There is much evidence that our psychological features depend upon states and events in our brains. A brain's continued existence need not be all-or-nothing. Physical connectedness can be a matter of degree. And there are countless actual cases in which psychological connectedness holds only in certain ways, or to some reduced degree.

We have sufficient evidence to reject the Non-Reductionist View. The Reductionist View is, I claim, the only alternative. I considered possible third views, and found none that was both non-Reductionist and a view that we had sufficient reasons to accept. More exactly, though these other views differ in other ways, the plausible views do not deny a Reductionist's central claim. They agree that we are *not* separately existing entities, distinct from our brains and bodies, whose existence must be all-or-nothing.…

WHAT DOES MATTER— LIBERATION FROM THE SELF

The truth is very different from what we are inclined to believe. Even if we are not aware of this, most of us are Non-Reductionists. If we considered my imagined cases, we would be strongly inclined to believe that our continued existence is a deep further fact, distinct from physical and psychological continuity, and a fact that must be all-or-nothing. This belief is not true.

Is the truth depressing? Some may find it so. But I find it liberating, and consoling. When I believed that my existence was such a further fact, I seemed imprisoned in myself. My life seemed like a glass tunnel, through which I was moving faster every year, and at the end of which there was darkness. When I changed my view, the walls of my glass tunnel disappeared. I now live in the open air. There is still a difference between my life and the lives of other people. But the difference is less. Other people are closer. I am less concerned about the rest of my own life, and more concerned about the lives of others.

When I believed the Non-Reductionist View, I also cared more about my inevitable death. After my death, there will be no one living who will be me. I can now redescribe this fact. Though there will later be many experiences, none of these experiences will be connected to my present experiences by chains of such direct connections as those involved in experience-memory, or in the carrying out of an earlier intention. Some of these future experiences may be related to my present experiences in less direct ways. There will later be some memories about my life. And there may later be thoughts that are influenced by mine, or things done as the result of my advice. My death will break the more direct relations between my present experiences and future experiences, but it will not break various other relations. This is all there is to the fact that there will be no one living who will be me. Now that I have seen this, my death seems to me less bad.

[handwritten margin note: dis-agree]

Personal Identity Is Essential

Christine M. Korsgaard

THE UNITY OF AGENCY

Suppose Parfit has established that there is no deep sense in which I am identical to the subject of experiences who will occupy my body in the future....I will argue that I nevertheless have reasons for regarding myself as the same rational agent as the one who will occupy my body in the future. These reasons are not metaphysical, but practical.

To see this, first set aside the problem of identity over time, and think about the problem of identity at any given time. Why do you think of yourself as one person now? This problem should seem especially pressing if Parfit has convinced you that you are not unified by a Cartesian Ego which provides a common subject for all your experiences. Just now you are reading this article. You may also be sitting in a chair, tapping your foot, and feeling hot or tired or thirsty. But what makes it one person who is doing and experiencing all this? We can add to this a set of characteristics which you attribute to yourself, but which have only an indirect bearing on your conscious experiences at any given time. You have loves, interests, ambitions, virtues, vices, and plans. You are a conglomerate of parts, dispositions, activities, and experiences. As Hume says, you are a bundle. What makes you one person even at one time?

In *On the Soul*, Aristotle says that the practical faculty of the soul must be one thing. We think of it as having parts, of course, because we sometimes have appetites that are contrary to practical reason, or experience conflict among our various desires. Still, the faculty that originates motion must be regarded as a single thing, because we do act. Somehow, the conflicts are resolved, and no matter how many different things you want to do, you in fact do one rather than another.

Your conception of yourself as a unified agent is not based on a metaphysical theory, nor on a unity of which you are conscious. Its grounds are practical, and it has two elements. First, there is the raw necessity of eliminating conflict among your various motives. In making his argument for Reductionism, Parfit appeals to a real-life example which has fascinated contemporary philosophers: persons with split brains. When the corpus callosum, the network of nerves between the two hemispheres of the brain, is cut, the two hemispheres can function separately. In certain experimental situations, they do not work together and appear to be wholly unconscious of each other's activities. These cases suggest that the two hemispheres of the brain are not related in any metaphysically deeper way than, say, two people who are married. They share the same quarters and, with luck, they communicate. Even their characteristic division of labor turns out to be largely conventional, and both can perform most functions. So imagine that the right and left halves of your brain disagree about what to do. Suppose that they do not try to resolve their differences, but each merely sends motor orders, by way of the nervous system, to your limbs. Since the orders are contradictory, the two halves of your body try to do different things. Unless they can come to an agreement, both hemispheres of your brain are ineffectual....You are a unified person at any given time because you must act, and you have only one body with which to act.

The second element of this pragmatic unity is the unity implicit in the *standpoint* from which you deliberate and choose. It may be that what actually happens when you make a choice is that the strongest of your conflicting desires wins. But that is not the way you think of it when you deliberate. When you deliberate, it is as if there were something over and above all your desires, something that is *you,* and that *chooses* which one to act on. The idea that you choose among your conflicting desires, rather than just waiting to see which one wins, suggests that you have reasons for or against acting on them. And it is these reasons, rather than the desires themselves, which are expressive of your will. The strength of a desire may be counted *by you* as a reason for acting on it; but this is different from *its* simply winning. This means that there is some principle or way of choosing that you regard as expressive of *yourself,* and that provides reasons that regulate your choices among your desires. To identify with such a principle or way of choosing is to be "a law to yourself," and to be unified as such. This does not require that your agency be located in a separately existing entity or involve a deep metaphysical fact. Instead, it is a practical necessity imposed upon you by the nature of the deliberative standpoint.

It is of course important to notice that the particular way you choose which desires to act on *may* be guided by your beliefs about certain metaphysical facts. Parfit evidently thinks that it should. When he argues about the rationality of concern about the future, Parfit assumes that my attitude about the desires of the

future inhabitant of my body should be based on the metaphysics of personal identity. That is, I should treat a future person's desires as *mine* and so as normative for me if I have some metaphysical reason for supposing that she is *me.* But this argument from the metaphysical facts to normative reasons involves a move from "is" to "ought" which requires justification. I will argue shortly that there may be other, more distinctively normative grounds for determining which of my motives are "my own"; metaphysical facts are not the only possible ground for this decision. For now, the important points are these: First, the *need* for identification with some unifying principle or way of choosing is imposed on us by the necessity of making deliberative choices, not by the metaphysical facts. Second, the metaphysical facts do not obviously settle the question: I must still decide whether the consideration that some future person is "me" has some special normative force for me. It is practical reason that requires me to construct an identity for myself; whether metaphysics is to guide me in this or not is an open question.

The considerations I have adduced so far apply to unification at any given moment, or in the context of any given decision. Now let us see whether we can extend them to unity over time. We might start by pointing out that the body which makes you one agent now persists over time, but that is insufficient by itself. The body could still be a series of agents, each unified pragmatically at any given moment. More telling considerations come from the character of the things that human agents actually choose. First of all, as Parfit's critics often point out, most of the things we do that matter to us take up time. Some of the things we do are intelligible only in the context of projects that extend over long periods. This is especially true of the pursuit of our ultimate ends. In choosing our careers, and pursuing our friendships and family lives, we both presuppose and construct a continuity of identity and of agency. On a more mundane level, the habitual actions we perform for the sake of our health presuppose ongoing identity. It is also true that we think of our activities and pursuits as interconnected in various ways; we think that we are carrying out plans of life. In order to carry out a rational plan of life, you need to be one continuing person. You normally think you lead one continuing life because you are one person, but according to this argument the truth is the reverse. You are one continuing person because you have one life to lead.

You may think of it this way: suppose that a succession of rational agents *do* occupy my body. I, the one who exists now, need the cooperation of the others, and they need mine, if together we are going to have any kind of a *life*. The unity of our life is forced upon us, although not deeply, by our shared embodiment, together with our desire to carry on long-term plans and relationships. But actually this is somewhat misleading. To ask why the present self should cooperate with the future ones is to assume that the present self has reasons with which it already identifies, and which are independent of those of later selves. Perhaps it is natural to think of the present self as necessarily concerned with present satisfaction. But it is mistaken. In order to make deliberative choices, your present self must identify with something from which you will derive your reasons, but not necessarily with something present. The sort of thing you identify yourself with may carry you automatically into the future; and I have been suggesting that this will very likely be the case. Indeed, the choice of any action, no matter how trivial, takes you some way into the future.

And to the extent that you regulate your choices by identifying yourself as the one who is implementing something like a particular plan of life, you need to identify with your future in order to be *what you are even now*. When the person is viewed as an agent, no clear content can be given to the idea of a merely present self.

Still, Parfit might reply that all this concedes his point about the insignificance of personal identity. The idea that persons are unified as agents shares with Reductionism the implication that personal identity is not very deep. If personal identity is just a prerequisite for coordinating action and carrying out plans, individual human beings do not have to be its possessors. We could, for instance, always act in groups. The answer to this is surely that for many purposes we do; there *are* agents of different sizes in the world. Whenever some group wants or needs to act as a unit, it must form itself into a sort of person—a legal person, say, or a corporation. Parfit himself likes to compare the unity of persons to the unity of nations. A nation, like a person, exists, but it does not amount to anything more than "the existence of its citizens, living together in certain ways, on its territory." In a similar way, he suggests, a person just amounts to "the existence of a brain and body, and the occurrence of a series of interrelated physical and mental events." On the view I am advancing, a better comparison would be the state. I am using "nation" here, as Parfit does, for a historical or ethnic entity, naturalistically defined by shared history and traditions; a state, by contrast, is a moral or formal entity, defined by its constitution and deliberative procedures. A state is not merely a group of citizens living on a shared territory. We have a state only where these citizens have constituted themselves in to a single agent. They have, that is, adopted a way of resolving conflicts, making decisions, interacting with other states, and planning together for an ongoing future. For a group of citizens to view themselves as a state, or for us to view them as one, we do not need to posit the state as a separately existing entity. All we need is to grant an authoritative status to certain choices and decisions made by certain citizens or bodies, as its legislative voice. Obviously, a state is not a deep metaphysical entity underlying a nation, but rather something a nation can make of itself. Yet the identity of states, for practical reasons, must be regarded and treated as more determinate than the identity of nations.

But the pragmatic character of the reasons for agent unification does not show that the resulting agencies are not *really* necessary. Pragmatic necessity can be overwhelming. When a group of human beings occupy the same territory, for instance, they have an imperative need to form a unified state. And when a group of psychological functions occupy the same human body, they have an even more imperative need to become a unified person. This is why the human body must be conceived as a unified agent. As things stand, it is the basic kind of agent.

Of course if our technology were different, individual human bodies might not be the basic kind of agent. My argument supports a physical criterion of identity, but only a conditional one. *Given the technology we have now*, the unit of action is a human body. But consider Thomas Nagel's concept of a "series-person." Nagel imagines a society in which persons are replicated in new matter once every year after they reach the age of thirty. This prevents them from aging, and barring accidents and incurable diseases, may even make them immortal. On my concept, a series-person, who would be able to carry out unified plans and projects, and have

ongoing relations with other persons, would be a person. But the fact that the basic unit of action might be different if technology were different is neither here nor there. The relevant necessity is the necessity of acting and living, and it is untouched by mere technological possibilities. The main point of the argument is this: a focus on agency makes more sense of the notion of personal identity than a focus on experience. There is a necessary connection between agency and unity which requires no metaphysical support.

THE UNITY OF CONSCIOUSNESS

Many will feel that my defense of personal unity simply bypasses what is most unsettling in Parfit's arguments. Parfit's arguments depend on what we may broadly call an "Aristotelian" rather than a "Cartesian" metaphysics of the person. That is, matter is essentially particular; form is essentially copiable; and form is what makes the person what she is, and so is what is important about her. The "Cartesian" metaphysics, by contrast, holds that the important element of a person is something essentially particular and uncopiable, like a Cartesian Ego. What tempts people to believe this is an entrenched intuition that something like a Cartesian Ego serves as the locus of the particular consciousness that is mine and no one else's. And my argument about the unity of agency in no way responds to this intuition.

Parfit writes: "When I believed that my existence was a further fact, I seemed imprisoned in myself. My life seemed like a glass tunnel, through which I was moving faster every year, and at the end of which there was darkness. When I changed my view, the walls of my glass tunnel disappeared. I now live in the open air." Parfit's glass tunnel is a good image of the way people think of the unity of consciousness. The sphere of consciousness presents itself as something like a room, a place, a lit-up area, within which we do our thinking, imagining, remembering, and planning, and from out of which we observe the world, the passing scene. It is envisioned as a tunnel or a stream, because we think that one moment of consciousness is somehow directly continuous with others, even when interrupted by deep sleep or anesthesia. We are inclined to think that memory is a deeper thing than it is, that it is *direct* access to an earlier stage of a continuing self, and not merely one way of knowing what happened. And so we may think of amnesia, not merely as the loss of knowledge, but as a door that blocks an existing place.

The sense that consciousness is in these ways unified supports the idea that consciousness requires a persisting psychological subject. The unity of consciousness is supposed to be explained by attributing all one's experiences to a single psychological entity. Of course, we may argue that the hypothesis of a unified psychological subject does nothing to *explain* the unity of consciousness. It is simply a figure for or restatement of that unity. Yet the idea of such a subject seems to have explanatory force. It is to challenge this intuition that Parfit brings up the facts about persons with divided brains. People are often upset by these facts because they think that they cannot imagine what it is like to be such a person. When the hemispheres function separately, the person seems to have two streams of consciousness. If consciousness is envisioned as a sort of place, then this is a person who seems to be in two places at the same time. If consciousness requires a subject, then this person's body seems, mysteriously, to have become occupied by two subjects. Here, the hypothesis of a psychological subject brings confusion rather than clarity.

Parfit's own suggestion is that the unity of consciousness "does not need a deep explanation. It is simply a fact that several experiences can be co-conscious, or be the objects of a single state of awareness." Split-brain people simply have experiences which are not co-conscious, and nothing more needs to be said. This seems to me close to the truth but not quite right. Privileging the language of "having experiences" and "states of awareness" gives the misleading impression that we can count the experiences we are now having, or the number of objects of which we are aware, and then ask what unifies them. The language of activities and dispositions enables us to characterize both consciousness and its unity more accurately.

Consciousness, then, is a feature of certain activities which percipient animals can perform. These activities include perceiving; various forms of attending such as looking, listening, and noticing; more intellectual activities like thinking, reflecting, recalling, remembering, and reading; and moving voluntarily. Consciousness is not a state that makes these activities possible, or a qualification of the subject who can perform them. It is a feature of *the activities themselves.* It is misleading to say that you must be conscious in order to perform them, because your being able to perform them is all that your being conscious amounts to.

Voluntary motion is an important example because of a distinction that is especially clear in its case. When we move voluntarily, we move consciously. But this is not to say we are conscious that we are moving. Much of the time when we move nothing is further from our minds than *the fact* that we are moving. But of course this does not mean that we move unconsciously, like sleepwalkers. It is crucial, in thinking about these matters, not to confuse *being engaged in a conscious activity* with *being conscious of an activity.* Perhaps such a confusion lies behind Descartes' bizarre idea that nonhuman animals are unconscious. In the direct, practical sense, an adult hunting animal which is, say, stalking her prey, knows exactly what she is doing. But it would be odd to say that she is aware *of* what she is doing or that she knows anything *about* it. What she is aware of is her environment, the smell of her prey, the grass bending quietly under her feet. The consciousness that is inherent in psychic activities should not be understood as an inner *observing* of those activities, a theoretic state. An animal's consciousness can be entirely practical.

The unity of consciousness consists in one's ability to coordinate and integrate conscious activities. People with split brains cannot integrate these activities in the same way they could before. This would be disconcerting, because the integration itself is not something we are ordinarily aware of. But it would not make you feel like two people. In fact, such persons learn new ways to integrate their psychic functions, and appear normal and normally unified in everyday life. It is only in experimental situations that the possibility of unintegrated functioning is even brought to light.

What makes it possible to integrate psychic functions? If this is a causal question, it is a question for neurologists rather than philosophers. But perhaps some will still think there is a conceptual necessity here—that such integration requires a common psychological subject. But think again of persons with split brains. Presumably, in ordinary persons the corpus callosum provides means of communication between the two hemispheres; it transmits signals. When split-brain persons are not in experimental situations, and they function normally, the reason appears to be simply that the two hemispheres are able

to communicate by other means than the corpus callosum. For example, if the left hemisphere turns the neck to look at something, the right hemisphere necessarily feels the tug and looks too. Activities, then, may be coordinated when some form of communication takes place between the performers of those activities. But communication certainly does not require a common psychological subject. After all, when they can communicate, two different people can integrate their functions, and, for purposes of a given activity, become a single agent.

Communication and functional integration do not require a common subject of conscious experiences. What they do require, however, is the unity of agency. Again, there are two aspects of this unity. First, there is the raw practical necessity. Sharing a common body, the two hemispheres of my brain, or my various psychic functions, must work together. The "phenomenon" of the unity of consciousness is nothing more than the *lack* of any perceived difficulty in the coordination of psychic functions. To be sure, when I engage in psychic activities *deliberately*, I regard myself as the subject of these activities. *I* think, *I* look, *I* try to remember. But this is just the second element of the unity of agency, the unity inherent in the deliberative standpoint. I regard myself as the employer of my psychic capacities in much the same way that I regard myself as the arbiter among my conflicting desires.

If these reflections are correct, then the unity of consciousness is simply another instance of the unity of agency, which is forced upon us by our embodied nature.

AGENCY AND IDENTITY

At this point it will be useful to say something about why I take the view I am advancing to be a Kantian one. Kant believed that as rational beings we may view ourselves from two different standpoints. We may regard ourselves as objects of theoretical understanding, natural phenomena whose behavior may be causally explained and predicted like any other. Or we may regard ourselves as agents, as the thinkers of our thoughts and the originators of our actions. These two standpoints cannot be completely assimilated to each other, and the way we view ourselves when we occupy one can appear incongruous with the way we view ourselves when we occupy the other. As objects of theoretical study, we see ourselves as wholly determined by natural forces, the mere undergoers of our experiences. Yet as agents, we view ourselves as free and responsible, as the authors of our actions and the *leaders* of our lives. The incongruity need not become contradiction, so long as we keep in mind that the two views of ourselves spring from two different relations in which we stand to our actions. When we look at our actions from the theoretical standpoint our concern is with their explanation and prediction. When we view them from the practical standpoint our concern is with their justification and choice. These two relations to our actions are equally legitimate, inescapable, and governed by reason, but they are separate. Kant does not assert that it is a matter of theoretical fact that we are agents, that we are free, and that we are responsible. Rather, we must view ourselves in these ways when we occupy the standpoint of practical reason—that is, when

we are deciding what to do. This follows from the fact that we must regard ourselves as the causes—the first causes—of the things that we will. And this fundamental attitude is forced upon us by the necessity of making choices, regardless of the theoretical or metaphysical facts.

From the theoretical standpoint, an action may be viewed as just another experience, and the assertion that it has a subject may be, as Parfit says, "because of the way we talk." But from the practical point of view, actions and choices must be viewed as having agents and choosers. This is what *makes* them, in our eyes, our own actions and choices rather than events that befall us. In fact, it is only from the practical point of view that actions and choices can be distinguished from mere "behavior" determined by biological and psychological laws. This does not mean that our existence as agents is asserted as a further fact, or requires a separately existing entity that should be discernible from the theoretical point of view. It is rather that from the practical point of view our relationship to our actions and choices is essentially *authorial*: from it, we view them as *our own*. I believe that when we think about the way in which our own lives matter to us personally, we think of ourselves in this way. We think of living our lives, and even of having our experiences, as something that we *do*. And it is this important feature of our sense of our identity that Parfit's account leaves out....

THE CONTINUING DEBATE:
Who Am I?

What Is New

Narrative models have recently been proposed—both in psychology and philosophy—as a possible solution to the quandaries of personal identity. On the narrative view, we make our identity by the narratives we develop of our own lives. That doesn't mean, of course, that we can write any narrative we like: if I attempt to structure the narrative of my life around my fabulous success as an NFL quarterback or a concert violinist, then the narrative will soon degenerate into incoherence or fantasy. Nor does it mean that I must actually write a memoir. I can have a meaningful life narrative even if I am illiterate, and without formally constructing a life story. My life narrative is the way I give meaning and significance to the events of my life, weave the episodic elements into a cohesive whole, and give value and structure to my decisions and activities. On this narrative view, my personal identity is made, not found or presupposed.

Where to Find More

There are several excellent collections of papers on the question of personal identity: Owen Flanagan and Amélie Oksenberg Rorty, *Identity, Character, and Morality* (Cambridge, Mass.: MIT Press, 1990); H. Harris, editor, *Identity* (Oxford: Oxford University Press, 1995); Raymond Martin and John Barresi, editors, *Personal Identity* (Oxford: Blackwell Publishing, 2003)—the editors include a clear and extensive historical introductory survey; and earlier collections by Amélie Oksenberg Rorty, *The Identities of Persons* (Berkeley: University of California Press, 1976), and by John Perry, *Personal Identity* (Berkeley: University of California Press, 1975). A very good and thought-provoking anthology of feminist perspectives on personal identity is edited by Diana Tietjens Meyer, Alison Jaggar, and Virginia Held, *Feminists Rethink the Self* (Boulder, Col.: Westview Press, 1997).

Personal Identity, by Sidney Shoemaker and Richard Swinburne (Oxford: Blackwell Publishing, 1984) offers sustained arguments and responses by Shoemaker (a materialist) and Swinburne (a dualist) on the questions surrounding personal identity.

A superb introduction to the issue of personal identity is Harold W. Noonan, *Personal Identity*, 2nd Edition (London: Routledge, 2003); an earlier very readable introduction is John R. Perry, *A Dialogue on Personal Identity and Immortality* (Indianapolis: Hackett, 1978).

Among the most influential contemporary philosophers on personal identity are Sydney Shoemaker, *Self-Knowledge and Self-Identity* (Ithaca, N.Y.: Cornell University Press, 1963) and *Identity, Cause, and Mind* (Cambridge: Cambridge University Press, 1984); and Peter Van Inwagen, whose writings on the subject include *Material Beings* (Ithaca: Cornell University Press, 1990), and "What Do I Refer to When I Say 'I'?" in R. Gale, editor, *The Blackwell Guide to Metaphysics* (Oxford: Blackwell Publishers, 2002).

Studies in psychopathology have stimulated difficult questions and interesting arguments concerning personal identity; see Mark T. Brown, "Multiple Personality and Personal Identity," *Philosophical Psychology*, volume 14 (2001): 435–448; Daniel Kolak, "Finding Our Selves: Identification, Identity and Multiple Personality," *Philo-*

sophical Psychology, volume 6 (2001): 363–386; R. W. Sperry, "Hemisphere Deconnection and Unity in Conscious Awareness," *American Psychologist*, volume 23, number 10 (1968); Roland Puccetti, "The Case for Mental Duality: Evidence from Split-Brain and Other Considerations," *Behavioral and Brain Sciences*, volume 4 (1981): 83–128, including commentaries; George Graham and G. Lynn Stephens, *When Self-Consciousness Breaks: Alien Voices and Inserted Thoughts* (Cambridge: MIT Press, 2000); and particularly George Graham and G. Lynn Stephens, editors, *Philosophical Psychopathology* (Cambridge, Mass.: MIT Press, 1994).

A leader in the development of narrative accounts of personal identity is Alasdair MacIntrye, in *After Virtue* (Notre Dame, Indiana: University of Notre Dame Press, 1981). Others employing this approach are Charles Taylor, *Sources of the Self: The Making of the Modern Identity* (Cambridge, Mass.: Harvard University Press, 1989); and Ronald Dworkin, *Life's Dominion* (New York: Knopf, 1993). The psychological research of D. P. McAdams has also been important to narrative accounts; see *The Stories We Live By: Personal Myths and the Making of the Self* (New York: William Morrow and Company, 1993). A good anthology on this approach is Gary D. Fireman, Ted E. McVay, and Owen J. Flanagan, editors, *Narrative and Consciousness: Literature, Psychology, and the Brain* (New York: Oxford University Press, 2003).

The Stanford Encyclopedia of Philosophy article on Personal Identity, by Eric T. Olson, is a good overview of the contemporary debate; it can be found at http://plato.stanford.edu/entries/identity-personal/.

For a very entertaining foray into personal identity issues, go to http://www.philosophersnet.com/games/identity.htm and play "Staying Alive: The Personal Identity Game."

7   DO WE HAVE FREE WILL?

Genuine Free Will Requires Nondeterminism

ADVOCATE: Robert Kane, University Distinguished Teaching Professor at the University of Texas at Austin; author of *Free Will and Values* (1985), *Through the Moral Maze* (1994), and *The Significance of Free Will* (1996), and editor of *The Oxford Handbook of Free Will* (2002).

SOURCE: "Free Will and Responsibility: Ancient Dispute, New Themes," *The Journal of Ethics*, volume 4 (2000): 315–322.

Free Will Is Compatible with Determinism

ADVOCATE: John Martin Fischer, Professor of Philosophy at the University of California, Riverside; author of *The Metaphysics of Free Will: An Essay on Control* (1994), and (with Mark Ravizza) *Responsibility and Control: A Theory of Moral Responsibility* (1998).

SOURCE: "Responsibility, History and Manipulation," *The Journal of Ethics*, volume 4 (2000): 385–391.

You freely chose which college you would attend, and what major you would pursue. You chose freely when you went to the beach last spring break, when you chose a salad for lunch, and when you went to the tavern last night instead of reading philosophy. Or at least, it *seemed* you were choosing freely at the time. But were you really acting from your own free will, or was your choice shaped and caused and *determined* by past events? You've studied biology, and you know that illnesses once attributed to chance or to a capricious God are actually caused by subtle factors we had not understood. You've studied astronomy and physics, and you know that the comet that appears to move in a totally unpredictable path is actually held in place by precise gravitational forces: Halley's Comet does not appear by chance, nor is it a miracle; rather, it is a predictable determined motion. And you have studied psychology, and you know that people's behavior is caused by subtle conditioning and situational factors that typically operate without our being aware of them. So maybe there are more causes operating on our behavior and our choices than we recognize. Maybe *everything* we do and choose is caused by past events and earlier conditioning. Maybe all our behavior—and everything that happens—is *determined*; and if so, maybe we don't have free will at all.

That is the conclusion drawn by the 19th Century German philosopher, Arthur Schopenhauer:

> Let us imagine a man who, while standing on the street, would say to himself: "It is six o'clock in the evening, the working day is over. Now I can go for a walk, or I can go to the club; I can also climb up the tower to see the sun set; I can go to the theater; I can visit this friend or that one; indeed, I also can run out of the gate, into the wide world, and never return. All of this is strictly up

to me, in this I have complete freedom. But still I shall do none of these things now, but with just as free a will I shall go home to my wife." This is exactly as if water spoke to itself: "I can make high waves (yes! in the sea during a storm), I can rush down hill (yes! in the river bed), I can plunge down foaming and gushing (yes! in the waterfall), I can rise freely as a stream of water in the air (yes! in the fountain), I can, finally, boil away and disappear (yes! at a certain temperature); but I am doing none of these things now, and am voluntarily remaining quiet and clear water in the reflecting pond."

As the water can do all those things only when the determining causes operate for the one or the other, so that man can do what he imagines himself able to do not otherwise than on the same condition. Until the causes begin to operate, this is impossible for him; but then, he *must*, as the water must, as soon as it is placed in the corresponding circumstances. "Essay on the Freedom of the Will," translated by Konstantine Kolenda.

The great Scottish philosopher, David Hume (1711–1776), was also a champion of determinism, but he believed that determinism posed no threat to free will: determinism (which Hume calls "necessity") and free will (Hume's "liberty") are compatible.

But to proceed in this reconciling project with regard to the question of liberty and necessity…it will not require many words to prove that all mankind have ever agreed in the doctrine of liberty as well as in that of necessity.…For what is meant by liberty when applied to voluntary actions? We cannot surely mean that actions have so little connection with motives, inclinations, and circumstances that one does not follow with a certain degree of uniformity from the other.…For these are plain and acknowledged matters of fact. By liberty, then, we can only mean *a power of acting or not acting according to the determinations of the will*; that is, if we choose to remain at rest, we may; if we choose to move, we also may. Now this hypothetical liberty is universally allowed to belong to everyone who is not a prisoner and in chains. Here then is no subject of dispute. *An Inquiry Concerning Human Understanding*, Section 8 (1748).

Determinism has long seemed a threat to free will. Determinism is the view that everything that happens, without exception, is the precise result of earlier states of affairs governed by causal laws: every movement, storm, thought, battle, wish, and breath is the product of prior events and causal laws. The major positions taken concerning free will and moral responsibility are shaped by reactions to determinism, and they fall into three major categories. First, there are *hard determinists*, who believe in determinism and reject free will. Second are the *libertarians*. Libertarians believe that *if* determinism were true, there could be no free will or moral responsibility; but fortunately determinism is *false*. Most libertarians maintain that we have a special creative power to be the *sole authors* of our choices, and such choices are the result of very special mysterious—even miraculous—powers of will. Robert Kane, however, is a naturalistic libertarian who rejects mysterious miraculous powers. While most libertarians insist that free will is a special creative power and reject the idea that our free choices involve chance, Kane embraces an essential element of chance. His libertarian rejection of determinism appeals to microlevel quantum indeterminacy, and uses that to build an account of choices which are neither determined nor mysterious, and for which the chooser has *ultimate* responsibility (because either way the open choice goes, it comes from the agent's own will). Without such an injection of indeterminacy—of chance, or randomness—Kane believes that we could not have genuine free will.

John Martin Fischer represents the third view, which he shares with Hume: *compatibilism*. Fischer maintains that determinism and free will are *compatible*, that once we understand the real nature of free will, we recognize that free will is not in conflict with determinism. When do you act freely? As you read this debate over free will, you are acting freely. No one is holding a gun to your head and forcing you to read, you are not in chains or behind bars, you can put the book down whenever you wish. If you *are* coerced you are not acting freely. But if you are reading because *you choose* to read, because you enjoy reading about philosophy, then you are acting *freely*. Don't worry about all the causal forces that shaped you to be who you are with the preferences and values you have. *Of course* (compatibilists would say) there are causes for why you enjoy reading, and why you chose to read this essay; but so long as you are acting from your *own* choices and values, then you are acting freely and with full moral responsibility for your acts.

Some causes do destroy your freedom: a gun to your head is an obvious example; causes that derive from psychological problems may be less obvious, but they can also destroy free will: my obsessive-compulsive desire to continually wash my hands is my own desire, but it hardly seems to result in free choices. I can be as much a prisoner of my psychological compulsion as I am of a prison cell. So compatibilists must explain why most determining causes are *not* like guns and chains and obsessions, but are instead compatible with free will. Frankfurt is a famous contemporary compatibilist who believes that we act freely when we not only act from our own desires, but we also deeply approve of those desires. Fischer rejects Frankfurt's version of compatibilisim; according to Fischer, when the determining causes are based on our own *reasons* then they do not undercut free will.

POINTS TO PONDER

➤ Robert Kane sets a very high standard for what counts as free will: free will requires that agents be "the ultimate creators (or originators) and sustainers of their own ends and purposes." Does this set the standard for free will too high?

➤ One key question in contemporary debates over free will has been the question of "alternative possibilities": in order to exercise free will, must it be possible for us to act differently, follow an alternative path? For example, suppose that you love Pat, and you deeply approve of your love for Pat (this is not some hopeless passion you would like to get over), and given your own nature and circumstances you *could not avoid* loving Pat. In that case, when you *cannot do otherwise*, but are still doing *as you wish*, do you have free will?

➤ John Martin Fischer claims that moral responsibility requires that we "take responsibility" for our actions; and by that he means we must regard ourselves as "a fair target in the social game of responsibility." Is that a sufficient condition for responsibility? Is it a necessary condition?

Genuine Free Will Requires Nondeterminism

ROBERT KANE

Free will, as I understand it, is "the power of agents to be the ultimate creators (or originators) and sustainers of their own ends and purposes." So understood, free will is to be distinguished from freedom of action. To act freely is to be unhindered in the pursuit of your own purposes; to will freely is to be the ultimate source or creator of your own purposes.

I think this is the traditional idea of free will that has been in dispute for centuries. Such an idea inevitably arises when humans reach an advanced state of self-consciousness about the ways in which the world may influence their behavior. Historical concerns about determinism in its various forms—physical or scientific, psychological, theological, logical and fatalistic—are indications that this advanced state of self-consciousness has been reached. It is therefore no accident that determinism in its varied historical manifestations has been thought to be a threat to free will. This same traditional conception of free will (which I believe is incompatible with determinism) has been under withering attack in the modern era of Western philosophy from the seventeenth century to the twentieth, where it has been dismissed by many philosophers and scientists as an obscure and outdated notion that no longer fits with modern images of human beings in the natural and human sciences.

These modern attacks on free will have brought to the forefront four basic questions about it: (1) The Compatibility Question ("Is free will compatible or incompatible with determinism?"), (2) the Significance Question ("What kind of free will is worth wanting?"), (3) the Intelligibility Question ("Can we make sense of a free will that is incompatible with determinism or is it, as many claim, essentially mysterious or obscure?") and (4) the Existence Question ("Can such a free will exist in the natural order and, if so, where?")....

First, on the Compatibility Question, most recent and past philosophical debate has focused on the question of whether determinism is compatible with "the condition of alternative possibilities" (AP)—the requirement that the free agent "could have done otherwise." Arguments about AP have reached new levels of sophistication in the past thirty years, with new incompatibilist arguments attempting to show that determinism is not compatible with the power to do otherwise....At the same time, new compatibilist and semi-compatibilist arguments have surfaced attempting to show either that determinism is compatible with alternative possibilities or AP, or that AP is not in fact required for free will or moral responsibility....

All in all, these recent debates, both for and against the incompatibility of freedom and responsibility with determinism have spawned an enormous recent literature and advanced our understanding of free will issues immensely. But they have tended to stalemate over differing interpretations of "can," "power," "ability" and "could have done otherwise."...there is a good reason for these stalemates. For I think that AP alone provides too thin a basis on which to rest the case for incompatibilism: the Compatibility Question cannot be resolved by focusing on alternative possibilities alone.

Fortunately, there is another place to look. I argue that in the long history of free will debate one can find another criterion fueling incompatibilist intuitions that is even more important than AP, though comparatively neglected. I call it the condition of ultimate responsibility or UR. The idea is this: to be ultimately responsible for an action, the agent must be responsible for anything that is a sufficient reason (condition, cause or motive) for the action's occurring. If, for example, a choice issues from, and can be sufficiently explained by, an agent's character and motives (together with background conditions), then to be ultimately responsible for the choice, the agent must be at least in part responsible by virtue of choices or actions voluntarily performed in the past for having the character and motives he or she now has. Compare Aristotle's claim that if a man is responsible for wicked acts that flow from his character, he must at some time in the past have been responsible for forming the wicked character from which these acts flow.

This UR condition accounts for the "ultimate" in the original definition of free will: "the power of agents to be the *ultimate* creators and sustainers of their own ends or purposes." UR does not require that we could have done otherwise (AP) for every act done of our own free wills. But it does require that we could have done otherwise with respect to some acts in our past life histories by which we formed our present characters (in my book, I call these "self-forming actions," or SFAs, or sometimes "self-forming willings," SFWs). Thus, we may admit that Martin Luther…was literally right when he said "Here I stand, I can do no other" upon breaking with Rome, without denying that Luther was responsible (even *ulti-*

mately responsible) for his act by virtue of many earlier struggles and self-forming choices that brought him to this point where he could do no other. Often we act from a will already formed, but it is "our own free will," by virtue of the fact that we formed it by other choices or actions in the past (SFAs) for which we could have done otherwise. If that were not so, there is nothing we could have ever done to make ourselves different than we are—a consequence, I believe, that is incompatible with our being (at least to some degree) ultimately responsible for what we are.

If the case for incompatibility of free will and determinism cannot be made on AP alone, it can be made if UR is added; and thus, I suggest, the too-often neglected UR should be moved to center stage in free will debates. If agents must be responsible to some degree for anything that is a sufficient cause or motive for their actions, an impossible infinite regress of past actions would be required unless some actions in the agent's life history did not have either sufficient causes or motives (and hence were undetermined). But this new route to incompatibility raises a host of further questions, including how actions lacking both sufficient causes and motives could themselves be free and responsible actions, and how, if at all, such actions could exist in the natural order where we humans live and have our being. These are versions of the Intelligibility and Existence questions respectively, to which I now turn.

The problem of intelligibility is an ancient one: if free will is not compatible with determinism, it does not seem to be compatible with indeterminism either. An undetermined or chance event occurs spontaneously and is not controlled by anything, hence not controlled by the agent. Here we encounter the oft-repeated charges that if free choices or actions were the result of indeterminism or chance, they would be "arbitrary," "capricious," "random," "irrational," "uncontrolled" and "inexplicable," hence not free and responsible actions at all. If, for example, a choice occurred by virtue of a quantum jump or other undetermined event in the brain it would seem a fluke or accident rather than a responsible choice. Undetermined events in the brain or body, say critics of indeterminist freedom, would turn out to be a nuisance—or perhaps a curse, like epilepsy—rather than an enhancement of our freedom.

Defenders of an incompatibilist or libertarian free will have a dismal record of answering these familiar charges. Realizing that free will cannot merely be indeterminism or chance, they have appealed to various obscure or mysterious forms of agency or causation to make up the difference— noumenal selves, non-material egos, immanent or non-event causation, *sui generis* acts of will, and the like. These stratagems have reinforced the view, now widespread among philosophers and scientists, that a traditional incompatibilist or libertarian free will is essentially mysterious and unintelligible, and has no place in the modern scientific picture of the world.

…I disavow all such traditional appeals to special forms of agency or causation and ask whether incompatibilist free will can be made intelligible without mystery, and in such a way that we can say how it might exist in the natural order.…

As indicated, not all acts done "of our own free wills" and for which we are "ultimately responsible" have to be undetermined and such that we could have done otherwise. Often we act responsibly from a will already formed, but it is "our own" free will by virtue of other past "self-forming" choices or other actions that were undetermined and by which we made ourselves into the kinds of persons we are. I believe

that these undetermined self-forming actions (SFAs) occur at those difficult times of life when we are torn between competing visions of what we should do or become. Perhaps we are torn between doing the moral thing or acting from ambition, or between powerful present desires and long-term goals, or we are faced with a difficult task for which we have an aversion. In all such cases, we are faced with competing motivations and have to make an effort to overcome temptation to do something else we also strongly want. There is tension and uncertainty in our minds about what to do at such times that, I suggest, is reflected in appropriate regions of our brains by movement away from thermodynamic equilibrium—in short, a kind of stirring up of chaos in the brain that makes it sensitive to micro-indeterminacies at the neuronal level. Thus, the uncertainty and inner tension we feel at such soul-searching moments of self-formation is reflected in the indeterminacy of our neural processes. What is experienced phenomenologically as uncertainty corresponds physically to the opening of a window of opportunity that temporarily screens off complete determination by influences of the past. (By contrast, when we act from predominant motives or settled dispositions, the uncertainty or indeterminacy is muted. If it did play a role in such cases, it *would* be a mere nuisance or fluke.)

When we do decide under such conditions of uncertainty, the outcome is not determined because of the preceding indeterminacy—and yet it can be willed (and hence rational and voluntary) either way owing to the fact that in such self-formation, the agents' prior wills are divided by conflicting motives. If we overcome temptation, it will be the result of our effort, and if we fail, it will be because we did not *allow* our effort to succeed. And this is due to the fact that, while we willed to overcome temptation, we also willed to fail, for quite different and incommensurable reasons. When we decide in such circumstances, and the indeterminate efforts we are making become determinate choices, we make one set of competing reasons or motives prevail over the others then and there by *deciding*.

Now let us add a further piece to the puzzle. Indeterminism in and of itself does not necessarily undermine control and responsibility. Suppose you are trying to think through a difficult problem, say a mathematical problem, and there is some indeterminacy in your neural processes complicating the task—a kind of chaotic background. It would be like trying to concentrate and solve a problem with background noise or distraction. Whether you are going to succeed in solving the problem is uncertain and undetermined because of the distracting noise. Yet, if you concentrate and solve the problem nonetheless, we have reason to say you did it and are responsible for it even though it was undetermined whether you would succeed. The indeterministic noise would have been an obstacle which you nevertheless overcame by your effort. Returning now to the mind divided between tempting alternatives, imagine in this case that the indeterministic noise which is providing an obstacle to your overcoming temptation is not coming from an external source but is coming from your own will, since you also deeply desire to do the opposite. Imagine that two crossing (recurrent) neural networks are involved, each influencing the other. The input of one of them consists in your reasons for, say, acting morally and its output a moral choice, the input of the other, your self-interested reasons and its output, a self-interested choice. The two networks are connected so that the indeterministic noise which is

an obstacle to your making one of the choices is coming from your desire to make the other, and *vice versa*—the indeterminism thus arising from a conflict in the will, as we said (that the networks are recurrent, and hence non-linear, is an important factor as well). Now, in these circumstances, when either of the pathways "wins" (i.e., reaches an activation threshold, which amounts to choice), it will be like your solving the mathematical problem by overcoming the background noise produced by the other. And just as when you solved the mathematical problem by overcoming the distracting noise, one can say you did it and are responsible for the outcome, so one can say this as well, I argue, in the present case, *whichever one is chosen*. The network that succeeds (i.e., reaches a choice threshold) will have overcome the obstacle in the form of indeterministic noise generated by the other.

Note that, under such conditions, the choices either way will not be inadvertent, accidental, capricious, or merely random because they will be *willed* by the agents either way when they are made, and done for *reasons* either way—reasons that the agents then and there endorse. These are the conditions usually required to say something is done "on purpose," rather than accidentally, capriciously or merely by chance. Moreover, these conditions taken together, I argue, rule out each of the reasons we have for saying that agents act, but do not have *control* over their actions (compulsion, coercion, constraint, inadvertence, accident, control by others, etc.). Of course, for undetermined SFAs, agents cannot control or determine which choice outcome will occur *before* it occurs; but it does not follow that, because one cannot control or determine which of a set of outcomes is going to occur before it occurs, one does not control which of them occurs, *when* it occurs.

When the above conditions for SFAs are satisfied, agents exercise control over their future lives *then and there* by deciding. They have what I call "plural voluntary control" over the options. They can choose either way, as we say, "at will."

Note also that this account of SFAs amounts to a kind of "doubling" of the mathematical problem. It is as if an agent faced with an SFA is *trying* or making an effort to solve *two* cognitive problems at once, or to complete two competing (deliberative) tasks at once—e.g., to make a moral choice and to make a conflicting self-interested choice (corresponding to the two competing neural networks mentioned). Each task is being thwarted by the indeterminism coming from the other, so it might fail. But if it succeeds, then the agents can be held responsible because, as in the case of solving the mathematical problem, they will have succeeded in doing what they were *knowingly and voluntarily trying to do*. There are many examples in which we can be held responsible for succeeding in doing what we were voluntarily trying to do, even if by *chance* or *indeterminism*, we might have failed. The example of solving the mathematical problem is one. Another is the case of an assassin who is trying to shoot the prime minister, but, owing to an undetermined jerk of his arm, might miss. If he succeeds, despite the probability of failure, he is responsible for killing the prime minister, because he will have succeeded in doing what he was trying to do. And so it is, I suggest, with SFAs, except that in the case of SFAs, *whichever way the agents choose*, they will have succeeded in doing what they were voluntarily trying to do because they were simultaneously trying to make both choices, and one is going to succeed. (Does it make sense to talk about the agent's trying to do two competing things at once

this way? Well, we know that the brain is a parallel processor and such a capacity is I think essential to the exercise of free will.)

Consider…a businesswoman who faces a conflict of will of the kind typically involved in the self-forming actions just described. She is on the way to a business meeting important to her career when she observes an assault taking place in an alley. An inner struggle ensues between her moral conscience, to stop and call for help, and her career ambitions which tell her she cannot miss this meeting. She has to make an effort of will to overcome the temptation to go on to the meeting, but she does so and eventually turns back to help. Now another way that our intuitions can go astray in considering these matters is the following. Since the outcome of the woman's effort (the choice) is undetermined up to the last minute, we may have the image of her first making an effort to overcome temptation and then at the last instant "chance takes over" and decides the issue for her. But this is a misleading image that fuels the wrong intuitions. On my view, one cannot separate the indeterminism and the effort of will, so that first the effort occurs *followed* by chance or luck (or vice versa). One must think of the effort and the indeterminism as fused; the effort *is* indeterminate and the indeterminism is a *property* of the effort, not something separate that occurs after or before the effort. The fact that the effort has this property of being indeterminate does not make it any less the woman's *effort*. The complex recurrent neural network that realizes the effort of will in the brain is circulating impulses in feedback loops and there is some indeterminacy in these circulating impulses. But the whole process *is* her effort of will and it persists right up to the moment when the choice is made. There is no point at which the effort stops and chance "takes over." She chooses as a result of the effort, even though she might have failed.

One might argue also that a residual arbitrariness remains in such undetermined SFAs since there cannot in principle be sufficient or overriding prior reasons for making one choice and one set of reasons prevail over the other (this of course does not mean the agent lacks good prior reasons for choosing, but only that they are not overriding until made so by choosing). I grant this, but argue that such arbitrariness relative to prior reasons tells us something important about free will. It tells us that "every free choice (which is an SFA) is the initiation of a 'value experiment' whose justification lies in the future and is not fully explained by the past. Making such a choice we say, in effect, 'Let's try this. It is not required by my past, but is consistent with my past and is one branching pathway my life could now meaningfully take. I am willing to take responsibility for it one way or the other.'"

Free Will Is Compatible with Determinism

John Martin Fischer

Before I start my presentation, let me say a few things about what Professor Kane said in his session earlier....We were talking about the issue of whether causal determinism in the actual sequence rules out moral responsibility directly and not in virtue of alternative possibilities. One thing he said is that encoded in some of our common sense practices is the demand for the lack of determination.... Consider...a hypothetical case, though obviously it is very similar to actual cases. A young man brutally raped a young woman....People are very angry. But then they attend the trial and they find out that the man was abused as a young child, sexually and otherwise. It then becomes unclear what the appropriate response is. What Professor Kane concludes from such a situation is that feeling confident in holding this individual responsible requires that we find some sort of lack of determination, as he put it.

First of all it is interesting that Gary Watson writes about just such a case of Robert Alton Harris in California. Harris brutally murdered a couple of young boys. Later he laughed about it and ate their sandwiches after he murdered them. But then there were long articles in the *L.A. Times* talking about his horrible upbringing. Gary Watson in his interesting piece talks about what an appropriate reply would be. But for the purposes of our discussion today, what I would say is that the example does not show that encoded within our common practices is the demand for the lack of determination. It shows that we demand the lack of a *certain sort of determination*. What was problematic was certain kinds of determination, such as sexual abuse. But the example doesn't show that determination *per se* rules out responsibility according to common sense.

You can see that by contrasting that sort of case with the example of Leopold and Loeb. In this sort of case someone very affluent and wealthy goes to a judge and says "Well no, I was not sexually abused. I was not physically abused. I killed because I wanted to commit the perfect crime. But by the way, I am not morally responsible because causal determinism is true." He would be laughed out of court. No one would take that seriously....In summary, I think that we do demand that causation not be of certain sorts. But it is not clear that we demand the lack of causation.

What I want to talk about today is my claim that moral responsibility is essentially an historical notion. I want to say a little bit about that, and about my account of a specific way in which it is an historical notion and how that might be promising in dealing with certain cases involving direct manipulation.

Certain phenomena or notions are historical, and, in contrast, certain phenomena are current time-slice notions. A current time-slice notion is something that does not depend in any crucial way on its history being a certain way rather than another. A current time-slice notion supervenes on snapshot properties—properties that one could in principle take a snapshot of at a given time. Size, weight, height, something's being shiny or metallic, or smooth, round, bright, colorful, symmetric: these are all examples of current time-slice properties. For example, something's being symmetric is a matter of its snapshot properties. It does not depend on its past being a certain way. However, I think that there are other notions that are essentially historical. To begin, I am going to use two examples from Al Mele. Something's being a sunburn is an historical notion. You can look at someone's face and see that it is red and burned, etc. But it can only be a sunburn if it was caused by the sun. Something being genuine currency rather than counterfeit is an historical notion. It is not just a matter of how it looks at a certain point in time but rather how it came into being. Also, something's being a genuine Picasso rather than a fake is an historical notion. Something that is molecule for molecule isomorphic, type-identical to a genuine Picasso is not necessarily a genuine Picasso....

Robert Nozick indicated, actually, in his book *Anarchy, State*, and *Utopia* in a very suggestive passage, that love is also an historical notion. There has been an interesting discussion of that claim. You can distinguish a couple different elements of the claim that love is historical. One is the idea that love is non-fungible. What I mean by that is illustrated by the ghoulish scenarios in which you are asked to imagine that you are coming home and as you arrive your wife and your children are hit by lightning bolts—suddenly vaporized. Yet, just at that same moment, due to a cosmic accident, molecule for molecule duplicates of your wife and your children are created. They come into being quite independent of the event that destroyed your wife and children. Obviously a very wildly implausible scenario, but seemingly conceivable. Now we can ask ourselves, assuming that you do love your wife and

your children, would it be appropriate for you to continue to have these attitudes towards these new individuals? Some argue that, no, love is *historical* in the sense that it would be inappropriate for you to transfer that set of attitudes constitutive of love to these new individuals because they are different individuals and love relates to particular individuals with whom you have had interactions in the past.

There is a separate idea involved in the claim that love is historical. This is the claim that it is conceptually impossible, or necessarily false that one can have "love at first sight." Carl (Ginet) was telling us that when he first met his wife Sally, it was love at first sight. But according to this view, you can't have love at first sight. It is like the claim that you can't have virtue pills that induce virtue suddenly, that you need a certain process. Well, I don't know what I think exactly about these claims about love. But that gives you a kind of flavor of some of the notions that people have claimed are historical. You could ask the same kinds of questions about reference, the reference of terms, and claims of knowledge, and justification of beliefs. For instance, certain epistemologists argue that belief can be justified only if the belief in question was formed as the result of the right sort of process. It is not just a matter of looking at a time-slice and considering the relationship between the evidence and the belief, but it is a matter of how the belief came into being. That is of course controversial. Others ("internalists") would argue against these sorts of "externalist" views.

So there are current time-slice notions and historical notions. My claim is that moral responsibility is an historical notion. Harry Frankfurt has contended vigorously on a number of occasions (although I am not sure he has *argued*) that moral responsibility is a current time-slice notion—that it doesn't matter what the history is; rather it is just a matter of how the different elements of our psychic harmony are related. On his view there are first-order desires and second-order desires. The first-order desire on which we act is called the will. For Frankfurt this is a stipulative definition. Then the second-order desire about which first-order desire should be our will is called one's second-order volition. If there is a mesh between one's second-order volition and one's will, that is supposed to be sufficient (for Frankfurt) for moral responsibility. Or at least in some of his earlier writings it looked like that was what he was saying. So then it would just be a matter of looking at psychic elements and their arrangements and not caring how those elements and that arrangement came into being. Basically, that is Frankfurt's view: assessing moral responsibility is a matter of looking at the elements that exist at a certain time but not looking at the history behind them.

I actually believe that this view is false. I am not sure that I can argue for the falsity of it, but I have contended vigorously that it is false! I would try to motivate the historicity claim in two ways. One, it seems to me that there are cases in which one freely puts oneself in a position in which one is out of control and yet one is responsible for those later acts. The existence of those scenarios makes it possible to consider two kinds of cases. The one case would be like what happened to Cary Grant in *North by Northwest*, the Hitchcock film. Someone forces the agent to drink, pouring liquor down his throat. Later he is drunk and out of control. He gets in a car and runs over an innocent person because he is not in control. That is very different from a case in which someone who is not an alcoholic freely gets very drunk and gets in a car and does the same thing. My point is that if you

look at the drunk drivers in the two cases, there may be no differences between them in terms of their current time-slice characteristics (at the time of the drunk driving). Their central nervous systems could be molecule for molecule isomorphic resulting in the same level of drunkenness and consequent lack of responsiveness. But one is morally responsible for what he did and the other isn't. The difference is a matter of their histories, of how they got to be the way they were. So that is the first kind of motivation for the claim that responsibility is essentially historical.

One can also motivate the idea by thinking about cases of hypnosis, direct electronic stimulation of the brain, and brainwashing. Again, one could look at two individuals at a certain time. Assume again that the two people have the same arrangement at that time of psychic elements, the same first-order desires and second-order desires, or in a different terminology, the same preferences and values. Yet one has got those in the normal way of human moral development and the other has, unbeknownst to him, been directly stimulated, or he has had subliminal advertising applied to him and he has never consented, or hypnosis to which he did not consent. To me, the idea is that if you look at these two individuals at a certain time, there may be no difference, and yet the moral responsibility characteristics of the two individuals differ based on their histories. Another way of putting the point is that it is possible to have two individuals who, in terms of the current time-slice properties, are exactly the same, type identical, and yet one is responsible and the other isn't. So responsibility doesn't supervene on the current time-slice properties. It is a matter of history.

More specifically, what kind of history do we need? In my view, in order to be responsible we have to *take responsibility*. So it is a kind of subjective approach to moral responsibility. That is just one element. I think that one also has to act from appropriately reasons-responsive mechanisms. But those mechanisms have to be one's own in some sense. The way that you make those mechanisms your own is by taking responsibility for them. Let me just sketch in a rough way what I mean by "taking responsibility." I don't mean that you ever say, "I take responsibility for my actions" or even explicitly think about taking responsibility. It is a kind of stipulative notion of taking responsibility. What it means is coming to have a certain set of beliefs about oneself. First of all, one must believe that one's choices and bodily movements are actually efficacious, that certain upshots in the world in fact result from one's own deliberations, choices and bodily movements. One can think, of course, in terms of the ordinary course of human moral development. Consider first, how a child, fairly early on, realizes that when he chooses to punch his sister and he moves his arm in such a way that his sister is hit, she cries as a result of his choices and bodily movements. So that seems to be a minimal condition. Then what I want to say is that one has to see oneself as an apt or fair target of the reactive attitudes, at least in certain contexts, on the basis of one's bodily movements and choices. You have to see yourself as a fair target in the social game of responsibility, which involves certain attitudes such as indignation, resentment, and gratitude (among others). And, finally, these beliefs about yourself can't just appear out of nowhere or by accident, or on the basis of no evidence. They have to be based on one's evidence in the appropriate way.

In the typical instance, that third condition is supposed to capture what is plausible about normal human moral development. As we grow up we learn that when

we punch our sister, our parents have certain reactive attitudes on the basis of what we have done. We learn over time that on the basis of moving our bodies and creating certain upshots in the world, in certain contexts we should expect, or it is appropriate to expect, the reactive attitudes. So the condition is supposed to capture what (to some extent) is going on in human moral development. I want to add to these conditions the claim that we take responsibility in the first instance for *kinds* of mechanisms or *kinds* of processes that issue in our behavior. There is, for instance, the ordinary human mechanism of practical reasoning. There is also action from unreflective habit. Consider a case in which we are punished, and in which we first deliberated about the pertinent action. Suppose we say, "Boy, my sister's birthday presents look really intriguing!" Suppose we go ahead and we say, "She won't really mind if I open one." Then we open it. Well, that is a deliberative context. We learn that if we deliberate and we make those kinds of choices, it is reasonable to expect that there will be certain reactive attitudes taken by or held by others. But also a crucial milestone comes when we learn that we can also be held accountable for our actions that come from nonreflective habit.

So we take responsibility at a certain point for the kinds of mechanism that issue in our actions. And I think that this is a part of what it is to be responsible. To be explicit: To be responsible is to act from a mechanism that is one's own appropriately reasons-sensitive mechanism. Part of what is involved in being one's own mechanism is that one takes responsibility for it, and one takes responsibility for it by having the beliefs described above.

...I want to end with this: I think that manipulation cases are compatibilism's dirty little secret. Compatibilists don't like to admit that this is a problem. It is to Bob Kane's and other incompatibilists' credit that they have pushed us to confront cases of covert non-constraining control. There can be thorough-going global kinds of manipulation. We compatibilists have to deal with this. In my view, honestly, Harry Frankfurt really has not addressed that problem. He has discussed it in different ways and in different places and it doesn't add up to anything—in my view. But I would like to suggest that at least the approach that Mark Ravizza and I have begun to develop has some promise of usefully illuminating the manipulation cases. We would say that when your brain is being directly manipulated in one of the covert non-constraining control cases, one's behavior does not issue from *one's own mechanism*. One has presumably in the typical case taken responsibility for practical reasoning and for the kind of mechanism which is ordinary human practical reasoning, and perhaps also for unreflective action from habit. But one has not (thereby) also taken responsibility for action as a result of a scientist manipulating one's brain—a different kind of mechanism. That is not my own mechanism because I have not taken responsibility for it....

THE CONTINUING DEBATE:
Do We Have Free Will?

What Is New

In the long debate over free will, a key question has concerned *alternative possibilities*. Libertarian writers—who reject determinism—insisted that free will requires the ability to do otherwise, the ability to take different paths, the opportunity to pursue alternative possibilities; and (the libertarians argued) determinism eliminates alternative possibilities, and so eliminates free will. Compatibilists typically responded by arguing that the requisite "alternative possibilities" need not be so dramatic: Free will requires only that we could do otherwise had we *wished* to do otherwise. Of course our wishes and desires are determined, so we will not actually pursue some other alternative; but (compatibilists claimed) free will does not require that we actually take some alternative path. So how we defined alternative possibilities was an intense subject of debate; but the need for alternative possibilities was assumed by all.

That alternative possibilities assumption was challenged by Harry G. Frankfurt and Gerald Dworkin, who argued that we can be free and morally responsible even though we plainly *could not have done otherwise*, and no alternative possibilities existed. Harry Frankfurt's famous example was of a *willing addict*. Imagine a drug addict who is enslaved to his addiction, and will take drugs no matter what, and cannot do otherwise. But this *willing* addict deeply approves of his addiction, is glad that he is addicted, and has no wish whatsoever to stop taking drugs. Frankfurt maintains that such an addict has no available alternatives to taking drugs, but is nonetheless acting with free will. Obviously not everyone accepts this version of compatibilism, but it has had a great impact, and shifted the focus of the debate over free will.

Where to Find More

Robert Kane's *Free Will and Values* (Albany: State University of New York Press, 1985) is an excellent sustained argument for the incompatibilist position, and a clear presentation of his own indeterminacy version of libertarianism; Kane's introduction to that book is a superb critical survey of the history, issues, and literature of the free will controversy. *The Significance of Free Will* (New York: Oxford University Press, 1996) is a more detailed development of his position, taking account of many critical reactions to his views. His anthology, *Free Will* (Oxford: Blackwell Publishers, 2002) is a very good collection of papers on the positions and arguments that have shaped the free will debate. Kane's *A Contemporary Introduction to Free Will* (New York: Oxford University Press, 2005) is a very clear, thorough, and even-handed introduction to the continuing debate on free will and responsibility.

John Martin Fischer has been a very influential proponent of compatibilism, in works such as *The Metaphysics of Free Will: A Study of Control* (Oxford: Blackwell, 1994) and (with Mark Ravizza) *Responsibility and Control: A Theory of Moral Responsibility* (Cambridge: Cambridge University Press, 1998).

Harry G. Frankfurt's compatibilist views are widely anthologized, and can be found in two collections of his essays: *Necessity, Volition, and Love* (Cambridge: Cambridge University Press, 1999), and *The Importance of What We Care About* (New York: Cambridge University Press, 1988); Gerald Dworkin's views are made quite clear in his *The Theory and Practice of Autonomy* (Cambridge: Cambridge University Press, 1988). A good collection of essays on the continuing debate can be found in David Widerker and Michael McKenna, editors, *Moral Responsibility and Alternative Possibilities* (Burlington, Vt.: Ashgate, 2003).

There are many excellent anthologies on free will; perhaps the best small collection is Gary Watson's *Free Will* (Oxford: Oxford University Press, 1982). An excellent recent anthology is edited by Laura Waddell Ekstrom, *Agency and Responsibility* (Boulder, Col.: Westview Press, 2001); another very good recent collection is *Philosophical Perspectives 14, Action and Freedom, 2000*, edited by James E. Tomberlin (Oxford: Blackwell, 2000).

A superb website on free will, determinism, fatalism, and moral responsibility—it contains a number of excellent links and is beautifully organized—is available at the Determinism and Freedom Philosophy Website, at http://www.ucl.ac.uk/~uctytho/dfwIntroIndex.htm. A very nice collection of online papers on free will has been compiled by David Chalmers, and are available at his home page: http://jamaica.u.arizona.edu/~chalmers/online2.html#freewill. Naturalism.org at http://www.naturalism.org/freewill.htm offers a number of excellent papers and reviews on issues related to free will.

The suggested readings for debates 8 and 9 are also relevant here.

8 DOES RECENT PSYCHOLOGICAL RESEARCH UNDERMINE FREE WILL AND RESPONSIBILITY?

Research in Situationist Psychology Poses a Serious Threat to Traditional Accounts of Freedom and Responsibility

ADVOCATE: John Doris, Associate Professor of Philosophy, Washington University in St. Louis; author of *Lack of Character: Personality and Moral Behavior* (Cambridge: Cambridge University Press, 2002) and numerous papers.

SOURCE: *Lack of Character: Personality and Moral Behavior* (Cambridge: Cambridge University Press, 2002).

The Situationist Challenge to Freedom and Responsibility Is Limited

ADVOCATE: Dana K. Nelkin, teaches philosophy at University of California, San Diego; works primarily in the area of moral psychology.

SOURCE: "Freedom, Responsibility and the Challenge of Situationism," in *Midwest Studies in Philosophy*, volume 29, 2005.

Throughout ancient and medieval history, and well into the modern period, the appearance of a comet was regarded as a terrifying break in the pattern of events. The stars and planets moved in a glorious clockwork, until some brilliant celestial object with a bright tail disrupted the entire pattern. Whether messengers from God or signals of doom, comets were the clearest example of unpredictability and capriciousness. But in the early 18th Century, Edmund Halley—using the laws of motion recently formulated by Isaac Newton—predicted the time and path of the comet now named in his honor. This successful prediction had an enormous impact: if something as strange and mysterious as a comet can be predicted and understood as a determined process, then perhaps *everything*—including the strange and apparently capricious behavior of humans—could also follow determined paths. Of course the Newtonian account of the determined motion of planets and comets is not proof that human behavior is likewise determined, but the amazing success of Newtonian physics made the idea of universal determinism much more attractive. As Voltaire stated:

> It would be very singular that all nature, all the planets, should obey eternal laws, and that there should be a little animal five foot high, who, in contempt of these laws, could act as he pleases, solely according to his caprice.

We might not yet know all the causal laws governing human behavior, but it seemed much more plausible to suppose that the discovery of such laws awaited only the emergence of another Newton who would demonstrate that—like the movement of comets—the apparent freedom and unpredictability of human behavior actually followed causal laws. Psychological research—with its efforts to understand the causes and paths of human behavior—has continued to be a potent source of challenge for belief in special human free will: the behavioral studies of B.F. Skinner and other behavioral scientists challenge that belief, as do recent neuropsychological studies of the brain. The challenges posed by the impressive research findings of contemporary situationist psychology are the subject of this debate.

We have traditionally believed that we make autonomous choices based on our character, our deep values, and our strong will power; and that these free choices are the result of our own independent decision making rather than being dictated by the environment or situation we happen to be in. Of course our choice-making can be severely limited, or even defeated, by extreme circumstances: if I am in chains, or threatened by someone aiming a gun at me, or drugged, or overwhelmed by catastrophic events, or caught in a raging torrent, then I may have little or no free choice. The storied demand of the highwayman—"your money or your life"—might leave some range of choice, but handing over my gold under the threat of sword and pistol hardly seems like a healthy exercise of free autonomous choice. But in normal circumstances, we make free choices that are shaped by our character, our reflection, our own independent decision.

Or so the traditional story goes. But recent psychological research—research into *situationist* psychology, research on the strong influence of our situation and our immediate environment on our behavior—has raised serious doubts about the traditional account. Research indicates that our environmental influences (including influences that seem so trivial that we are hardly even aware of them) have a profound and surprising influence on our choices and our behavior. John Doris takes these subtle but powerful influences very seriously; and while he does not believe that they totally destroy our free will and moral responsibility, he does claim that the research findings of situationist psychology require significant changes in the way we think of free will and moral character.

Dana Nelkin maintains that the ability to recognize and act from *good reasons* is essential to freedom and responsibility; and for Nelkin, the problem raised by situationist research is that it shows people often acting without good reasons, and sometimes even contrary to their reasons, and in these situations they appear to be blocked from recognizing and responding to good reasons. Though Nelkin regards the situationist research results as significant, she believes that their threat to freedom and responsibility is quite limited. For Nelkin, the key question is not whether in some situations there are subtle factors that may lead us astray; rather, the question is whether persons in those situations still have the capacity to recognize and respond to good reasons. If they do, they may be acting freely, and can legitimately be held responsible for failure to be carefully attentive to and guided by good reasons. Limited situations that undercut one's ability to recognize good reasons may well exist, but Nelkin does not see them as a large-scale threat to free will and responsibility; to the contrary, they can accentuate the central importance of reason-responsiveness for genuine free will.

POINTS TO PONDER

> John Doris suggests that in light of situationist research, our focus should be less on shaping good *character* and more on avoiding *situations* that prompt bad behavior. If you want to avoid alcoholic overindulgence, don't rely on your strong

will power; instead, stay away from bars and parties that encourage heavy drinking. In your own experience, which approach seems to work better?

➤ Doris believes that situationism calls for important revisions in our views, but we can still have a use for the concept of responsibility: We are not really responsible for acting badly in situations that promote bad behavior; rather, we are responsible for carefully *avoiding* such situations. *If* situationism is true, is it consistent with the concept of responsibility suggested by Doris?

➤ Nelkin maintains that in some situations in which many people *fail* to recognize and respond to good reasons, they still *could* have done so; and thus they can still be held responsible for their bad behavior in those situations. And in fact, in the same situations in which most people act very badly (as in the Milgram experiment) some few do manage to act well. Does the existence of that small minority show that those (the majority) who *failed* to act well were acting freely, and that they are morally responsible for their bad behavior?

Research in Situationist Psychology Poses a Serious Threat to Traditional Accounts of Freedom and Responsibility

JOHN DORIS

PRÉCIS

It's commonly presumed that good character inoculates against shifting fortune, and English has a rich vocabulary for expressing this belief: *steady, dependable, steadfast, unwavering, unflinching.* Conversely, the language generously supplies terms of abuse marking lack of character: *weak, fickle, disloyal, faithless, irresolute.* Such locutions imply that character will have regular behavioral manifestations: the person of good character will do well, even under substantial pressure to moral failure, while the person of bad character is someone on whom it would be foolish to rely. In this view it's character, more than circumstance, that decides the moral texture of a life; as the old saw has it, character is destiny.

This conception of character is both venerable and appealing, but it is also deeply problematic. For me, this judgment is motivated by reflection on a longstanding "situationist" research tradition in experimental social psychology. A large part

of my project is to articulate this tradition, but situationalism's fundamental observation can at the start be stated plainly enough: behavior is—*contra* the old saw about character and destiny—extraordinarily sensitive to variation in circumstance. Numerous studies have demonstrated that minor situational variations have powerful effects on helping behavior: hurried passersby step over a stricken person in their path, while unhurried passersby stop to help; passersby who find a bit of change stop to help a woman who has dropped her papers, while passersby who are not similarly fortunate do not. Situations have also been shown to have a potent influence on harming: ordinary people are willing to torture a screaming victim at the polite request of an experimenter, or perpetrate all manner of imaginative cruelties while serving as guards in a prison simulation. The experimental record suggests that situational factors are often better predictors of behavior than personal factors, and this impression is reinforced by careful examination of behavior outside the confines of the laboratory. In very many situations it looks as though personality is less than robustly determinative of behavior. To put things crudely, people typically lack character.

Situationism's three central theoretical commitments concern behavioral variation, the nature of traits, and personality organization.

(1) Behavioral variation across a population owes more to situational differences than dispositional differences among persons. Individual dispositional differences are not so behaviorally individuating as might have been supposed; to a surprising extent it is safest to predict, for a particular situation, that a person will behave in a fashion similar to the population norm.

(2) Systematic observation problematizes the attribution of robust traits. People will quite typically behave inconsistently with respect to the attributive standards associated with a trait, and whatever behavioral consistency is displayed may be readily disrupted by situational variation.

(3) Personality is not often evaluatively integrated. For a given person, the dispositions operative in one situation may have an evaluative status very different from those manifested in another situation; evaluatively inconsistent dispositions may "cohabitate" in a single personality.

MORAL CHARACTER, MORAL BEHAVIOR

Totalitarianism specializes in the dissolution of fortitude, whether by the extremes of physical torture or by the psychological degradation of "thought reform" or "brainwashing." These practices are repellent, but their effects are not unexpected. Russell remarked that the will withstands the tyrant only so long as the tyrant is unscientific. Situationism teaches something more surprising and, in a sense, more disturbing. The unsettling observation doesn't concern behavior in extremis, but behavior in situations that are rather less than extreme; the problem is not that substantial situational factors have substantial effects on what people do, but that seemingly insubstantial situational factors have substantial effects on what people do. The disproportionate impact of these "insubstantial" situational factors presses charges of empirical inadequacy against characterological moral psychology: If dispositional structures were typically so robust as familiar conceptions of character and personality lead one to believe, insubstantial factors would not so frequently have such impressive effects.

HELPING BEHAVIOR
Mood Effects

Imagine a person making a call in a suburban shopping plaza. As the caller leaves the phone booth, along comes Alice, who drops a folder full of papers that scatters in the caller's path. Will the caller stop and help before the only copy of Alice's magnum opus is trampled by the bargain-hungry throngs? Perhaps it depends on the person: Jeff, an entrepreneur incessantly stalking his next dollar, probably won't, while Nina, a political activist who takes in stray cats, probably will. Nina is the compassionate type; Jeff isn't. In these circumstances we expect their true colors to show. But this may be a mistake, as an experiment by Isen and Levin shows. There the paper-dropper was an experimental assistant, or "confederate." For one group of callers, a dime was planted in the phone's coin return slot; for the other, the slot was empty. Here are the results:

	Helped	Did Not Help
Found dime	14	2
Did not find dime	1	24

If greedy Jeff finds the dime, he'll likely help, and if compassionate Nina doesn't, she very likely won't. The situation, more than the person, seems to be making the difference.

On Isen and Levin's reading, the determinative impact of finding the dime proceeds by influencing affective states; apparently, this small bit of good fortune elevates mood, and "feeling good leads to helping." The crucial observation is not that mood influences behavior—no surprise there—but just how unobtrusive the stimuli that induce the determinative moods can be. Finding a bit of change is something one would hardly bother to remark on in describing one's day, yet it makes the difference between helping and not.

A rather trivial situational factor may have a nontrivial impact on prosocial behavior; Baron found subjects near a fragrant bakery or coffee shop more likely to change a dollar bill when asked than those near a neutral-smelling dry goods store.

Good Samaritans

In one of the most widely discussed situationist experiments, Darley and Batson invited students at the Princeton Theological Seminary to participate in a study of "religious education and vocations." Subjects began experimental procedures by filling out questionnaires in one building and then reported to a nearby building for the second part of the experiment, which consisted in their giving a short verbal presentation. Before leaving the first site, subjects were told either that they were running late ("high hurry" condition), were right on time ("medium hurry" condition), or were a little early ("low hurry" condition); thus the conditions exerted a different degree of time pressure on the subjects. The behavior of interest occurred on the walk between the two sites, when each seminarian passed an experimental

confederate slumped in a doorway, apparently in some sort of distress.

One might expect that most individuals training for a "helping profession" like the ministry would be strongly disposed to assist the unfortunate victim or at the very least inquire as to his condition. Instead, helping varied markedly according to the degree of hurry.

| | **Degree of Hurry** | | |
	Low	Medium	High
Percentage of helping	63	45	10

It's no surprise that haste can have people paying less regard to others. But the apparent disproportion between the seriousness of the situational pressures and the seriousness of the omission is surprising: The thought of being a few minutes late was enough to make subjects not notice or disregard a person's suffering.

We find considerable helping even amongst strangers: Numerous studies of staged emergencies have found impressive rates of intervention, in some conditions approaching 100 percent. The situationist point is not that helping is rare, but that helping is situationally sensitive.

DESTRUCTIVE BEHAVIOR

The Milgram Experiments

So far, we have examined experimental manipulations which appear to generate omissions of compassion, failures to act where one might fairly expect a person of ordinary moral stature to do so. Social psychologists have also performed experimental manipulations of active harming behavior, laboratory inducements to destructive behaviors one would expect a person of ordinary moral stature to quite readily avoid. The classic studies in this vein are the famous, or infamous, "obedience experiments" conducted by Stanley Milgram. While they are among the most widely recognized, and among the most important, of all psychological demonstrations, it is not obvious that we have come fully to grips with the notorious "experiments where they shocked people." Nor is it the case that philosophers have been especially engaged with Milgram's work, despite its apparent ethical significance.

Milgram's experiments show how apparently noncoercive situational factors may induce destructive behavior despite the apparent presence of contrary evaluative and dispositional structures. Furthermore, personality research has failed to find a convincing explanation of the Milgram results that references individual differences. Accordingly, Milgram gives us reason to doubt the robustness of dispositions implicated in compassion-relevant moral behavior; his experiments are powerful evidence for situationism.

From 1960 to 1963, Milgram ran various permutations of his experiment with approximately 1,000 subjects drawn from various socioeconomic groups in the New Haven area—postal clerks, high school teachers, salesmen, engineers, and laborers—who responded to newspaper and mail solicitations seeking paid participants for a study of memory and learning at Yale University. Here's how the story goes.

On arrival at the site, the subject is met by a lab-coated "experimenter" who introduces him to another ostensible subject, actually a confederate, and explains that the study concerns the effects of punishment on learning. There is a drawing to determine experimental roles, rigged so that the subject is designated "teacher" and the confederate "learner." The learner, an affable middle-aged accountant, is strapped into a chair "to prevent excessive movement." An electrode is attached to his wrist with electrode paste "to avoid blisters and burns." The experimenter assures par-

ticipants that the shocks used as punishment, although they can be extremely painful, will cause no "permanent tissue damage." The teacher is administered an uncomfortable sample shock to convince him of the scenario's authenticity; however, the "shocks" administered the learner are fake, and he experiences no pain.

The teacher is then led to another room and seated in front of an imposing "shock generator" that the experimenter explains is wired to the electrode on the learner, who is now hidden from view in the first room. The teacher next remotely administers a word-association test to the learner; the learner's answers are displayed above the shock generator, and with each wrong answer, the teacher administers a shock, which is increased in intensity one increment for each wrong answer. The learner responds incorrectly on a pre-arranged schedule, so that shock intensity steadily increases. If the teacher expresses concern about this process, as many subjects did, the experimenter responds with a standardized series of verbal prods: (1) "Please continue," (2) "The experiment requires that you continue," (3) "It is absolutely essential that you continue," (4) "You have no other choice, you *must* go on." The sequence begins again at (1) each time the subject balks and progresses through (4) if he continues to refuse. The experimenter may also repeat the reassurance that the shocks "cause no permanent tissue damage" if the subject expresses concern over the learner's safety. If the subject refuses to continue after prod (4), the experiment terminates, and the subject is counted "disobedient"; subjects who comply with all instructions and proceed to the maximum shock are termed "obedient." According to Milgram, the experimenter's tone of voice is "at all times firm, but not impolite."

With each error, the teacher ups the voltage one increment, gradually moving across the control panel to increasingly ominous designations and increasingly vehement protests. After the last protest, at 330 volts, the learner is unresponsive. Has he had a heart attack? What is the teacher to do? According to the experimenter, the teacher is to treat no answer as a wrong answer and continue the progression. We are left with the indelible image of two-thirds doing so until the bitter end.

The experiment does not suggest that Milgram had stumbled onto an aberrant pocket of sadists in the New Haven area and still less does it suggest that all of us are a bunch of meanies. Trait-contrary behavior does not necessarily signal the possession of a contrary trait; even active failures of compassion do not necessarily imply sadism. What the experiments do highlight, once more, is the power of the situation; the majority of subjects were willing to torture another individual to what seemed the door of death without any more direct pressure than the polite insistence of the experimenter. But it is badly mistaken to think that the obedient subjects generally found their job easy— the experiment does not show that people are blindly obedient to authority. The most striking feature of the demonstration is not blind obedience but *conflicted* obedience. Horribly conflicted obedience: Subjects were often observed to "sweat, tremble, stutter, bite their lips, groan, and dig their fingernails into their flesh."

The story is not quite so depressing as it sounds. Ross imagines a "panic button" placed on Milgram's shock generator together with prominent instructions from a "human subjects committee" stating that the subject should push the button if he wants to stop. Actual human subjects review boards would very likely prohibit putting matters to the test, but Ross conjectures that obedience rates would be much lower than those obtained by Mil-

gram, because the panic button would provide a situational "channel" facilitating subjects acting on their distress. This seems exactly right. Milgram's lesson is not simply that situational pressures may induce particular *undesirable* behaviors, but that situational pressures may induce particular behaviors, *period*. Situational sensitivity is not always a bad thing. But in bad situations, it may very well result in bad behavior.

The Stanford Prison Experiment

In the early 1970s, Zimbardo and colleagues devised a "functional representation" of an American prison in the basement of the Stanford University psychology building. Male college students with no history of crime, emotional disability, physical handicap, or intellectual and social disadvantage were selected from a pool of 75 applicants; those chosen were "judged to be most stable (physically and mentally), most mature, and least involved in anti-social behavior." The 21 participants were randomly assigned the role of "prisoner" or "guard"; prisoners were confined 24 hours a day in a simulated penitentiary complete with barred cells and a small closet for solitary confinement, which became known as the "Hole." This is what happened.

Five prisoners were released prematurely due to "extreme emotional depression, crying, rage and acute anxiety," symptoms that developed as early as two days into the experiment; one subject developed a psychosomatic rash over portions of his body. Conversely, most of the guards seemed rather to enjoy their roles. Prohibited by experimenters from employing physical punishment, they improvised all manner of creative sadisms such as requiring prisoners to clean out toilets with their bare hands. On the second day there was a prisoner insurrection quashed by guards hosing down prisoners with fire extinguishers. At the end of six days, the alarmed investigators terminated the scheduled two-week experiment. Once again, it appears that persons are swamped by situations.

JUDGING CHARACTER

Attribution and Overattribution

Social psychologists have long noted that people—at least, people in the West— tend to inflate the importance of dispositions and neglect the importance of situations in explaining behavior. This has been variously called the "fundamental attribution error," the "correspondence bias," and—to use my favored term—"overattribution."

When asked to describe people or explain behavior, Americans strongly favor trait attribution; in typical studies subjects appeal to dispositions such as "kind" and "shy" two to three times as frequently as specific behaviors and contexts like "disturbs class by being loud." Of course, if dispositional attributions are typically well founded, there is little cause for concern. Unfortunately, this is not often the case.

Luck in Circumstance

The topic of person evaluation invites unsettling discussion of "moral luck." Despite familiar convictions to the effect that the moral quality of our lives is somehow "up to us" or "in our control," people's moral status may to a disquieting degree be hostage to the vagaries of fortune. Of particular relevance to situationalism is luck in circumstances, the thought that every person may have behaved very differently than they actually did, were their circumstances different. Had I lived in Germany, Rwanda, or any number of places during the wrong historical moment, I might have led a life that was morally reprehensible, despite the fact that the life I lead now is perhaps no worse than morally mediocre. That, but for the grace of God, do I.

This observation does not equally problematize all aspects of ethical thought. Luck in circumstance doesn't cause any obvious trouble for responsibility assessment, for the simple reason that people are held responsible for what they actually do. I don't get credit for the heroic deeds I would have done had the world gone differently, nor am I excoriated for the nefarious deeds I would have done had I been unfortunate enough to live in more interesting times. However, taking luck in circumstances seriously does seem to make familiar practices of person evaluation look very uncertain. How can one be sure that a person is really a decent sort if that person would have done horrible things in altered circumstances?

Think of someone you admire, and then ask what might ground your confidence that she would not have gone along with the Nazis had she lived under the Third Reich. A likely answer appeals to features of her character: Someone that principled, decent, or kind would not participate in or condone atrocities no matter how deranged her country's politics. Since skepticism about character in effect prohibits this kind of thought, it might be thought to erode the bulwarks against luck in circumstance. Indeed, situationism appears to make things still worse: It tells me I might have behaved poorly had I been in a hurry or had I not found a dime. The queasy realization turns out to be not "had things been different" but "had things been *just a little* different."

SITUATION AND RESPONSIBILITY

Responsibility and Reactive Attitudes

Human beings, unlike rocks, raccoons, and rainstorms, are sometimes subjects of moral responsibility. But which human beings are responsible for their actions, and when? These are notoriously incorrigible questions, and I won't say much here to make them easier. Indeed, I raise them because my arguments exacerbate the difficulty: I advocate eschewing central forms of character assessment, while responsibility attribution seems to presuppose such assessments.

According to Hume, a person is responsible only for actions that proceed from her "characters and disposition"; to attribute responsibility is to attribute behavior to an enduring feature of character. People apparently have a more intimate relation to behaviors that are an "expression of their character" than to behaviors that are not such expressions; my impassioned political activism says rather more about me than does my paying the electric bill, and it seems perfectly natural that I get credit (or blame) for the one and not the other. If such intuitions lead to a view like Hume's, situationism undermines responsibility attribution.

Responsibility and Deep Assessment

Responsibility assessment, we might say, has "depth"; moral praise and blame look beyond the surface properties of actions to associated psychological states such as belief, desire, and motive. But situationist skepticism about character may appear to preclude this. If (1) deep responsibility assessment must be properly psychological assessment, and (2) properly psychological assessment involves character assessment, then (3) skepticism about character precludes deep responsibility assessment. This argument fails, because we should reject the second premise. An *acharacterological* account of responsibility need not be *apsychological*: Situationist moral psychology is not prevented from looking deep.

It is not obvious, then, that situationism unduly complicates standard approaches to the infamous "problem of free will." Their troubles—if one thinks they have troubles—are of their own making.

My trouble is that I think situationism does uniquely problematize two notions central to thinking on responsibility—normative competence and identification—notions important in developing compatibilisms with enough psychological texture to provide satisfying underpinnings for the reactive attitudes. While everyone may not place these ideas as close to the heart of things as I do, I think it can be shown that the problems I adduce are of quite general concern.

Situations and Self-Control

It is plausible to think that "powers of reflective self-control" are requisite for responsibility; if an individual generally lacks such powers, she may be in exempting conditions, and if particular circumstances undermine the exercise of such powers, she may be in excusing conditions. Actually, there are two sorts of "powers" relevant here: "powers of reflection" and "powers of self-control." I've argued that situational factors are pervasively implicated in substantial cognitive and motivational failures. Could the lesson of situationism be that exculpating impairments in the powers of reflective self-control are, contra American legal practice, more the rule than the exception?

We've seen how noncoercive situational factors may result in "ordinary, decent" people acting in ways they know to be wrong: Milgram's subjects tearing their hair as they shocked their victim, a Stanford Prison Experiment "guard" awash in self-loathing as he abused "inmates," and the anxiety experienced by some passive bystanders in the experiments of Darley and colleagues. Such data suggest "weakness of will," "incontinence," or as Aristotle called it, *akrasia*—cases where a person knowingly acts other than as she thinks best. This phenomenon, although puzzling, is not unfamiliar; it certainly appears that people often, too often, act in ways other than they know they ought. But situationist experiments *are* surprising: I should shock a man to the door of death because a laboratory technician politely asks me to do so? In such cases we are not merely *akratic*, but as one might put it, *radically akratic*: Our wills are not merely weak but positively anemic. Furthermore, if the ease with which such behaviors are experimentally induced is any indication, alarming failures of the will are alarmingly widespread. Does this problematize attributing powers of self-control?

One might think, as Aristotle seemed to, that it is pardonable when someone is overcome by extremely intense pleasures and pains but not when someone is overcome by pleasures or pains most people can resist. The person who reveals state secrets under torture is not condemned as a traitor, while the person who does so for a modest payoff is; the agonies of torture are something few can resist, while the lure of minor financial gain is something most can.

When we find that a majority of those in a prima facie low-intensity situation engage in unusual or untoward behavior, we will want to reexamine the case, but this needn't force substantive conceptual revision in the practice of responsibility assessment, such as dropping the intensity criterion in favor of a frequency criterion. Situationism does, however, present epistemological difficulty for the practice: It suggests that unobtrusive high-intensity stimuli very often obtain, with the result that people may sometimes be in undetected excusing conditions. This does not mean that confident assessments of responsibility are impossible. It does mean that making such assessments may take a lot of work, since there may be more—much more—to the circumstances of behavior than meets the eye. Yet if situationism raises a problem in this regard, it also provides materials in the direction of a so-

lution, since situationist research can help uncover the sorts of inobvious motivational phenomena, such as mood effects and group effects, that sensitive responsibility assessment must consider, even if this consideration does not always, or even often, compel excusing judgments. I don't pretend that a realistic and fairminded practice of responsibility assessment is easy to achieve, but I don't see that coming to terms with the vagaries of human motivation—what some might call the vicissitudes of will—prevents the realization of such a practice.

Normative Competence

Even if the foregoing is right, trouble remains for our "powers of reflection." The worry, let me emphasize again, is not simply that situationism tells a causal story about the origins of behavior. It's not *that* the relevant psychological states are caused, but rather *how* they are caused. The causal stories the situationist tells, as we shall see, raise questions about the reflective capacities requisite for responsibility.

Attributions of responsibility presuppose their object possesses normative competence, a complex capacity enabling the possessor to appreciate normative considerations, ascertain information relevant to particular normative judgments, and engage in effective deliberation.

Normative competence involves, among other things, whatever cognitive capacities are required for effective deliberation. Deliberation is effective when it secures conformity between the deliberator's evaluative commitments and the plan, policy, or decision the deliberator endorses; the effective deliberator is one able to determine what is conducive to the "implementation" of her values. My deliberation is effective if, in light of my commitment to making you happy, my deliberation effects decisions, plans, or policies suited to bringing about your happiness. If my deliberation works to impede the implementation of your commitment—suppose I arrive at a decision that results in your being hurt or offended, despite my good intentions—my deliberation is ineffective.

Here deliberation concerns "instrumental" rationality, having to do with selection of means best suited to secure one's aims. But the difficulty engendered by situationism does not concern substantive deliberation. I'm happy to allow that human beings are quite able to reflect on and maintain settled evaluative commitments; the problem is that situationism raises questions about our prospects for deliberation conducive to the effective implementation of these commitments.

The requisite conformity between evaluative commitment and deliberative outcome can't come about just any old way—conformity secured by you boxing my ears doesn't look like an exercise of competence on my part. The exercise of normative competence involves not only securing the requisite conformity, but also something like reflection or deliberation, a process of ratiocination involving consideration of alternatives, an awareness of salient considerations, and the like. How involved and explicit this process needs to be is a difficult question that will recur, but reliable conformity alone is not enough for competence.

Here now is the problem deriving from situationism. Our default position regarding "normal" adults is to hold them responsible for their actions; unlike the hopelessly deranged, we assume that they do not suffer global impairments of normative competence. But any normal adult might be in circumstances which effect local impairments of normative competence, such as difficult-to-interpret situations that prevent acquisition of morally significant information. In these circum-

stances, normal adults have something importantly in common with the legally insane; they are unable to properly appreciate normatively relevant considerations. The difficulty is that situationism suggests such circumstances may be pervasive. If this were true, our default position would be quite wrong; instead, the sensible default would be a general agnosticism about responsibility attribution, since we could never confidently rule out the presence of competence defeaters. This result, it seems to me, would radically undermine the practice of the reactive attitudes.

But this is not to propose radical adjustments in our thinking on responsibility; once more, what is needed is closer and more nuanced attention to particular circumstances with an eye to the possibility that legitimate excusing conditions may be unexpectedly unobtrusive.

However, there is a more insidious problem having to do with "internally directed" normative competence. In surveying subjects' reports on their thinking during experimental manipulations of cognitive processes, Nisbett and Wilson observe that people very often fail to accurately report on stimuli experimentally shown to be determinative; they worry that this phenomenon threatens a general skepticism regarding introspective access to cognitive processes. Nisbett and Wilson acknowledge that people may correctly report the causes of their judgments, especially when the relevant causes are readily ascertainable, intuitively plausible, and not masked by intuitively plausible but causally noninfluential explanatory factors. But situationism suggests that these happy conditions often fail to hold. Critical stimuli may be extremely difficult to ascertain and, when brought to light, seem highly implausible as compared with lay psychological heuristics. As a result, people quite typically have a rather tenuous grasp on their own cognitive operations; we may reasonably wonder whether this has a detrimental effect on normative competence. In fact, the force of Nisbett and Wilson's point is not limited to cognition; it generalizes to the motivational processes implicated in overt moral behaviors.

For example, Latané and Darley found that questioning subjects influenced by the group effect invited confabulation.

> We asked this question every way we knew how: subtly, directly, tactfully, bluntly. Always we got the same answer. Subjects persistently claimed that their behavior was not influenced by the other people present. This denial occurred in the face of results showing that the presence of others did inhibit helping.

People may be quite unaware of determinative situational factors; indeed, they may be frankly incredulous when these factors are brought to their attention. It is difficult to say precisely how pervasive such "sneaky" stimuli are, but the exact extent of the phenomena needn't be decided for us to feel real concern, for there is no easy way to rule out their presence. Why was I so curt? Perhaps because the salesperson was inattentive. Or perhaps it's that I'm standing on a wool carpet, or that the ambient temperature is 67.2 degrees. Why was I so amorous? Perhaps I'm in love. Or perhaps it was the smell of garlic or the feel of polyester. If situationism is right, we can play this game with every action. Worse, why should we be confident we've played it well? If we survey 1,000 situational factors, how can we be sure that number 1,001 wasn't doing the work? Our grip on our motivational universe appears alarmingly frail; we may quite frequently be in the dark or dead wrong about why we do what we do.

Situation and Deliberation

I'm urging a certain redirection of our ethical attention. Rather than striving to develop characters that will determine our behavior in ways substantially independent of circumstance, we should invest more of our energies in attending to the features of our environment that influence behavioral outcomes.

Reflection on situationism has an obvious benefit: It reminds us that the world is a morally dangerous place. In a study related to his obedience experiments, Milgram asked respondents to predict the maximum intensity shock they would deliver were they subjects "required" to punish the confederate "victim" with incrementally increasing shocks. The mean prediction was around 150 volts (level 10), and no subject said they would go beyond 300 volts (level 20). When these respondents were asked to predict the behavior of others, they predicted that at most 1 or 2 percent of subjects would deliver the maximum shock of 450 volts (level 30). In fact, for a standard permutation of the experiment, the mean maximum shock was 360 (level 24), and 65 percent continued to 450 volts (level 30). The usual expectation seems to be that behavior is much more situation-independent than it actually is; apparently, people tend to see character traits as substantially robust, with typical dispositions to moral decency serving as guarantors against destructive behavior. Milgram's study indicates that perception and reality are markedly discrepant in this regard. The consequence of this discrepancy, I contend, is an increased probability of moral failure; many times their confidence in character is precisely what puts people at risk in morally dangerous situations. Far from being practically indispensable, characterological discourse is a heuristic we often have very good reason to purge from deliberation.

The way to get things right more often, I suggest, is by attending to the determinative features of situations. We should try, so far as we are able, to avoid "near occasions for sin"—ethically dangerous circumstances. At the same time, we should seek near occasions for happier behaviors—situations conducive to ethically desirable conduct. The determinants of ethical success or failure often emerge earlier in an activity than might be thought. In our example, the difficulty to be addressed lies less in an exercise of will after dinner than in deciding to engage the situation in the first place, a decision that may occur in a lower pressure, relatively "cool," context where even exquisitely situation-sensitive creatures such as ourselves may be able to act in accordance with their values. For instance, it may be easier to "do the right thing" over the phone than it would be in the ethical "hot zone" of a candlelit dinner. Then condemnation for ethical failure might very often be directed not at a particular failure of the will but a certain culpable naiveté or insufficiently careful attention to situations. The implication of this is that our duties may be surprisingly complex, involving not simply obligations to particular actions but a sort of "cognitive duty" to attend, in our deliberations, to the determinative features of situations.

If this sort of situational sophistication can be regularly exercised in cooler decision contexts, the suggested approach might effect a considerable reliability in ethical behavior. Unfortunately, I doubt our optimism here should be unbounded. Those with knowledge of the Milgram paradigm, for example, are perhaps unlikely to be obedient dupes in highly similar situations. But this knowledge may be difficult to apply in dissimilar circumstances. Furthermore, many dangerous features of situations will have a degree of subtlety that will make them difficult to unmask, however one tries. People may often be in "Milgram situations" without being so aware—at a seminar or in a meeting. So my approach cannot offer guarantees. But it can, I submit, focus ethical attention where it may do the most good: deliberation contexts where reflection on one's values will be most likely to make a difference.

The Situationist Challenge to Freedom and Responsibility Is Limited

DANA K. NELKIN

I. INTRODUCTION

We have now learned that over the course of months in the Abu Ghraib prison in Iraq during the fall and winter of 2003–04, United States soldiers serving as guards inflicted severe physical and psychological pain on their Iraqi prisoners while appearing to revel in the experience. The news prompted an outcry—across the United States and across the world—and a demand to punish those responsible for the atrocious acts. Interestingly, although courts-martial of the participating soldiers are on-going, as are investigations into the higher ranks of the military, it has not been treated by everyone as obvious that the prison guards themselves are morally responsible. For at least some of the participants seem to be basically decent people who were in some sense victims of the situation in which they found themselves. A friend of perhaps the most well-known participant, Private Lynddie England, put it this way: "…It's so not her. It's not in her nature to do something like that. There's not a malicious bone in her body."

As has been well-documented, the behavior of the U.S. soldiers is eerily reminiscent of the Stanford Prison Experiment, conducted by Zimbardo and colleagues in 1971, in which adult male undergraduates were asked to participate in a simulation of a prison, with some being randomly assigned to be "guards" and some "prisoners." The results were both astounding and disturbing, revealing the employment of humiliation and other psychological abuse on the part of some prison guards, and an unwillingness to interfere on the part of all the others. Although the experiment was planned to last two weeks, it was halted after just six days in the face of escalating abuse on the part of the guards and despondency and extreme anxiety on the part of prisoners.

The Stanford Prison Experiment is one part of a vast literature known as "situationist." Many of the experiments in this tradition lack the high stakes of the Stanford Prison Experiment, showing simply that apparently unimportant situational factors such as finding a dime or the presence of a stranger can exert surprising influence on whether we help someone, for example. But all have, at one time or other, been associated under the common rubric of situationism. While there is some controversy among psychologists as to how exactly to characterize the situationist thesis, I will here understand situationism to be the thesis that

(S) traditional personality or character traits like honesty, kindness, or cowardice play less of a role in predicting and explaining behavior than do particular situational factors.

And a kind of corollary of this claim is that people make what is called the "Fundamental Attribution Error":

(FAE) "People's inflated belief in the importance of personality traits and dispositions, together with their failure to recognize the importance of situational factors in affecting behavior."

In other words, we fail to recognize the truth of situationism.

Now the wide variety of situationist experiments is disturbing for a variety of reasons. One very general reason is that they seem to call into question our everyday assumption that we—and our fellow human beings—are free and responsible agents to be blamed and praised. For if they reveal that we are acting the way we do primarily because of situational factors that we don't expect to exert such influence, then how can our actions be "up to us"? (This is a question about freedom.) And how can they accrue to our moral account? (This is a question about responsibility.) Beginning to answer these questions is the task of this paper.

II. SOME KEY EXPERIMENTS

Hartshorne and May

Hartshorne and May conducted a study of 8,000 schoolchildren in the late 1920s that tested for honest behavior across a wide range of situations, such as willingness to lie to avoid getting another student into trouble, to cheat on a test, or to steal change left on a table. They found that almost none of the schoolchildren behaved "consistently" honestly across the situations, and concluded that honesty is not an internal trait.

Latané and Rodin

In a study replicating the results of Latané and Darley, the subjects were 120 male undergraduates who had agreed to participate in a study for a market research organization. A representative met each at the door, and after asking each subject to fill out a questionnaire in the waiting room, opened a curtained partition to an adjoining room, and closed the partition. While in the waiting room, the subjects heard a loud crash from an adjoining room, a scream and "Oh my God, my foot...I...I...can't move it.

Oh...my ankle...I...can't get this...thing...off me." They hear crying and moaning for about a minute more. The entire episode took about 130 seconds. The question was whether subjects would intervene to help, and under what conditions. When a subject was alone in the waiting room, 70% offered to help the victim. When a subject was in the room with a confederate playing a fellow subject who simply shrugged off the victim's cries and did not offer to help, only 7% of subjects intervened. The response rate rose to 40% when two subjects who were strangers to each other were in the waiting room together, and again to 70% when the two subjects were friends. Latané and Rodin conducted post-experimental interviews in which subjects acknowledged very little influence on their behavior by their co-workers. For example, in the passive confederate situation, "subjects reported, on the average, that they were 'very little' influenced by the stooge." And yet, when considering the overall statistical results, the presence or absence of others seems to have made an important contribution.

Asch

An earlier set of studies on group effects is also a classic in the situationist literature. In one variation, Asch placed a subject in a group with seven other individuals whom the subject believed to be fellow subjects, but who in fact were confederates of the experimenter. Each member of the group was asked to match the length of a given line with one of three other lines. The confederates of the subject each gave what would appear to be obviously incorrect answers. A third of all the estimates by the subjects were errors either identical with or in the direction of the mistaken estimates of the other members of the group. In contrast, there were virtually no errors in control groups in which subjects were simply asked to write down their answers privately.

In these studies, there were serious individual differences. For example, some individuals never conformed to the majority, while others conformed nearly each time. But anywhere from 50% to 80% of the subjects, depending on the particular study, conformed to the incorrect majority view at least once.

The results were surprising in that subjects were willing to make statements that appeared to be contradicted by the best evidence of their senses.

[Nelkin also describes the Isen and Levin, Darley and Batson, and Milgram experiments.]

In each of the experiments described, certain aspects of the situation were surprisingly influential. Whether one found oneself in an empty room with some change on the table, found a dime, was in a hurry, was near a stranger, or was politely asked by an experimenter to continue to shock a fellow human being, for example, played a larger than expected role in subjects' behavior. Each of these cases has been taken to support situationism. For in each case, certain situational factors seem to play a large role in determining behavior, whereas whether we would have described the subjects antecedently as generous or sadistic or sensitive appears to be less important. While these cases are among the most well known, they represent a small sampling of cases in the situationist tradition.

III. POSSIBLE ROUTES TO THE THREAT

Again, these cases seem troubling, at least in part because they raise the question of whether we really are free and responsible agents. Why?

Characterological Views of Freedom and Responsibility

A natural suggestion is that situationism threatens freedom and responsibility because (1) it undermines any attribution of robust character traits and dispositions, and (2) actions are free and responsible only to the extent that they issue from one's character and dispositions.

It is true that a number of philosophers, Hume notable among them, appeal to a notion of character in setting out conditions of freedom and responsibility and offer them as intuitive.

Such a view could be a plausible and implicitly accepted account of freedom or responsibility. And the account itself could actually gain support by appealing to the fact that it offers a simple and straightforward explanation of why the situationist literature appears to threaten freedom and responsibility. So we need to take seriously the question of whether a character based account of either freedom or responsibility does in fact explain the challenge of situationism.

In fact, we are faced with a plethora of apparent counterexamples to characterological views. We do not always withhold praise and blame when people appear to act out of character. We probably all have stories like this one: a person I would describe as wonderfully conscientious misses an appointment without a very good excuse. She is responsible for missing the appointment, even blameworthy, despite the fact that in some sense she acted "out of character." Now we can always re-evaluate her character on the basis of this new information, but reflection on the case suggests that acting from traditional character traits is not a requirement for being responsible. Nor does it seem required for acting freely.

If characterological views of freedom and responsibility do not have a great deal of plausibility, then situationism is not threatening to freedom and responsibility in virtue of its apparent undermining of character. At the same time, when someone acts out of character, it suggests that something is amiss, and gives us an opportunity to explore whether she is in fact responsible for her action. When our apparently conscientious friend misses her appointment, our first thought might be whether she is all right. Only when we find out that she has not been in an accident, and so on, can we think of blaming her for missing the appointment. For this reason, in undermining characterological explanations, situationism might appear to raise an indirect threat to freedom and responsibility.

But we can already draw an important lesson here. Even if we reject characterological views as implausible, this does not eliminate the challenge posed by the situationist literature. It does not, for example, eliminate all question as to whether we should assign responsibility—or perhaps blame, in particular—to the subjects of the Milgram experiments, or assign praise to the subjects of the Isen and Levin experiments who helped pick up papers. And this in turn suggests that we would do well to distinguish explicitly between a threat posed by situationism — that is, (S), the substantive thesis concerning the role of traditional character traits in our behavior—and a threat posed by the situationist *literature*. In other words, even if freedom and responsibility do not appear to be threatened by (S) itself, the experiments that have been taken to support (S) may still raise very real questions for our assumption that we are quite generally free and responsible agents. Once we make this crucial distinction between situation*ism* and the situationist literature that details the experimental results, we are free to see that

different experiments can be troubling for different reasons, even if psychologists have drawn the conclusion that they all support situationism. Further, we can see that the situationist literature raises important questions for freedom and responsibility whether the truth of (S) is ultimately borne out or not.

The Fundamental Attribution Error

Another route from the situationist literature to the apparent undermining of freedom and responsibility that looks tempting is through the FAE. On this view, to act freely and responsibly requires self-knowledge, and the FAE shows that we lack it in a fundamental way.

I think that there is an important insight here. But interestingly, the FAE turns out not to be essential to it. The reason is that although we regularly use characterological explanations for the behavior of other people, we much more frequently use situational factors to explain our own behavior. A variety of studies reveal that actors tend to offer fewer dispositional explanations for their behavior than observers. For example, Nisbett and colleagues conducted a study in which they asked subjects why they chose their college major and why they dated the person they did. Subjects tended to explain their own choices in situational terms (e.g., "I date her because she's a very warm person."). On the other hand, observers tended to explain subjects' choices in terms of subjects' dispositions (e.g., "He dates her because he's very dependent and needs a nonthreatening girlfriend.") And there are natural theories to explain this asymmetry. As Nisbett and Ross put it, "when we observe another person, an actor, it is the actor who is 'figure' and the situation that is 'ground.'" In contrast, for the actor, the situation is presumably "figure" against the "ground" of oneself. So it seems that we do not make the FAE as often when it comes to ourselves.

Still, the situationist literature contains evidence that we lack self-knowledge. For example, in the debriefings of studies by Latané and Darley and Latané and Rodin, like those described earlier on group effects, subjects systematically deny that the presence of others had an effect on their actions, even though the overall statistical picture seems to undermine the claims of at least some subjects.

There is also indirect evidence of a lack of self-knowledge provided by cases like the Milgram experiments in which, as we saw earlier, people who were asked to predict the behavior of subjects in the experiments radically underestimated the number of people who would "shock" their fellow subjects. Since the subjects themselves were not obviously different in relevant ways from those making the predictions, it is not too great a leap to suppose that many would not have predicted their own behavior in the experimental situation. And this in turn suggests some sort of lack of self-knowledge, as well.

Importantly, then, there *is* a reason to worry about self-knowledge, but not primarily because of its support for either situationism or the FAE. Many situationist cases are troubling, not because they purport to show that we mistakenly attribute our actions to our characters when they really depend on situational factors, but because they seem to show that we *mis*identify the particular situational factors that really bring about our actions. What we need to do, I believe, is distinguish between the FAE and problems of self-knowledge—and even knowledge more generally.

Having made these key distinctions, we can see that some of the experiments do seem worrisome because they indicate a lack of self-knowledge.

IV. THE SITUATIONIST EXPERIMENTS AND REASONS-RESPONSIVENESS

One way of seeing the situationist cases—or at least some of them—as troubling is this: simply put, the subjects seem to be acting for bad reasons, or at least not acting for good reasons, and they seem stuck doing so. At the same time, having the ability to act for good reasons is essential to freedom and/or responsibility. In the dime and the phone booth case, it would be nice if the subjects acted primarily because they picked up on a stranger's need for help, the lack of sacrifice on their part that would be required to help, and so on. Acting because of a mood boost is not as appealing. With more at stake, but in a similar way, the subjects in Milgram's experiments seem not to be acting for good reasons. Perhaps they are acting out of a desire to please the experimenter. Whatever the case, it seems that they are not acting for good reasons.

The idea is that the experimental results threaten our attributions of freedom and responsibility because they suggest that we aren't—and are perhaps systematically blocked from—responding to good reasons. So an account of responsibility that requires the capacity to act for good reasons gains support from reflection on the experiments.

Fischer and Ravizza, for example, suggest that responsibility should be understood, at least in part, in terms of what they call "moderate reasons-responsiveness," which is, in turn, understood as acting on a mechanism that is both sensitive to reasons and can translate those reasons into actions. In particular,

(FR) In order to be morally responsible, an agent must "act on a mechanism that is regularly receptive to reasons, some of which are moral reasons, and at least weakly reactive to reason."

Particular experimental results may be threatening in different ways. But ultimately, many of them seem problematic because the subjects in them don't seem to be acting for good reasons, or at least their behavior raises a question about whether they are. And further, the way in which the subjects seem to proceed raises a question about whether they *can* act for good reasons—in some important sense of "can."

Thinking of a lack of reasons-responsiveness as providing a fundamental threat from the situationist literature allows for a unifying explanation of at least some of our responses to the experiments. It can also help explain the temptation of some of the other suggestions we have canvassed.

For example, knowing about one's own motives can be seen as one kind of knowledge needed to respond well to reasons. Other sorts of knowledge, too, other than self-knowledge are crucial, and might be thought to be missing in some of the situationist experiments. For example, do the seminarians simply not *see* the person slumped in the doorway? Does the observation not register as a morally salient piece of information? If so, then this suggests that the situationist experiments call into question knowledge of a variety of kinds and even perhaps the ability to acquire them that is essential to having the ability to respond to reasons.

Second, return to the question of self-control. While the situationist experiments do not obviously suggest a wide-scale epidemic of intense temptations to act against our better judgment, they might suggest that we have trouble translating our commitments into actions. And this can be accommodated by reasons-responsive views, as well. For the problem can be seen as a problem in applying our correct conception of general moral—and

other—principles to particular situations. While it seems so obvious to observers that subjects in Milgram's experiments should not "shock" their fellow subjects to the point of heart failure, we have good reason to think that were some group of those observers actually in the situation, they would most likely act in ways very different from their predictions about others. It seems then that for many there is a failure to apply their general commitments in the particular situation.

Finally, return to robust character traits. It may be that we usually expect free and responsible people to act from character (or at least to act with that ability). And this general, and perhaps defeasible, expectation can be explained as follows: we expect that if we have the ability to act from good reasons, those reasons should hang together in a way that might resemble the endorsement of character traits. For example, acting for good reasons in the Stanford Prison Experiment might require recognizing that there is a need to stand up for what is right in order to save people unnecessary pain. If one adopts this as a general reason for action, then one might naturally endorse acting from both bravery and compassion.

V. WHERE WE ARE

First, let me summarize some modest conclusions as to how the situationist literature should affect our thinking about freedom and responsibility. Distinguishing between situationism and the situationist literature, and between the FAE and self knowledge (and knowledge generally), is liberating in an important way. It allows us to see different experiments as threatening to freedom and responsibility for different reasons. One ultimate reason the situationist literature appears to undermine freedom and responsibility is that the experiments challenge the idea that we can control our actions on the basis of good reasons.

Now what should we conclude about whether we really are free and responsible? Fortunately—or unfortunately, depending on your point of view—there is no simple answer to this question. Since situationism does not provide a monolithic threat to either freedom or responsibility, we do not face global skepticism when we explore the situationist literature. At the same time, the situationist experiments raise serious questions about whether we are free and responsible, albeit questions that ultimately must be answered on a case-by-case basis. In each case, we must look at whether the agent has the normative and other capacities required for freedom and responsibility. For example, does she have the knowledge —of herself and of the salient aspects of the world—to allow her to recognize good reasons, and does she have the capacity to translate those reasons into motives and actions?

Answering these questions is not easy, and depends on filling in both theoretical and empirical gaps in our understanding. What is it to have the relevant capacities, for example? And what exactly is the state of particular agents? Consider the subjects of the Isen and Levin experiments, for example. Perhaps the mood boost that results from finding a dime actually serves to enhance the capacity to recognize and respond to good reasons for acting, in which case those who helped may very

well be responsible. We are not forced by the evidence to see the mood boost as circumventing one's reason-seeking capacities. Similarly, those who didn't help pick up papers are not necessarily off the hook because they failed to receive a mood boost. Whether they acted with the relevant normative capacities is a question to ask about each subject.

Even more importantly, what is the state of someone like Private England? What knowledge was available to her? Was she deceived in various ways about relevant aspects of her situation? Did her *particular* situation provide some sort of obstacle to the exercise of her capacity to recognize facts like the suffering and humanity of the prisoners or her ability to translate her knowledge into action? The existence of situationist experiments does not provide a blanket answer for these questions. At the same time, the experiments help highlight which specific questions to ask.

In conclusion, then, the situationist literature provides a rich area of exploration for those interested in freedom and responsibility. Interestingly, it does not do so primarily because it is *situationist* in the sense of supporting the substantive thesis about the role of character traits. Rather it is because it makes us wonder whether we really do act on a regular basis with the particular normative, epistemic, and reactive capacities that are central to our identity as free and responsible agents.

THE CONTINUING DEBATE:
Does Recent Psychological Research Undermine
Free Will and Responsibility?

What Is New

Psychological research poses a number of interesting challenges to traditional accounts of free will and moral responsibility. While Doris and Nelkin examine the implications of situationist research, others have been concerned with findings from a variety of neuropsychological studies. Some neuropsychological research indicates that our experience of *conscious willing*—exerting an effort of will to get out of bed or tackle a difficult problem or start an unpleasant task—is illusory. Rather than the conscious willing being the cause of our willed behavior, the actual cause occurs earlier in the brain, without our being conscious of it at all; and the experience of "conscious willing" is merely a signal to our conscious thought that the causal process is now in motion. Though this research and its interpretation remain controversial, it has obvious implications for any theory of free will that relies heavily on our experience of willed choice.

Where to Find More

The major situationist social psychology research includes S. Milgram, "Behavioral Study of Obedience," *Journal of Abnormal and Social Psychology*, volume 67 (1963); J. M. Darley and C. D. Batson, "'From Jerusalem to Jericho': A Study of Situational and Dispositional Variables in Helping Behavior," *Journal of Personality and Social Psychology*, volume 27 (1973); A. Isen and P. Levin, "Effect of Feeling Good on Helping: Cookies and Kindness," *Journal of Personality and Social Psychology*, volume 21 (1972); G. Blevins and T. Murphy, "Feeling Good and Helping: Further Phone Booth Findings," *Psychological Reports*, volume 34 (1974); R. Baron and M. Bronfen, "A Whiff of Reality: Empirical Evidence Concerning the Effects of Pleasant Fragrances on Work-Related Behavior," *Journal of Applied Social Psychology*, volume 24 (1994): 1179–1203; R. Nisbet and L. Ross, *The Person and the Situation: Perspectives of Social Psychology* (New York: McGraw-Hill, 1991). An early review of situationist research is available in G. Allport, "Traits Revisited," *American Psychologist*, volume 21 (1966): 1–10. For more recent work on the Milgram experiment, see T. Blass, editor, *Obedience to Authority: Current Perspectives on the Milgram Paradigm* (Mahwah, N.J.: Erlbaum, 2000). Recent psychological work that looks favorably on character traits includes A. Colby, J. B. James and D. Hart (editors), *Competence and Character Through Life* (Chicago: University of Chicago Press, 1998); and N. Emler, "Moral Character," in V. J. Derlega and B. A. Winstead (editors), *Personality: Contemporary Theory and Research*, 2nd edition, pp. 376–404 (Chicago: Nelson-Hall, 1999).

Gilbert Harman examines the philosophical and ethical implications of situationist psychology in "Moral Philosophy Meets Social Psychology: Virtue Ethics and the Fundamental Attribution Error," *Proceedings of the Aristotelian Society*, volume 99 (1999): 315–332. Among the many responses to Harman is James Montmarquet, "Moral Character and Social Science Research," *Philosophy*, volume 78 (2003): 355–368; and Nafsika Athanassoulis, in "A Response to Harman: Virtue Ethics and

Character Traits," *Proceedings of the Aristotelian Society*, volume 100 (2000): 216–221. Harman responds to Athanassoulis in "The Nonexistence of Character Traits," *Proceedings of the Aristotelian Society*, volume 100 (2000): 223–226.

A book by neuropsychologist Daniel M. Wegner—*The Illusion of Conscious Will* (Cambridge, Mass.: Bradford Books, 2002)—examines decades of neuropsychological research, and its often surprising and perhaps disturbing impact on traditional belief in free will. Daniel C. Dennett critiques some of this work in *Freedom Evolves* (New York: Viking, 2003). *The Volitional Brain: Towards a Neuroscience of Free Will*, edited by Benjamin Libet, Anthony Freeman, and Keith Sutherland (Thorverton, Exeter: Imprint Academic, 1999) is an excellent collection of essays on the implications of contemporary neuroscience for questions of free will. Another good anthology is by Sabine Maasen, Wolfgang Prinz, and Gerhard Roth, editors, *Voluntary Action: Brains, Minds, and Sociality* (Oxford: Oxford University Press, 2003). Antonio D'Amasio is a distinguished neuropsychologist who has written some fascinating and very accessible books on the implications of neuropsychological research for a variety of philosophical questions; see *Descartes' Error: Emotion, Reason, and the Human Brain* (New York: G. P. Putnam's Sons, 1994), and *Looking for Spinoza: Joy, Sorrow, and the Feeling Brain* (Orlando: Harcourt, 2003). Martin E. P. Seligman has raised some important questions about the subtle undermining of free choice and free will by environmental influences; see his classic *Helplessness: On Depression, Development, and Death* (New York: W. H. Freeman, 1975).

See also the suggested readings following debates 7 and 9.

9 ARE WE MORALLY RESPONSIBLE FOR WHAT WE DO?

Moral Responsibility Makes Sense

ADVOCATE: Daniel C. Dennett, Austin B. Fletcher Professor of Philosophy and Director of the Center for Cognitive Studies, Tufts University; author of *Darwin's Dangerous Idea* (New York: Simon & Schuster, 1995), *Elbow Room* (Cambridge, Mass.: The MIT Press, 1984), and many other works.

SOURCE: *Freedom Evolves* (New York: Viking, 2003).

Moral Responsibility Is Ultimately Unjustified

ADVOCATE: Saul Smilansky, Professor of Philosophy, University of Haifa; author of *Free Will and Illusion* (Oxford: Oxford University Press, 2000).

SOURCE: "Compatibilism: The Argument from Shallowness," *Philosophical Studies*, volume 115, 2003: 257–282.

Patricia Hearst—a college student who was the daughter of a wealthy newspaper publisher, William Randolph Hearst—was kidnapped from her apartment by members of a radical group, the Symbionese Liberation Army. She was threatened and brainwashed over a period of several months, and ultimately this caused her to become a member of the group and adopt their views. Over the following months she participated in armed robberies, at one point firing an automatic weapon into the front of a store. Although she had numerous opportunities to escape, she chose to stay with the group and join in their cause. Ultimately most of the group was killed, and Patricia Hearst was arrested. She was charged with several counts of armed robbery and placed on trial. She was found guilty, and spent several years in prison. Apparently she *chose* to participate in the robberies, she *willingly* stayed with the group. However, she certainly did not volunteer to be kidnapped, and she had no control over the brainwashing process that converted her to the Symbionese Liberation Army cause. Did Patricia Hearst *justly deserve* to be imprisoned? Was she *morally responsible* for the crimes she helped commit?

The debate over moral responsibility has a long history in theology and law, as well as in philosophy, and the controversy continues. The contemporary philosopher, Thomas Nagel, raises strong questions concerning moral responsibility:

> If one cannot be responsible for consequences of one's acts due to factors beyond one's control, or for antecedents of one's acts that are properties of temperament not subject to one's will, or for the circumstances that pose one's moral choices, then how can one be responsible even for the stripped-down acts of the will itself, if *they* are the product of antecedent consequences outside of the will's control?

The area of genuine agency, and therefore of legitimate moral judgment, seems to shrink under this scrutiny to an extensionless point. Everything seems to result from the combined influence of factors, antecedent and posterior to action, that are not within the agent's control. Since he cannot be responsible for them, he cannot be responsible for their results...: "Moral Luck," in *Mortal Questions* (Cambridge: Cambridge University Press, 1979).

In contrast, the mid-20th Century French existentialist, Jean-Paul Sartre, insisted on broad responsibility, extending it far beyond ordinary bounds:

...man being condemned to be free carries the weight of the whole world on his shoulders; he is responsible for the world and for himself as a way of being. We are taking the word "responsibility" in its ordinary sense as "consciousness of being the incontestable author of an event or of an object." In this sense the responsibility of the for-itself is overwhelming since he is the one by whom it happens that there is a world; since he is also the one who makes himself be, then whatever may be the situation in which he finds himself, the for-itself must wholly assume this situation with its peculiar coefficient of adversity, even though it be insupportable. He must assume the situation with the proud consciousness of being the author of it, for the very worst disadvantages or the worst threats which can endanger my person have meaning only in and through my project; and it is on the ground of the engagement which I am that they appear. It is therefore senseless to think of complaining since nothing foreign has decided what we feel, what we live, or what we are. "Being and Doing: Freedom," from *Being and Nothingness*, trans by H. E. Barnes (New York: Philosophical Library, 1956).

The dispute between Daniel Dennett and Saul Smilansky is a dispute between philosophers who agree on many points. Both are determinists; or rather, both are *naturalists*. That is, they may allow for quantum indeterminacy at the subatomic level, but they insist that the phenomena we observe and experience can be explained naturalistically, without appeal to miracles or mysteries. Furthermore, both believe that determinism/naturalism is compatible with free will. However, while Dennett champions the standard *compatibilist* view that determinism is compatible with both free will *and* moral responsibility, Smilansky argues that determinism is compatible with free will and responsibility but *in*compatible with *ultimate* moral responsibility.

The sort of responsibility that is in dispute is *moral* responsibility; that is, the concept of responsibility that would justify reward and punishment, that would provide good grounds for the justice of blaming and praising, and would serve as a foundation for the *fairness* of treating people in radically different ways: giving some special beneficial rewards, while subjecting others to harmful punitive measures. There are other meanings of responsibility that must be carefully distinguished from the *moral* responsibility of just deserts. We might say that Hurricane Katrina was *causally responsible* for enormous destruction on the Gulf Coast, though there is no question of a hurricane being *morally* responsible. Likewise, Albert can be causally responsible for the crash without being morally responsible (for example, if he suffered a severe stroke or heart attack while he was driving). Another important sense of responsibility, role-responsibility, was described by H. L. A. Hart. Jane has *role*-responsibility for leading her philosophy seminar next week: she has agreed to and accepted that important responsibility. If she does an excellent job, then she has done well in her role-responsibility; but that is quite different from being *morally* responsible and justly deserving praise and reward for her outstanding efforts. After all, we might dispute her moral responsibility while agreeing that she did splendidly in her role-responsibility: "Jane performed her role very well, true enough; but she deserves no special credit for the superb outcome; after all, her mother is a brilliant philosopher, and she coached Jane all week in exactly what to say." Or we might agree that Jane was wonderfully role-responsible, but deny that she is *morally* responsible: "Jane did great, true enough; but she was just lucky, because she has the philosophy gene, she inherited it from her mother, and anyone lucky enough to have the philosophy gene can run great philosophy seminars; Jane no more deserves special reward for her splendid philosophical abilities than Harshad deserves special reward for being handsome. In both cases, it's just genetic good luck." Of course, someone might dispute the claim that Jane is not morally responsible, as well as role-responsible. But since there *is* a question to dispute—we agree that Jane is role-responsible, but there is controversy concerning her moral responsibility—it is obvious that the two senses of responsibility are distinct. Whether *moral* responsibility can be justified (and whether it is worth trying to save) is the basic issue between Dennett and Smilansky.

POINTS TO PONDER

➤ Daniel Dennett confidently asserts that "ought implies can": that I cannot have an *obligation* to do something that I *cannot* do. But is that slogan correct? My friend Rachel is in the hospital, and needs cheering up, and I *ought* to go visit her. However, I have a profound fear of hospitals, and I *cannot* bring myself to enter the building. Is this a counterexample to the principle of "ought implies can"?

➤ Dennett suggests that when people *agree* that they are just targets of punishment—when they assert a *right* to be punished—that is good reason to suppose that they are morally responsible and genuinely deserving of punishment. Do you agree?

➤ Saul Smilansky distinguishes the *compatibilist* level of freedom and control from the *ultimate* level, and he claims that looking deeply we recognize that compatibilism is ethically *shallow* and basically *unfair*. However, Smilansky also claims that "compatibilism captures much of fairness and justice." Can those claims be reconciled?

➤ Smilansky states that "we often want a person to blame himself, feel guilty, and even see that he deserves to be punished." Dennett would certainly agree. So where do their views divide?

Moral Responsibility Makes Sense

Daniel C. Dennett

THE FUTURE OF HUMAN FREEDOM

Where will it all end? There is no more potent source of anxiety about free will than the image of the physical sciences engulfing our every deed, good or bad, in the acid broth of causal explanation, nibbling away at the soul until there is nothing left to praise or blame, to honor, respect, or love. Or so it seems to many people. And so they try to erect one barrier or another, some absolutist doctrine designed to keep these corrosive ideas at bay. This is a doomed strategy, a relic from the last millennium. Thanks to our growing understanding of nature, we have learned that such bastions only postpone catastrophe, and often make it worse. If you want to live on the beach, you had better be prepared to move when the beach shifts, as beaches do, slowly but surely. Breakwaters can "save" the shoreline only by destroying some of the features that made the shoreline such a fine place to live in the first place. The wiser move is to study the situation and then agree on some guidelines about how close to the edge is too close to build a house. But times change, and policies that made sense for decades or centuries can become obsolete and need revision. It is often said that we have to work with nature, not against it, but of course this is just the rhetoric of moderation; every human artifice thwarts or redirects some trend of nature; the trick is to figure out enough about how nature's patterns are put together so that our interference in them will achieve the results we want.

HOLDING THE LINE AGAINST CREEPING EXCULPATION

As we learn more and more about how people make up their minds, the assumptions underlying our institutions of praise and blame, punishment and treatment, education and medication will have to adjust to honor the facts as we know them, for one thing is clear: Institutions and practices based on obvious falsehoods are too brittle to trust. Few people will be willing to wager their futures on a fragile myth that they themselves can see the cracks in. In fact, our attitudes on these matters have been shifting gradually over the centuries. We now uncontroversially exculpate or mitigate in many cases that our ancestors would have dealt with much more harshly. Is this progress or are we all going soft on sin? To the fearful, this revision looks like erosion, and to the hopeful it looks like growing enlightenment, but there is also a neutral perspective from which to view the process. It looks to an evolutionist like a rolling equilibrium, never quiet for long, the relatively stable outcome of a series of innovations and counter-innovations, adjustments and meta-adjustments, an arms race that generates at least one sort of progress: growing self-knowledge, growing sophistication about who we are and what we are, and what we can and cannot do. And from this self-understanding, we fashion and refashion our conclusions about what we ought to do.

What, in fact, are the qualifications for being a genuinely culpable miscreant, and could anybody actually meet them? Nobody's perfect, and besides, a perfect *miscreant* is a concept in danger of self-contradiction, a point that has been appreciated since Socrates. Doesn't there have to be *something* amiss in anybody who sets out knowingly to do evil? How shall we draw the line between exculpatory pathology of various sorts—he didn't know, he couldn't control himself—and people who do evil "of their own free will," knowing what they are doing? If we set the threshold too high, everybody gets off the hook; if we set it too low, we end up punishing scapegoats. The various libertarian proposals aimed at this problem land wide of the target: Frankly mysterious agent causation, quantum indeterminacy in the faculty of practical reason, moral levitation performed by immaterial souls or other spectral puppeteers—at best these doctrines cajole us into diverting our attention from a difficult puzzle and fixating on a conveniently insoluble mystery. So let's return to the problem: How *do* we draw the line, and what keeps it from retreating in the face of all the pressure from science?

Imagine trying to devise an aptitude test that would measure the flexibility of mind, general knowledge, social comprehension, and impulse-control that are arguably the minimal requirements of moral agency. Such a test could operationalize the ideal implied by our tacit understanding of responsibility: Normal adults have it, and you either have it or you don't. We could design it to have a "ceiling effect": You can't get more than 100 out of 100 points, and most people get 100. (We have no legitimate interest in differences in competence above the threshold. Unimaginative Smith may not have known what he was doing quite as clearly as his accomplice, brilliant Jones, but Smith knew quite well enough to be held accountable.) The rationale for such a policy is clear and familiar, and it seems to work well in such simple applications as automobile driver's licenses. You have to be sixteen (or fifteen, or seventeen…) and you have to pass a test of aptitude and knowledge of the rules. Thereafter, you are given the freedom of the road and treated as equal to any other driver. Such a policy can then be adjusted as we learn more about its effects on highway safety; nighttime restrictions, apprenticeship periods, exceptions for identifiable disabilities or other special circumstances can be considered in a cost-benefit trade-off between maximizing safety and maximizing freedom.

Just such a balancing process can also be discerned to be operating in the debates over grounds for exculpation or mitigation of responsibility in general. As we learn more about patterns of relative disability and their effects, we discover grounds for relocating individuals relative to the threshold, usually but not always in the direction of exculpating some class of people heretofore seen as clearly culpable. This creates the appearance of an ever-retreating threshold, but we need to examine that appearance more dispassionately. It is quite possible for us to make major revisions in our policies about whom we incarcerate and whom we treat, for instance, without any revision in our philosophical background assumptions. After all, we don't change our concepts of guilt and innocence when we discover that some individual in prison was falsely convicted. We remove that unfortunate person from the set of those deemed guilty, but we don't change the criterion for set membership. It is precisely because we adhere to our standard understanding of the concept of guilt that we recognize that this person is not guilty after all. Similarly, on the strength of new evidence a *category* of individuals could be removed from the set of those deemed responsible without any change—in particular, without any "erosion"—of our concept of moral responsibility. We would just learn that there were fewer morally responsible people in our society than we had heretofore supposed.

The anxious mantra returns: "But where will it all end?" Aren't we headed toward a 100 percent "medicalized" society in which nobody is responsible, and everybody is a victim of one unfortunate feature of their background or another (nature or nurture)? No, we are not, because there are forces—not mysterious metaphysical forces, but readily explainable social and political forces—that oppose this trend, and they are of the same sort, really, as the forces that prevent the driving age from rising to, say, thirty! People *want* to be held accountable. The benefits that accrue to one who is a citizen in good standing in a free society are so widely and deeply appreciated that there is always a potent presumption in favor of inclusion. Blame is the price we pay for credit, and we pay it gladly under most circumstances. We pay dearly, accepting punishment and public humiliation for a chance to get back in the game after we have been caught out in some transgression. And so the best strategy for holding the line against creeping exculpation is clear: Protect and enhance the value of the games one gets to play if one is a citizen in good standing. It is erosion of these benefits, not the onward march of the human and biological sciences, that would threaten the social equilibrium.

Since there will always be strong temptations to make yourself really small, to externalize the causes of your actions and deny responsibility, the way to counteract these is to make people an offer they can't refuse: If you want to be free, you must *take* responsibility. But what about the poor slobs who just can't hold their lives together, whose ability to resist temptation is so impaired that they are well-nigh certain to live a life of transgression and punishment? Isn't this unfair to them, a coercive offer that only masquerades as a free choice? They can't really hold up their end of the bargain, and then they get punished. They make useful scapegoats, perhaps, since the example we set with them keeps vivid the anticipation of punishment that actually deters those with slightly more self-control, but isn't this obviously unjustifiable? After all, "they couldn't do otherwise." There is a sense of this well-worn phrase that belongs in this context, but it is not the sense that incompatibilists worry about, as we shall see.

The dynamics of the process of negotiated thresholds is perhaps most visible in the extreme cases that occasionally come before the public. What should we do, for instance, about convicted pedophiles? The recidivism rate is appalling—you really can't teach these old dogs new tricks, apparently—and the harm they can do if allowed their freedom is even more appalling. There is, however, a treatment that studies have shown to be effective in endowing pedophiles with the self-control that would render them safe enough to return to society (under some further supervision): castration. A dire remedy for a dire condition. Can it be justified? Is it "cruel and unusual punishment"? It is important that many convicted pedophiles volunteer for castration, as a vastly preferable alternative to indefinite incarceration. (One hears less complaint about the cruel and unusual punishment of releasing a sex offender into a community of quite appropriately terrified and outraged citizens bent on forming vigilante groups to hound the dangerous individual out of town.) The issue is far from resolved and is complicated by many factors. Castration achieves its main effect by stopping the flow of testosterone into the body, and this can be done chemically or surgically. Chemical castration requires repeated injections and is in general reversible, but the drugs have some bad side effects; surgical castration is not readily reversible in one regard, but its main effect on behavior can be sidestepped by self-administering testosterone—if one really wants to. But why would one want to do this?

The symbolic effect of castration is obviously part of what makes the issue so highly charged. If the surgical removal of, say, the appendix, had as dramatic effect on the self-control of those who underwent the treatment, it is hard to believe there would be as much vehemence in the opposition to this option. I know from experience that discussing this issue in this context is going to make some readers' heads swim. "He ends up advocating castration!" No, I have raised the policy as a serious alternative but expressed no opinion on its ultimate wisdom. After all, there may well be some better, and less dire, treatment just around the corner. Moreover, suppose for the sake of argument that the recidivism rate for pedophiles is 50 percent (not far off the mark), and suppose that many pedophiles voluntarily undergo castration as the price they are willing to pay for freedom. Roughly half of those will be "unnecessary" castrations: They wouldn't have re-offended in any case. The problem is that we can't identify them (now) in advance. But presumably with growing knowledge this will improve. What should we do in the meantime? There are compelling reasons for shunning castration, and compelling reasons for advocating it. I am using castration as an example, and inviting readers to reflect on how strong they find the urge to respond to such an "unspeakable" proposal by turning off their minds and turning up the volume on their "hearts." This is part of the problem. So sure are some

people that they are being invited onto a buttered slide to perdition that they just can't let themselves think about such issues. Philosophers are supposed to be above such pressures, dispassionate contemplators of every conceivable option, insulated in their ivory towers, but that is a myth. In fact, philosophers rather relish the role of early warning scouts, heading off a dimly imagined catastrophe before it gets a chance to come into focus.

Castration is a useful example, since it exposes inconsistencies in the thinking of advocates on both sides. There are those who eagerly seek prescription drugs for themselves to help them keep to their diets or control blood pressure that they cannot make themselves control through proper exercise, while denying all such high-tech crutches to boost or supplement the willpower of those with other temptations. If it is rational, and responsible, for them to recognize their own weaknesses and take whatever steps are currently available to heighten their own self-control, how can they disparage the same policies in others? The new gastric bypass surgery that seems to be a major breakthrough for some cases of chronic obesity caused by obsessive eating is a drastic measure, but the ambient opinion *today* in many quarters is that seriously overweight people who *resist* having the operation are being irresponsible. This may well change as we learn more about the long-term effects, both on the obsessive eaters and on the surrounding society and its attitudes. Such attitudes play a powerful role in setting the conditions in which free choices are made. For instance, eating disorders such as bulimia and anorexia nervosa are much less common among women in Muslim countries, in which the physical attractiveness of women plays a muted role relative to Westernized countries. Even minor revisions of societal norms, as Gibbard notes, can have a profound effect on how individuals think about the choices they make, and this is a key feature distinguishing human choice from animal choice.

Suppose you have a big purple spot on your back. This is a biological feature, but probably not a very important psychological feature. Suppose instead that you have a big purple spot on your nose. This is a much greater misfortune, since although both discolorations may be physiologically harmless, the blotch on your nose will no doubt interfere profoundly with your self-image, because it affects how others see you and treat you, and how you react to that treatment, and how they react to those re-actions, and so forth. A purple nose is a huge psychological handicap. Its being such a handicap is, however, something that is itself readily recognizable by many, which can lead to the endorsement of social policies, practices, and attitudes that tend to minimize, or at any rate channel, the ef-fects. What starts out as a superficial bio-logical feature of an organism is turned into a psychological feature and, in turn, be-comes a political feature in the wider world. This sort of thing doesn't happen to any great extent in the animal world. Field ethologists routinely capture and tag the animals they study, to help with re-identifi-cation of individuals over time. Many thousands of birds have lived their lives with a colored band on one leg, and per-haps as many mammals have conducted their affairs with numbered metal tags quite visible on their ears, and so far as any-one can tell, these markers do not interfere seriously with their lives, neither diminish-ing nor enhancing their opportunities. A human being who had to appear in public with a metal tag affixed to one ear would have to make major adjustments in life hopes and plans, and thus there is a politi-cal dimension to any decision, self-imposed or otherwise, to display such a feature.

This sensitivity to social and political reverberations that distinguishes human agency from animal agency also provides the grounds for founding human respon-sibility on something more promising than quantum indeterminacy. The politi-cal negotiations out of which our current practices and presumptions about respon-sibility emerge have nothing to do with determinism or mechanism in general, but do concern the assessment of the in-evitability—or evitability—of particular features of particular agents and types of agents. Can you teach these old dogs new tricks, or not? There is an unproblematic sense in which there can be growth in ability over time in a deterministic world, as well as a widening of opportunities and what is made of them by particular deter-ministic agents. Such increase in ability over time is utterly invisible to the mind-set that adopts the narrow vision of possi-bility enshrined in the definition of deter-minism: "There is at any instant exactly one physically possible future." According to that vision, in a deterministic world, at any time t, nothing *can do* anything other than the one thing it is determined at t to do, and in an indeterministic world, at any time t, a thing *can do* as many differ-ent things—at least two—as that brand of indeterminism allows for, presumably a deep and immutable fact of physics that could not be perturbed by changes in practices or knowledge or technology. The obvious fact that people today *can do* more than people used to be able to do disappears from sight if we can under-stand possibility this way, and yet this fact is as important as it is obvious.

Indeed, failure to deal with the impli-cations of *this* kind of "can" now confronts ethical theorists of every persuasion. One of the few uncontroversial propositions in ethics, deserving its own simple slogan, is "*ought* implies *can*"—you are only obligated to do something you are able to do. If you are frankly unable to do X, then it is not true that you ought to do X. It is sometimes supposed that right here we see the fundamental—and obvious—connection between free will and responsibility: Since we are responsible only for what is *in our power*, and since if determinism is true, we *can* do only whatever we are determined to do, it is never the case that we *ought* to do something else, nothing else ever being in our power. But at the same time, it is even more obvious that the explosive growth of *can-do* in recent human history is rendering obsolete many of our traditional moral notions about determinism or indeterminism. The sense of "can" that has the moral import is not the sense of "can" (if there is one) that depends on indeterminism.

Suppose a competent but diseased adult asked you for assistance in putting his living body into cryogenic suspension of life pending some low-probability discovery of a cure for the disease somewhere down the road. Wouldn't that be assisted suicide? Today, arguably, it is; tomorrow it may be as obviously justifiable as assisting in the administration of anesthesia to somebody about to undergo potentially life-saving surgery. We never used to have to worry about the ethics of cloning, or omnipresent electronic surveillance, or mind-altering drugs used by athletes, or genetic enhancement of embryos, and we have never had to worry much about the prospect of effective prosthetic enhancements of the ability of human agents to control themselves, but as such innovations arise, we need to have in place an understanding of responsibility that is robust enough to accommodate them gracefully.

"THANKS, I NEEDED THAT!"

The key shift in perspective that will enable this is an inversion described by Stephen White in *The Unity of the Self* (1991, Chapter 8, "Moral Responsibility"). Don't try to use metaphysics to ground ethics, he argues; put it the other way around: Use ethics to fix what we should mean by our "metaphysical" criterion. First, show how there can be an internal justification for some agent acquiescing in his own punishment—saying, in effect, "Thanks, I needed that!"—and then use that understanding to anchor and support a reading of our pivotal phrase, *could have done otherwise:* "An agent could have done other than he or she did just in case the ascription of responsibility and blame to that agent for the action in question is justified." In other words, the fact that free will *is* worth wanting can be used to anchor our conception of free will in a way metaphysical myths fail to do. The basic argument is meant to cover all moral praise and blame, but we can simplify the reasoning if we focus on cases of punishment by authority ("the state") as a stand-in for the broader class of cases in which although no *crime* has been committed one individual blames another for a misdeed. In many cases in the broader class, there may be no anticipated punishment other than being scolded—or just resented, thought ill of. We can monitor the generality of the argument by shifting every now and then between a legal setting (the state vs. Jones) and a moral setting (a parent admonishing a child, for instance).

The ideal for an institution of punishment, White argues, would be that every punishment should be justified *in the eyes of the person punished*. This presupposes that agents eligible for punishment are intelligent, rational, knowledgeable enough to be competent judges of the purported justification of that punishment. Their (imagined) acquiescence in their own punishment serves as a reference or pivot point for setting the threshold. Those who are incompetent to make such a judgment are surely not competent to enjoy the freedoms of citizenship without supervision, so we don't blame them (not yet, if they are young children). Those who are competent enough to appreciate the justification, and accept it, are unproblematic instances of culpable miscreants—they say so themselves, and we have no plausible grounds for not taking them at their word. That leaves those who are apparently competent but who resist acquiescence. These are the problem cases, but they are squeezed from both sides: On the one hand, they presumably desire the status of competent citizen, with its many benefits, and on the other hand, they dread the punishment, which they can escape only by declaring themselves—or revealing themselves—to be too small. (If you make yourself really small, you can externalize virtually everything.) White notes, slyly, that even the rational psychopath will have an internal justification for supporting laws that punish psychopaths, since they protect him from other psychopaths and allow him the freedom to pursue his interests as best he can.

Whether or not such a ceremony of justification is actually performed, we can imagine the scenario. Suppose you are the culprit. The state says to you, in effect: "You erred. Tough luck, but for the good of the state you are hereby asked to undergo punishment." You hear the charges, the evidence, the verdict. Let's suppose that you are guilty as charged. (The checks and balances of the system will keep pressure on the state to make its cases well, and you are encouraged to exploit that presumption in your defense.) But now the question is whether you are responsible for the act committed. We *may* frame this as the question "Could you have done otherwise?" but we wouldn't then seek testimony from metaphysicians or quantum physicists. We would seek *specific* evidence of your competence, or extenuating circumstances. Consider, in particular, a defense that cites factors that were beyond your control, factors that were put in place many years before you were born, for instance. These are relevant only insofar as you could not have known about them. If you knew that the ground on which you were building the house had been contaminated by factory refuse a hundred years ago, or *if you should have known*, you cannot cite this as a factor beyond your control. But could you have known? ("Ought" implies "can.") As we come to have greater and greater powers for acquiring knowledge about the factors that play a causal role in our actions, we become increasingly liable for not knowing about factors both external (e.g., the contaminated soil) and internal (e.g., your well-understood obsession with making a quick buck—you should have done something about that!). A defense of "I could not have done otherwise" that would have passed muster in olden days is no longer acceptable. You are obliged by the prevailing attitudes of society to keep up with the latest know-how on all matters over which you wish to exercise some responsibility.

The state invites you to acquiesce in your punishment and, of course, you may not acquiesce, but if the state has done its job right, you ought to. That is, the state can offer you a reason that it can defend without blushing. If you don't get it, that's your problem. If there are lots of folks that don't get it, that's the state's problem; they have set the threshold too low, or in some other way done a bad job framing the laws. How do we handle the penumbra of cases in the real, non-ideal world of people who can't get it, or whose acquiescence is a result of brainwashing or coercion? The existence of a non-empty set of punished culprits who do not competently acquiesce in their own punishment is *inevitable*, but it is not *inevitably large*. In fact, the system of negotiated thresholds has the nice property of being adjustable *over time* to minimize the set of those misclassified. As we learn of miscarriages of justice, we consider them as grounds for revision of our policies, and when we learn of categories of individuals who fall below the currently defended threshold for self-control, we face a political question of the same sort as the question we face about whether to adjust the rules for driver's licenses. And if new technologies (surgery or drugs or treatments or prosthetic devices or educational systems or warning lights or…) can be effective in adjusting the abilities of those who fall short, we will confront the cost-benefit trade-off of whether the good effects outweigh the harm.

Can pedophiles do otherwise? Some can and some can't, and we should consider steps that might be taken to move more of the latter group into the former. Those who can do otherwise are those who, *if* they lapse, would insist on their *right* to be punished. And when they make this claim, we should not prejudge their presumption of competence to make it—although that will be an issue in the trial. But wouldn't the occurrence of a lapse, any lapse, show that after all, they could *not* have done otherwise—at least not on the specific occasion? No. That is an illicit return to the narrow notion of the term "can." We anchor the broader notion to our practices and *hold* such individuals responsible. In the relevant sense, they could have done otherwise.

But, knowing there will almost certainly be some recidivists who do lapse, isn't this just too risky a policy to adopt? Perhaps it is, but this is a political question about how much risk we are prepared to live with, not a philosophical question

about whether pedophiles have some sort of metaphysical free will after all, or even a scientific question about just what makes pedophiles do what they do. As we learn more and more about the conditions—neurochemical, social, genetic—that predispose for pedophilia (and the shifting limits of evitability of these conditions), we will surely shrink the uncertainty, and hence the risk, of releasing such people from confinement, but there will always be risk. The political question is about how much risk we are prepared to tolerate in order to maintain our freedom as a society.

For centuries we've lived by the rule that no one can be punished, or detained, for *being likely to commit a crime*, but for all that time we've been quite aware of the fact that this admirable principle has its risks. What do we do about the heretofore law-abiding citizen who approaches his intended victim with a dangerous weapon? Just when may we intervene? At what point does our fellow citizen forfeit his freedom from interference? Does he have the *right* to a first blow before we can take action against him? As we learn more and more about the probabilities, and the conditions that underlie them, there will be more and more pressure to adjust our admirable principle in the interests of public safety. Notice that we have a host of clever innovations in the law that already serve this purpose—they preserve the admirable principle by creating new crimes for people to commit on their way to their main crime. We make a law that prohibits people from carrying certain dangerous weapons in public, for instance, or that institutes the new crime of conspiracy to commit another crime. It is already a crime for people with certain medical conditions to conceal that fact when they apply for certain high-risk positions. We have ways of putting the burden of knowledge on individuals so that they can make decisions parallel to the dire choice of the pedophile. And—this is the important point—if we maintain the requirement that these innovations must pass the "Thanks, I needed that!" test, we can preserve our institution of responsibility; we can keep the specter of creeping exculpation at bay. Ask yourself: Suppose you *knew* (because of lots of good science) that you suffered from a condition that made you highly likely to injure people in some way unless you submitted to treatment Z, which would make such a calamity much more *evitable*; and suppose undergoing this treatment preserved your competence in (virtually) every way. Would you be willing to undergo the treatment? Would you be in favor of a law that made undergoing the treatment a condition of preserving your freedom? In other words, are you sure that under those conditions you would have a *right* to strike the first blow? You could say, at your trial, "I have a condition, Your Honor; it was outside my control! I couldn't do otherwise," but this would be disingenuous if you knew about the opportunity. What if such a treatment had to be undergone in childhood, before the age of informed consent? Are we prepared to consider the ethical wisdom of such preemptive interventions? What standard of evidence should we require before endorsing such a "public health" measure across the board? (We already have laws mandating inoculation, even though we know to a moral certainty that some children will have bad reactions to them and die or be disabled.) The more we know, the more we can do; the more we can do, the more obligations we face. We may yearn for the good old days when ignorance was a better excuse than it is today, but we cannot turn back the clock.

Presumably everybody has a breaking point; those who happen to encounter their personal breaking point break! How can it be fair to hold them responsible and punish them, just because some *other* person wouldn't have broken if faced with exactly their predicament? Isn't he just the victim of bad luck? And isn't it just your good luck not to have succumbed to temptation or had your weaknesses exploited by some conspiracy of events? Yes, luck figures heavily in our lives, all the time, but since we know this, we take the precautions we deem appropriate to minimize the untoward effects of luck, and then take responsibility for whatever happens.

Moral Responsibility Is Ultimately Unjustified

SAUL SMILANSKY

1. THE FREE WILL PROBLEM AND SOME ALTERNATIVES

In compact form, the free will problem can be presented as the conjunction of two questions:

a. The first question is whether there is libertarian free will, and it can be called the libertarian Coherence/Existence Question. Libertarians think that there is libertarian free will; everyone else disagrees. This question is metaphysical, or ontological, or possibly logical.

b. The second question is whether—if there is no libertarian free will—our situation is still satisfactory. It can be called the Compatibility Question, namely, are moral responsibility and related notions such as desert and justice compatible with determinism (or with the absence of libertarian free will irrespective of determinism)? Compatibilism and hard determinism are the opponents on the Compatibility Question. This question, as we will understand it here, is both ethical and personal-existential.

The traditional positions can be seen clearly from their answers to these questions:

First, *libertarian free will*. We are all, more or less, familiar with the idea of libertarian free will. For our purposes it can be characterized roughly as the ability to control one's action and actually do otherwise in exactly the same situation, with internal and external conditions held constant. People naturally assume that they have libertarian free will, and it has formed the basis of most of the ethical teaching of the Western religions and of major ethical systems such as Kant's. To help us intuitively hook on to it, it is the sort of freedom that determinism would preclude (although indeterminism would also not help and in fact the issue of determinism is not important). Libertarianism of course answers yes to the first question. Typically libertarians are incompatibilists, that is they think that if we did not have libertarian free will we would be in trouble, and there would not be, for example, moral responsibility. But luckily, we do have libertarian free will. In other words, the libertarian is *demanding* but *optimistic*.

Compatibilism is, roughly, the position that the forms of free will most people clearly have to some degree, such as the ability to deliberate and do as they wish, suffice to meet the requirements of morality and personal life insofar as they are affected by the issue of free will. In particular, the compatibilist rejects the idea that some sort of "metaphysical" or "libertarian" notion of free will, such as would be negated by a completely deterministic ontology, is necessary in order to have moral responsibility. Hence, the term "compatibilism": the compatibilist insists that free will, moral responsibility, and their concomitant notions are compatible with determinism (or with the absence of libertarian free will). For example, the compatibilist would claim that most people in the West choose a career with some measure of freedom, and are morally responsible for this choice, although it follows from their desires and beliefs. Lack of relevant freedom would result only from atypical causes eliminating or severely curtailing control (such as pathological compulsion or external coercion). It is important to stress that compatibilism maintains contact with the traditional paradigm requiring control for moral responsibility, and moral responsibility for blameworthiness and desert. Compatibilists maintain that the traditional paradigm can be sustained even in a deterministic world, and does not require libertarian free will. On the *compatibilist level* of deliberating, choosing, and acting, most people are basically free, such matters are within their control, and it is this that matters. The compatibilist is *non-demanding* and hence *optimistic*.

Hard determinism, despite its misleading name, is not only a position on determinism or on the existence of libertarian free will (although it is of course that as well). It is the opponent of compatibilism, which is sometimes called "soft-determinism," on the second question. In other words, hard determinism is a normative position according to which, given that there is no libertarian free will in the world, moral responsibility and desert are impossible. Libertarian free will is required, but does not exist. The hard determinist is the pessimist in our cast of characters: she agrees with the libertarian that compatibilist free will is insufficient and that we require libertarian free will; hence, both are incompatibilists. But, like the compatibilist, the hard determinist believes that libertarian free will does not exist. Consider again the example of the person who chose his career freely according to the compatibilist: the hard determinist would claim that on the *ultimate level* the career-choice was not up to the person, who could not in the end form the sources of his motivation. These sources, the hard

determinist will emphasise, are the basis for his "free" choice on the compatibilist level. In certain cases—such as the man choosing a criminal career—this absence of ultimate control is what matters, and eliminates moral responsibility. The hard determinist is *demanding* and *pessimistic*.

2. FUNDAMENTAL DUALISM ON FREE WILL—AND THE LIMITED VALIDITY OF COMPATIBILISM

A complex recent alternative that I have proposed provides the basis for understanding free will-related matters: Fundamental Dualism. This position incorporates two elements, corresponding to the two basic questions that, as we saw above, make up the free will problem:

a. The rejection of libertarian free will.

b. The attempt to *combine* the insights of both compatibilism and hard determinism.

In its answer to the first question, the Fundamental Dualism is at one with compatibilism and hard determinism. We shall assume the absence of libertarian free will in this discussion, for our concern lies with the answer to the second, Compatibility Question, which asks about the implications of this absence.

The second, and for us more significant element of the Fundamental Dualism is its dualism—the combination of compatibilism and hard determinism. This dual perspective can be explored concerning various matters: morality, desert, justice, self-respect, and so on. We shall see it emerging in the various spheres where the shallowness of compatibilism will be demonstrated. Initially, I shall explain the dualism by considering moral responsibility, blameworthiness and justice.

The free will problem is about control: it issues from the core normative intuition that we must take human agency, control and its absence very seriously, particularly when judging ourselves and others. To punish a person for an act that he did not commit is a paradigm of injustice: control is a condition for moral responsibility, moral responsibility is a condition for blameworthiness, and blameworthiness is a condition for just punishment. The absence of control precludes guilt and blameworthiness, and hence punishment would be manifestly unjust. Control is also crucial for our self-evaluative and reactive attitudes, even beyond morality, as we shall see later on.

It turns out, however, that the pertinent forms of control are fundamentally *dualistic*: on the one hand, we need to take seriously distinctions in local compatibilist control, if we are to treat people as we ought. Questions about the existence of control, as well as about degrees of control, make sense and are morally and personally central. On the compatibilist level we take the person as a "given," and ask about his or her control in pedestrian ways: did he willingly do X? Was he coerced? Was he under some uncontrollable psychological compulsion? Most people most of the time do have compatibilist control over their actions, even if there is no libertarian free will (say, if determinism applies to all human actions). The kleptomaniac or alcoholic are not in control of their pertinent actions in the way that, respectively, the common thief or occasional mild drinker are in control, irrespective of determinism. And this often matters. If we are to respect persons, we need to establish and maintain a social order and human relationships that broadly follow the compatibilist distinctions in terms of local control.

But we can ask the question about control also on the ultimate level. Given that there is no libertarian free will, asking about "ultimate control" lands us with the hard determinist conclusion, where ultimately there can be no control. Any person whom we could agree was on the compatibilist level free (that is, could reflect on his options, decide to do what he wanted, was not coerced, etc.) would be seen in a new light: under the ultimate perspective, the sources of his character and motivation would also be queried. And if we have no libertarian free will, then ultimately we are just "given," with our desires and beliefs, and any change in them is ultimately down to our earlier selves, which we ultimately cannot control. We are what we are, and from the ultimate perspective, with all our compatibilist choosing and doing, we operate as we were molded.

Compatibilist Justice is the sort of justice which exists when we follow compatibilist distinctions in terms of local control: in other words, when the pertinent results of the social order suffered and enjoyed by persons, reflect their free choices (on the compatibilist level). For instance, those who choose to keep to the law will be safe, while those breaking it may be punished. Ultimate Injustice is the sort of injustice that, I claim, may follow when we do not take account of the absence of ultimate control, and follow Compatibilist Justice. Such injustice occurs, for example, when we punish the compatibilistically-guilty. We may well morally need to do so, overall, and as we noted doing so along compatibilist lines is just in a way that, say, punishment based on factors beyond people's control such as race would not be—because (compatibilist level) control and its absence is not being respected. But we must not hide from ourselves the (ultimate level) injustice that following Compatibilist Justice would involve.

In my view we have to take account of both valid perspectives on control, the compatibilist and the ultimate hard determinist, for they are each part of the complex truth on the free will problem. Hence a Fundamental Dualism encompassing both perspectives. In sum, many of the practices of a community based on such compatibilist distinctions, a Community of Responsibility, would be *in one way* unjust, owing to the absence of libertarian free will which implies that our actions are on the ultimate level not up to us, and that to hold us responsible for them is therefore morally arbitrary. Nevertheless, working according to such distinctions might be just *in another way*, because they correspond to a sense of being up to us, existing to some degree in specific cases— and which in cases such as kleptomania would not be applicable, and therefore it would be an injustice to treat in the same way. To *fail* to create a Community of Responsibility is also in one sense to fail to create a feasible non-arbitrary moral order, hence to fail in the proper respect for persons. There is a basis for working with compatibilist level control, even though we lack the sort of deep grounding in the "ultimately guilty self" that libertarian free will was thought to provide. Moreover, we are required by the core intuitions pertaining to free will to work in this way. But doing so has often a "hard determinist" moral price. We must recognize both the frequent need to be compatibilists and the need to confront that price. Both compatibilist control and ultimate-level arbitrariness and lack of control are morally relevant. The intuitive power of the requirement for control manifests itself in dual ways. *We see why the Community of Responsibility is deeply (non-consequentially) morally imperative, and why its results are deeply morally disturbing.*

Now, the immediate reaction of both compatibilists and hard determinists to such a dualistic account is likely to involve an attempt to discredit the other side's portion. "Ultimate" injustice does not matter, the compatibilist might say, after all: you yourself tend to admit that we can distinguish between the guilty and innocent, and meet common intuitions about the way to treat various cases. Why care about "ultimate fantasies" when people can have control of their lives, reform and even partially create themselves, and behave responsibly? The hard determinist is likely to attack me from the other side, saying that all talk about moral distinctions and about desert is groundless—do I not myself admit that any person, even the manifestly guilty in the compatibilist's eyes, is not ultimately responsible for being whoever he happens to be, and for the actions which result from this? What sort of control is it that is merely an unfolding of pre-set factors?

Both sets of arguments have some strength, which is why I think that any "monistic" position is inadequate. However, once we make the conscious attempt to rid our minds of the assumption that either compatibilism or hard determinism must be exhaustively true (as there is no libertarian free will), we begin to see that there are aspects of the compatibilist case that the hard determinist cannot plausibly deny, and likewise with the hard determinist case. Since people tend to be immediately inclined in one way or the other, each reader will have to work on himself or herself *in order to see* the side he or she is blind to. One has to try to conquer one's blind side, and try to grasp how it is to inhabit it.

However deeply we might feel that all people are ultimately innocent, it is unconvincing to deny the difference between the control possessed by the common thief and that of the kleptomaniac, and to ignore the moral inadequacy of social institutions that would fail to take account of this difference. We have an intimate experience of control (or its lack). If a man believes that he is Napoleon then he is deluded, and his belief is *false*. But a woman's belief that her decision to see a movie and not a play is up to her is, even in a deterministic world, well founded on the compatibilist level. She did not ultimately create the sources of her motivation, and this hard determinist insight is sometimes important, but her sense of local control is *not* illusory, although it is only part of the truth about her state. Irrespective of the absence of libertarian free will, the kleptomaniac is simply not in a condition for membership in a Community of Responsibility of which most people, having the required control, *can be*, and *would want to be* members.

The hard determinist is right to say that any punishment is in some sense unjust, but wrong when she denies that some punishments are more unjust than others because of the issue of compatibilist control. The eradication of free will-related distinctions does not make the hard determinist more humane and compassionate, but morally blind and a danger to the conditions for a civilised, sensitive moral environment. The same distinctions also apply to individual acts: there is a sense in which you may be properly blamed for not coming to class if you did not feel like coming and did not overcome this urge, but not if you were abducted (unless being abducted resulted from factors under your control). To blame a person who was abducted would be barbarous. The realisation of the absence of libertarian free will does not erase all these moral distinctions. We must take account of them and maintain the Community of Responsibility, in order to respect persons. An order not taking account of the compatibilist level distinctions is morally monstrous and inhuman.

Similarly, once we grant the compatibilist that his distinctions have *some* foundation and are partially morally required, there is no further reason to go the *whole* way with him, to claim that the absence of libertarian free will is of no great moral significance, and to deny the fact that without libertarian free will even a vicious and compatibilistically-free criminal who is being punished is in some important sense a victim of his circumstances. If we reflect upon the fact that many people are made to undergo acute misery while the fact that they have developed into criminals is ultimately beyond their control, it is hard to dismiss this matter in the way compatibilists are wont to do. Given the absence of libertarian free will, the appropriate notion of justice incorporates pity into the very fabric of justice. There is a sense in which Compatibilist Justice is very often, at best, "justified injustice," and in which the proper compatibilist order can be seen as, in one way, morally outrageous. The valid requirement to form, maintain, and enhance this moral order is hence tragic.

3. THE SHALLOWNESS OF COMPATIBILISM

Let us review where we are. We are assuming that there is no libertarian free will. The implications were seen to be inherently dualistic: neither the compatibilist interpretation nor the hard determinist one covers all that needs to be said. Fundamental Dualism hence means that both traditional approaches are inadequate. Of hard determinists who reject all possibility of making sense of moral responsibility and of a moral order based on it we say that they are over-reacting. Here the compatibilists will be quick to agree. This side of the debate is not the topic of this paper. Of compatibilists who rest content with moral responsibility and the concomitant notions even in the face of the absence of libertarian free will, we say that they are morally, "personally" and even pragmatically shallow. This does not follow from some error in compatibilist presentations of their views; on the contrary, compatibilists today present sophisticated positions and have made genuine philosophical progress. Nevertheless, the inherent limitations of the compatibilist perspective mean that it is shallow. Now we shall proceed to defend this charge.

The Ethical Shallowness of Compatibilism

Since in our presentation of the dualistic picture we have focused upon moral responsibility and justice, the materials for seeing the moral shallowness of compatibilism are close at hand. Let us focus on an individual criminal who is justly being harmed, in terms of Compatibilist Justice. Even if this criminal significantly shaped his own identity he could not, in a non-libertarian account, have created the original "he" that formed his later self (an original "he" that could not have created his later self differently). If he suffers on account of whatever he is, he is a *victim* of injustice, simply by being. Even if people can be morally responsible in compatibilist terms they lack ultimate responsibility: this lack is often morally significant, and in cases such as the one we have considered having people pay dearly for their compatibilistically-responsible actions is unjust. Not to acknowledge this prevailing injustice would be morally unperceptive, complacent, and unfair.

Consider the following quotation from a compatibilist:

> The incoherence of the libertarian conception of moral responsibility arises from the fact that it requires not only authorship of the action, but also, in a sense, authorship of one's self, or of one's character. As was shown, this requirement is

unintelligible because it leads to an infinite regress. The way out of this regress is *simply to drop* the second-order authorship requirement, which is what has been done here.

The difficulty, surely, is that there is an *ethical basis* for the libertarian requirement, and, even if it cannot be fulfilled, the idea of "simply dropping it" masks how *problematic* the result may be in terms of fairness and justice. The fact remains that if there is no libertarian free will a person being punished *may suffer justly* in compatibilist terms for what is ultimately her luck, for what follows from being what she is—ultimately without her control, a state which she had no real opportunity to alter, hence not her responsibility and fault.

Consider a more sophisticated example. Jay Wallace maintains the traditional paradigmatic terminology of moral responsibility, desert, fairness and justice. Compatibilism captures what needs to be said because it corresponds to proper compatibilist distinctions, which in the end turn out to require less than incompatibilist stories made us believe. According to Wallace, "it is reasonable to hold agents morally accountable when they possess the power of reflective self-control; and when such accountable agents violate the obligations to which we hold them, they deserve to be blamed for what they have done."

I grant the obvious difference in terms of fairness that would occur were we to treat alike cases that are very different compatibilistically, say, were we to blame people who lacked any capacity for reflection or self-control. I also admit, pace the incompatibilists, that there is an important sense of desert and of blameworthiness that can form a basis for the compatibilist practices that should be implemented. However, the compatibilist cannot form a sustainable barrier, either normatively or metaphysically, that will *block* the incompatibilist's *further* inquiries, about all of the central notions: opportunity, blameworthiness, desert, fairness and justice. It is *unfair* to blame a person for something not ultimately under her control, and, given the absence of libertarian free will, ultimately nothing *can* be under our control. Ultimately, no one can *deserve* such blame, and thus be truly blame-*worthy*. Our decisions, even as ideal compatibilist agents, reflect the way we were formed, and we have had no opportunity to have been formed differently. If in the end it is only our bad luck, then in a deep sense it is not morally our fault—*anyone* in "our" place would (tautologically) have done the same, and so everyone's not doing this, and the fact of *our* being such people as do it, is ultimately just a matter of luck. Matters of luck, by their very character, are the opposite of the moral—how can we ultimately hold someone accountable for what is, after all, a matter of luck? How can it be fair, when all that compatibilists have wanted to say is heard, that the person about to be, e.g., punished "pay" for this?

Without libertarian free will, no matter how sophisticated the compatibilist formulation of control is, and whether it focuses on character, reflection, ability to follow reasons or anything else available at the compatibilist level, in the end *no one can have ultimate control over that for which one is being judged*. While "forms of life" based on the compatibilist distinctions about control are possible and morally required, they are also superficial and deeply problematic in ethical and personal terms. When ultimate control is seen to be impossible, we must take notice.

Note that my own claim is not that Ultimate Injustice is all that there is of free will-related justice: I acknowledge that compatibilism captures much of fairness and justice, and indeed that compatibilist

distinctions are to have a dominant role in establishing social practices. The compatibilist cannot dismiss the dualist by saying, as she might attempt to do in response to the hard determinist, that the hard determinist is denying the manifest moral differences between cases and the very conditions for a civilized moral order. The dualist, after all, *acknowledges* all this. What the dualist resists is the claim that this is all that matters, and that the ultimate arbitrariness of it all is, somehow, of no moral import. The proper description of such a case is indeed dualistic: given that we need to order social life within certain constraints, we are obliged to follow compatibilist distinctions in terms of control and its absence, if we are to respect persons. But those who pay the price, by ultimately acting as they have been molded, are in the end victims as well. Their treatment is hence, on a deep view, manifestly morally disturbing. This needs to be acknowledged.

Let us take a step back and reflect on the compatibilist task. There are two ways in which this task can be understood: first, as a project of defending the compatibilist distinctions, of making some sense of what the compatibilists value. Hence, focusing on this task, then, once they manage to show the unreasonable reductionism of the typical incompatibilists, who group together the compatibilistically free and unfree, compatibilists understandably think that they have triumphed. Any claim that something is amiss is dismissed as the denial of the obvious, namely, that compatibilist distinctions in term of control *are* manifestly salient. However, as my dualistic argumentation showed, it is not sufficient for compatibilists to show the limitations of those who deny their case: there is a second compatibilist task, that of showing that the compatibilist captures *everything* important that is at stake. And while on the first task the compatibilists are successful, this does not seem to be the case with the second one. The dualistic case I presented allows, as it were, the compatibilist to enter the house, but denies her claim to take full control of it. Valid compatibilist insights need to share the pertinent philosophical accommodation with hard determinist insights.

The Pragmatic Shallowness of Compatibilism

We by now understand what the moral and personal-existential shallowness consists of: avoiding to take seriously what must be taken seriously, and not pursuing the same control-valuing principle that the compatibilist herself affirms up to the worrisome level, where that very principle comes up with the ultimate negative result. But what is pragmatic shallowness? By this I understand the corresponding lack of seriousness as to the grave dangers that recognizing the implications of the absence of libertarian free will can have. In a word, the deep practical *complacency* of compatibilism in the face of what is perhaps the most serious conceptual, ethical, and personal-existential challenge of modernity. The naturalistic-deterministic picture challenges our most central values and self-images. Compatibilists, who think that their half-way substitutes, for all of their limited validity, suffice, are simply naïve.

A number of brief illustrations should make the point. We often want a person to blame himself, feel guilty, and even see that he deserves to be punished. There is no viable picture of the moral life that can completely bypass this need. Such a person is not as likely to do all this if he internalized the ultimate perspective, according to which, in the actual world, nothing else could in fact have occurred, and he could not strictly have done anything else except

what he did do. But, as we saw, it was not very difficult to enter the ultimate perspective, at least in one's thoughts. Compatibilists hardly seem to notice the very difficulty. Here, it seems to me, the common person's incompatibilist intuitions, for all of their vagueness and crudeness, have captured something that has escaped philosophical compatibilists. A realization of the absence of the sort of tacit libertarian free will that is typically assumed by most people (at least in the West) is likely to be detrimental to the acceptance of responsibility and accompanying emotions.

There are perhaps two levels at which we can consider this. One is the level at which people are in fact eager to look for excuses. How, for instance, would we be able to develop a sense of responsibility in children if there was the culturally available possibility of using the ultimate perspective as a way of escaping responsibility for one's past actions or omissions? The partial validity of compatibilism is likely to be pragmatically defeated when confronted with the eagerness to put forward the fruits of a deeper look, as an excuse. On another level, even good will and eagerness to accept responsibility would not suffice. One can surrender the right to make use of the "ultimate level excuse" for normative reasons, and yet perhaps not be able to hold oneself truly responsible (e.g., to engage in remorse), if one has no grain of belief in something like libertarian free will. One can, after all, accept responsibility for matters that were not up to one in any sense, such as for the actions of others, for normative reasons. But here we are dealing with a different matter: not with the acceptance of responsibility in the shallow sense of "willingness to pay," but rather with feeling *compunction*. Compunction seems conceptually problematic and psychologically (non-pathologically) dubious when it concerns matters that, it is understood, ultimately one could not help doing. But such genuine feelings of responsibility (and not mere acceptance of it) are crucial for being responsible selves.

Consider now briefly the issue of self-respect and respect for others that we touched upon before. Clearly, if people really thought of themselves or of their parents as determined outcomes of what existed a century ago (perhaps with some small random indeterminism thrown in), this would make a substantial difference to their attitudes of (self-)respect and pride. The appreciation of achievement or lack of it cannot emerge unscathed from such reflection: in retrospect, we might tend to say of an achiever that "Well, *he had it in him.*" When applied to ourselves or to others, such deprecatory thoughts can be extremely damaging to our sense of achievement, worth, and self-respect. For if *any virtue that one has exhibited*, if *all that one has achieved*, was "in the cards," just an unfolding of one's predetermined self, one's view of oneself (or important others) cannot, surely, remain the same.

It seems that the shallowness of the substantive compatibilist diagnosis of the situation in moral and personal-existential terms translates into blindness as to the pragmatic dangers.

THE CONTINUING DEBATE:
Are We Morally Responsible for What We Do?

What Is New

As psychologists and biologists have continued to increase the range and detail of their explanations of human behavior, the justification for moral responsibility has been subjected to severe challenge. While some are willing to base moral responsibility on inexplicable mystery or miraculous human will power, few contemporary philosophers find such appeals persuasive. There are still many who believe that moral responsibility is compatible with contemporary scientific views and endeavor to give an account of moral responsibility that squares it with scientific naturalism. But a number of philosophers have taken a somewhat different approach. Following an approach developed by P. F. Strawson, they argue that whatever the scientific study of human behavior should reveal, our culture and our institutions simply cannot function without the concept of moral responsibility; and that furthermore, the denial of moral responsibility would impoverish our emotional lives and deprive us of psychological elements that are essential for full rich human relationships. So whatever scientific studies might reveal, it would be psychologically unhealthy and socially disastrous to give up belief in moral responsibility. In fact—this position claims—belief in moral responsibility is so deeply woven into our social and psychological lives that it cannot be undermined by either scientific or philosophical argument, and any argument that asks us to deny moral responsibility is a futile exercise that asks us to do the impossible.

Where to Find More

Daniel Dennett has written two very entertaining and readable books that take a compatibilist view on free will: *Elbow Room* (Cambridge, Mass.: The MIT Press, 1984); and *Freedom Evolves* (New York: Viking, 2003). Saul Smilansky has written a variety of very perceptive articles regarding free will and moral responsibility; for a clear and well-argued account of his views, see his *Free Will and Illusion* (Oxford: Clarendon Press, 2000).

The classic presentation of both determinism and compatibilism is David Hume, *An Inquiry Concerning Human Understanding*, section 8, and in his *Treatise of Human Nature*, Book II, Part III. Thomas Hobbes developed an earlier similar account (1651) in *Leviathan*, chapter 2. A more recent argument for compatibilism can be found in A. J. Ayer, "Freedom and Necessity," in his *Philosophical Essays* (London: Macmillan, 1954).

P. F. Strawson's "Freedom and Resentment" was originally published in 1962; widely anthologized, it offers a very influential compatibilist view, arguing that we simply can't get along without our basic concepts of free will and responsibility.

Philosophers who deny the existence of free will and moral responsibility altogether (generally because they favor determinism and believe determinism and free will are incompatible) include Baron D'Holbach (1770) and Arthur Schopenhauer, *Essay on the Freedom of the Will* (first published in 1841, reissued by New York: Liberal Arts Press, 1960).

A very clear and creative contribution to the debate over free will and moral responsibility is made by Richard Double in *The Non-Reality of Free Will* (New York: Oxford University Press, 1991) and *Metaphilosophy and Free Will* (New York: Oxford University Press, 1996).

H. L. A. Hart, who wrote a number of influential works in the philosophy of law, draws very clear distinctions among types of responsibility in *Punishment and Responsibility* (Oxford: Clarendon Press, 1968).

Some very good anthologies on moral responsibility are John Martin Fischer, editor, *Moral Responsibility* (Ithaca, N.Y.: Cornell University Press, 1986); Ferdinand Schoeman, editor, *Responsibility, Character, and the Emotions: New Essays in Moral Psychology* (Cambridge: Cambridge University Press, 1987); John Christman, editor, *The Inner Citadel: Essays on Individual Autonomy* (New York: Oxford University Press, 1989); Owen Flanagan and Amélie Oksenberg Rorty, editors, *Identity, Character, and Morality: Essays in Moral Psychology* (Cambridge, Mass.: MIT Press, 1990); John Martin Fischer and Mark Ravizza, editors, *Perspectives on Moral Responsibility* (Ithaca: Cornell University Press, 1993); Laura Waddell Ekstrom, editor, *Agency and Responsibility* (Boulder, Col.: Westview, 2001); and volume 29 of *Midwest Studies in Philosophy* (2005). For an anthology that collects the key historical writings on free will and responsibility, as well as many important legal essays on the subject, see Herbert Morris, editor, *Freedom and Responsibility* (Stanford, Cal.: Stanford University Press, 1961).

For more suggested readings, see debates 7 and 8.

10   ARE THERE OBJECTIVE ETHICAL TRUTHS?

Reason Cannot Discover Ethical Truths

ADVOCATE: Bernard Williams was Monroe Deutsch Professor of Philosophy at the University of California, Berkeley, and a Fellow of All Souls College, Oxford.

SOURCE: *Ethics and the Limits of Philosophy* (Cambridge, Mass.: Harvard University Press, 1985).

Reason Can Discover Ethical Truths

ADVOCATE: Thomas Nagel, University Professor of Philosophy at New York University; author of *The View from Nowhere* (New York: Oxford University Press, 1986).

SOURCE: *The Last Word* (New York: Oxford University Press, 1997).

Steve believes that capital punishment is morally *wrong*, while Katrina believes it is morally *right*. Their differences may stem from different opinions on questions that are not really questions of ethical values, but instead questions of criminology: Does the death penalty deter crime, are there effective alternative methods of protecting society, how expensive is capital punishment compared to life imprisonment? But suppose that Steve and Katrina *agree* that capital punishment is not an effective deterrent, that life imprisonment effectively protects society, and that capital punishment is more expensive than imprisonment. There may still remain a fundamental difference in values: Steve maintains that it is *wrong* to kill another human, whether by murder or by state sanctioned execution, and that two wrongs do not make a right. Katrina holds that it is *right* to execute those who have committed terrible crimes, that *justice* demands such ultimate penalties, and failure to carry out such executions is itself unjust. If Steve and Katrina reach this level of fundamental value dispute, can their conflict be resolved by *reason*? Are there any rational arguments that can conclusively establish moral truths or moral principles? Thomas Nagel and Bernard Williams are grappling with what is perhaps the central ethical issue of the last two and a half millennia. In Plato's *Republic*, Thrasymachus asserts that "the just is nothing else than the advantage of the stronger": there are no objective moral principles, and might makes right. Socrates takes up the challenge, arguing that principles of ethics and justice can be established by reason (and only by reason). This debate has raged ever since, taking many forms: Can reason discover ethical truths, or must they be revealed by God? Are ethical truths known by reason, or is ethics based on our emotions and affections (or our intuitions, or perhaps our empirical experience)? Can reason reveal ethical truths, or is the notion of objective ethical truth an illusion? For modern philosophy, the defining figures in the continuing controversy are Immanuel Kant, who argued that objective universal ethical truths can be known purely and ex-

clusively by reason; and David Hume, who maintained that ethics is derived solely from our feelings. Kant's view is that:

> I do not…need any far-reaching penetration to discern what I have to do
> in order that my will may be morally good.…I only ask myself: Canst thou
> also will that thy maxim should be a universal law? If not, then it must be
> rejected,…because it cannot enter as a principle into a possible universal leg-
> islation, and reason extorts from me immediate respect for such legislation.
> Kant, *Fundamental Principles of the Metaphysic of Morals*, "Transition from the
> Common Rational Knowledge of Morality to the Philosophical," trans.
> Thomas K. Abbott, 1785.

In contrast, Hume holds that:

> 'Tis not contrary to reason to prefer the destruction of the whole world to
> the scratching of my finger.…But can there be any difficulty in proving, that
> vice and virtue are not matters of fact, whose existence we can infer by reason?
> Take any action allow'd to be vicious. Wilful murder, for instance. Examine it
> in all lights, and see if you can find that matter of fact, of real existence, which
> you call *vice*. In which-ever way you take it, you find only certain passions,
> motives, volitions and thoughts. There is no other matter of fact in the case.
> The vice entirely escapes you, as long as you consider the object. You never can
> find it, till you turn your reflexion into your own breast, and find a sentiment
> of disapprobation, which arises in you, towards this action. Here is a matter of
> fact, but 'tis the object of feeling, not of reason. It lies in yourself, not in the
> object. David Hume, *A Treatise of Human Nature*, "Of the Influencing
> Motives of the Will," 1739–1740.

In our debate, Thomas Nagel follows in the Kantian tradition while Williams
champions a position more like Hume's. The basic question that divides them is this
long contested issue: if we are guided by *reason* and function as rational beings, does
that in itself presuppose substantive ethical principles (such as an obligation of impartiality among ourselves and other rational beings)? The Kantian approach does not
start with a quest for moral truth that we somehow discover as an end result of our
inquiries; rather, Kantians maintain that the very process of practical reasoning involves or presupposes substantive moral principles and obligations that apply to all
who use practical reason: moral obligations are inherent in the practical reasoning
process itself. That basic Kantian claim is the pivot point for the debate between
Williams and Nagel.

POINTS TO PONDER

➢ Bernard Williams denies that rational deliberation can establish an impartial ethical standpoint that respects the interests of all persons, because—Williams
argues—practical deliberation is a personal process of deciding about my own
preferences (and is distinct from factual deliberation concerning the world, which
does involve impartial rational deliberation). Is there (contrary to Williams'
claims) an essential element of impartiality in personal practical deliberation?
That is, could it be argued that impartiality is an essential element of *all* rational
deliberation?

➤ Thomas Nagel asserts that "someone who abandons or qualifies his basic methods of moral reasoning on historical or anthropological grounds alone is nearly as irrational as someone who abandons a mathematical belief on other than mathematical grounds....Moral considerations occupy a position in the system of thought that makes it illegitimate to subordinate them completely to anything else." Thus on Nagel's view, biology or psychology or anthropology might lead us to modify some of our moral beliefs (for example, learning more about chimpanzees might lead us to believe we are morally obligated to change our treatment of them); but those disciplines could never legitimately lead us to abandon or modify our methods of moral reasoning. Do you agree? Can you think of any possible scientific finding that could cause you to radically revise your basic perspective on the nature of morality and moral deliberation?

➤ Nagel argues that when psychological (or other scientific) accounts give a causal explanation for our moral beliefs, it is always possible to step back and look impersonally at our moral principles *in light of* the new information about their origin; and from that new broader perspective, we can always ask whether we now have good reason for believing in those moral principles. Thus scientific research could never destroy our belief in objective morality, since it is always open to us to take account of that research, reflect upon it, and (with the new information in hand) make a rational decision about what moral principles it is now most reasonable to hold. Of course, at some point we might give up and decide that scientific accounts have undermined all reasonable belief in the rational objectivity of our moral beliefs; but, according to Nagel, "to give up would be nothing but moral laziness." Do you agree? Could there come a point (following several levels of debunking causal explanation of why we hold what we thought were rationally derived moral principles) at which it would be *unreasonable* (rather than "morally lazy") to claim that at a higher reflective level we can still make an objectively reasonable moral evaluation?

Reason Cannot Discover Ethical Truths

BERNARD WILLIAMS

FOUNDATIONS: PRACTICAL REASON

There is a project that tries to start from the ground up. It offers certain structural or formal features of ethical relations. Instead of relying on a specific teleology of human nature, it starts from a very abstract conception of rational agency. It still tries to give an answer to Socrates' question, though a minimal one. It gives the answer to each agent, merely because the agent can ask the question. Hence its answers are more abstract and less determinately human than those in the Aristotelian style. This type of argument yields, if anything, general and formal principles to regulate the shape of relations between rational agents. These are the concerns of Kant.

This may seem a surprising thing to say. Kant's name is associated with an approach to morality in which, it is often supposed, there can be no *foundations* for morality at all. He insisted that morality should be "autonomous," and that there could be no reason for being moral. A simple argument shows why, in the Kantian framework, this must be so. Any reason for being moral must be either a moral or a nonmoral reason. If it is moral, then it cannot really be a reason for being moral, since you would have to be already inside morality in order to accept it. A nonmoral reason, on the other hand, cannot be a reason for being *moral*; morality requires a purity of motive, a basically moral intentionality (which Kant took to be obligation), and that is destroyed by any nonmoral inducement. Hence there can be no reason for being moral, and morality presents itself as an unmediated demand, a categorical imperative.

It is specifically *morality* that Kant introduces. Kant's outlook indeed requires that there be no reason for morality, if that means a motivation or inducement for being moral, but it does not imply that morality has no foundations. Kant thought that we could come to understand why morality should rightly present itself to the rational agent as a categorical demand. It was because rational agency itself involved accepting such a demand, and this is why Kant described morality in terms of laws laid down by practical reason for itself.

In his extraordinary book *The Groundwork of the Metaphysic of Morals*, he tries to explain how this can be. I do not want to try to set out the argument, however, by directly expounding Kant. That would involve many special problems of its own. I shall treat his outlook as the destination rather than the route and shall develop in the first place an argument that will be simpler and more concrete than Kant's.

Is there anything that rational agents necessarily want? That is to say, is there anything they want (or would want if they thought hard enough about it) merely as part or precondition of being agents?

When they are going to act, people necessarily want, first of all, some outcome: they want the world to be one way rather than another. You can want an outcome without wanting to produce that outcome—you might prefer that the outcome merely materialize. Indeed, there are some cases in which the outcome you want will count only if you do not directly produce it (you want her to fall in love with you). But, in direct contrast to that possibility, in many cases you essentially want not only the outcome, but to produce the outcome. To put it another way (a way that is complicated but still conceals some complications), the outcome you want itself includes the action that your present deliberations will issue in your doing.

We do not merely want the world to contain certain states of affairs (it is a deep error of consequentialism to believe that this is all we want). Among the things we basically want is to act in certain ways. But even when we basically want some state of affairs, and would be happy if it materialized, we know that we do not live in a magical world, where wanting an outcome can make it so. Knowing, therefore, that it will not come about unless we act to produce it, when we want an outcome we usually also want to produce it. Moreover, we do not want it merely to *turn out* that we produced it; we want these thoughts of ours to produce it. The wants involved in our purposive activities thus turn out to be complex. At the very least, what we want is that the outcome should come about because we wanted it, because we believed certain things, and because we acted as we did on the basis of those wants and beliefs. Similar considerations apply to keeping things that we want to keep.

This adds up, then, to the following: on various occasions we want certain outcomes; we usually want to produce those outcomes; we usually want to produce them in a way that expresses our want to produce them. Obviously enough, on those occasions we do not want to be frustrated, for instance by other people. Reflecting on all this, we can see that we have a general, dispositional, want not to be frustrated, in particular by other people. We have a general want, summarily put, for freedom.

It is not enough, though, for this freedom merely that we should not be frustrated in doing whatever it is we want to do. We might be able to do everything we wanted, simply because we wanted too little. We might have unnaturally straitened or impoverished wants. This consideration shows that we have another general want, if an indeterminate one: we want (to put it vaguely) an adequate range of wants.

It does not follow from all this that we want our choices to be as little limited as possible, by anything or anyone. We do not want our freedom to be limitless. It may seem to follow, but to accept it would be to leave out another vital condition of rational agency. Some things, clearly, are accessible to an agent at a given time and others are not. Moreover, what is accessible, and how easily, depends on features both inside and outside the agent. He chooses, makes up plans, and so on, in a world that has a certain practicable shape, in terms of where he is, what he is, and what he may become. The agent not only knows this is so (that is to say, he is sane), but he also knows, on reflection, that it is necessary if he is indeed going to be a rational agent. Moreover, he cannot coherently think that in an ideal world he would not need to be a rational agent. The fact that there are restrictions on what he can do is what requires him to be a rational agent, and it also makes it possible for him to be one; more than that, it is also

the condition of his being some particular person, of living *a* life at all. We may think sometimes that we are dismally constrained to be rational agents, and that in a happier world it would not be necessary. But that is a fantasy (indeed it is *the* fantasy).

Similar conditions apply to the agent's knowledge. Acting in a particular situation, he must want his plans not to go wrong through ignorance or error. But even in that particular case, he does not want to know everything, or that his action should have no unintended consequences. Not to know everything is, once more, a condition of having a life—some things are unknown, for instance, because they will form one's future. If you cannot coherently want to know everything, then you also cannot coherently want never to be in error. They are not the same thing (omniscience is not the same as infallibility), but there are many considerations between them. For one thing, as Karl Popper has always emphasized, you must make errors, and recognize them, if you are going to extend such knowledge as you have.

These last considerations have concerned things a rational agent does not need to want, indeed needs not to want, as a condition of being such an agent. They assume him or her to be a finite, embodied, historically placed agent.

As rational agents, then, we want what I have summarily called freedom, though that does not mean limitless freedom. Does this commit us to thinking that our freedom is a good and that it is a good thing for us to be free? One path leading to this conclusion would be to say that when an agent wants various particular outcomes, he must think that those various outcomes are good. Then he would be bound to think that his freedom was a good thing, since it was involved in securing those outcomes.

Is it true that if we want something and purposively pursue it, then we think of our getting that thing as good? This is a traditional doctrine, advanced in Plato's *Meno* and hallowed in a saying of scholastic philosophy, *omne appetitum appetitur sub specie boni*, everything pursued is pursued as being something good. It seems to me not true. In any ordinary understanding of *good*, surely, an extra step is taken if you go from saying that you want something or have decided to pursue it to saying that it is good, or (more to the point) that it is good that you should have it. The idea of something's being good imports an idea, however minimal or hazy, of a perspective in which it can be acknowledged by more than one agent as good. An agent who merely has a certain purpose may of course think that his purpose is good, but he does not have to. The most he would commit himself to merely by having a purpose would presumably be that it would be good *for him* if he succeeded in it, but must even this much be involved? Even this modest claim implies a perspective that goes somewhere beyond the agent's immediate wants, to his longer-term interests or well-being. To value something, even relatively to your own interests, as you do in thinking that it would be better "for me," is always to go beyond merely wanting something. I might indeed come to put all the value in my life into the satisfaction of one desire, but if I did, it would not simply be because I had only one desire. Merely to have one desire might well be to have no value in my life at all; to find all the value in one desire is to have just one desire that *matters* to me.

Even if we give up the traditional doctrine, however, so that I do not have to see everything I want as good, it might still be true that I should see my freedom as good. "Good for me," I suggested, introduces some reference to my interests or well-being that goes beyond my immediate purposes, and my freedom is one of my fundamental interests. So perhaps I must regard my own freedom as a good. But if so, I must not be misled into thinking that my freedom constitutes a good, period. This would be so only if it were a good, period, that I should be a rational agent, and there is no reason why others should assent to that. In fact, it is not even clear that *I* have to assent to it. This begins to touch on some deeper questions about my conception of my own existence.

Everything said so far about the basic conditions and presuppositions of rational action seems to be correct. The argument that tries to provide a foundation for morality attempts to show that, merely because of those conditions, each agent is involved in a moral commitment. Each agent, according to this argument, must think as follows. Since I necessarily want my basic freedom, I must be opposed to courses of action that would remove it. Hence I cannot agree to any arrangement of things by which others would have the right to remove my basic freedom. So when I reflect on what arrangement of things I basically need, I see that I must claim a *right* to my basic freedom. In effect, I must lay it down as a rule for others that they respect my freedom. I claim this right solely because I am a rational agent with purposes. But if this fact alone is the basis of my claim, then a similar fact must equally be the basis of such a claim by others. If, as I suppose, I legitimately and appropriately think that they should respect my freedom, then I must recognize that they legitimately and appropriately think that I should respect their freedom. In moving from my need for freedom to "they ought not to interfere with me," I must equally move from their need to "I ought not to interfere with them."

If this is correct, then each person's basic needs and wants commit him to stepping into morality, a morality of rights

fundamental

and duties, and someone who rejects that step will be in a kind of pragmatic conflict with himself. Committed to being a rational agent, he will be trying to reject the commitments necessarily involved in that. But is the argument correct? Its very last step—that if in my case rational agency alone is the ground of a right to noninterference, then it must be so in the case of other people—is certainly sound. It rests on the weakest and least contestable version of a "principle of universalizability," which is brought into play simply by *because* or *in virtue of.* If a particular consideration is really enough to establish a conclusion in my case, then it is enough to establish it in anyone's case. That must be so if enough is indeed enough. If the conclusion that brings in morality does not follow, it must be because of an earlier step. Granted that the original claims are correct about a rational agent's wants and needs, the argument must go wrong when I first assert my supposed right.

It is useful to consider what the agent might say in thinking out his claims. It could be put like this:

I have certain purposes.

I need freedom to pursue these or any other purposes.

So, I need freedom.

I prescribe: let others not interfere with my freedom.

Call the one who is thinking this, the agent A. Assume for the moment that we know what a "prescription" is, and call this prescription of A's, *Pa*. Then A also thinks

Pa is reasonable,

where what this means is that *Pa* is reasonably related to his, A's, being a rational agent. A can of course recognize that another agent, say B, can have thoughts just like his own. He knows, for instance, that

B prescribes: let A not interfere with my freedom,

and, calling B's prescription *Pb*, the principle of universability will require A to agree that

Pb is reasonable.

It may look as if he has now accepted B's prescription as reasonable in the sense of making some claim on himself. This is what the argument to morality requires. But A has not agreed to this. He has agreed only that *Pb* is reasonable in the same sense that *Pa* is, and what this means is only that *Pb* is reasonably related to B's being a rational agent—that is to say, B is as rational in making his prescription as A is rational in making his. It does not mean that B would be rational in accepting *Pa* (or conversely) if in accepting it he would be committing himself not to interfere with A's freedom.

The same point comes out in this: one could never get to the required result, the entry into the ethical world, just from the consideration of the *should* or *ought* of rational agency itself, the *should* of the practical question. The reasons that B has for doing something are not in themselves reasons for another's doing anything. The *should* of practical reason has, like any other, a second and a third person, but these forms merely represent my perspective on your or his interests and rational calculations, the perspective of "if I were you." Considering in those terms what B should do, I may well conclude that he should interfere with my freedom.

But can I "prescribe" this for him? What does it mean? Certainly I do not want him to interfere with my freedom. But does this, in itself, generate any prescription that leads to obligations or rights? The argument suggests that if I do not prescribe that others ought not to interfere with my freedom, I shall be logically required to admit that they *may* interfere with it—which I do not want to do. What the argument claims is that I must either give them the right to interfere with my freedom or withhold that right from them. The argument insists, in effect, that if I am to be consistent, I must make a rule to the effect that others should not interfere with my freedom, and nothing less than this rule will do. But the rule, of course, just because it is a general rule, will equally require me not to interfere with their freedom.

But why must I prescribe any rule? If I am in the business of making rules, then clearly I will not make one enjoining others to interfere with my freedom, nor will I make one permitting them to do so. But there is another possibility: I do not regard myself as being in this business, and I make no rule either way. I do not have to be taken as giving permission. If there is a system of rules, then no doubt if the rules are silent on a certain matter (at least if the rules are otherwise wide enough in their scope), that fact can naturally be taken to mean permission. The law, like other sovereign agencies, can say something by remaining silent. But if there is no law, then silence is not meaningful, permissive, silence: it is simply silence. In another sense, of course, people "may" interfere with my freedom, but that means only that there is no law to stop, permit, or enjoin. Whether they "may" means they "can" depends on me and what I can do. As the egoist Max Stirner put it: "The tiger that assails me is in the right, and I who strike him down am also in the right. I defend against him not my *right*, but *myself*."

I can also ask why, if I am going to prescribe that much, I should not more ambitiously prescribe that no one interfere with whatever particular purposes I may happen to have. I *want* the success of my particular projects, of course, as much as any-

thing else, and I want other people not to interfere with them. Indeed, my need for basic freedom was itself derived from that kind of want. But the argument is certainly not going to allow me to prescribe for all my particular wants.

The argument depends on a particular conception of the business of making rules, a conception that lies at the heart of the Kantian enterprise. If I were in a position to make any rules I liked and to enforce them as an instrument of oppression, then I could make a law that suited my interests and attacked the competing interests of others. No one else would have a reason to obey such a law, except the reason I gave him. But the laws we are considering in these arguments are not that kind of law, have no external sanction, and respond to no inequalities between the parties. They are *notional* laws. The question "what law could I make?" then becomes "what law could I make that I could reasonably expect others to accept?" When we reflect on the fact that everyone asks it from an equal position of powerlessness—since these are laws for a kingdom where power is not an issue—we see that the question could equally be "what law could I accept?" and so, finally, "what laws should there be?"

If this is the question, asked in such a spirit, for such a kingdom, then we can see why its answer should be on the lines of Kant's fundamental principle of action, the Categorical Imperative of morality, which requires you to "act only on that maxim through which you can at the same time will that it should become a universal law." But the problem immediately becomes: Why should one adopt such a picture? Why should I think of myself as a legislator and—since there is no distinction—at the same time a citizen of a republic governed by these notional laws? This remains a daunting problem, even if one is already within ethical life and is considering how to think about it. But it is a still more daunting problem when this view of things is being demanded of any rational agent. The argument needs to tell us what it is about rational agents that requires them to form this conception of themselves as, so to speak, abstract citizens.

It might be thought that the question answers itself because, simply as rational agents, there is nothing else for them to be, and there is no difference among them. But to arrive at the model in this way would be utterly unpersuasive. We are concerned with what any given person, however powerful or effective he may be, should reasonably do as a rational agent, and this is not the same thing as what he would reasonably do if he were a rational agent *and no more*. Indeed, that equation is unintelligible, since there is no way of being a rational agent and no more. A more sensible test would be to ask what people should reasonably do if they did not know anything about themselves except that they were rational agents; or, again, what people should do if they knew more than that, but not their own particular powers and position. This is an interesting test for some things; in particular, it is a possible test for justice, and in that role it can be proposed to those with a concern for justice. But it is not a persuasive test for what you should reasonably do if you are not already concerned with justice. Unless you are already disposed to take an impartial or moral point of view, you will see as highly unreasonable the proposal that the way to decide what to do is to ask what rules you would make if you had none of your actual advantages, or did not know what they were.

The Kantian project, if it is to have any hope, has to start farther back. It has to be, in a vital way, more like Kant's own project than the argument I have just outlined. The argument started from what ra-

tional agents need, and while what it said about that was true, it was not enough to lead each agent into morality. Kant started from what in his view rational agents essentially *were*. He thought that the moral agent was, in a sense, a rational agent and no more, and he presented as essential to his account of morality a particular metaphysical conception of the agent, according to which the self of moral agency is what he called a "noumenal" self, outside time and causality, and thus distinct from the concrete, empirically determined person that one usually takes oneself to be.

What we are looking for is an argument that will travel far enough into Kant's territory to bring back the essential conclusion that a rational agent's most basic interests must coincide with those given in a conception of himself as a citizen legislator of a notional republic; but does not bring back the more extravagant metaphysical luggage of the noumenal self. The argument might go something like this. We have already agreed that the rational agent is committed to being free, and we have said something about what is required for that freedom. But we have not yet reached a deep enough understanding of what that freedom must be. The idea of a rational agent is not simply the third-person idea of a creature whose behavior is to be explained in terms of beliefs and desires. A rational agent acts *on* reasons, and this goes beyond his acting in accordance with some regularity or law, even one that refers to beliefs and desires. If he acts *on* reasons, then he must not only be an agent but reflect on himself as an agent, and this involves his seeing himself as one agent among others. So he stands back from his own desires and interests, and sees them from a standpoint that is not that *of* his desires and interests. Nor is it the standpoint of anyone else's desires and interests. That is the standpoint of impartiality. So it is appropriate for the rational agent, with his aspiration to be genuinely free and rational, to see himself as making rules that will harmonize the interests of all rational agents.

In assessing this line of argument, it is important to bear in mind that the kind of rational freedom introduced by it is manifested, according to Kant, not only in decisions to act but also in theoretical deliberation, thought about what is true. It is not merely freedom as an agent—the fact (roughly speaking) that what I do depends on what I decide—that leads to the impartial position, but my reflective freedom as a thinker, and this applies also to the case of factual thought. In both cases, Kant supposed, I am not merely caused to arrive at a conclusion: I can stand back from my thoughts and experiences, and what otherwise would merely have been a cause becomes *a consideration for me*. In the case of arriving by reflection at a belief, the sort of item that will be transmuted in this way will be a piece of evidence, or what I take to be evidence: it might for instance be a perception. In the case of practical deliberation, the item is likely to be a desire, a desire which I take into consideration in deciding what to do. In standing back from evidence, or from my desires, so that they become considerations in the light of which I arrive at a conclusion, I exercise in both cases my rational freedom. When, in the practical case, I adopt the standpoint outside my desires and projects, I may endorse my original desires, as in the factual case I may endorse my original disposition to believe. If I do this my original desire may in the outcome be my motive for action (though someone who uses this picture would naturally say that on some occasions what I eventually do will be motivated by none of the desires I originally had, but is radically produced by my reflection).

The fact that Kant's account of rational freedom is meant to apply to factual deliberation as much as to practical brings out what is wrong with the Kantian argument. What it says about reflection does indeed apply to factual deliberation, but it does so because factual deliberation is not essentially first-personal. It fails to apply to practical deliberation, and to impose a necessary impartiality on it, because practical deliberation is first-personal, radically so, and involves an *I* that must be more intimately the *I* of my desires than this account allows.

When I think about the world and try to decide the truth about it, I think *about the world*, and I make statements, or ask questions, which are about it and not about me. I ask, for instance,

Is strontium a metal?

or confidently say to myself

Wagner never met Verdi.

Those questions and assertions have first-personal shadows, such as

I wonder whether strontium is a metal,

or

I believe that Wagner never met Verdi.

But these are derivative, merely reflexive counterparts to the thoughts that do not mention me. I occur in them, so to speak, only in the role of one who has this thought.

What should I think about this question?

where that has the same effect as

What is the truth about this question?

is again a case in which *I* occurs only derivatively: the last question is the primary one.

Because of this, the *I* of this kind is also impersonal. The question,

> What should I think about this question?

could as well be

> What should anyone think about this question?

This is so, even when it means

> What should I think about this on the evidence I have?

This must ask what anyone should think about it on that evidence. Equally, what anyone truly believes must be consistent with what others truly believe, and anyone deliberating about the truth is committed, by the nature of the process, to the aim of a consistent set of beliefs, one's own and others'.

It is different with deliberation for action. Practical deliberation is in every case first-personal, and the first person is not derivative or naturally replaced by *anyone*. The action I decide on will be mine, and (on the lines of what was said earlier about the aims of action) its being mine means not just that it will be arrived at by this deliberation, but that it will involve changes in the world of which I shall be empirically the cause, and of which these desires and this deliberation itself will be, in some part, the cause. It is true that I can stand back from my desires and reflect on them, and this possibility can indeed be seen as part of the rational freedom at which any rational agent aims. This goes somewhat beyond the considerations about freedom and intentionality acknowledged earlier in the discussion, but it still does not give the required result in relation to morality. The *I* of the reflective practical deliberation is not required to take the result of anyone else's properly conducted deliberation as a datum, nor be committed from the outset to a harmony of everyone's deliberations—that is to say, to making a rule from a standpoint of equality. Reflective deliberation about the truth indeed brings in a standpoint that is impartial and seeks harmony, but this is because it seeks truth, not because it is reflective deliberation, and those features will not be shared by deliberation about what to do simply because it too is reflective. The *I* that stands back in rational reflection from my desires is still the *I* that has those desires and will, empirically and concretely, act; and it is not, simply by standing back in reflection, converted into a being whose fundamental interest lies in the harmony of all interests. It cannot, just by taking this step, acquire the motivations of justice.

Indeed, it is rather hard to explain why the reflective self, if it is conceived as uncommitted to all particular desires, should have a concern that any of them be satisfied. The reflective self of theoretical or factual deliberation has a unity of interest with prereflective belief: each in its way aims at truth, and this is why the prereflective disposition to believe yields so easily, in the standard case, to corrective reflection. But on the model we are considering there is not an identity of interest between the reflective practical self and any particular desires, my own or others'. It is unclear, then, why the reflective self should try to provide for the satisfaction of those desires. This is just another aspect of the mistake that lies in equating, as this argument does, reflection and detachment.

What has been shown, I believe, is that there is no route to the impartial standpoint from rational deliberation alone.

Reason Can Discover Ethical Truths

Thomas Nagel

ETHICS

I

I take it for granted that the objectivity of moral reasoning does not depend on its having an external reference. There is no moral analogue of the external world—a universe of moral facts that impinge on us causally. Even if such a supposition made sense, it would not support the objectivity of moral reasoning. Science, which this kind of reifying realism takes as its model, doesn't derive its objective validity from the fact that it starts from perception and other causal relations between us and the physical world. The real work comes after that, in the form of active scientific reasoning, without which no amount of causal impact on us by the external world would generate a belief in Newton's or Maxwell's or Einstein's theories, or the chemical theory of elements and compounds, or molecular biology.

If we had rested content with the causal impact of the external world on us, we'd still be at the level of sense perception. We can regard our scientific beliefs as objectively true not because the external world causes us to have them but because we are able to *arrive at* those beliefs by methods that have a good claim to be reliable, by virtue of their success in selecting among rival hypotheses that survive the best criticisms and questions we can throw at them. Empirical confirmation plays a vital role in this process, but it cannot do so without theory.

Moral thought is concerned not with the description and explanation of what happens but with decisions and their justification. It is mainly because we have no comparably uncontroversial and well-developed methods for thinking about morality that a subjectivist position here is more credible than it is with regard to science. But just as there was no guarantee at the beginnings of cosmological and scientific speculation that we humans had the capacity to arrive at objective truth beyond the deliverances of sense-perception—that in pursuing it we were doing anything more than spinning collective fantasies—so there can be no decision in advance as to whether we are or are not talking about a real subject when we reflect and argue about morality. The answer must come from the results themselves. Only the effort to reason about morality can show us whether it is possible—whether, in thinking about what to do and how to live, we can find methods, reasons, and principles whose validity does not have to be subjectively or relativistically qualified.

Since moral reasoning is a species of practical reasoning, its conclusions are desires, intentions, and actions, or feelings and convictions that can motivate desire, intention, and action. We want to know how to live, and why, and we want the answer in general terms, if possible. Hume famously believed that because a "passion" immune to rational assessment must underly every motive, there can be no such thing as specifically practical reason, nor specifically moral reason either. That is false, because while "passions" are the source of some reasons, other passions or desires are themselves motivated and/or justified by reasons that do not depend on still more basic desires. And I would contend that either the question whether one should have a certain desire or the question whether, given that one has that desire, one should act on it, is always open to rational consideration.

The issue is whether the procedures of justification and criticism we employ in such reasoning, moral or merely practical, can be regarded finally as just something we do—a cultural or societal or even more broadly human collective practice, within which reasons come to an end. I believe that if we ask ourselves seriously how to respond to proposals for contextualization and relativistic detachment, they usually fail to convince. Although it is less clear than in some of the other areas we've discussed, attempts to get entirely outside of the object language of practical reasons, good and bad, right and wrong, and to see all such judgments as expressions of a contingent, nonobjective perspective will eventually collapse before the independent force of the first-order judgments themselves.

II

Suppose someone says, for example, "You only believe in equal opportunity because you are a product of Western liberal society. If you had been brought up in a caste society or one in which the possibilities for men and women were radically unequal, you wouldn't have the moral convictions you have or accept as persuasive the moral arguments you now accept." The second, hypothetical sentence is probably true, but what about the first— specifically the "only"? In general, the fact that I wouldn't believe something if I hadn't learned it proves nothing about the status of the belief or its grounds. It may be impossible to explain the learning without invoking the content of the belief itself,

and the reasons for its truth; and it may be clear that what I have learned is such that even if I hadn't learned it, it would still be true. The reason the genetic fallacy is a fallacy is that the explanation of a belief can sometimes confirm it.

To have any content, a subjectivist position must say more than that my moral convictions are my moral convictions. That, after all, is something we can all agree on. A meaningful subjectivism must say that they are *just* my moral convictions—or those of my moral community. It must *qualify* ordinary moral judgments in some way, must give them a self-consciously first-person (singular or plural) reading. That is the only type of antiobjectivist view that is worth arguing against or that it is even possible to disagree with.

But I believe it is impossible to come to rest with the observation that a belief in equality of opportunity, and a wish to diminish inherited inequalities, are merely expressions of our cultural tradition. True or false, those beliefs are essentially objective in intent. Perhaps they are wrong, but that too would be a nonrelative judgment. Faced with the fact that such values have gained currency only recently and not universally, one still has to try to decide whether they are right—whether one ought to continue to hold them. That question is not displaced by the information of contingency: The question remains, at the level of moral content, whether I would have been in error if I had accepted as natural, and therefore justified, the inequalities of a caste society, or a fairly rigid class system, or the orthodox subordination of women. It can take in additional facts as material for reflection, but the question of the relevance of those facts is inevitably a moral question: Do these cultural and historical variations and their causes tend to show that I and others have less reason than we had supposed to favor equality of opportunity? Presentation of an array of historically and culturally conditioned attitudes, including my own, does not disarm first-order moral judgment but simply gives it something more to work on—including information about influences on the formation of my convictions that may lead me to change them. But the relevance of such information is itself a matter for moral reasoning—about what are and are not good grounds for moral belief.

When one is faced with these real variations in practice and conviction, the requirement to put oneself in everyone's shoes when assessing social institutions—some version of universalizability—does not lose any of its persuasive force just because it is not universally recognized. It dominates the historical and anthropological data: Presented with the description of a traditional caste society, I have to ask myself whether its hereditary inequalities are justified, and there is no plausible alternative to considering the interests of all in trying to answer the question. If others feel differently, they must say why they find these cultural facts relevant—why they require some qualification to the objective moral claim. On both sides, it is a moral issue, and the only way to defend universalizability or equal opportunity against subjectivist qualification is by continuing the moral argument. It is a matter of understanding exactly what the subjectivist wants us to give up, and then asking whether the grounds for those judgments disappear in light of his observations.

In my opinion, someone who abandons or qualifies his basic methods of moral reasoning on historical or anthropological grounds alone is nearly as irrational as someone who abandons a mathematical belief on other than mathematical grounds. Even with all their uncertainties and liability to controversy and distortion, moral considerations occupy a position in the system of human thought that makes it illegitimate to subordinate them completely to anything else. Particular moral claims are constantly being discredited for all kinds of reasons, but moral considerations per se keep rising again to challenge in their own right any blanket attempt to displace, defuse, or subjectivize them.

This is an instance of the more general truth that the normative cannot be transcended by the descriptive. The question "What should I do?" like the question "What should I believe?" is always in order. It is always possible to think about the question in normative terms, and the process is not rendered pointless by any fact of a different kind—any desire or emotion or feeling, any habit or practice or convention, any contingent cultural or social background. Such things may in fact guide our actions, but it is always possible to take their relation to action as an object of further normative reflection and ask, "How should I act, given that these things are true of me or of my situation?"

The type of thought that generates answers to this question is practical reason. But, further, it is always possible for the question to take a specifically moral form, since one of the successor questions to which it leads is, "What should anyone in my situation do?"—and consideration of that question leads in turn to questions about what everyone should do, not only in this situation but more generally.

Such universal questions don't always have to be raised, and there is good reason in general to develop a way of living that makes it usually unnecessary to raise them. But if they are raised, as they always can be, they require an answer of the appropriate kind—even though the answer may be that in a case like this one may do as one likes. They cannot be ruled out of order by pointing to something more fundamental—psychological, cultural, or biological—that brings the request for justification to an end. Only a justification can bring the request for justifications to an end. Normative questions in general are not undercut or rendered idle by anything, even though particular normative answers may be. (Even when some putative justification is exposed as rationalization, that implies that something else could be said about the justifiability or nonjustifiability of what was done.)

III

The point of view to defeat, in a defense of the reality of practical and moral reason, is in essence the Humean one. Although Hume was wrong to say that reason was fit only to serve as the slave of the passions, it is nevertheless true that there are desires and sentiments prior to reason that it is not appropriate for reason to evaluate—that it must simply treat as part of the raw material on which its judgments operate. The question then arises how pervasive such brute motivational data are, and whether some of them cannot perhaps be identified as the true sources of those grounds of action which are usually described as reasons. Hume's theory of the "calm" passions was designed to make this extension, and resisting it is not a simple matter—even if it is set in the context of a minimal framework of practical rationality stronger than Hume would have admitted.

If there is such a thing as practical reason, it does not simply dictate particular actions but, rather, governs the *relations* among actions, desires, and beliefs—just as theoretical reason governs the relations among beliefs and requires some specific material to work on. Prudential rationality, requiring uniformity in the weight accorded to desires and interests situated at different times in one's life, is an example—and the example about which Hume's skep-

ticism is most implausible, when he says it is not contrary to reason "to prefer even my own acknowledged lesser good to my greater, and have a more ardent affection for the former than the latter." Yet Hume's position always seems a possibility, because whenever such a consistency requirement or similar pattern has an influence on our decisions, it seems possible to represent this influence as the manifestation of a systematic second-order desire or calm passion, which has such consistency as its object and without which we would not be susceptible to this type of "rational" motivation. Hume need then only claim that while such a desire (for the satisfaction of one's future interests) is quite common, to lack it is not contrary to reason, any more than to lack sexual desire is contrary to reason. The problem is to show how this misrepresents the facts.

The fundamental issue is about the order of explanation, for there is no point in denying that people have such second-order desires: the question is whether they are sources of motivation or simply the manifestation in our motives of the recognition of certain rational requirements. A parallel point could be made about theoretical reason. It is clear that the belief in modus ponens, for example, is not a rationally ungrounded *assumption* underlying our acceptance of deductive arguments that depend on modus ponens: Rather, it is simply a recognition of the validity of that form of argument.

The question is whether something similar can be said of the "desire" for prudential consistency in the treatment of desires and interests located at different times. I think it can be and that if one tries instead to regard prudence as simply a desire among others, a desire one happens to have, the question of its appropriateness inevitably reappears as a normative question, and the answer can only be given in terms of the principle itself. The normative can't be displaced by the psychological.

If I think, for example, "What if I didn't care about what would happen to me in the future?" the appropriate reaction is not like what it would be to the supposition that I might not care about movies. True, I'd be missing something if I didn't care about movies, but there are many forms of art and entertainment, and we don't have to consume them all. Note that even this is a judgment of the *rational acceptability* of such variation—of there being no reason to regret it. The supposition that I might not care about my own future cannot be regarded with similar tolerance: It is the supposition of a real failure—the paradigm of something to be regretted—and my recognition of that failure does not reflect merely the antecedent presence in me of a contingent second-order desire. Rather, it reflects a judgment about what is and what is not relevant to the justification of action against a certain factual background.

Relevance and consistency both get a foothold when we adopt the standpoint of decision, based on the total circumstances, including our own condition. This standpoint introduces a subtle but profound gap between desire and action, into which the free exercise of reason enters. It forces us to the idea of the difference between doing the right thing and doing the wrong thing (here, without any specifically ethical meaning as yet)—given our total situation, *including* our desires. Once I see myself as the subject of certain desires, as well as the occupant of an objective situation, I still have to decide what to do, and that will include deciding what justificatory weight to give to those desires.

This step back, this opening of a slight space between inclination and decision, is the condition that permits the operation of reason with respect to belief as well as with respect to action, and that poses the

demand for generalizable justification. The two kinds of reasoning are in this way parallel. It is only when, instead of simply being pushed along by impressions, memories, impulses, desires, or whatever, one stops to ask "What should I do?" or "What should I believe?" that reasoning becomes possible—and, having become possible, becomes necessary. Having stopped the direct operation of impulse by interposing the possibility of decision, one can get one's beliefs and actions into motion again only by thinking about what, in light of the circumstances, one should do.

The controversial but crucial point, here as everywhere in the discussion of this subject, is that the standpoint from which one assesses one's choices after this step back is not just first-personal. One is suddenly in the position of judging what one ought to do, against the background of all one's desires and beliefs, in a way that does not merely flow from those desires and beliefs but *operates* on them—by an assessment that should enable anyone else also to see what is the right thing for you to do against that background.

It is not enough to find some higher order desires that one happens to have, to settle the matter: such desires would have to be placed among the background conditions of decision along with everything else. Rather, even in the case of a purely self-interested choice, one is seeking the right answer. One is trying to decide what, given the inner and outer circumstances, *one should do*—and that means not just what *I* should do but what *this person* should do. The same answer should be given to that question by anyone to whom the data are presented, whether or not he is in your circumstances and shares your desires. That is what gives practical reason its generality.

The objection that has to be answered, here as elsewhere, is that this sense of unconditioned, nonrelative judgment is an illusion—that we cannot, merely by stepping back and taking ourselves as objects of contemplation, find a secure platform from which such judgment is possible. On this view whatever we do, after engaging in such an intellectual ritual, will still inevitably be a manifestation of our individual or social nature, not the deliverance of impersonal reason—for there is no such thing.

But I do not believe that such a conclusion can be established a priori, and there is little reason to believe it could be established empirically. The subjectivist would have to show that all purportedly rational judgments about what people have reason to do are really expressions of rationally unmotivated desires or dispositions of the person making the judgment—desires or dispositions to which normative assessment has no application. The motivational explanation would have to have the effect of *displacing* the normative one—showing it to be superficial and deceptive. It would be necessary to make out the case about many actual judgments of this kind and to offer reasons to believe that something similar was true in all cases. Subjectivism involves a positive claim of empirical psychology.

Is it conceivable that such an argument could succeed? In a sense, it would have to be shown that all our supposed practical reasoning is, at the limit, a form of rationalization. But the defender of practical reason has a general response to all psychological claims of this type. Even when some of his actual reasonings are convincingly analyzed away as the expression of merely parochial or personal inclinations, it will in general be reasonable for him to add this new information to the body of his beliefs about himself and then step back once more and ask, "What, in light of all this, do I have reason to do?" It is logically conceivable that the subjectivist's strategy might succeed by exhaustion; the

rationalist might become so discouraged at the prospect of being once again undermined in his rational pretensions that he would give up trying to answer the recurrent normative question. But it is far more likely that the question will always be there, continuing to appear significant and to demand an answer. To give up would be nothing but moral laziness.

More important, as a matter of substance I do not think the subjectivist's project can be plausibly carried out. It is not possible to give a debunking psychological explanation of prudential rationality, at any rate. For suppose it is said, plausibly enough, that the disposition to provide for the future has survival value and that its implantation in us is the product of natural selection. As with any other instinct, we still have to decide whether acting on it is a good idea. With some biologically natural dispositions, both motivational and intellectual, there are good reasons to resist or limit their influence. That this does not seem the right reaction to prudential motives (except insofar as we limit them for moral reasons) shows that they cannot be regarded simply as desires that there is no reason to have. If they were, they wouldn't give us the kind of reasons for action that they clearly do. It will never be reasonable for the rationalist to concede that prudence is just a type of consistency in action that he happens, groundlessly, to care about, and that he would have no reason to care about if he didn't already.

The null hypothesis—that in this unconditional sense there are no reasons—is acceptable only if from the point of view of detached self-observation it is superior to the alternatives; and as elsewhere, I believe it fails that test.

IV

Bernard Williams is a prominent contemporary representative of the opposite view.

In chapter 4 of *Ethics and the Limits of Philosophy*, he argues that reflective practical reason, unlike reflective theoretical reason, always remains first-personal: One is always trying to answer the question "What shall (or should) *I* do?" and the answer must derive from something internal to what he calls one's "motivational set." Williams says that in theoretical reasoning, by contrast, while it is true that one is trying to decide what to believe, the question "What should I believe?" is in general replaceable by a substantive question which need make no first-person reference: a question like "Did Wagner ever meet Verdi?" or "Is strontium a metal?" This means that the pursuit of freedom through the rational, reflective assessment of the influences on one's beliefs leads, in the theoretical case, to the employment of objective, non-first-personal standards. To decide what to believe, I have to decide, in light of the evidence available to me, and by standards that it would be valid for anyone to use in drawing a conclusion from that evidence, what is probably true.

But Williams holds that in deciding what to do, even if I try to free myself from the blind pressures of my desires and instincts by reflecting on those influences and evaluating their suitability as reasons for action, such reflection will never take me outside of the domain of first-personal thought. Even at my most reflective, it will still be a decision about what *I* should do and will have to be based on *my* reflective assessment of my motives and reasons. To believe that at some point I will reach a level of reflection where I can consider truly objective reasons, valid for anyone, that reveal what *should be done* by this person in these circumstances, is to deceive myself. In the practical domain, there is no such standpoint of assessment.

It has to be admitted that phenomenologically, the subjectivist view is more plausible in ethics than in regard to theoretical reason. When I step back from my practical reasonings and ask whether I can endorse them as correct, it is possible to experience this as a move to a deeper region of myself rather than to a higher universal standpoint. Yet at the same time there seems to be no limit to the possibility of asking whether the first-personal reasoning I rely on in deciding what to do is also objectively acceptable. It always seems appropriate to ask, setting aside that the person in question is oneself, "What ought to happen? What is the right thing to do, in this case?"

That the question can take this form does not follow merely from the fact that it is always possible to step back from one's present intentions and motives and consider whether one wishes to change them. The fact that the question "What should I do?" is always open, or reopenable, is logically consistent with the answer's always being a first-personal answer. It might be, as Williams believes, that the highest freedom I can hope for is to ascend to higher order desires or values that are still irreducibly my own—values that determine what kind of person I as an individual wish to be—and that all apparently objective answers to the question are really just the first person masquerading as the third. But do values really disappear into thin air when we adopt the external point of view? Since we can reach a *descriptive* standpoint from which the first person has vanished and from which one regards oneself impersonally, the issue is whether at that point description outruns evaluation. If it does not, if evaluation of some sort keeps pace with it, then we will finally have to evaluate our conduct from a non-first-person standpoint.

Clearly, description can outrun some evaluations. If I don't like shrimp, there simply is no higher order evaluation to be made of this preference. All I can do is to observe that I have it; and no higher order value seems to be involved when it leads me to refrain from ordering a dish containing shrimp or to decline an offer of shrimp when hors d'oeuvres are passed at a cocktail party. However external a view I may take of the preference, I am not called on either to defend it or to endorse it: I can just accept it. But there are other evaluations, by contrast, that seem at least potentially to be called into question by an external, descriptive view, and the issue is whether those questions always lead us finally to a first-person answer.

Suppose I reflect on my political preferences—my hope that candidate X will not win the next presidential election, for example. What external description of this preference, considered as a psychological state, is consistent with its stability? Can I regard my reasons for holding it simply as facts about myself, as my dislike of shrimp is a fact about myself? Or will any purely descriptive observation of such facts give rise to a further evaluative question—one that cannot be answered simply by a reaffirmation that this is the kind of person I am?

Here, as elsewhere, I don't think we can hope for a decisive proof that we are asking objective questions and pursuing objective answers. The possibility that we are deceiving ourselves is genuine. But the only way to deal with that possibility is to think about it, and one must think about it by weighing the plausibility of the debunking explanation against the plausibility of the ethical reasoning at which it is aimed. The claim that, at the most objective level, the question of what we should do becomes meaningless has to compete head-to-head with specific claims about what in fact we should do, and their grounds. So in the end, the contest is between the credibility of substantive ethics and the credibility of an external psychological reduction of that activity....

VI

The first step on the path to ethics is the admission of *generality* in practical judgments. That is actually equivalent to the admission of the existence of reasons, for a reason is something one person can have only if others would also have it if they were in the same circumstances (internal as well as external). In taking an objective view of myself, the first question to answer is whether I have, in this generalizable sense, any reason to do anything, and a negative answer is nearly as implausible as a negative answer to the analogous question of whether I have any reason to believe anything. Neither of those questions—though they are, to begin with, about me—is essentially first-personal, since they are supposed not to depend for their answers on the fact that I am asking them.

It is perhaps less impossible to answer the question about practical reasons in the negative than the question about theoretical reasons. (And by a negative answer, remember, we mean the position that there *are* no reasons, not merely that I have no reason to believe, or do, anything rather than anything else—the skeptical position, which is also universal in its grounds and implications.) If one ceased to recognize theoretical reasons, having reached a reflective standpoint, it would make no sense to go on having beliefs, though one might be unable to stop. But perhaps action wouldn't likewise become senseless if one denied the existence of practical reasons: One could still be moved by impulse and habit, without thinking that what one did was justified in any sense—even by one's inclinations—in a way that admitted generalization.

However, this seems a very implausible option. It implies, for example, that none of your desires and aversions, pleasures and sufferings, or your survival or death, give you any generalizable reason to do anything—that all we can do from an objective standpoint is to observe, and perhaps try to predict, what you *will* do. The application of this view to my own case is outlandish: I can't seriously believe that I have *no reason* to get out of the way of a truck that is bearing down on me in the street—that my motive is a purely psychological reaction not subject to rational endorsement. Clearly I have a reason, and clearly it is generalizable.

The second step on the path to familiar moral territory is the big one: the choice between agent-relative, essentially egoistic (but still general) reasons and some alternative that admits agent-neutral reasons or in some other way acknowledges that each person has a noninstrumental reason to consider the interests of others. It is possible to understand this choice partly as a choice of the way in which one is going to value oneself and one's own interests. It has strong implications in that regard.

Morality is possible only for beings capable of seeing themselves as one individual among others more or less similar in general respects—capable, in other words, of seeing themselves as others see them. When we recognize that although we occupy only our own point of view and not that of anyone else, there is nothing cosmically unique about it, we are faced with a choice. This choice has to do with the relation between the value we naturally accord to ourselves and our fates from our own point of view, and the attitude we take toward these same things when viewed from the impersonal standpoint that assigns to us no unique status apart from anyone else.

One alternative would be not to "transfer" to the impersonal standpoint in any form those values which concern us from the personal standpoint. That would mean that the impersonal standpoint would remain purely descriptive and our

lives and what matters to us as we live them (including the lives of other people we care about) would not be regarded as mattering at all if considered apart from the fact that they are ours, or personally related to us. Each of us, then, would have a system of values centering on his own perspective and would recognize that others were in exactly the same situation.

The other alternative would be to assign to one's life and what goes on in it some form of impersonal as well as purely perspectival value, not dependent on its being one's own. This would then imply that everyone else was also the subject of impersonal value of a similar kind.

The agent-relative position that all of a person's reasons derive from his own interests, desires, and attachments means that I have no reason to care about what happens to other people unless what happens to them matters to me, either directly or instrumentally. This is compatible with the existence of strong derivative reasons for consideration of others—reasons for accepting systems of general rights, and so forth—but it does not include those reasons at the ground level. It also means, of course, that others have no reason to care about what happens to me—again, unless it matters to them in some way, emotionally or instrumentally. All the practical reasons that any of us have, on this theory, depend on what is valuable *to us*.

It follows that we each have value only to ourselves and to those who care about us. Considered impersonally, we are valueless and provide no intrinsic reasons for concern to anyone. So the egoistic answer to the question of what kinds of reasons there are amounts to an assessment of oneself, along with everyone else, as *objectively worthless*. In a sense, it doesn't matter (except to ourselves) what happens to us: Each person has value only *for himself*, not *in himself*.

Now this judgment, while it satisfies the generality condition for reasons, and while perfectly consistent, is in my opinion highly unreasonable and difficult to honestly accept. Can you really believe that objectively, it doesn't matter whether you die of thirst or not—and that your inclination to believe that it does is just the false objectification of your self-love? One could really ask the same question about anybody else's dying of thirst, but concentrating on your own case stimulates the imagination, which is why the fundamental moral argument takes the form, "How would you like it if someone did that to you?" The concept of reasons for action faces us with a question about their content that it is very difficult to answer in a consistently egoistic or agent-relative style.

THE CONTINUING DEBATE:
Are There Objective Ethical Truths?

What Is New

Nagel states that "in the end, the contest [over rational moral objectivity] is between the credibility of substantive ethics and the credibility of an external psychological reduction of that activity." Thus debates 8 and 9, which examine some specific attempts to use psychological research to undermine or at least modify some elements of ethics, have direct relevance to the issues raised in this debate: such appeals to psychological research to modify ethical methodology or moral principles are an attempt to accomplish what Nagel claims cannot be done.

Where to Find More

Among Bernard Williams' many important works (in addition to *Ethics and the Limits of Philosophy*) are *Moral Luck* (Cambridge: Cambridge University Press, 1981); *Shame and Necessity* (Berkeley: University of California Press, 1993); and *Making Sense of Humanity* (Cambridge: Cambridge University Press, 1995).

In addition to *The Last Word* and *The View from Nowhere,* Thomas Nagel's major works include *Mortal Questions* (London: Cambridge University Press, 1979), *Equality and Partiality* (Oxford: Oxford University Press, 1991), and *Concealment and Exposure* (Oxford: Oxford University Press, 2002). Though Nagel represents the Kantian position in this debate, many of his views are quite different from those of Kant—see, in particular, Nagel's *The View from Nowhere.*

Among Kant's classic works on ethics are *Groundwork of the Metaphysic of Morals,* trans. H. J. Paton, as *The Moral Law* (London: Hutchinson, 1953); *Critique of Practical Reason,* trans. L. W. Beck (Indianapolis: Bobbs-Merrill, 1977); and *Religion Within the Limits of Reason Alone,* trans. T. M. Greene and H. H. Hudson (New York: Harper and Row, 1960).

Excellent works on Kant's ethics include Lewis White Beck's *A Commentary on Kant's Critique of Practical Reason* (Chicago: University of Chicago Press, 1960); and Onora O'Neill, *Constructions of Reason: Explorations of Kant's Practical Philosophy* (Cambridge: Cambridge University Press, 1989). A fascinating brief challenge to Kant's ethical system is Rae Langton's "Maria von Herbert's Challenge to Kant," which can be found in Peter Singer, editor, *Ethics* (Oxford: Oxford University Press, 1994).

Many outstanding contemporary philosophers follow—to at least some degree—the Kantian tradition in ethics. A small sample would include Kurt Baier, *The Moral Point of View* (Ithaca, N.Y.: Cornell University Press, 1958); Alan Donagan, *The Theory of Morality* (Chicago: University of Chicago Press, 1977); Alan Gewirth, *Reason and Morality* (Chicago: University of Chicago Press, 1978); Stephen Darwall, *Impartial Reason* (Ithaca, N.Y.: Cornell University Press, 1983) and *Philosophical Ethics* (Boulder, Col.: Westview Press, 1998); Onora O'Neill, *Constructions of Reason: Explorations of Kant's Practical Philosophy* (Cambridge: Cambridge University Press, 1989); Marcia W. Baron, *Kantian Ethics Almost Without Apology* (Ithaca, N.Y.: Cornell University Press, 1995); and Christine Korsgaard, *Creating the Kingdom of Ends* (Cambridge: Cambridge University Press, 1996).

Kantian ethics can seem cold and austere. For a more engaging perspective on Kantian ethics, see Thomas E. Hill, Jr., a Kantian who writes with clarity and charm in *Respect, Pluralism, and Justice: Kantian Perspectives* (Oxford: Oxford University Press, 2000); and *Human Welfare and Moral Worth: Kantian Perspectives* (Oxford: Oxford University Press, 2002).

David Hume has two classic works on ethics and emotions (though both works also contain much more). The first is *A Treatise of Human Nature*, originally published in 1738. A good edition is by L. A. Selby-Bigge (Oxford: Clarendon Press, 1978). The second is *An Inquiry Concerning Human Understanding*, originally published in 1751. A good edition is L. A. Selby-Bigge's *Hume's Enquiries*, 2nd ed. (Oxford: Clarendon Press, 1902).

Kai Nielsen, *Why Be Moral?* (Buffalo, N.Y.: Prometheus Books, 1989) is a very readable defense of nonobjectivist ethics based in emotions.

IS ETHICS BASED
ON A SOCIAL CONTRACT?

Social Contract Theory Offers the Best Grounds for Ethics

ADVOCATE: David Gauthier, a native of Toronto, is Distinguished Service
Professor of Philosophy and Senior Research Fellow at the Center for
Philosophy of Science at the University of Pittsburgh. His *Morals by
Agreement* (Oxford: Oxford University Press, 1986) is widely regarded
as one of the most significant and influential contemporary works on
social contract theory.

SOURCE: "Why Contractarianism?" from Peter Vallentyne, Editor,
*Contractarianism and Rational Choice: Essays on David Gauthier's Morals
by Agreement* (New York: Cambridge University Press, 1991), pages
15–30.

Social Contract Theory Is an Inadequate Account of Ethics

ADVOCATE: Jean Hampton was Professor of Philosophy at the University of
California, Davis; she was the author of *Hobbes and the Social Contract
Tradition* (Cambridge: Cambridge University Press, 1986) and (with
Jeffrie Murphy) *Forgiveness and Mercy* (Cambridge: Cambridge
University Press, 1988).

SOURCE: "Two Faces of Contractarian Thought," from Peter Vallentyne,
Editor, *Contractarianism and Rational Choice: Essays on David
Gauthier's Morals by Agreement* (New York: Cambridge University Press,
1991), pages 31–55.

Maybe we don't find ethical principles through either reason or deep feelings or intuitions; maybe we don't find them at all, but instead we *make* ethical rules through our agreements. Suppose we have just invented the game of baseball, and we decide to play a game. If a batted ball is caught before it hits the ground, should the batter be out? We can't discover the correct rule through reason or intuition; rather, we *decide* among ourselves what the rules will be, and we enforce them. If the rule is that you're out if the ball is caught in the air, then it's *wrong* for you to claim that you are safe when your fly ball is caught. It's wrong, because those are the rules we all agreed upon. The agreed upon and mutually enforced *rules* determine what is right and wrong. We don't discover the moral rules through either reason or feelings, because we don't *discover* them at all: we make them.

There are many versions of social contract theory, but the most famous was by Thomas Hobbes, the 17th Century British philosopher and political theorist; and the classic source is his *Leviathan*:

To this war of every man, against every man, this also is consequent: that nothing can be unjust. The notions of right and wrong, justice and injustice have there no place. Where there is no common power, there is no law; where no law, no injustice. Force, and fraud, are in war the two cardinal virtues. Justice, and injustice are none of the faculties neither of the body, or mind. If they were, they might be in a man that were alone in the world....They are qualities, that relate to men in society, not in solitude.

Social contract theorists start from a "state of nature" with no laws or restraints: a "war of all against all," where life is "nasty, brutish, and short," and the only rule is to do unto others *before* they do unto you. Finally people recognize that it is in their own individual best interests to contract with one another for a more peaceful, law-abiding, and rights-recognizing existence. Of course there was not literally a time when everyone suspended murder and mayhem and sat together drawing up a social contract. Social contract theory is neither history nor anthropology; rather, it offers a model for judging when the rules of a society or state are just and fair. *If*—as a self-interested contractor— you would agree to accept a set of rules, then those rules are reasonably just.

There have been two major developments in contemporary social contract theory. First, John Rawls used social contract theory to develop an account of "justice as fairness," in which he considered what rules of social justice we would approve from "behind the veil of ignorance." That is, suppose you will be born into a society as a human being with the standard needs and desires of our species, but you know nothing else about your position or characteristics or capacities. You have no idea of your gender, race, ethnic group; whether you will be lazy or industrious, bright or dull, athletic or clumsy, poor or privileged. From behind this veil of ignorance, what social rules would you favor? Rawls' social contract theory pushes us to think hard about what rules and systems we would regard as fair and just if we set aside our biases of race and gender, privilege and inherited wealth, special interests and individual talents.

David Gauthier, whose work is the focus of our readings, brings a new twist to social contract theory by his very effective use of the Prisoner's Dilemma. Suppose that Alice and Barbara have been caught with stolen money. The police suspect they were the robbers, but can't prove it. If both keep quiet, each will serve a 2 year sentence. But Alice and Barbara, in separate cells, are offered the same deal: If you squeal on your friend, and your friend keeps silent, your sentence will be reduced to one year; your friend will be sentenced to10 years. If you both talk you'll both be convicted for the bank job, but your cooperation will net each of you a 5 year sentence. Being a self-interested criminal, Alice reaches a quick conclusion: "If I keep quiet, the best I can get is a 2 year sentence, assuming that Barbara also keeps her mouth shut. But if that rat squeals on me, I'll get ten. If I talk, the best I can get is a one year sentence, and the worst is 5. Whether Barbara talks or clams up, my best bet is to talk." The problem is, Barbara is thinking the same thing. They both talk, and both get 5 year sentences. If they could have reliably cooperated both would have been better off. The moral of the story is simple but important: There are circumstances when my individual interests are best served by cooperating rather than seeking the maximum benefits I could gain individually. As a purely self-interested individual, social cooperation—even involving personal sacrifices—is my best policy. And that is sufficient cooperative foundation to build a social contract society.

Jean Hampton challenges social contract theory at its individualistic foundation, arguing that it cannot support belief in intrinsic human worth, and therefore it cannot support an adequate system of morality.

197

➤ In constructing his moral system, Gauthier starts from an assumption of rationally self-interested nonmoral beings. Some critics consider this too austere: humans are after all a profoundly social species. What advantages or disadvantages are there in Gauthier's starting point?

➤ Gauthier proposes his social contract morality as a means of "resolving morality's foundational crisis." Does such a crisis exist?

➤ Hampton claims that traditional contract theory (such as Hobbes' theory) embraces a "radical individualism" that "goes too far in trying to represent us as radically separate from others." The United States, founded on a social contract model, has a strongly individualistic, "make it on your own or suffer the consequences" social structure (for example, the U.S. is the only developed country that does not provide health care for all its citizens). Has social contract thinking shaped U.S. "rugged individualism"?

➤ Hampton's key criticism is that Gauthier's moral system is not as purely individualistic as Gauthier supposes. Is that a legitimate criticism? *If* it is, what effect would that have on Gauthier's moral system?

Social Contract Theory Offers the Best Grounds for Ethics

DAVID GAUTHIER

I

Morality faces a foundational crisis. Contractarianism offers the only plausible resolution of this crisis. These two propositions state my theme. What follows is elaboration.

Nietzsche may have been the first, but he has not been alone, in recognizing the crisis to which I refer. Consider these recent statements. "The hypothesis which I wish to advance is that in the actual world which we inhabit the language of morality is in…[a] state of grave disorder…we have—very largely, if not entirely—lost our comprehension, both theoretical and practical, of morality" (Alasdair MacIntyre). "The resources of most modern moral philosophy are not well adjusted to the modern world" (Bernard Williams).

"There are no objective values.…[But] the main tradition of European moral philosophy includes the contrary claim" (J. L. Mackie). "Moral hypotheses do not help explain why people observe what they observe. So ethics is problematic and nihilism must be taken seriously.…An extreme version of nihilism holds that morality is simply an illusion.…In this version, we should abandon morality, just as an atheist abandons religion after he has decided that religious facts cannot help explain observations" (Gilbert Harman).

I choose these statements to point to features of the crisis that morality faces. They suggest that moral language fits a world view that we have abandoned—a view of the world as purposively ordered. Without this view, we no longer truly understand the moral claims we continue to make. They suggest that there is a lack of fit between what morality presupposes—objective values that help explain our behavior, and the psychological states—desires and beliefs—that, given our present world view, actually provide the best explanation. This lack of fit threatens to undermine the very idea of a morality as more than an anthropological curiosity. But how could this be? How could morality *perish*?

II

To proceed, I must offer a minimal characterization of the morality that faces a foundational crisis. And this is the morality of justified constraint. From the standpoint of the agent, moral considerations present themselves as constraining his choices and actions, in ways independent of his desires, aims, and interests. Later, I shall add to this characterization, but for the moment it will suffice. For it reveals clearly what is in question—the ground of constraint. This ground seems absent from our present world view. And so we ask, what reason can a person have for recognizing and accepting a constraint that is independent of his desires and interests? He may agree that such a constraint would be *morally* justified; he would have a reason for accepting it *if* he had a reason for accepting morality. But what justifies paying attention to morality, rather than dismissing it as an appendage of outworn beliefs? We ask, and seem to find no answer.

Fortunately, I do not have to defend *normative* foundationalism. One problem with accepting moral justification as part of our ongoing practice is that, as I have suggested, we no longer accept the world view on which it depends. But perhaps a more immediately pressing problem is that we have, ready to hand, an alternative mode for justifying our choices and ac-

tions. In its more austere and, in my view, more defensible form, this is to show that choices and actions maximize the agent's expected utility, where utility is a measure of considered preference. In its less austere version, this is to show that choices and actions satisfy, not a subjectively defined requirement such as utility, but meet the agent's objective interests. Since I do not believe that we have objective interests, I shall ignore this latter. But it will not matter. For the idea is clear; we have a mode of justification that does not require the introduction of moral considerations.

Let me call this alternative nonmoral mode of justification, neutrally, deliberative justification. Now moral and deliberative justification are directed at the same objects—our choices and actions. What if they conflict? And what do we say to the person who offers a deliberative justification of his choices and actions and refuses to offer any other? We can say, of course, that his behavior lacks *moral* justification, but this seems to lack any hold, unless he chooses to enter the moral framework. And such entry, he may insist, lacks any deliberative justification, at least for him.

If morality perishes, the justificatory enterprise, in relation to choice and action, does not perish with it. Rather, one mode of justification perishes, a mode that, it may seem, now hangs unsupported. But not only unsupported, for it is difficult to deny that deliberative justification is more clearly basic, that it cannot be avoided insofar as we are rational agents, so that if moral justification conflicts with it, morality seems not only unsupported but opposed by what is rationally more fundamental.

Deliberative justification relates to our deep sense of self. What distinguishes human beings from other animals, and provides the basis for rationality, is the capacity for semantic representation. You can, as your dog on the whole cannot, represent a state of affairs to yourself, and consider in particular whether or not it is the case, and whether or not you would want it to be the case. You can represent to yourself the contents of your beliefs, and your desires or preferences. But in representing them, you bring them into relation with one another. You represent to yourself that the Blue Jays will win the World Series, and that a National League team will win the World Series, and that the Blue Jays are not a National League team. And in recognizing a conflict among those beliefs, you find rationality thrust upon you. Note that the first two beliefs could be replaced by preferences, with the same effect.

Since in representing our preferences we become aware of conflict among them, the step from representation to choice becomes complicated. We must, somehow, bring our conflicting desires and preferences into some sort of coherence. And there is only one plausible candidate for a principle of coherence—a maximizing principle. We order our preferences, in relation to decision and action, so that we may choose in a way that maximizes our expectation of preference fulfillment. And in so doing, we show ourselves to be rational agents, engaged in deliberation and deliberative justification. There is simply nothing else for practical rationality to be.

The foundational crisis of morality thus cannot be avoided by pointing to the existence of a practice of justification within the moral framework, and denying that any extramoral foundation is relevant. For an extramoral mode of justification is already present, existing not side by side with moral justification, but in a manner tied to the way in which we unify our beliefs and preferences and so acquire our deep sense of self. We need not suppose that this deliberative justification is

itself to be understood foundationally. All that we need suppose is that moral justification does not plausibly survive conflict with it.

III

In explaining why we may not dismiss the idea of a foundational crisis in morality as resulting from a misplaced appeal to a philosophically discredited or suspect idea of foundationalism, I have begun to expose the character and dimensions of the crisis. I have claimed that morality faces an alternative, conflicting, deeper mode of justification, related to our deep sense of self, that applies to the entire realm of choice and action, and that evaluates each *action* in terms of the reflectively held concerns of its *agent*. The relevance of the agent's concerns to practical justification does not seem to me in doubt. The relevance of anything else, except insofar as it bears on the agent's concerns, does seem to me very much in doubt. If the agent's reflectively endorsed concerns, his preferences, desires, and aims, are, with his considered beliefs, constitutive of his self-conception, then I can see no remotely plausible way of arguing from their relevance to that of anything else that is not similarly related to his sense of self. And, indeed, I can see no way of introducing anything as relevant to practical justification except through the agent's self-conception. My assertion of this practical individualism is not a conclusive argument, but the burden of proof is surely on those who would maintain a contrary position. Let them provide the arguments—if they can.

Deliberative justification does not refute morality. Indeed, it does not offer morality the courtesy of a refutation. It ignores morality, and seemingly replaces it. It preempts the arena of justification, apparently leaving morality no room to gain purchase. Let me offer a controversial comparison. Religion faces—indeed, has faced—a comparable foundational crisis. Religion demands the worship of a divine being who purposively orders the universe. But it has confronted an alternative mode of explanation. Although the emergence of a cosmological theory based on efficient, rather than teleological, causation provided warning of what was to come, the supplanting of teleology in biology by the success of evolutionary theory in providing a mode of explanation that accounted in efficient-causal terms for the *appearance* of a purposive order among living beings, may seem to toll the death knell for religion as an intellectually respectable enterprise. But evolutionary biology and, more generally, modern science do not refute religion. Rather they ignore it, replacing its explanations by ontologically simpler ones. Religion, understood as affirming the justifiable worship of a divine being, may be unable to survive its foundational crisis. Can morality, understood as affirming justifiable constraints on choice independent of the agent's concerns, survive?

There would seem to be three ways for morality to escape religion's apparent fate. One would be to find, for moral facts or moral properties, an explanatory role that would entrench them prior to any consideration of justification. One could then argue that any mode of justification that ignored moral considerations would be ontologically defective. I mention this possibility only to put it to one side. No doubt there are persons who accept moral constraints on their choices and actions, and it would not be possible to explain those choices and actions were we to ignore this. But our explanation of their behavior need not commit us to their view. Here the comparison with religion should be straightforward and uncontroversial.

We could not explain many of the practices of the religious without reference to their beliefs. But to characterize what a religious person is doing as, say, an act of worship, does not commit us to supposing that an object of worship actually exists, though it does commit us to supposing that she believes such an object to exist. Similarly, to characterize what a moral agent is doing as, say, fulfilling a duty does not commit us to supposing that there are any duties, though it does commit us to supposing that he believes that there are duties. The skeptic who accepts neither can treat the apparent role of morality in explanation as similar to that of religion. Of course, I do not consider that the parallel can be ultimately sustained, since I agree with the religious skeptic but not with the moral skeptic. But to establish an explanatory role for morality, one must first demonstrate its justificatory credentials. One may not assume that it has a prior explanatory role.

The second way would be to reinterpret the idea of justification, showing that, more fully understood, deliberative justification is incomplete, and must be supplemented in a way that makes room for morality. There is a long tradition in moral philosophy, deriving primarily from Kant, that is committed to this enterprise. This is not the occasion to embark on a critique of what, in the hope again of achieving a neutral characterization, I shall call universalistic justification. But critique may be out of place. The success of deliberative justification may suffice. For theoretical claims about its incompleteness seem to fail before the simple practical recognition that it works. Of course, on the face of it, deliberative justification does not work to provide a place for morality. But to suppose that it must, if it is to be fully adequate or complete as a mode of justification, would be to assume what is in question, whether moral justification is defensible.

If, independent of one's actual desires, and aims, there were objective values, and if, independent of one's actual purposes, one were part of an objectively purposive order, then we might have reason to insist on the inadequacy of the deliberative framework. An objectively purposive order would introduce considerations relevant to practical justification that did not depend on the agent's self-conception. But the supplanting of teleology in our physical and biological explanations closes this possibility, as it closes the possibility of religious explanation.

I turn then to the third way of resolving morality's foundational crisis. The first step is to embrace deliberative justification, and recognize that morality's place must be found within, and not outside, its framework. Now this will immediately raise two problems. First of all, it will seem that the attempt to establish any constraint on choice and action, within the framework of a deliberation that aims at the maximal fulfillment of the agent's considered preferences, must prove impossible. But even if this be doubted, it will seem that the attempt to establish a constraint *independent of the agent's preferences*, within such a framework, verges on lunacy. Nevertheless, this is precisely the task accepted by my third way. And, unlike its predecessors, I believe that it can be successful; indeed, I believe that my recent book, *Morals by Agreement*, shows how it can succeed.

Let me sketch briefly those features of deliberative rationality that enable it to constrain maximizing choice. The key idea is that in many situations, if each person chooses what, given the choices of the others, would maximize her expected utility, then the outcome will be mutually disadvantageous in comparison with some alternative—everyone could do better.

Equilibrium, which obtains when each person's action is a best response to the others' actions, is incompatible with (Pareto-)optimality, which obtains when no one could do better without someone else doing worse. Given the ubiquity of such situations, each person can see the benefit, to herself, of participating with her fellows in practices requiring each to refrain from the direct endeavor to maximize her own utility, when such mutual restraint is mutually advantageous. No one, of course, can have reason to accept any unilateral constraint on her maximizing behavior; each benefits from, and only from, the constraint accepted by her fellows. But if one benefits more from a constraint on others than one loses by being constrained oneself, one may have reason to accept a practice requiring everyone, including oneself, to exhibit such a constraint. We may represent such a practice as capable of gaining unanimous agreement among rational persons who were choosing the terms on which they would interact with each other. And this agreement is the basis of morality.

Consider a simple example of a moral practice that would command rational agreement. Suppose each of us were to assist her fellows only when either she could expect to benefit herself from giving assistance, or she took a direct interest in their well-being. Then, in many situations, persons would not give assistance to others, even though the benefit to the recipient would greatly exceed the cost to the giver, because there would be no provision for the giver to share in the benefit. Everyone would then expect to do better were each to give assistance to her fellows, regardless of her own benefit or interest, whenever the cost of assisting was low and the benefit of receiving assistance considerable. Each would thereby accept a constraint on the direct pursuit of her own concerns, not unilaterally, but given a like acceptance by others. Reflection leads us to recognize that those who belong to groups whose members adhere to such a practice of mutual assistance enjoy benefits in interaction that are denied to others. We may then represent such a practice as rationally acceptable to everyone.

This rationale for agreed constraint makes no reference to the content of anyone's preferences. The argument depends simply on the *structure* of interaction, on the way in which each person's endeavor to fulfill her own preferences affects the fulfillment of everyone else. Thus, each person's reason to accept a mutually constraining practice is independent of her particular desires, aims and interests, although not, of course, of the fact that she has such concerns. The idea of a purely rational agent, moved to act by reason alone, is not, I think, an intelligible one. Morality is not to be understood as a constraint arising from reason alone on the fulfillment of nonrational preferences. Rather, a rational agent is one who acts to achieve the maximal fulfillment of her preferences, and morality is a constraint on the manner in which she acts, arising from the effects of interaction with other agents.

Hobbes's Foole now makes his familiar entry onto the scene, to insist that however rational it may be for a person to agree with her fellows to practices that hold out the promise of mutual advantage, yet it is rational to follow such practices only when so doing directly conduces to her maximal preference fulfillment. But then such practices impose no real constraint. The effect of agreeing to or accepting them can only be to change the expected payoffs of her possible choices, making it rational for her to choose what in the absence of the practice would not be utility maximizing. The practices would offer only true prudence, not true morality.

The Foole is guilty of a twofold error. First, he fails to understand that real acceptance of such moral practices as assisting one's fellows, or keeping one's promises, or telling the truth is possible only among those who are disposed to comply with them. If my disposition to comply extends only so far as my interests or concerns at the time of performance, then you will be the real fool if you interact with me in ways that demand a more rigorous compliance. If, for example, it is rational to keep promises only when so doing is directly utility maximizing, then among persons whose rationality is common knowledge, only promises that require such limited compliance will be made. And opportunities for mutual advantage will be thereby forgone.

Consider this example of the way in which promises facilitate mutual benefit. Jones and Smith have adjacent farms. Although neighbors, and not hostile, they are also not friends, so that neither gets satisfaction from assisting the other. Nevertheless, they recognize that, if they harvest their crops together, each does better than if each harvests alone. Next week, Jones's crop will be ready for harvesting; a fortnight hence, Smith's crop will be ready. The harvest in, Jones is retiring, selling his farm, and moving to Florida, where he is unlikely to encounter Smith or other members of their community. Jones would like to promise Smith that, if Smith helps him harvest next week, he will help Smith harvest in a fortnight. But Jones and Smith both know that in a fortnight, helping Smith would be a pure cost to Jones. Even if Smith helps him, he has nothing to gain by returning the assistance, since neither care for Smith nor, in the circumstances, concern for his own reputation, moves him. Hence, if Jones and Smith know that Jones acts straightforwardly to maximize the fulfillment of his preferences, they know that he will not help Smith. Smith, therefore, will not help Jones even if Jones pretends to promise assistance in return. Nevertheless, Jones would do better could he make and keep such a promise—and so would Smith.

The Foole's second error, following on his first, should be clear; he fails to recognize that in plausible circumstances, persons who are genuinely disposed to a more rigorous compliance with moral practices than would follow from their interests at the time of performance can expect to do better than those who are not so disposed. For the former, constrained maximizers as I call them, will be welcome partners in mutually advantageous cooperation, in which each relies on the voluntary adherence of the others, from which the latter, straightforward maximizers, will be excluded. Constrained maximizers may thus expect more favorable opportunities than their fellows. Although in assisting their fellows, keeping their promises, and complying with other moral practices, they forgo preference fulfillment that they might obtain, yet they do better overall than those who always maximize expected utility, because of their superior opportunities.

In identifying morality with those constraints that would obtain agreement among rational persons who were choosing their terms of interaction, I am engaged in rational reconstruction. I do not suppose that we have actually agreed to existent moral practices and principles. Nor do I suppose that all existent moral practices would secure our agreement, were the question to be raised. Not all existent moral practices need be justifiable—need be ones with which we ought willingly to comply. Indeed, I do not even suppose that the practices with which we ought willingly to comply need be those that would secure our present agreement. I suppose that justifiable moral practices

are those that would secure our agreement ex ante, in an appropriate premoral situation. They are those to which we should have agreed as constituting the terms of our future interaction, had we been, per impossible, in a position to decide those terms. Hypothetical agreement thus provides a test of the justifiability of our existent moral practices.

IV

Many questions could be raised about this account, but here I want to consider only one. I have claimed that moral practices are rational, even though they constrain each person's attempt to maximize her own utility, insofar as they would be the objects of unanimous ex ante agreement. But to refute the Foole, I must defend not only the rationality of agreement, but also that of compliance, and the defense of compliance threatens to preempt the case for agreement, so that my title should be "Why Constraint?" and not "Why Contractarianism?" It is rational to dispose oneself to accept certain constraints on direct maximization in choosing and acting, if and only if so disposing oneself maximizes one's expected utility. What then is the relevance of agreement, and especially of hypothetical agreement? Why should it be rational to dispose oneself to accept only those constraints that would be the object of mutual agreement in an appropriate premoral situation, rather than those constraints that are found in our existent moral practices? Surely it is acceptance of the latter that makes a person welcome in interaction with his fellows. For compliance with existing morality will be what they expect, and take into account in choosing partners with whom to cooperate.

I began with a challenge to morality—how can it be rational for us to accept its constraints? It may now seem that what I have shown is that it is indeed rational for us to accept constraints, but to accept them whether or not they might be plausibly considered moral. Morality, it may seem, has nothing to do with my argument; what I have shown is that it is rational to be disposed to comply with whatever constraints are generally accepted and expected, regardless of their nature. But this is not my view.

To show the relevance of agreement to the justification of constraints, let us assume an ongoing society in which individuals more or less acknowledge and comply with a given set of practices that constrain their choices in relation to what they would be did they take only their desires, aims, and interests directly into account. Suppose that a disposition to conform to these existing practices is prima facie advantageous, since persons who are not so disposed may expect to be excluded from desirable opportunities by their fellows. However, the practices themselves have, or at least need have, no basis in agreement. And they need satisfy no intuitive standard of fairness or impartiality, characteristics that we may suppose relevant to the identification of the practices with those of a genuine morality. Although we may speak of the practices as constituting the morality of the society in question, we need not consider them morally justified or acceptable. They are simply practices constraining individual behavior in a way that each finds rational to accept.

Suppose now that our persons, as rational maximizers of individual utility, come to reflect on the practices constituting their morality. They will, of course, assess the practices in relation to their own utility, but with the awareness that their fellows will be doing the same. And one question that must arise is: Why these practices? For they will recognize that the set of actual moral practices is not the only possible set of constraining practices that would yield mutually advantageous, optimal outcomes. They will recognize the possibility of alternative moral orders. At this point it will not be enough to say that, as a matter of fact, each person can expect to benefit from a disposition to comply with existing practices. For persons will also ask themselves: Can I benefit more, not from simply abandoning any morality, and recognizing no constraint, but from a partial rejection of existing constraints in favor of an alternative set? Once this question is asked, the situation is transformed; the existing moral order must be assessed, not only against simple noncompliance, but also against what we may call alternative compliance.

To make this assessment, each will compare her prospects under the existing practices with those she would anticipate from a set that, in the existing circumstances, she would expect to result from bargaining with her fellows. If her prospects would be improved by such negotiation, then she will have a real, although not necessarily sufficient, incentive to demand a change in the established moral order. More generally, if there are persons whose prospects would be improved by renegotiation, then the existing order will be recognizably unstable. No doubt those whose prospects would be worsened by renegotiation will have a clear incentive to resist, to appeal to the status quo. But their appeal will be a weak one, especially among persons who are not taken in by spurious ideological considerations, but focus on individual utility maximization. Thus, although in the real world, we begin with an existing set of moral practices as constraints on our maximizing behavior, yet we are led by reflection to the idea of an amended set that would obtain the agreement of everyone, and this amended set has, and will be recognized to have, a stability lacking in existing morality.

The reflective capacity of rational agents leads them from the given to the agreed, from existing practices and principles requiring constraint to those that would receive each person's assent. The same reflective capacity, I claim, leads from those practices that would be agreed to, in existing social circumstances, to those that would receive ex ante agreement, premoral and presocial. As the status quo proves unstable when it comes into conflict with what would be agreed to, so what would be agreed to proves unstable when it comes into conflict with what would have been agreed to in an appropriate presocial context. For as existing practices must seem arbitrary insofar as they do not correspond to what a rational person would agree to, so what such a person would agree to in existing circumstances must seem arbitrary in relation to what she would accept in a presocial condition.

What a rational person would agree to in existing circumstances depends in large part on her negotiating position vis-à-vis her fellows. But her negotiating position is significantly affected by the existing social institutions, and so by the currently accepted moral practices embodied in those institutions. Thus, although agreement may well yield practices differing from those embodied in existing social institutions, yet it will be influenced by those practices, which are not themselves the product of rational agreement. And this must call the rationality of the agreed practices into question. The arbitrariness of existing practices must infect any agreement whose terms are significantly affected by them. Although rational agreement is in itself a source of stability, yet this stability is undermined by the arbitrariness of the circumstances in which it takes place. To escape this arbitrariness, rational persons will revert from actual to hypothetical agreement, considering what practices they would have agreed to from an initial position not structured by existing institutions and the practices they embody.

The content of a hypothetical agreement is determined by an appeal to the equal rationality of persons. Rational persons will voluntarily accept an agreement only insofar as they perceive it to be equally advantageous to each. To be sure, each would be happy to accept an agreement more advantageous to herself than to her fellows, but since no one will accept an agreement perceived to be less advantageous, agents whose rationality is a matter of common knowledge will recognize the futility of aiming at or holding out for more, and minimize their bargaining costs by coordinating at the point of equal advantage. Now the extent of advantage is determined in a twofold way. First, there is advantage internal to an agreement. In this respect, the expectation of equal advantage is assured by procedural fairness. The step from existing moral practices to those resulting from actual agreement takes rational persons to a procedurally fair situation, in which each perceives the agreed practices to be ones that it is equally rational for all to accept, given the circumstances in which agreement is reached. But those circumstances themselves may be called into question insofar as they are perceived to be arbitrary—the result, in part, of compliance with constraining practices that do not themselves ensure the expectation of equal advantage, and so do not reflect the equal rationality of the complying parties. To neutralize this arbitrary element, moral practices to be fully acceptable must be conceived as constituting a possible outcome of a hypothetical agreement under circumstances that are unaffected by social institutions that themselves lack full acceptability. Equal rationality demands consideration of external circumstances as well as internal procedures.

But what is the practical import of this argument? It would be absurd to claim that mere acquaintance with it, or even acceptance of it, will lead to the replacement of existing moral practices by those that would secure presocial agreement. It would be irrational for anyone to give up the benefits of the existing moral order simply because he comes to realize that it affords him more than he could expect from pure rational agreement with his fellows. And it would be irrational for anyone to accept a long-term utility loss by refusing to comply with the existing moral order, simply because she comes to realize that such compliance affords her less than she could expect from pure rational agreement. Nevertheless, these realizations do transform, or perhaps bring to the surface, the character of the relationships between persons that are maintained by the existing constraints, so that some of these relationships come to be recognized as coercive. These realizations constitute the elimination of false consciousness, and they result from a process of rational reflection that brings persons into what, in my theory, is the parallel of Jürgen Habermas's ideal speech situation. Without an argument to defend themselves in open dialogue with their fellows, those who are more than equally advantaged can hope to maintain their privileged position only if they can coerce their fellows into accepting it. And this, of course, may be possible. But coercion is not agreement, and it lacks any inherent stability.

Stability plays a key role in linking compliance to agreement. Aware of the benefits to be gained from constraining practices, rational persons will seek those that invite stable compliance. Now compliance is stable if it arises from agreement among persons each of whom considers both that the terms of agreement are sufficiently favorable to herself that it is ra-

tional for her to accept them, and that they are not so favorable to others that it would be rational for them to accept terms less favorable to them and more favorable to herself. An agreement affording equally favorable terms to all thus invites, as no other can, stable compliance.

V

In defending the claim that moral practices, to obtain the stable voluntary compliance of rational individuals, must be the objects of an appropriate hypothetical agreement, I have added to the initial minimal characterization of morality. Not only does morality constrain our choices and actions, but it does so in an impartial way, reflecting the equal rationality of the persons subject to constraint. Although it is no part of my argument to show that the requirements of contractarian morality will satisfy the Rawlsian test of cohering with our considered judgments in reflective equilibrium, yet it would be misleading to treat rationally agreed constraints on direct utility maximization as constituting a morality at all, rather than as replacing morality, were there no fit between their content and our pretheoretical moral views. The fit lies, I suggest, in the impartiality required for hypothetical agreement.

The foundational crisis of morality is thus resolved by exhibiting the rationality of our compliance with mutual, rationally agreed constraints on the pursuit of our desires, aims, and interests. Although bereft of a basis in objective values or an objectively purposive order, and confronted by a more fundamental mode of justification, morality survives by incorporating itself into that mode. Moral considerations have the same status, and the same role in explaining behavior, as the other reasons acknowledged by a rational deliberator. We are left with a unified account of justification, in which an agent's choices and actions are evaluated in relation to his preferences—to the concerns that are constitutive of his sense of self. But since morality binds the agent independently of the particular content of his preferences, it has the prescriptive grip with which the Christian and Kantian views have invested it.

In incorporating morality into deliberative justification, we recognize a new dimension to the agent's self-conception. For morality requires that a person have the capacity to commit himself, to enter into agreement with his fellows secure in the awareness that he can and will carry out his part of the agreement without regard to many of those considerations that normally and justifiably would enter into his future deliberations. And this is more than the capacity to bring one's desires and interests together with one's beliefs into a single coherent whole. Although this latter unifying capacity must extend its attention to past and future, the unification it achieves may itself be restricted to that extended present within which a person judges and decides. But in committing oneself to future action in accordance with one's agreement, one must fix at least a subset of one's desires and beliefs to hold in that future. The self that agrees and the self that complies must be one. "Man himself must first of all have become *calculable, regular, necessary*, even in his own image of himself, if he is to be able to stand security for *his own future*, which is what one who promises does!"

In developing *"the right to make promises,"* we human beings have found a contractarian bulwark against the perishing of morality.

Social Contract Theory is an Inadequate Account of Ethics

JEAN HAMPTON

I

Although Hobbes's masterpiece *Leviathan* is primarily concerned with presenting a contract argument for the institution of a certain kind of state (one with an absolute sovereign), if one looks closely, one also sees a sketch of a certain kind of contractarian approach to morality, which has profoundly influenced contemporary moral theorists such as Gauthier.

Hobbes's approach to morality does not assume there are natural moral laws or natural rights that we discern through the use of our reason or intuition. It is not an approach that assumes there is a naturally good object in the world (such as Aristotle's *Summum Bonum*) that moral action serves and that people ought to pursue. It is not an approach that explains moral action as "natural," for example, as action generated by powerful other-regarding sentiments; Hobbes did not believe that such sentiments were very important or powerful in human life. And it is not an approach that justifies morality as a set of laws commanded by God—although Hobbes believed that his moral imperatives were *also* justified as commands of God. Using his contractarian method, he seeks to define the nature and authority of moral imperatives by reference to the desires and reasoning abilities of human beings, so that regardless of their religious commitments, all people will see that they have reason to act morally. So without repudiating the divine origin of the laws, Hobbes invokes contract language in order to develop an entirely *human* justification of morality.

Let me simply state here the features of what I take to be the Hobbesian moral theory.

1. What is valuable is what a person desires, not what he ought to desire (for no such prescriptively powerful object exists); and rational action is action that achieves or maximizes the satisfaction of desire (where it is a fact that the desire for self-preservation is our primary desire, and that human beings are, by and large, mutually unconcerned).

2. Moral action is rational for a person to perform if and only if such action advances his interests.

3. Morality is, in part, a body of causal knowledge about what human actions lead to peace, an end which it is common knowledge people desire and which they can all share, so that such actions are rational for them and "mutually agreeable." (This precept rests on the Hobbesian belief that people are not self-sufficient, and that they are roughly equal in strength and mental ability.)

4. Peace-producing action is only individually rational to perform (hence only moral action) when there is a convention in the community that people perform such action (so that I know that if I behave cooperatively, then others will do so too, and vice versa). These conventions comprise the institution of morality in our society. The rationality of performance is, however, subject to two provisos:

Proviso 1: In order to be moral, an action must be not only peace producing and performed in the knowledge that others are willing to do so, but also an action that involves no net loss for the agent.

Proviso 2: Human beings are not, as a group, rational enough to be able to institute moral conventions, and hence must create a sovereign who can use his power to generate them.

5. Defining justice or equitable treatment in situations of conflict is done by considering what principles of justice the people involved "could agree to" or "what they would be unreasonable to reject," where the reasonableness of rejection is determined by a calculation comparing the benefits and costs of accepting an arbitrator's resolution with the benefits and costs of resorting to violence to resolve the conflict. An impartial judge, therefore, arbitrates according to the principle "to each according to his threat advantage in war."

Let us reflect, for a moment, on the interesting features and strengths of a moral theory with this structure. Consider, first of all, that the Hobbesian approach relies on a very strong conception of individuality. According to Hobbes, cooperative social interaction is presented neither as inevitable nor as something that people value for its own sake, but rather as something that asocially defined individuals find instrumentally valuable given their primary (nonsocially defined) desires. To think that cooperative behavior needs to be encouraged and justified, so that we must be *persuaded* to behave socially toward one another, is to believe that, even if society has some affect on us, it does not determine our fundamental or "intrinsic" nature as human beings, which is a nature that "dissociates us, and renders us apt to invade and destroy one another."

Moreover, notice that there are two quite different ways in which this moral contractarian theory uses the notion of agreement. Features 2 and 3 capture the idea that the behavior enjoined by Hobbes's laws of nature is "agreeable," that is, that such action helps to secure the most-desired objects and/or states of affairs for each individual. Feature 5 captures the idea for which moral contractarians are famous; namely, that certain features of morality (e.g., fair resolution of conflict) can be understood as the *object* of agreement. However, there is a connection, in Hobbes's theory, between the latter way of using agreement and the former. To resolve conflicts via the use of arbitrators and agreement procedures is to resolve them peacefully and with much less cost to the parties than more violent resolution procedures. Hobbes commends the use of arbitrators as individually rational for disputants, and warns the arbitrators that their usefulness to the disputants depends on the extent to which their peaceful resolution is more acceptable than going to war to resolve the dilemma. It is therefore conducive to self-preservation to use a cooperative agreement procedure to resolve conflict, so that defining moral behavior through agreement is itself, for Hobbes, a mutually agreeable—that is, mutually self-preserving—behavior.

But perhaps most important of all, we should appreciate that all five features of Hobbes's moral view fit into a moral theory that is committed to the idea that morality is a *human-made institution*, which is justified only to the extent that it effectively furthers human interests. That is, Hobbes seeks to explain the *existence* of morality in society by appealing to the convention-creating activities of human beings, while arguing that the *justification* of morality in any human society depends upon how well its moral conventions serve individuals' desires.

In fact, there is a connection between Hobbes's contractarian approach to the state and this approach to morality. His decision to justify absolute sovereignty by reference to what people "could agree to" in a prepolitical society is an attempt to explain and legitimate the state's authority by appealing neither to God nor to any natural features of human beings that might be thought to explain the subordination of some to others, but solely to the needs and desires of the people who will be subjects of political realms. In the same manner, he insists that existing moral rules have power over us because they are social conventions for behavior (where Hobbes would also argue that these conventions only exist because of the power of the sovereign).

But Hobbes does not assume that existing conventions are, in and of themselves, justified. By considering "what we *could* agree to" if we had the chance to reappraise and redo the cooperative conventions in our society, we are able to determine the extent to which our present conventions are "mutually agreeable" and so *rational* for us to accept and act on. So Hobbes's moral theory invokes both actual agreements (i.e., conventions) and hypothetical agreements (which involve considering what conventions would be "mutually agreeable") at different points in his theory; the former are what he believes our moral life consists of; the latter are what he believes our moral life *should* consist of—that is, what our actual moral life should model. The contractarian methodology is useful in defining and justifying morality for one who believes that morality is man-made because considering what moral laws "people could agree to" (as well as what laws they have agreed to) is a way of confirming *that* morality is man-made, and a way of appraising how well the present institution serves the powerful self-regarding interests that virtually all of us have.

Note that this way of cashing out the language of hypothetical agreement makes the agreement-talk only a kind of metaphor, and not a device that reveals, in and of itself, the nature of morality or justice. What rational agents could all agree to is the securing of an object and/or state of affairs, the benefits of which they could all share and for which there is a rational argument using premises that all rational agents would take as a basis for deliberation. Hence, to determine what these agents "could all agree to," one must perform a deduction of practical reason, something that Hobbes believes he has done in Chapters 14 and 15 of *Leviathan*.

Hence, the notion of contract or agreement does not do justificational work *by itself* in the Hobbesian moral theory. What we "could agree to" has moral force for Hobbes not because make-believe promises in hypothetical worlds have any binding force, but because this sort of agreement is a device that *reveals* the way in which the agreed-upon outcome is rational for all of us. The justificational force of this kind of contract theory is therefore carried within, but derived from sources other than, the contract or agreement in the theory.

II

There was enormous interest in this Hobbesian understanding of morality in the seventeenth century by both detractors and supporters alike.

In the latter half of the twentieth century, we find renewed enthusiasm for this approach and a sustained interest in developing it further. And I suspect that the source of the enthusiasm comes from contemporary philosophers' attraction to the most important and fundamental feature of this approach, the presumption that morality is a human creation.

The contemporary theory that most completely realizes the Hobbesian approach and that develops it in important ways is presented by David Gauthier in *Morals by Agreement*, where he attempts to "validate the conception of morality as a set of rational, impartial constraints on the pursuit of individual interest." Every one of the features of Hobbes's moral theory is embraced in some fashion by Gauthier. On his view, moral behavior is rational and mutually advantageous behavior (features 1 and 2) that will lead to a cooperative state of affairs that is desired by everyone (feature 3), assuming, of course, that they are equal in rationality and technology, when (and only when) people become disposed to engage in such behavior on a widespread basis (i.e., when a convention to behave cooperatively exists—feature 4). Gauthier also argues that resolution of conflict by such individuals should proceed via principles arrived at by considering the outcome of a hypothetical bargain among equals (feature 5). The people in this theory are quite clearly determinate individuals, who are defined prior to the morality that their contractual agreement is supposed to justify. While Gauthier does not explicitly say that the constraints traditionally endorsed as "moral" in human societies are human inventions, that idea, as well as the idea that these constraints can be "reinvented" to better serve human purposes, appears to be the assumption behind his philosophical project, which aims to show what conventions people *would* agree to if they were the sort of perfectly rational people we are all striving to become.

However, what makes Gauthier's moral contractarianism so interesting is the way in which it develops certain features of Hobbes's moral theory to produce not only a more sophisticated moral theory than Hobbes's own, but also one that is more palatable to twentieth-century moral theorists. Consider again feature 4 of Hobbes's theory: that it would only be ra-

tional to act cooperatively if others are disposed to do so. In general, Hobbes seems to be right that cooperative situations have a game-theoretic structure such that people are rational to act cooperatively together, but irrational to act cooperatively alone. Yet sometimes cooperation is surely going to have a Prisoner's Dilemma structure, so that even when others are disposed to cooperate, the individual agent is still rational *not* to cooperate. This suggests that the correct moral attitude is one that says, in essence: "I will cooperate with others, when they are willing to do so, except in situations where, by not cooperating, I can gain benefits from them with impunity," but this attitude is hardly what one would call "moral." Hume explicitly worries about this problem when he discusses the "sensible knave" who has exactly the attitude I have just described:

> And though it is allowed that, without a regard to property, no society could subsist; yet according to the imperfect way in which human affairs are conducted, a sensible knave, in particular incidents, may think that an act of iniquity or infidelity will make a considerable addition to his fortune, without causing any considerable breach in the social union or confederacy. That *honesty is the best policy*, may be a good general rule, but is liable to many exceptions; and he, it may perhaps be thought, conducts himself with most wisdom, who observes the general rule, and takes advantage of all the exceptions.

The knave is essentially saying that he will cooperate if and only if it is utility maximizing for him to do so, and thus will be prepared not to do so in situations, such as the Prisoner's Dilemma, despite the existence of a moral convention to perform the cooperative act in that sort of situation. And what does Hume say to this sensible knave? Essentially nothing. Given the difficulties that Hobbes himself had providing an answer to the same knavish question, we see that it is difficult for anyone who embraces the Hobbesian approach to morality to persuade someone who has no natural sentiments against exploitation of his fellow man not to exploit them when he can do so with impunity. Yet such a person is very far from being moral.

Gauthier attempts, however, to answer the knave, inspired by a line of argumentation that he believes Hobbes suggests (but does not develop adequately) in an attempt to answer the "foole"—who offers roughly the same challenge as Hume's knave. It is rational, says Gauthier, for people to become "disposed" to cooperate in such situations (assuming, however, that a sufficient number of others will become similarly disposed). By doing so, they become "constrained maximizers" rather than knavish "straightforward maximizers," where the former are people who pursue their advantage but who do so respecting a constraint against exploitative noncooperation in Prisoner's Dilemmas, where they have good reason to believe that their partners are inclined to cooperate. Such people are willing to forego benefit in Prisoner's Dilemmas; hence, they are not straightforwardly maximizing utility. Yet they have chosen to be disposed to act in this way because they have determined that they can amass more utility by having this disposition than by not having it. A constrained maximizer refrains from taking advantage of any person who is also disposed to constrain his maximizing behavior because "he is not the sort of person that is disposed to do that sort of thing." That is the "moral" attitude that the sensible knave lacks. But the constrained maximizer has that "moral" atti-

tude because of a prior determination that is individually maximizing to have it. So, true to Hobbesian principles, Gauthier is arguing that moral behavior is utility maximizing and, in the long run, behavior that involves no net cost.

Contemporary Hobbesians and Humeans would certainly *want* to embrace Gauthier's argument if they could. It offers them a way to explain how collectively rational cooperative action that involves forgoing exploitative opportunities, but which is not dangerous, is also *individually rational* for the agent. But I am not so sure that they can embrace it. First, the idea that one could "will" to be disposed to act as Gauthier describes is dubious if one accepts Hobbesian psychology, and perhaps just as dubious on more plausible contemporary psychological theories. Second, it remains to be seen whether or not Gauthier's argument that it is rational to become disposed to act as a constrained maximizer actually succeeds. If Peter Danielson is right it is rational to adopt the more "knavish" cooperative attitude called "reciprocal cooperation," which differs from Gauthier's constrained maximization in that it directs us to exploit (rather than cooperate with) unconditional cooperators. Finally, it might be even more rational only to *pretend* to be disposed to cooperate in either Gauthier's or Danielson's sense, ready to exploit others whenever one can do so with impunity.

The jury is, therefore, still out on the question of whether constrained maximization is rational for individuals to adopt. But other of Gauthier's modifications of Hobbes's project face what seem to be even more serious difficulties. For example, Gauthier argues that Hobbes was wrong to think that we could not establish moral conventions voluntarily, and that we need a sovereign to make their creation possible (although he admits that a limited political power would be needed to handle those among us who are not rational). Not only are most people able to constrain their maximizing tendencies for long-term gain on his view, but they are also able to recognize and act from a principle of acquisition that will provide a rational starting point for further agreement on the terms of cooperation. This principle is what Gauthier calls the "Lockean Proviso"—which directs that one is to acquire goods in a way that leaves no one worse off; and the principle defining fair terms of cooperation that rationally proceeds from a bargain based on this proviso is what Gauthier calls the principle of "minimax relative concession" (hereafter the MRC principle), which essentially directs that the parties are to accept that outcome that is the result of their making equal concessions to one another in the bargaining process.

It may appear that Hobbes has no equivalent of the proviso or the MRC principle since, in his view, there is no way that people could develop a peaceful method of acquiring or dividing goods outside of civil society. But this is not quite so; as we saw, he does consider the kind of principle that an arbitrator (were such a thing possible in the state of nature) would be rational to use in resolving disputes about the acquisition or the division of goods: "to each according to his threat advantage in war." Clearly, there is a big difference between this principle and Gauthier's cooperative rules! Is either theorist's argument for his approach effective?

James Buchanan comes down on the side of Hobbes. Imagine, says Buchanan, a state of nature in which people are competing for some scarce good x:

> Each would find it advantageous to invest effort, a "bad," in order to secure the good x. Physical strength, cajolery, stealth—all these and other personal qualities might determine

the relative abilities of the individuals to secure and protect for themselves quantities of x...as a result of the actual or potential conflict over the relative proportions of x to be finally consumed, some "natural distribution" will come to be established.

It is this "natural distribution" that then becomes the baseline for any further contractual agreements. And it is that distribution that then "defines the individual" for purposes of future bargaining.

This future bargaining should occur, according to Buchanan, because everyone has a motive for resolving disputes and allocating goods peacefully given the substantial costs of predation and defense. Successful resolution of conflict through peaceful means would free up the resources used in warfare, and any agreement reached regarding the distribution of these resources, or any portions of the good x not appropriated, will proceed from the natural distribution. What Buchanan does not notice is that the natural distribution also generates the principle to be used in the peaceful resolution of these sorts of competitive conflicts: it is the principle "to each according to what he would have received in war." Consider the following passage from *Leviathan*:

> if *a man be trusted to judge between man and man*, it is a precept of the law of nature, *that he deale Equally between them*. For without that, the controversies of men cannot be determined but by War. He therefore that is partial in judgement, doth what in him lies, to deter men from the use of Judges, and Arbitrators; and consequently (against the fundamental Law of Nature) is the cause of War.

Hobbes is saying here that an arbitrator in a dispute must beware not to be "partial" in his resolution of the conflict or else the parties will ignore his resolution and go to war to resolve their dispute. But the knowledge that warfare may be deemed rational by the parties if the outcome is not to their liking will affect how the arbitrator resolves the conflict. He must try, as far as possible, to mimic the distribution of the goods or the resolution of the conflict that the parties believe warfare between them will likely effect (assuming that each would stop short of attempting to kill the other). To do otherwise would be to risk one party deciding, "I won't accept this resolution: I can get more if I go to war." Of course, there are costs to going to war that are not involved in accepting an arbitrator's resolution of the conflict, so that even if the arbitrator got the resolution wrong, he might be close enough to the division each thinks warfare would effect such that no party would feel it was worth the cost of warfare to try to get more. On the other hand, one or both of them may be vainglorious and believe (falsely) that he can win a fight over the other and wrest away everything that he wants, in which case there is no way the arbitrator can resolve their dispute that both will find acceptable. But when both are at least fairly realistic in assessing their powers, the arbitrators can peacefully decide conflicts between them using the maxim "To each according to his threat advantage in a conflict between them."

Gauthier argues that the initial bargaining position is misidentified with the noncooperative outcome, and although his argument is directed at Buchanan, it would clearly apply to Hobbes as well. Why, Gauthier asks, should people behave in a way that maintains the effects of predation after it has been banned?

Were agreement to lapse, then what might I expect? Buchanan depends on the threat implicit in the natural distribution to elicit compliance. But a return to the natural distribution benefits no one. The threat is unreal. What motivates compliance is the absence of coercion rather than the fear of its renewal.

Gauthier is, I believe, trying to make the following point. If people have decided to enter a world in which their interactions are cooperative rather than coercive, then coercive power and the goods that this power has amassed no longer define the parties' bargaining positions; instead, it is their power as cooperators that determines their clout in the bargain, as the MRC principle is meant to represent. If Buchanan and Hobbes reply that past coercers can threaten a return to predation and warfare unless they get them, then Gauthier will counter that such a return is extremely expensive for them, so expensive that it would be a threat they would never feel they could carry out. Not only would they lose the resources that had been freed up by the ban on predation, but they would also give up any productive returns that those freed-up resources may have been able to yield in cooperative investments with others. Gauthier argues that distribution according to predative power should be abandoned, and that initial distribution rationally proceeds according to the Lockean Proviso, while the results of further cooperation should be distributed by the market or, when the market fails, according to the MRC principle.

But Buchanan and Hobbes can defend their claim that predative power should still be understood as the foundation of the parties' bargaining on distribution of a cooperative surplus. Imagine a world in which predation has gone on for some time. The predators would certainly prefer to the MRC principle the Hobbesian "warfare threat advantage" principle, which would give every party at least what she would have gotten in the state of war, plus some of the resources that previously went into predation and defense. The predators would point out that no one would lose, and everyone would gain, from this deal, although the weak would not gain as much from this principle as they would from MRC. But why should the weak, who may have considerable co-operative potential, go along with this deal? Doesn't such potential generate a new threat advantage, so that the result of the agreement will be (loosely) "To each according to his production in the cooperative endeavour"? I want to propose that the strong may have a strategy for ensuring that it does not by invoking the very notion of commitment that Gauthier himself thought so powerful in his answer to the knave. The strong would be rational to turn the situation into a two-move game and use what game theorists call a "precommitment strategy," which is essentially just the same as Gauthier's technique of "constraining oneself for gain." On the first move they would perform two actions. They would:

(a) make a threat to reassemble the means of war for as long as it took to persuade the noncompliers to go along with the threat-advantage principle;

and then they would

(b) dispose themselves to keep their threats, no matter how expensive it is to do so.

The second move would be made by the weak. What is their rational response to the first move of the strong? Clearly, they would find it utility maximizing to accept the threat-advantage principle rather than to hold out for a principle more favorable to them. Hence, by transforming the situation into a two-move game and using the first move to make a threat that they would then commit themselves to keep,

the strong would be able to insist on ensuring that the structure of future mutual cooperation respects their past predative power.

In response, Gauthier could try to contend that this kind of two-move strategy would be unavailable to the people in his bargaining situation. For example, he might argue that insofar as the weak are perfectly rational, they would know that this strategy would be rational for the strong, and would do their best to block it. But precisely because they *are* weak, blocking this strategy might be difficult. Indeed, it is difficult for Gauthier to *prove* that the weak could block it. His bargaining situation is so sparsely described and highly idealized that we can find nothing in the structure of that situation to rule out this kind of precommitment strategy by the strong, so that it seems possible for both the starting point and the results of a Gauthierian initial contract to be alarmingly Hobbesian.

These remarks make me appear strangely unappreciative of Gauthier's attempt to mount a plausible neo-Hobbesian moral theory. It seems that I am commending to contemporary contractarians the meanest and most unappealing aspects of Hobbes's approach to justice and property. But those mean and unappealing aspects are quite clearly and strongly linked with Hobbes's requirement that moral action involve no net loss to the agent. There are no free giveaways or free rides on Hobbes's theory; you get what it is in your interest to get and what it is in others' interest to let you have. The results of this kind of thinking are not, I think, very attractive. Contemporary Hobbesians like Gauthier try to accept the self-interested underpinnings of the theory but dress up or deny the conclusions that Hobbes claims they force one to draw. I have attempted to suggest in these remarks that

Hobbes is right to insist on them. I suspect that if Gauthier or other theorists sympathetic to the structure of Hobbesian theory long for "nicer" principles of morality and justice than those that Hobbes develops, they need to find a non-Hobbesian foundation for them. And as I now discuss, there are signs that Gauthier himself suspects this is so.

III

Consider what many have found a particularly ugly side to Hobbesian morality: its radical individualism. Recall that the people in Hobbes's or Gauthier's contracting world are fully developed, asocially defined individuals. But when *Leviathan* was originally published, some readers were shocked by the idea that the nature of our ties to others was interest-based. Aristotelian critics contended that Hobbes's theory goes too far in trying to represent us as radically separate from others. Their worries are also the worries of many twentieth-century critics. Do not our ties to our mothers and fathers, our children and our friends define, at least in part, who we are? Isn't it true that our distinctive tastes, projects, interests, characteristics, and skills are defined by and created within a social context? So how can a moral theory that does not take this into account be an accurate representation of our moral life? It would seem that we *must* bring into our moral theory noninstrumental ties with others that are not based on our affections because it is through such ties that we *become* individuals.

Hobbes would either not understand or else resist the claims of our social definition. But Gauthier, a member of our place and time, accepts them, and this has strange consequences for his moral theory. Gauthier is moved by the criticism that it is unfair to use allocation procedures, such as the market, to distribute goods in circum-

stances where the society permits—even encourages—one class of people to prevent development in another class of people of those talents that allow one to do well in a system using that allocation procedure. Thus, he suggests that we see his contract on the fair terms of cooperation not as an agreement among determinate, already defined, individuals, but as an agreement at a hypothetical "Archimedean Point" among "protopeople"—people who have a certain genetic endowment and who are concerned to select principles that will structure their society such that they will develop well:

> The principles chosen from the Archimedean point must therefore provide that each person's expected share of the fruits of social interaction be related, not just to what he actually contributes, since his actual contribution may reflect the contingent permissions and prohibitions found in any social structure, but *to the contributions he would make* in that social structure most favorable to the actualization of his capacities and character traits, and to the fulfillment of his preferences, provided that this structure is a feasible alternative meeting the other requirements of the Archimedean choice. (My emphasis)

No longer does Gauthier's contract talk presume fully determinate individuals, and no longer is the object of any contract a principle for the resolution of conflict among individuals. Now the contract methodology is used to choose principles that are "for" the structuring of the social system that plays a profound role in structuring individuals. Like Rawls, Gauthier is declaring that the first order of moral business is the definition of social justice.

This is not a benign addition to Gauthier's Hobbesian moral theory: it is an addition that essentially destroys its character as a Hobbesian theory. Of course, it undermines the individualism of the original Hobbesian theory; many will think that this is no great loss. But it was that individualism that much of the rest of the theory presupposed. Consider, for example, that a Hobbesian theory answers the "Why be moral?" question with the response, "Because it is in your interest to be so." But that answer no longer makes sense in a contract theory designed to pursue the nature of social justice using protopeople. Suppose the results of that theory call for a more egalitarian distribution of resources and opportunities open to talents that society will attempt to develop in all its members. If I am a white male in a society that accords white males privileged opportunities to develop talents that will allow them to earn well, then why is it rational for me to pursue a restructuring of social institutions in which this is no longer true?

Indeed, given that their development has already taken place, *why is it even rational for adult minority members or females to support this restructuring?* All of these people are already "made." Restructuring the social world such that it does a fairer job of creating a future generation of individuals is a costly and other-regarding enterprise. Why should these determinate individuals be rational to undertake it, given its cost, unless they just happened to be affected by sympathy for other members of their race or caste or sex, and so enjoyed the struggle? But the nontuistic perspective Gauthier encourages his bargainers to take encourages them to discount any benefits to others from their actions. So assuming the Hobbesian/Gauthierian theory of rationality, what it would be rational for "proto-me" to agree to in some extrasocietal bargain seems to have little bearing on what it is rational for "determinate-me" to accept now.

It is because the self-interest of *determinate* individuals does not seem sufficient to explain the commitment to the results of a bargain among *protopeople* that one wonders whether Gauthier's eventual interest in defining fair principles for the development of individual talents in a social system betrays a commitment to the intrinsic value of the individuals themselves. And it is the idea that individuals have intrinsic value that is missing from the Hobbesian approach. It has not been sufficiently appreciated, I believe, that by answering the "Why be moral?" question by invoking self-interest in the way that Hobbes does, one makes not only cooperative action, but the human beings with whom one will cooperate merely of *instrumental value*; and this is an implicit feature of Hobbes's moral theory that is of central importance. Now Hobbes is unembarrassed by the fact that in his view, "The *Value*, or WORTH of a man, is as of all other things, his Price; that is to say, so much as would be given for the use of his Power: and therefore is not absolute; but a thing dependent on the need and judgment of another." But this way of viewing people is not something that we, or even Gauthier, can take with equanimity. In the final two chapters of his book, Gauthier openly worries about the fact that the reason why we value moral imperatives on this Hobbesian view is that they are instrumentally valuable to us in our pursuit of what we value. But note *why* they are instrumentally valuable: in virtue of our physical and intellectual weaknesses that make it impossible for us to be self-sufficient, we need the cooperation of others to prosper. If there were some way that we could remedy our weaknesses and become self-sufficient, for example, by becoming a superman or superwoman, or by using a Ring of Gyges to make ourselves invisible and so steal from the stores of others with impunity, then it seems we would no longer value or respect moral constraints because they would no longer be useful to us—unless we happened to like the idea. But in this case sentiment, rather than reason, would motivate kind treatment. And without such sentiment, people would simply be "prey" for us.

Even in a world in which we are not self-sufficient, the Hobbesian moral theory gives us no reason to respect those with whom we have no need of cooperating, or those whom we are strong enough to dominate, such as old people, or the handicapped, or retarded children whom we do not want to rear, or people from other societies with whom we have no interest in trading. And I would argue that this shows that Hobbesian moral contrac-

tarianism fails in a very serious way to capture the nature of morality. *Regardless* of whether or not one can engage in beneficial cooperative interactions with another, our moral intuitions push us to assent to the idea that one owes that person respectful treatment simply in virtue of the fact that he or she is a *person*. It seems to be a feature of our moral life that we regard a human being, whether or not she is instrumentally valuable, as always intrinsically valuable. Indeed, to the extent that the results of a Hobbesian theory are acceptable, this is because one's concern to cooperate with someone whom one cannot dominate leads one to behave in ways that mimic the respect one ought to show her simply in virtue of her worth as a human being.

THE CONTINUING DEBATE:
Is Ethics Based on a Social Contract?

What Is New

While social contract theory—especially in the forms developed by Rawls and Gauthier—is a major focus of contemporary ethical theory, it is also a favorite target for some ethical theorists, particularly those who favor care (or feminist) ethics. The issue of whether social contract ethics promotes an overly narrow perspective that neglects important personal elements of ethical relations is currently much debated.

Where to Find More

Thomas Hobbes' *Leviathan*, the classic source for social contract theory, is available from Bobbs-Merrill (Indianapolis: 1958); it was originally published in 1651. John Locke's *Second Treatise on Government* was originally published in 1690; an accessible edition is Indianapolis: Bobbs-Merrill, Library of Liberal Arts, 1952. Rousseau's *Social Contract (Du Contrat Social)* was originally published in 1762; it is available in an edition edited by R. Masters (New York: St. Martin's Press, 1978).

The Iroquois Confederation was perhaps the most successful social contract in history. For more on the Iroquois Confederation, the development of the Iroquois social contract, and the influence of the Iroquois Confederation on the writing of the United States Constitution, see Bruce E. Johansen, *Forgotten Founders: Benjamin Franklin, the Iroquois and the Rationale for the American Revolution* (Ipswich, Mass.: Gambit Publishers, 1982). An account of the development of the Iroquois social contract, along with a link to the remarkably detailed and progressive agreement itself, can be found at the World Civilizations Website at Washington State University, at http://www.wsu.edu:8080/~dee/CULAMRCA/IRLEAGUE.HTM. The agreement or constitution is also available at http://Tuscaroras.com.

Discussions of social contract theory tradition include Jean Hampton, *Hobbes and the Social Contract Tradition* (Cambridge: Cambridge University Press, 1986); and P. Riley, *Will and Political Legitimacy: A Critical Exposition of Social Contract Theory in Hobbes, Locke, Rousseau, Kant, and Hegel* (Cambridge, Mass.: Harvard University Press, 1982).

Probably the best known philosophical book of the late 20th Century presented an updated version of social contract theory: John Rawls, *A Theory of Justice* (London: Oxford University Press, 1971). Robert Nozick, in *Anarchy, State and Utopia* (New York: Basic Books, 1974) develops a well-known opposing view to Rawls' position. David Gauthier, *Morals by Agreement* (Oxford: Oxford University Press, 1986), is a very interesting contemporary version of social contract theory. See Peter Vallentyne, Editor, *Contractarianism and Rational Choice: Essays on David Gauthier's Morals by Agreement* (New York: Cambridge University Press, 1991) for excellent discussion of Gauthier's work.

There is an extensive literature critiquing social contract theory from the care ethics perspective; see particularly Carole Pateman, *The Sexual Contract* (Stanford: Stanford University Press, 1988), who argues that contract theory preserves patriarchal domination rather than opening a path to freedom and equality; Virginia Held, *Feminist Morality: Transforming Culture, Society, and Politics* (Chicago: Chicago University Press, 1993), who claims that social contract theory reduces individuals to "economic man," and neglects the full rich range of human relationships; Eva Feder Kittay, *Love's Labor* (New York: Routledge, 1999), who raises objections based on who is left out of social contract considerations; and Martha Nussbaum, *Frontiers of Justice* (Cambridge, Mass.: Harvard University Press, 2006), who focuses on those— the disabled, persons in disadvantaged countries, nonhuman animals—who are better served by policies of strong social cooperation.

There are several good web sources that discuss social contract theory. See *The Internet Encyclopedia of Philosophy*, http://www.ut.edu/s/soc-cont.htm; the *Stanford Encyclopedia of Philosophy*, http://plato.stanford.edu/entries/contractarianism; and also see "game theory and ethics" in *Stanford Encyclopedia of Philosophy*, http://plato.stanford.edu/entries/game-ethics.

12 DO WOMEN HAVE A DISTINCTIVE ETHICAL PERSPECTIVE?

Women Have a Distinctive Ethical Perspective

ADVOCATE: Annette Baier was Distinguished Service Professor of Philosophy at the University of Pittsburgh until her retirement to her native New Zealand; she is the author of *Postures of the Mind: Essays on Mind and Morals* (Cambridge, Mass.: Harvard University Press, 1985), *A Progress of Sentiments* (Cambridge, Mass.: Harvard University Press, 1991), *Moral Prejudices: Essays on Ethics* (Cambridge, Mass.: Harvard University Press, 1994), and *The Commons of the Mind* (Chicago: Open Court, 1997).

SOURCE: "What Do Women Want in a Moral Theory?" *Noûs*, volume 19 (March 1985): 53–63. Reprinted in Annette Baier, *Moral Prejudices: Essays on Ethics* (Cambridge, Mass.: Harvard University Press, 1994).

Gender Does Not Ultimately Distinguish Different Moral Perspectives

ADVOCATE: Marilyn Friedman, Professor of Philosophy, Washington University in St. Louis; author of *What Are Friends For? Feminist Perspectives on Personal Relationships and Moral Theory* (Ithaca, N.Y.: Cornell University Press, 1993).

SOURCE: "Beyond Caring: The De-Moralization of Gender," from M. Hanen and K. Nielsen, eds., *Science, Morality, and Feminist Theory* (Calgary: Canadian Journal of Philosophy, 1987).

The idea that men and women have different moral rules and roles has a long history: Men should be decisive and courageous, women should be submissive and meek; men should pursue amorous conquests, women should be faithful and chaste; men should be warriors, and women nurturers; men should lead, women should quietly follow. One begins to suspect that most of those rules were made by the boys. Indeed, the idea that men and women have different moral rules and roles has been traditionally a source of oppression of women, and it is hardly surprising that many look upon such assertions of difference very skeptically. The contemporary philosopher Jean Grimshaw puts the point very well:

If ethical concerns and priorities arise from different forms of social life, then those which have emerged from a social system in which women have so often been subordinate to men must be suspect. Supposedly "female" values are not only the subject of little agreement among women: they are also deeply mired in conceptions of "the feminine" which depend on the sort of polarization between "masculine" and "feminine" which has itself been so closely related to the subordination of women. There is no autonomous realm of female values, or of female activities which can generate "alternative" values to those of the public sphere; and any conception of a "female ethic" which depends on these ideas cannot, I think, be a viable one. "The Idea of a Female Ethic," in Peter Singer, ed., *A Companion to Ethics* (Oxford: Blackwell, 1991), p. 498.

But there is another angle to consider. Perhaps there is a distinctive feminine ethical perspective that has been suppressed and hidden, a perspective that is a valuable element of ethics and an essential corrective to traditional male-dominated approaches to ethics. Not, of course, the perspective of submissiveness, but instead the distinctive ethical voice that the old submissiveness tradition silenced. This view was championed by the contemporary psychologist, Carol Gilligan, in her influential book, *In a Different Voice*:

> ...the moral judgments of women differ from those of men in the greater extent to which women's judgments are tied to feelings of empathy and compassion and are concerned with the resolution of real as opposed to hypothetical dilemmas. However, as long as the categories by which development is assessed are derived from research on men, divergence from the masculine standard can be seen only as a failure of development. Carol Gilligan, *In a Different Voice* (Cambridge, Mass.: Harvard University Press, 1982), pp. 69–70.

Gilligan's work is a response to the moral development research of Lawrence Kohlberg, who tracked a number of subjects from childhood well into their adult lives and charted their stages of moral development: from early preconventional stages (obey the rules to avoid punishment), through the conventional level (conform to the social rules and maintain good relationships), and finally into the postconventional principled level, involving loyalty to the rules of the social contract or (the highest level of all) recognition of universal ethical principles grasped through rational deliberation. The highest level postulated by Kohlberg was a distinctively Kantian ethics, guided by purely rational principles independently of feelings or personal relations. In Kohlberg's longitudinal study, a number of men reached the postconventional level, and some even achieved the postconventional principled level; but significantly fewer women achieved the level of postconventional moral development, and of those many later regressed to the conventional level. While Kohlberg sought an explanation for why women generally achieved less moral development than men, Carol Gilligan's work proposed a major shift in our understanding of moral development itself. For Gilligan, women's moral development was not inferior but fundamentally *different*. It emphasized moral goods and benefits that Kohlberg (and most moral philosophy, especially the Kantian ethics that Kohlberg assumed in his research) had sorely neglected: the goods associated with personal relationships and affection. In short, Gilligan represented the moral perspective more frequently held by women as different, but *not* inferior: a prominent theme for many contemporary advocates of care ethics.

Whatever one concludes about the existence of a distinctive moral perspective enjoyed (more often, but neither universally nor exclusively) by women, it is clear that there is no "women's moral viewpoint" shared by all members of the gender. Considering only the writings in this volume, the range of views represented by Christine M. Korsgaard, Jean Hampton, Marilyn Friedman, Annette Baier, and Martha Nussbaum reflect great diversity and considerable conflict.

In the current debate, Marilyn Friedman notes the common belief that women and men have distinctly different approaches to ethics, with women focusing more on care and personal relationships while men emphasize impersonal justice and rights. Friedman argues that this difference is only apparent, since in fact the two approaches to ethics are compatible, and in practice they become intermingled and indistinguishable. Annette Baier sees love and obligation as distinct, but believes that an account of "appropriate trust" might make good use of both.

POINTS TO PONDER

➤ Jean Grimshaw writes: "If ethical concerns and priorities arise from different forms of social life, then those which have emerged from a social system in which women have so often been subordinate to men must be suspect." *If* it is true that the distinctive features of care (feminist) ethics—such as its focus on sustaining particular relationships rather than judging by impersonal universal rules—developed out of an oppressive cultural system, does that cast doubt on the legitimacy of that ethical view?

➤ It is sometimes suggested that personal relationships suffer when they are governed by the impersonal principles of justice rather than by affection (or alternatively, that when personal relationships require justice considerations, they have already suffered a decline: If I must be prompted by considerations of justice and obligation to do a kind act for my friend, then that friendship is not all it should be). How would Friedman respond to such a claim? Is it a challenge to her view?

➤ Friedman acknowledges the importance of the "care" perspective, but she characterizes it as primarily a distinction between a focus on *particular* persons as opposed to focusing on *general* or universal *principles*. Would that way of drawing the distinction be acceptable for Annette Baier?

➤ Friedman concludes that "we need nothing less than to 'de-moralize' the genders"; would Baier agree (either partially or wholly)?

➤ Baier recommends the concept of "appropriate trust" as a means of bringing together the elements of obligation and love. Is "appropriate trust" just another name for Friedman's representation of care and obligation as compatible, or is Baier's account a distinctly different model of the relation between care (or love) and obligation? Are the views of Friedman and Baier compatible, though they emphasize different issues; or is there some basic area of disagreement between them?

Women Have a Distinctive Ethical Perspective

ANNETTE BAIER

When I finished reading Carol Gilligan's *In a Different Voice*, I asked myself the obvious question for a philosopher reader: what differences should one expect in the moral philosophy done by women, supposing Gilligan's sample of women to be representative and supposing her analysis of their moral attitudes and moral development to be correct? Should one expect women to want to produce moral theories, and if so, what sort of moral theories? How will any moral theories they produce differ from those produced by men?

Obviously one does not have to make this an entirely a priori and hypothetical question. One can look and see what sort of contributions women have made to moral philosophy. Such a look confirms, I think, Gilligan's findings. What one finds *is* a bit different in tone and approach from the standard sort of the moral philosophy as done by men following in the footsteps of the great moral philosophers (all men).

Although we find out what sort of moral philosophy women want by looking to see what they have provided, if we do that for moral theory, the answer we get seems to be "none." None of the contributions to moral philosophy by women really counts as a moral theory, nor is seen as such by its author.

The paradigm examples of moral theories—those that are called by their authors "moral theories"—are distinguished not by the comprehensiveness of their internally coherent account but by the *sort* of coherence which is aimed at over a fairly broad area. Their method is not the mosaic method but the broad brushstroke method. Moral theories, as we know them, are, to change the art form, vaults rather than walls—they are not built by assembling painstakingly made brick after brick. In *this* sense of theory—a fairly tightly systematic account of a large area of morality, with a keystone supporting all the rest—women moral philosophers have not yet, to my knowledge, produced moral theories or claimed that they have.

What key concept or guiding motif might hold together the structure of a moral theory hypothetically produced by a reflective woman, Gilligan-style, who has taken up moral theorizing as a calling? What would be a suitable central question, principle, or concept to structure a moral theory which might accommodate those moral insights which women tend to have more readily than men, and to answer those moral questions which, it seems, worry women more than men? I hypothesized that the women's theory, expressive mainly of women's insights and concerns, would be an ethics of love, and this hypothesis seems to be Gilligan's too, since she has gone on from *In a Different Voice* to write about the limitations of Freud's understanding of love as women know it. But presumably women theorists will be like enough to men to want their moral theory to be acceptable to all, so acceptable both to reflective women and to reflective men. Like any good theory, it will need not to ignore the partial truth of previous theories. It must therefore accommodate both the insights men have more easily than women and those women have more easily than men. It should swallow up its predecessor theories. So women theorists will need to connect their ethics of love with what has been the men theorists' preoccupation, namely, obligation.

The great and influential moral theorists have in the modern era taken *obligation* as the key and the problematic concept, and have asked what justifies treating a person as morally bound or obliged to do a particular thing. Since to be bound is to be unfree, by making obligation central one at the same time makes central the question of the justification of coercion, of forcing or trying to force someone to act in a particular way. The concept of obligation as justified limitation of freedom does just what one wants a good theoretical concept to do—to divide up the field (as one looks at different ways one's freedom may be limited, freedom in different spheres, different sorts and versions and levels of justification) and at the same time to hold the subfields together. There must in a theory be some generalization and some speciation or diversification, and a good rich key concept guides one both in recognizing the diversity and in recognizing the unity in it. The concept of obligation has served this function very well for the area of morality it covers, and so we have some fine theories about that area. But as Aristotelians and Christians, as well as women, know, there is a lot of morality *not* covered by that concept, a lot of very great importance even for the area where there are obligations.

This is fairly easy to see if we look at what lies behind the perceived obligation to keep promises. Unless there is some good moral reason why someone should assume the responsibility of rearing a child to be *capable* of taking promises seriously, once she understands what a promise is, the obligation to obey promises will not effectively tie her, and any force applied to punish her when she breaks promises or makes fraudulent ones will be of questionable justice. Is there an *obligation* on someone to make the child into a morally competent promiser? If so, on whom? Who has failed in his or her obligations when, say, war orphans who grew up without parental love or any other love arrive at legal adulthood very willing to be untrue to their word? Who failed in what obligation in all those less extreme cases of attempted but unsuccessful moral education? The liberal version of our basic moral obligations tends to be fairly silent on who has what obligations to new members of the moral community, and it would throw most theories of the justification of obligations into some confusion if the obligation to rear one's children lovingly were added to the list of obligations. Such evidence as we have about the conditions in which children do successfully "learn" the morality of the community of which they are members suggests that we cannot substitute "conscientiously" for "lovingly" in this hypothetical extra needed obligation. But an obligation to love, in the strong sense needed, would be an embarrassment to the theorist, given most accepted versions of "ought implies can."

Reliance on a recognized obligation to turn oneself into a good parent or else to avoid becoming a parent would be a problematic solution. Good parents tend to be the children of good parents, so this obligation would collapse into the obligation to avoid parenthood unless one expected to be a good parent. That, given available methods of contraception, may itself convert into the obligation, should one expect not to be a good parent, to sexual abstinence, or sterilization, or resolute resort to abortion when contraception fails. The conditional obligation to abort, and in effect also the conditional obligation to sterilization, falls on the women. There may be conditions in which the rational moral choice is between obligatory sexual abstinence and obligatory sterilization, but obligatory abortion, such as women in China now face, seems to me a moral monster.

No liberal moral theorist, as far as I know, is advocating obligatory abortion or obligatory sterilization when necessary to prevent the conception of children whose parents do not expect to love them. My point rather is that they escape this conclusion only by avoiding the issue of what is to ensure that new members of the moral community do get the loving care they need to become morally competent persons. Liberal moral theories assume that women either will provide loving maternal care, or will persuade their mates to provide loving paternal care, or when pregnant will decide for abortion, encouraged by their freedom-loving men. These theories, in other words, exploit the culturally encouraged maternal instinct and/or the culturally encouraged docility of women. The liberal system would receive a nasty spanner in its works should women use their freedom of choice as regards abortion to choose *not* to abort, and then leave their newborn children on their fathers' doorsteps. That would test liberal morality's ability to provide for its own survival.

At this point it may be objected that every moral theory must make some assumptions about the natural psychology of those on whom obligations are imposed. Why shouldn't the liberal theory count on a continuing sufficient supply of good loving mothers, as it counts on continuing self-interest and, perhaps, on a continuing supply of pugnacious men who are able and willing to become good soldiers, without turning any of these into moral *obligations*? Why waste moral resources recognizing as obligatory or as virtuous what one can count on getting without moral pressure? If, in the moral economy, one can get enough good mothers and good warriors "for free," why not gladly exploit what nature and cultural history offer? I cannot answer this question fully here, but my argument does depend upon the assumption that a decent morality will *not* depend for its stability on forces to which it gives no moral recognition. Its account books should be open to scrutiny, and there should be no unpaid debts, no loans with no prospect of repayment. I also assume that once we are clear about these matters and about the interdependencies involved, our principles of justice will not allow us to recognize either a special obligation on every woman to initiate the killing of the fetus she has conceived, should she and her mate be, or think they will be, deficient in parental love, or a special obligation on every young man to kill those his elders have labelled enemies of his country. Both such "obligations" are prima facie suspect, and difficult to make consistent with any of the principles supposedly generating obligations in modern moral theories. I also assume that, on reflection, we will not want to recognize as *virtues* the character traits of women and men which lead them to supply such life and death services "for free." Neither maternal servitude, nor the resoluteness needed to kill off one's children to prevent their growing up unloved, nor the easy willingness to go out and kill when ordered to do so by authorities seems to me to be a character trait a decent morality will encourage by labelling it a virtue. But the liberals' morality must somehow encourage such traits if its stability depends on enough people showing them. There is, then, understandable motive for liberals' avoidance of the question of whether such qualities are or are not morally approved of, and of whether or not there is any obligation to act as one with such character traits would act.

It is symptomatic of the bad faith of liberal morality as understood by many of those who defend it that issues such as whether to fight or not to fight, to have or not to have an abortion, or to be or not to be an unpaid maternal drudge are left to individual conscience. Since there is no coherent guidance liberal morality can give on these issues, which clearly are *not* matters of moral indifference, liberal morality tells each of us, "the choice is yours," hoping that enough will choose to be self-sacrificial life providers and self-sacrificial death dealers to suit the purposes of the rest.

Granted that the men's theories of obligation need supplementation, to have much chance of integrity and coherence, and that the women's hypothetical theories will want to cover obligation as well as love, then what concept brings them together? My tentative answer is—the concept of appropriate trust, oddly neglected in moral theory. This concept also nicely mediates between reason and feeling, those tired old candidates for moral authority, since to trust is neither quite to believe something about the trusted nor necessarily to feel any emotion towards them—but to have a belief-informed and action-influencing attitude. To make it plausible that the neglected concept of appropriate trust is a good one for the enlightened moral theorist to make central, I need to show, or begin to show, how it could include obligation, indeed shed light on obligations and their justification, as well as include love, the other moral concerns of Gilligan's women, and many of the topics women moral philosophers have chosen to address, mosaic fashion. I would also need to show that it could connect all of these in a way which holds out promise both of synthesis and of comprehensive moral coverage. A moral theory which looked at the conditions for proper

trust of all the various sorts we show, and at what sorts of reasons justify inviting such trust, giving it, and meeting it, would, I believe, not have to avoid turning its gaze on the conditions for the survival of the practices it endorses, so it could avoid that unpleasant choice many current liberal theories seem to have—between incoherence and bad faith. I do not pretend that we will easily agree once we raise the questions I think we should raise, but at least we may have a language adequate to the expression of both men's and women's moral viewpoints.

My trust in the concept of trust is based in part on my own attempts to restate and consider what is right and what wrong with men's theories, especially Hume's, which I consider the best of the lot. I have found myself reconstructing his account of the artifices of justice as an account of the progressive enlargement of a climate of trust, and have found that a helpful way to see it. It has some textual basis, but is nevertheless a reconstruction, and one I have found, immodestly, an improvement. So it is because I have tried the concept and explored its dimensions a bit—the variety of goods we may trust others not to take from us, the sort of security or insurance we have when we do, the sorts of defences or potential defences we lay down when we trust, the various conditions for reasonable trust of various types—that I am hopeful about its power as a theoretical, and not just an exegetical, tool. I also found myself needing to use it when I made a brief rash attempt at that women's topic, caring (invited in by a male philosopher, I should say). I am reasonably sure that trust does generalize some central moral features of the recognition of binding obligations and moral virtues and of loving, as well as of other important relations between persons, such as teacher-pupil, confider-confidante, worker to co-worker in the same cause, and professional to client. Indeed it is fairly obvious that love, the main moral phenomenon women want attended to, involves trust, so I anticipate little quarrel when I claim that, if we had a moral theory spelling out the conditions for appropriate trust and distrust, that would include a morality of love in all its variants—parental love, love of children for their parents, love of family members, love of friends, of lovers in the strict sense, of co-workers, of one's country and its figureheads, of exemplary heroines and heroes, of goddesses and gods.

Love and loyalty demand maximal trust of one sort, and maximal trustworthiness, and in investigating the conditions for maximal trust and maximal risk we must think about the ethics of love. More controversial may be my claim that the ethics of obligation will also be covered. I see it as covered because to recognize a set of obligations is to trust some group of persons to instill them, to demand that they be met, possibly to levy sanctions if they are not, and this is to trust persons with very significant coercive power over others. Less coercive but still significant power is possessed by those shaping our conception of the virtues and expecting us to display them, approving when we do, disapproving and perhaps shunning us when we do not. Such coercive and manipulative power over others requires justification, and is justified only if we have reason to trust those who have it to use it properly and to use the discretion which is always given when trust is given in a way which serves the purpose of the whole system of moral control, and not merely self-serving or morally improper purposes. Since the question of the justification of coercion becomes, at least in part, the question of the wisdom of trusting the coercers to do their job properly, the morality of obligation, in

as far as it reduces to the morality of coercion, is covered by the morality of proper trust. Other forms of trust may also be involved, but trusting enforcers with the use of force is the most problematic form of trust involved.

The coercers and manipulators are, to some extent, all of us, so to ask what our obligations are and what virtues we should exhibit is to ask what it is reasonable to trust us to demand, expect, and contrive to get from one another. It becomes, in part, a question of what powers we can in reason trust ourselves to exercise properly. But self-trust is a dubious or limit case of trust, so I prefer to postpone the examination of the concept of proper self-trust at least until proper trust of others is more clearly understood. Nor do we distort matters too much if we concentrate on those cases where moral sanctions and moral pressure and moral manipulation are not self-applied but applied to others, particularly by older persons to younger persons. Most moral pressuring that has any effect goes on in childhood and early youth. Moral sanctions may continue to be applied, formally and informally, to adults, but unless the criminal courts apply them it is easy enough for adults to ignore them, to brush them aside. It is not difficult to become a sensible knave, and to harden one's heart so that one is insensible to the moral condemnation of one's victims and those who sympathize with them. Only if the pressures applied in the morally formative stage have given one a heart that rebels against the thought of such ruthless independence of what others think will one see any reason *not* to ignore moral condemnation, not to treat it as mere powerless words and breath. Condemning sensible knaves is as much a waste of breath as arguing with them—all we can sensibly do is to try to protect children against their influence, and ourselves against their knavery. Adding to the criminal law will not be the way to do the latter, since such moves will merely challenge sensible knaves to find new knavish exceptions and loopholes, not protect us from sensible knavery. Sensible knaves are precisely those who exploit us without breaking the law. So the whole question of when moral pressure of various sorts, formative, reformative, and punitive, ought to be brought to bear by whom is subsumed under the question of whom to trust when and with what, and for what good reasons.

In concentrating on obligations, rather than virtues, modern moral theorists have chosen to look at the cases where more trust is placed in enforcers of obligations than is placed in ordinary moral agents, the bearers of the obligations. In taking, as contractarians do, contractual obligations as the model of obligations, they concentrate on a case where the very minimal trust is put in the obligated person, and considerable punitive power entrusted to the one to whom the obligation is owed (I assume here that Hume is right in saying that when we promise or contract, we formally subject ourselves to the penalty, in case of failure, of never being trusted as a promiser again). This is an interesting case of the allocation of trust of various sorts, but it surely distorts our moral vision to suppose that *all* obligations, let alone all morally pressured expectations we impose on others, conform to that abnormally coercive model. It takes very special conditions for it to be safe to trust persons to inflict penalties on other persons, conditions in which either we can trust the penalizers to have the virtues necessary to penalize wisely and fairly, or else we can rely on effective threats to keep unvirtuous penalizers from abusing their power—that is to say, rely on others to coerce the first coercers into proper behavior. But that reliance too will either be trust or

will have to rely on threats from coercers of the coercers of coercers, and so on. Morality on this model becomes a nasty, if intellectually intriguing, game of mutual mutually corrective threats. The central question of who should deprive whom of what freedom soon becomes the question of whose anger should be dreaded by whom (the theory of obligation), supplemented perhaps by an afterthought on whose favour should be courted by whom (the theory of the virtues).

Undoubtedly some important part of morality does depend in part on a system of threats and bribes, at least for its survival in difficult conditions when normal goodwill and normally virtuous dispositions may be insufficient to motivate the conduct required for the preservation and justice of the moral network of relationships. But equally undoubtedly life will be nasty, emotionally poor, and worse than brutish (even if longer), if that is all morality is, or even if that coercive structure of morality is regarded as the backbone, rather than as an available crutch, should the main support fail. For the main support has to come from those we entrust with the job of rearing and training persons so that they can be trusted in various ways, some trusted with extraordinary coercive powers, some with public decision-making powers, all trusted as parties to promise, most trusted by some who love them and by one or more willing to become co-parents with them, most trusted by dependent children, dependent elderly relatives, sick friends, and so on. A very complex network of a great variety of sorts of trust structures our moral relationships with our fellows, and if there is a *main* support to this network it is the trust we place in those who respond to the trust of new members of the moral community, namely, children, and prepare them for new forms of trust.

A theory which took as its central question "Who should trust whom with what, and why?" would not have to forego the intellectual fun and games previous theorists have had with the various paradoxes of morality—curbing freedom to increase freedom, curbing self-interest the better to satisfy self-interest, not aiming at happiness in order to become happier. For it is easy enough to get a paradox of trust to accompany or, if I am right, to generalize the paradoxes of freedom, self-interest, and hedonism. To trust is to make oneself or to let oneself be more vulnerable than one might have been to harm from others—to give them an opportunity to harm one, in the confidence that they will not take it, because they have no good reason to. Why would one take such a risk? For risk it always is, given the partial opaqueness to us of the reasoning and motivation of those we trust and with whom we cooperate. Our confidence may be, and quite often is, misplaced. That is what we risk when we trust. If the best reason to take such a risk is the expected gain in security which comes from a climate of trust, then in trusting we are always giving up security to get greater security, exposing our throats so that others become accustomed to not biting. A moral theory which made proper trust its central concern could have its own categorical imperative, could replace obedience to self-made laws and freely chosen restraint on freedom with security-increasing sacrifice of security, distrust in the promoters of a climate of distrust, and so on.

Such reflexive use of one's central concept, negative or affirmative, is an intellectually satisfying activity which is bound to have appeal to those system lovers who want to construct moral theories, and it may help them design their theory in an intellectually pleasing manner. But we should beware of becoming hypnotized by our slogans or of sacrificing truth to intellectual elegance. Any theory of proper trust should not *prejudge* the question of when distrust is proper. We might find more objects of proper distrust than just the contributors to a climate of reasonable distrust, just as freedom should be restricted not just to increase human freedom but to protect human life from poisoners and other killers. I suspect, however, that all the objects of reasonable distrust are more reasonably seen as falling into the category of ones who contribute to a decrease in the scope of proper trust than can all who are reasonably coerced be seen as themselves guilty of wrongful coercion. Still, even if all proper trust turns out to be for such persons and on such matters as increase the scope of reasonable distrust, overreliance on such nice reflexive formulae can distract us from asking all the questions about trust which need to be asked if an adequate moral theory is to be constructed around that concept. These questions should include when to *respond* to trust with *un*trustworthiness, when and when not to invite trust, as well as when to give and refuse trust. We should not assume that promiscuous trustworthiness is any more a virtue than is undiscriminating distrust. It is appropriate trustworthiness, appropriate trustingness, appropriate encouragement to trust which will be virtues, as will be judicious untrustworthiness, selective refusal to trust, discriminating discouragement of trust.

Women are particularly well placed to appreciate these last virtues, since they have sometimes needed them to get into a position even to consider becoming moral theorizers. The long exploitation and domination of women by men depended on men's trust in women and women's trustworthiness to play their allotted role and so to perpetuate their own and their daughters' servitude. However keen women now are to end the lovelessness of modern moral philosophy, they are unlikely to lose sight of the cautious virtue of appropriate distrust or of the tough virtue of principled betrayal of the exploiters' trust.

Gilligan's girls and women saw morality as a matter of preserving valued ties to others, of preserving the conditions for that care and mutual care without which human life becomes bleak, lonely, and after a while, as the mature men in her study found, not self-affirming, however successful in achieving the egoistic goals which had been set. The boys and men saw morality as a matter of finding workable traffic rules for self-assertors, so that they might not needlessly frustrate one another and so that they could, should they so choose, cooperate in more positive ways to mutual advantage. Both for the women's sometimes unchosen and valued ties with others and for the men's mutual respect as sovereigns and subjects of the same minimal moral traffic rules (and for their more voluntary and more selective associations of profiteers), trust is important. Both men and women are concerned with cooperation, and the dimensions of trust-distrust structure the different cooperative relations each emphasize. The various considerations which arise when we try to defend an answer to any question about the appropriateness of a particular form of cooperation with its distinctive form of trust or distrust, that is, when we look into the terms of all sorts of cooperation, at the terms of trust in different cases of trust, at what are fair terms and what are trust-enhancing and trust-preserving terms, are suitably many and richly interconnected. A moral theory (or family of theories) that made trust its central problem could do better justice to men's and women's moral intuitions than do the going men's theories. Even if we don't easily agree on the answer to the question of who should trust whom with what, who should accept and who should meet various sorts of trust, and why, these questions might enable us better to reason morally together than we can when the central moral questions are reduced to those of whose favour one must court and whose anger one must dread.

Gender Does Not Ultimately Distinguish Different Moral Perspectives

Marilyn Friedman

Carol Gilligan heard a "distinct moral language" in the voices of women who were subjects in her studies of moral reasoning. Though herself a developmental psychologist, Gilligan has put her mark on contemporary feminist moral philosophy by daring to claim the competence of this voice and the worth of its message. Her book, *In a Different Voice*, explored the concern with care and relationships which Gilligan discerned in the moral reasoning of women and contrasted it with the orientation toward justice and rights which she found to typify the moral reasoning of men.

According to Gilligan, the standard (or "male") moral voice articulated in moral psychology derives moral judgments about particular cases from abstract, universalized moral rules and principles which are substantively concerned with justice and rights. For justice reasoners: the major moral imperative enjoins respect for the rights of others; the concept of duty is limited to reciprocal noninterference; the motivating vision is one of the equal worth of self and other; and one important underlying presupposition is a highly individuated conception of persons.

By contrast, the other (or "female") moral voice which Gilligan heard in her studies eschews abstract rules and principles. This moral voice derives moral judgments from the contextual detail of situations grasped as specific and unique. The substantive concern for this moral voice is care and responsibility, particularly as these arise in the context of interpersonal relationships. Moral judgments, for care reasoners, are tied to feelings of empathy and

compassion; the major moral imperatives center around caring, not hurting others, and avoiding selfishness; and the motivating vision of this ethic is "that everyone will be responded to and included, that no one will be left alone or hurt."

While these two voices are not necessarily contradictory in all respects, they seem, at the very least, to be different in their orientation. Gilligan's writings about the differences have stimulated extensive feminist reconsideration of various ethical themes. In this paper, I use Gilligan's work as a springboard for extending certain of those themes in new directions.

THE GENDER DIFFERENCE CONTROVERSY

Gilligan had advanced at least two different positions about the care and the justice perspectives. One is that the care perspective is distinct from the moral perspective which is centered on justice and rights. Following Gilligan, I will call this the "different voice" hypothesis about moral reasoning. Gilligan's other hypothesis is that the care perspective is typically, or characteristically, a *woman's* moral voice, while the justice perspective is typically, or characteristically a *man's* moral voice. Let's call this the "gender difference" hypothesis about moral reasoning.

The truth of Gilligan's gender difference hypothesis has been questioned by a number of critics who cite what seems to be disconfirming empirical evidence. This evidence includes studies by the psychologist Norma Haan, who has discerned two distinct moral voices among her research subjects, but has found them to be utilized to approximately the same extent by both females and males.

In an attempt to dismiss the research-based objections to her gender difference hypothesis, Gilligan now asserts that her aim was not to disclose a statistical gender difference in moral reasoning, but rather simply to disclose and interpret the differences in the two perspectives. Psychologist John Broughton has argued that if the gender difference is not maintained, then Gilligan's whole explanatory framework is undermined. However, Broughton is wrong. The different voice hypothesis has a significance for moral psychology and moral philosophy which would survive the demise of the gender difference hypothesis. At least part of its significance lies in revealing the lopsided obsession of contemporary theories of morality, in both disciplines, with universal and impartial conceptions of justice and rights and the relative disregard of *particular*, interpersonal relationships based on partiality and affective ties.

But *what about* that supposed empirical disconfirmation of the gender difference hypothesis? Researchers who otherwise accept the disconfirming evidence have nevertheless noticed that many women readers of Gilligan's book find it to "resonate…thoroughly with their own experience." Gilligan notes that it was precisely one of her purposes to expose the gap between women's experience and the findings of psychological research, and, we may suppose, to critique the latter in light of the former.

These unsystematic, anecdotal observations that females and males do differ in ways examined by Gilligan's research should lead us either: (1) to question, and examine carefully, the methods of that empirical research which does not reveal such differences; or (2) to suspect that a gender difference exists but in some form which is not, strictly speaking, a matter of statistical differences in the moral reasoning of women and men. Gilligan has herself expressed the first of these alternatives. I would like to explore the second possibility.

Suppose that there were a gender difference of a sort, but one which was not a simple matter of differences among the form or substance of women's and men's moral reasonings. A plausible account might take this form. Among the white middle classes of such Western industrial societies as Canada and the United States, women and men are associated with different moral norms and values at the level of the stereotypes, symbols, and myths which contribute to the social construction of gender. One might say that morality is "gendered" and that the genders are "moralized." Our very conceptions of femininity and masculinity, female and male, incorporate norms about appropriate behavior, characteristic virtues, and typical vices.

Morality, I suggest, is fragmented into a "division of moral labor" along the lines of gender, the rationale for which is rooted in historic developments pertaining to family, state, and economy. The tasks of governing, regulating social order, and managing other "public" institutions have been monopolized by men as their privileged domain, and the tasks of sustaining privatized personal relationships have been imposed on, or left to, women. The genders have thus been conceived in terms of special and distinctive moral projects. Justice and rights have structured male moral norms, values, and virtues, while care and responsiveness have defined female moral norms, values, and virtues. The division of moral labor has had the dual function both of preparing us each for our respective socially defined domains and of rendering us incompetent to manage the affairs of the realm from which we have been excluded. That justice is symbolized in our culture by the figure of a woman is a remarkable irony; her blindfold hides more than the scales she holds.

To say that the genders are moralized is to say that specific moral ideas, values, virtues, and practices are culturally conceived as the special projects or domains of specific genders. These conceptions would determine which commitments and behaviors were to be considered normal, appropriate, and expected of each gender, which commitments and behaviors were to be considered remarkable or heroic, and which commitments and behaviors were to be considered deviant, improper, outrageous, and intolerable.

Social science provides ample literature to show that gender differences are alive and well at the level of popular perception. Both men and women, on average, still conceive women and men in a moralized fashion. For example, expectations and perceptions of women's greater empathy and altruism are expressed by both women and men. The gender stereotypes of women center around qualities which some authors call "communal." These include: a concern for the welfare of others; the predominance of caring and nurturant traits; and, to a lesser extent, interpersonal sensitivity, emotional expressiveness, and a gentle personal style.

By contrast, men are stereotyped according to what are referred to as "agentic" norms. These norms center primarily around assertive and controlling tendencies. The paradigmatic behaviors are self-assertion, including forceful dominance, and independence from other people. Also encompassed by these norms are patterns of self-confidence, personal efficacy, and a direct, adventurous personal style.

If I am right, then Gilligan has discerned the *symbolically* female moral voice, and has disentangled it from the *symbolically* male moral voice. The moralization of gender is more a matter of how we *think* we reason than of how we actually reason, more a matter of the moral concerns we *attribute* to women and men than of true statistical differences between women's and men's moral reasoning. Gilligan's findings resonate with the experiences of many people because those experiences are shaped, in part, by cultural myths and stereotypes of gender which even feminist theorizing may not dispel. Thus, both women and men in our culture *expect* women and men to exhibit this moral dichotomy, and, on my hypothesis, it is this expectation which has shaped both Gilligan's observations and the plausibility which we attribute to them. Or, to put it somewhat differently, *whatever* moral matters men concern themselves with are categorized, estimably, as matters of "justice and rights," whereas the moral concerns of women are assigned to the devalued categories of "care and personal relationships."

It is important to ask why, if these beliefs are so vividly held, they might, nevertheless, still not have produced a reality in conformity with them. How could those critics who challenge Gilligan's gender hypothesis be right to suggest that women and men show no significant differences in moral reasoning, if women and men are culturally educated, trained, pressured, expected, and perceived to be so radically different?

My admittedly *partial* answer to it depends upon showing that the care/justice dichotomy is rationally implausible and that the two concepts are conceptually compatible. This conceptual compatibility creates the empirical possibility that the two moral concerns will be intermingled in practice.

SURPASSING THE CARE/JUSTICE DICHOTOMY

I have suggested that if women and men do not show statistical differences in moral reasoning along the lines of a care/justice dichotomy, this should not be thought surprising since the concepts of care and justice are mutually compatible. People who treat each other justly can also care about each other. Conversely, personal relationships are arenas in which people have rights to certain forms of treatment, and in which fairness can be reflected in ongoing interpersonal relationships—which I will emphasize here.

Justice, at the most general level, is a matter of giving people their due, of treating them appropriately. Justice is relevant to personal relationships and to care precisely to the extent that considerations of justice itself determine appropriate ways to treat friends or intimates. Justice as it bears on relationships among friends or family, or on other close personal ties, might not involve duties which are universalizable, in the sense of being owed to all persons simply in virtue of shared moral personhood. But this does not entail the irrelevance of justice among friends or intimates.

One sort of role for justice in close relationships among people of comparable moral personhood may be discerned by considering that a personal relationship is a miniature social system, which provides valued mutual intimacy, support, and concern for those who are involved. The maintenance of a relationship requires effort by the participants. One intimate may bear a much greater burden for sustaining a relationship than the other participant(s) and may derive less support, concern, and so forth than she deserves for her efforts. Justice sets a constraint on such relationships by calling for an appropriate sharing, among the participants, of the benefits and burdens which constitute their relationship.

Justice is relevant to close personal relationships among comparable moral persons in a second way as well. The trust and intimacy which characterize special relationships create special vulnerabilities to harm. Commonly recognized harms, such as physical injury and sexual assault, become more feasible; and special relationships, in corrupt, abusive, or degenerate forms, make possible certain uncommon emotional harms not even possible in impersonal relationships. When someone is harmed in a personal relationship, she is owed a rectification of some sort, a righting of the wrong which has been done her. The notion of justice emerges, once again, as a relevant moral notion.

Thus, in a close relationship among persons of comparable moral personhood, care may degenerate into the injustices of exploitation, or oppression. Many such problems have been given wide public scrutiny recently as a result of feminist analysis of various aspects of family life and sexual relationships. Women battering, acquaintance rape, and sexual harassment are but a few of the many recently publicized injustices of "personal" life. The notion of distributive or corrective injustice seems almost too mild to capture these indignities, involving, as they do, violation of bodily integrity and an assumption of the right to assault and injure. But to call these harms injustices is certainly not to rule out impassioned moral criticism in other terms as well.

The two requirements of justice which I have just discussed exemplify the standard distinction between distributive and corrective justice. They illustrate the role of justice in personal relationships regarded in abstraction from a social context. Personal relationships may also be regarded in the context of their various institutional settings, such as marriage and family. Here justice emerges again as a relevant ideal, its role being to define appropriate institutions to structure interactions among family members, other household cohabitants, and intimates in general. The family, for example, is a miniature society, exhibiting all the major facets of large-scale social life: decision-making affecting the whole unit; executive action; judgments of guilt and innocence; reward and punishment; allocation of responsibilities and privileges, of burdens and benefits; and monumental influences on the life-chances of both its maturing and matured members. Any of these features *alone* would invoke the relevance of justice; together, they make the case overwhelming.

Women's historically paradigmatic role of monitoring of mothering has provided a multitude of insights which can be reconstructed as insights about the importance of justice in family relationships, especially those relationships involving remarkable disparities in maturity, capability, and power. In these familial relationships, one party grows into moral personhood over time, gradually acquiring the capacity to be a responsible moral agent. Considerations of justice pertain to the mothering of children in numerous ways. For one thing, there may be siblings to deal with, whose demands and conflicts create the context for parental arbitration and the need for a fair allotment of responsibilities and privileges. Then there are decisions to be made, involving the well-being of all persons in the family unit, whose immature members become increasingly capable over time of participating in such administrative affairs. Of special importance in the practice of raising children are the duties to nurture and to promote growth and maturation. These duties may be seen as counterparts to the welfare rights viewed by many as a matter of social justice. Motherhood continually presents its practitioners with moral problems best seen in terms of a complex framework which integrates justice with care, even though the politico-legal dis-

course of justice has not shaped its domestic expression.

I have been discussing the relevance of justice to close personal relationships. A few words about my companion thesis—the relevance of care to the public domain—is also in order. In its more noble manifestation, care in the public realm would show itself, perhaps, in foreign aid, welfare programs, famine or disaster relief, or other social programs designed to relieve suffering and attend to human needs. If untempered by justice in the public domain, care degenerates precipitously. The infamous "boss" of Chicago's old-time Democratic machine, Mayor Richard J. Daley, was legendary for his nepotism and political partisanship; he cared extravagantly for his relatives, friends, and political cronies.

In recounting the moral reasoning of one of her research subjects, Gilligan once wrote that the "justice" perspective fails "to take into account the reality of relationships." What she meant is that the "justice" perspective emphasizes a self's various rights to noninterference by others. Gilligan worried that if this is all that a concern for justice involved, then such a perspective would disregard the moral value of positive interaction, connection, and commitment among persons.

However, Gilligan's interpretation of justice is far too limited. For one thing, it fails to recognize positive rights, such as welfare rights, which may be endorsed from a "justice" perspective. But beyond this minor point, a more important problem is Gilligan's failure to acknowledge the potential for *violence and harm* in human interrelationships and human community. The concept of justice, in general, arises out of relational conditions in which most human beings have the capacity, and many have the inclination, to treat each other badly.

Thus, notions of distributive justice are impelled by the realization that people who together comprise a social system may not share fairly in the benefits and burdens of their social cooperation. Conceptions of rectificatory, or corrective, justice are founded on the concern that when harms are done, action should be taken either to restore those harmed as fully as possible to their previous state, or to prevent further similar harm, or both. And the specific rights which people are variously thought to have are just so many manifestations of our interest in identifying ways in which people deserve protection against harm by others. The complex reality of social life encompasses the human potential for helping, caring for, and nurturing others *as well as* the potential for harming, exploiting, and oppressing others. Thus, Gilligan is wrong to think that the justice perspective completely neglects "the reality of relationships." Rather, it arises from a more complex, and more realistic, estimate of the nature of human interrelationship.

In light of these reflections, it seems wise both to reconsider the seeming dichotomy of care and justice, and to question the moral adequacy of either orientation dissociated from the other. Our aim would be to advance "beyond caring," that is, beyond *mere* caring dissociated from a concern for justice. In addition, we would do well to progress beyond gender stereotypes which assign distinct and different moral roles to women and men. Our ultimate goal should be a nongendered, nondichotomized, moral framework in which all moral concerns could be expressed. We might, with intentional irony, call this project, "de-moralizing the genders."

COMMITMENTS TO PARTICULAR PERSONS

Even though care and justice do not define mutually exclusive moral frameworks, it is still too early to dispose of the "differ-

ent voice hypothesis." I believe that there is something to be said for the thesis that there are different moral orientations, even if the concepts of care and justice do not capture the relevant differences and even if the differences do not correlate statistically with gender differences.

My suggestion is that one important distinction has to do with the nature and focus of what may be called "primary moral commitments." Let us begin with the observation that, from the so-called "care standpoint," responsiveness to other persons in their wholeness and their particularity is of singular importance. This idea, in turn, points toward a notion of moral commitment which takes *particular persons* as its primary focus. A form of moral commitment which contrasts with this is one which involves a focus on general and abstract rules, values, or principles. It is no mere coincidence, I believe, that Gilligan found the so-called "justice" perspective to feature an emphasis on *rules*.

In the second part of this paper, I argued that the concepts of justice and care are mutually compatible and, to at least some extent, mutually dependent. Based on my analysis, the "justice perspective" might be said to rest, at bottom, on the assumption that the best way to *care* for persons is to respect their rights, and to accord them their due, both in distribution of the burdens and benefits of social cooperation, and in the rectification of wrongs done. But to uphold these principles, it is not necessary to respond with emotion, feeling, passion, or compassion to other persons. Upholding justice does not require the full range of mutual responsiveness which is possible between persons.

By contrast, the so-called "ethic of care" stresses an ongoing responsiveness. This ethic is, after all, the stereotypic moral norm for women in the domestic role of sustaining a family in the face of the harsh realities of a competitive marketplace and an indifferent polis. The domestic realm has been idealized as the realm in which people, as specific individuals, were to have been nurtured, cherished, and succored. The "care" perspective discussed by Gilligan is a limited one; it is not really about care in all its complexity, for, as I have argued, that notion *includes* just treatment. But it *is* about the nature of relationships to particular persons grasped as such. The key issue is the sensitivity and responsiveness to another person's emotional states, individuating differences, specific uniqueness, and whole particularity. The "care" orientation focuses on whole persons and deemphasizes adherence to moral rules.

Thus, the important conception which I am extracting from the so-called "care" perspective is that of commitment to particular persons. What is the nature of this form of moral commitment? Commitment to a specific person, such as a lover, child, or friend, takes as its primary focus the needs, wants, attitudes, judgments, behavior, and overall way of being of that particular person. It is specific to that individual and is not generalizable to others. We show a commitment to someone whenever we attend to her needs, enjoy her successes, defer to her judgment, and find inspiration in her values and goals simply because they are *hers*. If it is *who she is*, and not her actions or traits subsumed under general rules, which matters as one's motivating guide, then one's responsiveness to her reflects a person-oriented, rather than a rule-based, moral commitment.

Thus, the different perspectives which Gilligan called "care" and "justice" do point toward substantive differences in human interrelationship and commitment. Both orientations take account of relationships in some way; both may legitimately incorporate a concern for justice and for care, and both aim to avoid harm

to others and (at the highest stages) to the self. But from the standpoint of "care," self and other are conceptualized in their *particularity* rather than as instances for the application of generalized moral notions. This difference ramifies into what appears to be a major difference in the organization and focus of moral thought.

This analysis requires a subtle expansion. Like care and justice, commitments to particular persons and commitments to values, rules, and principles are not mutually exclusive within the entire panorama of one person's moral concerns. Doubtless, they are intermingled in most people's moral outlooks. Pat likes and admires Mary because of Mary's resilience in the face of tragedy, her intelligent courage, and her good-humored audacity. Pat thereby shows a commitment *in general* to resilience, courage, and good-humored audacity as traits of human personality.

However, in Mary, these traits coalesce in a unique manner: perhaps no one will stand by a friend in deep trouble quite so steadfastly as Mary; perhaps no one petitions the university president as effectively as Mary. The traits which Pat likes, in general, converge to make *Mary*, in Pat's eyes, an especially admirable human individual, a sort of moral exemplar. In virtue of Pat's loyalty to her, Mary may come to play a role in Pat's life which exceeds, in its weightiness, the sum total of the values which Pat sees in Mary's virtues, taken individually and in abstraction from any particular human personality.

Pat is someone with commitments both to moral abstractions and to particular persons. Pat is, in short, like most of us. When we reason morally, we can take up a stance which makes either of these forms of commitment the focal point of our attention. The choice of which stance to adopt at a given time is probably, like other moral alternatives, most poignant and difficult in situations of moral ambiguity or uncertainty when we don't know how to proceed. In such situations, one can turn *either* to the guidance of principled commitments to values, forms of conduct, or human virtues, *or* one can turn to the guidance which inheres in the example set by a trusted friend or associate—the example of how *she* interprets those same moral ambiguities, or how *she* resolves those same moral uncertainties.

Of course, the commitment to a particular person is evident in more situations than simply those of moral irresolution. But the experience of moral irresolution may make clearer the different sorts of moral commitment which structure our thinking. Following cherished values will lead one out of one's moral uncertainties in a very different way than following someone else's example.

Thus, the insight that each person needs some others in her life who recognize, respect, and cherish her particularity in its richness and wholeness is the distinctive motivating vision of the "care" perspective. The sort of respect for persons which grows out of this vision is not the abstract respect which is owed to all persons in virtue of their common humanity, but a respect for individual worth, merit, need, or, even, idiosyncrasy. It is a form of respect which involves admiration and cherishing, when the distinctive qualities are valued intrinsically, and which, at the least, involves toleration when the distinctive qualities are not valued intrinsically.

Indeed, there is an apparent irony in the notion of personhood which underlies some philosophers' conceptions of the universalized moral duties owed to all persons. The rational nature which Kant, for example, takes to give each person dignity and to make each of absolute value and, therefore, irreplaceable, is no more than an abstract rational nature in virtue of which we are all alike. But if we are all alike in this respect, it is hard to understand why we would be irreplaceable. Our common rational nature would seem to make us indistinguishable and, therefore, mutually interchangeable. Specific identity would be a matter of indifference, so far as absolute value is concerned. Yet it would seem that only in *virtue* of our distinctive particularity could we each be truly irreplaceable.

Of course, our particularity does not *exclude* a common nature, conceptualized at a level of suitable generality. We still deserve equal respect in virtue of our common humanity. But we are also *more* than abstractly and equivalently human. It is this "more" to which we commit ourselves when we care for others in their particularity.

Thus, as I interpret it, there is at least one important difference in moral reasoning brought to our attention by Gilligan's "care" and "justice" frameworks. This difference hinges on the primary form of moral commitment which structures moral thought and the resulting nature of the response to other persons. For so-called "care" reasoners, recognition of, and commitment to, persons in their particularity is an overriding moral concern.

Unlike the concepts of justice and care, which admit of a mutual integration, it is less clear that these two distinct forms of moral commitment can jointly comprise the focus of one's moral attention, in any single case. Nor can we respond to all other persons equally well in either way. The only integration possible here may be to seek the more intimate, responsive, committed relationships with people who are known closely, or known in contexts in which differential needs are important and can be known with some reliability, and to settle for rule-based equal respect toward that vast number of others whom one cannot know in any particularity.

At any rate, to tie together the varied threads of this discussion, we may conclude that nothing intrinsic to gender demands a division of moral norms which assigns particularized, personalized commitments to women and universalized, rule-based commitments to men. We need nothing less than to "de-moralize" the genders, advance beyond the dissociation of justice from care, and enlarge the symbolic access of each gender to all available conceptual and social resources for the sustenance and enrichment of our collective moral life.

THE CONTINUING DEBATE:
Do Women Have a Distinctive Ethical Perspective?

What Is New

Debate continues over whether women bring a uniquely enriching and enlarging perspective to ethical understanding, as well as over the best model for representing the ethical perspective of care. Sandra Lee Bartky and Jean Grimshaw emphasize that some elements of women's experience as caregivers may involve negatives: women are sometimes pushed into that role by being deprived of other opportunities, or because others refuse to share these important responsibilities. Friedman adds that some of these caring relations may occur in a patriarchal framework in which women's work is denigrated as subordinate and inferior, and she favors a friendship model of care rather than the traditional maternal or parenting model. In any case, the recognition that women have been—and often still are—socially and economically exploited continues to have an impact on the old but continuing debate over what (if anything) counts as the distinctive contribution of women to ethical theory. There is no doubt, however, that the recent emphasis among many ethicists on particular relations of caring and friendship (as opposed to an exclusive focus on impersonal universal principles) has been stimulated by writers on care ethics.

Where to Find More

Annette Baier's work (in addition to *Moral Prejudices*) includes *A Progress of Sentiments: Reflections on Hume's Treatise* (Cambridge, Mass.: Harvard University Press, 1991) and *The Commons of the Mind* (Chicago: Open Court, 1997).

Marilyn Friedman has written *What Are Friends For? Feminist Perspectives on Personal Relationships and Moral Theory* (Ithaca, N.Y.: Cornell University Press, 1993), as well as *Autonomy, Gender, Politics* (Oxford: Oxford University Press, 2003).

Lawrence Kohlberg's account of his research on moral development can be found in *The Philosophy of Moral Development: Moral Stages and the Idea of Justice* (New York: Harper and Row, 1981). A good brief description and critique of Kohlberg's work can be found in Laurence Thomas, "Morality and Psychological Development," in Peter Singer, editor, *A Companion to Ethics* (Oxford: Blackwell Publishers, 1991): 464–475.

Carol Gilligan, *In a Different Voice: Psychological Theory and Women's Development* (Cambridge, Mass: Harvard University Press, 1982), had a powerful impact on the contemporary development of care ethics.

For more on Kohlberg and Gilligan, see Lawrence Kohlberg and Owen Flanagan, "Virtue, Sex, and Gender," *Ethics*, volume 92, number 3 (April, 1982): 499–512; Lawrence Kohlberg, "A Reply to Owen Flanagan and Some Comments on the Puka-Goodpaster Exchange," *Ethics*, volume 92, number 3 (April, 1982): 513–528; Owen Flanagan and Kathryn Jackson, "Justice, Care, and Gender: The Kohlberg–Gilligan Debate Revisited," *Ethics*, volume 97 (1987): 622–637; and Lawrence Blum, "Gilligan and Kohlberg: Implications for Moral Theory," *Ethics*, volume 98, number 3 (April, 1988): 472–491.

Jean Grimshaw, "The Idea of a Female Ethic," in Peter Singer, editor, *A Companion to Ethics* (Oxford: Blackwell Publishers, 1991): 491–499, is a superb introduction to many of the issues surrounding this debate, and offers a strong critique of the view that women have a distinctly different approach to ethics. Sandra Lee Bartky, in her contribution to her edited volume, *Femininity and Domination* (New York: Routledge, 1990), offers an interesting analysis of caregiving in a larger (and sometimes quite negative) social context.

A brief survey of Alison M. Jaggar, editor, *Living With Contradictions: Controversies in Feminist Social Ethics* (Boulder, Col.: Westview Press, 1994) is sufficient evidence of the wide variety and divergence of positions held even among those who identify themselves as taking a feminist approach to ethics.

Virginia Held's edited collection, *Justice and Care* (Boulder, Co.: Westview Press, 1995), is an excellent collection of essays on the subject. A very good and wide–ranging anthology is Eva Feder Kittay and Diana T. Meyers, editors, *Women and Moral Theory* (Totowa, N.J.: Rowman & Littlefield, 1987). Mary Jeanne Larrabee, *An Ethic of Care: Feminist and Interdisciplinary Perspectives* (New York: Routledge, 1993), contains key essays, particularly on the Kohlberg-Gilligan debate.

Helpful internet resources include the Gender and Ethical Theory section of *Ethics Updates*, at http://ethics/acusd.edu/theories/Gender/index.html; and the Feminist Ethics entry (by Rosemary Tong) in the *Stanford Encyclopedia of Philosophy*, at http://plato.stanford.edu/entries/feminism-ethics.

Further readings are suggested in debate 11.

13   DO ANIMALS HAVE RIGHTS?

There Are No Moral Arguments for Animal Rights

ADVOCATE: Richard A. Posner, Judge for the U.S. Court of Appeals, 7th
Circuit, and Senior Lecturer at University of Chicago Law School, is
best known for his strong economic orientation to the law. He is the
author of many books, including *Economic Analysis of Law* (Boston:
Little, Brown, 1972); *The Economics of Justice* (Cambridge, Mass.:
Harvard University Press, 1981); and *The Problematics of Moral and
Legal Theory* (Cambridge, Mass.: Belknap Press of Harvard University
Press, 1999).

SOURCE: "Animal Rights: Legal, Philosophical, and Pragmatic Perspectives,"
from Cass R. Sunstein and Martha C. Nussbaum, Editors, *Animal
Rights* (New York: Oxford University Press, 2004): 51–77.

There Are Strong Moral Arguments for Animal Rights

ADVOCATE: Peter Singer, Ira W. DeCamp Professor of Bioethics at Princeton
University; *Animal Liberation* (1975) is perhaps his most famous book,
but he has written many important works, including *The Expanding
Circle* (New York: Farrar, Straus & Giroux, 1981). His *Writings on an
Ethical Life* (New York: HarperCollins, 2000) is a very readable and
engaging collection of his essays.

SOURCE: "Ethics Beyond Species and Beyond Instincts: A Response to
Richard Posner," from Cass R. Sunstein and Martha C. Nussbaum,
Editors, *Animal Rights* (New York: Oxford University Press, 2004):
78–92 (copyright by Cambridge University Press).

It's almost lunch time. You could stop by the local burger place and have a deli-
cious double burger—two big slabs of beef, maybe with some cheese on top. Or
you could go to a Chinese restaurant and enjoy some tofu sauteed with snow pea
pods and carrot slices. If you are concerned about your health or your weight, the
latter will obviously be a far superior choice. But is this also a moral question? Leave
aside the health issue. There are also important environmental issues: raising beef
animals is a very inefficient way of producing food, and it causes substantial environmental problems, but set that aside also. Suppose you prefer the taste of grilled
beef to the taste of grilled tofu. Is it morally acceptable to kill animals to satisfy that
taste preference?

The question of animal rights is a source of major contemporary controversy, but
the issue has been around for a long time, and the differences on this issue are dramatic. In the 18th Century, Immanuel Kant maintained that nonhuman animals
have no moral significance whatsoever, and it is not morally wrong to eat them, experiment on them, or even torture them:

...since animals exist only as means, and not for their own sakes, in that they have no self-consciousness, whereas man is the end,...it follows that we have no immediate duties to animals; our duties towards them are indirect duties to humanity....If a man has his dog shot, because it can no longer earn a living for him, he is by no means in breach of any duty to the dog, since the latter is incapable of judgment, but he thereby damages the kindly and humane qualities in himself, which he ought to exercise in virtue of his duties to mankind. *Lectures on Ethics*, translated by Peter Heath (Cambridge: Cambridge University Press, 1997), p. 212.

In contrast Jeremy Bentham, a 19th Century British utilitarian, insisted that all sentient living creatures are due moral consideration:

The day may come when the rest of the animal creation may acquire those rights which could never have been withholden from them but by the hand of tyranny. The French have already discovered that the blackness of the skin is no reason why a human being should be abandoned without redress to the caprice of a tormentor. It may one day come to be recognised that the number of the legs, the villosity of the skin, or the termination of the *os sacrum*, are reasons equally insufficient for abandoning a sensitive being to the same fate. What else is it that should trace the insuperable line? Is it the faculty of reason, or perhaps the faculty of discourse? But a full-grown horse or dog is beyond comparison a more rational, as well as a more conversable animal, than an infant of a day, or a week, or even a month. But suppose they were otherwise, what would it avail? The question is not, Can they reason? Nor can they talk? But *Can they suffer?* Jeremy Bentham, *Introduction to the Principles of Morals and Legislation*, Chapter 18, section 1.

The question of our moral obligations toward nonhuman animals is an ethical issue confronted daily when deciding what food to eat, what clothes to wear, and what laboratory experiments to pursue. Our religious views, our deepest beliefs about ourselves and our place in the world, and many of our most mundane daily practices involve our beliefs about animals and their appropriate treatment. It is hardly surprising, then, that questions about our treatment of animals provoke strong reactions on both sides of the issue.

The most obvious basis for extending ethical consideration to animals is utilitarian ethics. Though there are many varieties of utilitarianism, most utilitarians subscribe to something along the lines of the following basic principle: The right act is the act that produces the greatest balance of pleasure over suffering for all involved. On the utilitarian view suffering is suffering, whether the suffering is experienced by a human or a dog. Some utilitarians accept the idea of different degrees or levels or even qualities of pleasure and suffering, but all pleasures and pains are important, and the interests of all sentient creatures must be factored in when deciding what act is likely to produce the best consequences. Utilitarians are generally more focused on *consequences*, rather than general principles; but the consequences to be considered include long-term consequences, and consequences for all, and so utilitarian calculation of the right act can be a demanding exercise. Peter Singer is one of the leading contemporary proponents of utilitarian ethics, and he bases his arguments on broad utilitarian considerations.

The debate between Richard Posner and Peter Singer concerns the treatment of animals, but it also involves some basic questions about the nature of ethics. Richard Posner claims that no genuine arguments on this moral issue are possible; and that in any case, our deep instincts on these issues cannot be modified by argument, and are too strong to be successfully challenged by argument. Thus Posner employs a "humancentric" approach to the issue of how animals should be treated, maintaining that any consideration shown to nonhuman animals must be based on existing human sympathies and human interests rather than on principled ethical argument. In contrast, Singer argues that utilitarian principles—as well as basic considerations of fairness and consistency—can establish strong grounds for recognizing the genuine interests of nonhuman animals, and that those grounds are derived from moral obligation rather than accidental inclinations.

POINTS TO PONDER

➤ Some animal researchers—especially at universities—have made an effort to treat their animal research subjects more humanely: providing larger cages, imposing less isolation on social species, reducing suffering during experiments. Some who support animal rights see this as a valuable step in the right direction, while others deride such measures as part of the "clean cage movement": an effort to gain positive publicity without addressing the fundamental abuses of animals in experimentation. What is your view of programs to ameliorate the suffering of laboratory animals while continuing to run experiments that harm and ultimately kill the animals? What would Posner think of it?

➤ It is always possible—as a matter of religious doctrine—to insist that only humans have souls, and therefore only humans have rights (though at least some Eastern views, not to mention St. Francis of Assisi in the Christian tradition, would deny that other animals lack souls). But leaving aside such religious doctrines, *is* there any characteristic that would apply to *all* humans whom you would say have rights (including the demented, the severely retarded, small children) but would *not* apply to nonhuman animals (such as chimpanzees or pigs)?

➤ Think back to some moral belief that you once held, and that you now regard as wrong. *How* did that belief change? Did *moral argument* play any part in changing your view?

➤ Neither Posner nor Singer believe that the insights of Darwinian biology provide adequate grounds for ethical claims concerning the treatment of nonhuman animals; however, does an understanding of the evolutionary process have *any* important implications for your beliefs about how nonhuman animals should be treated?

There Are No Moral Arguments for Animal Rights

Richard A. Posner

PHILOSOPHIZING ABOUT ANIMAL RIGHTS

Where might we go, necessarily outside rather than inside law, for reasons for changing the law to entitle animals? I shall discuss two possible sources, which I shall call the *philosophical* and illustrate primarily with Peter Singer's utilitarian approach, and the *pragmatic* in the everyday sense of the word, the sense that equates it to "practical" and "down-to-earth." Conventional philosophizing over animal rights seeks for first principles to determine how we should treat animals. A utilitarian—someone who believes that our basic moral duty is to maximize happiness or the satisfaction of preferences and thus to minimize pain and disappointment—can readily argue that people should be forbidden to mistreat those animals that have a sufficiently developed nervous system to be able to experience pain, unless that mistreatment (perhaps then misnamed) minimizes pain, or maximizes pleasure, overall. That can easily happen; an example would be a case in which minor animal suffering was a sine qua non for developing a cure for a lethal disease of human beings. Or vice versa—for there is nothing in utilitarian theory to prevent arguing for medical experimentation on human beings that is designed to find cures for fatal animal illnesses, especially painful ones.

The utilitarian cannot, however, establish the validity of his major premise: that maximizing the satisfaction of preferences should be the goal of society. This is the standard problem of moral philosophy in a morally heterogeneous society: finding common ground from which to argue to normative conclusions. But what really undermines the utilitarian's position is the logical implications of his premise. By itself it has a certain appeal; only when one explores its implications does it become unpalatable and even bizarre. Animals experience pain and pleasure, so panspecies utilitarianism seems indeed entailed by the utilitarian premise. But in that case, the life of a healthy pig is likely to be worthier of legal protection than that of a severely retarded human being. Indeed, if pigs are naturally happier than human beings, or if because of their relatively small size the earth can support far more pigs than human beings, a world human population just large enough to support an enormous pig population might be the utilitarian optimum. We might, as I suggested in the last paragraph, have to allow medical experimentation on human beings for the sake of improving animal health.

At the same time, the utilitarian premise implies that killing an animal painlessly and without forewarning can be completely compensated for by creating a new animal to replace it and that carnivorous animals should be killed or sequestered to protect their prey. The first implication undermines the case for vegetarianism. Most people obtain great utility from eating meat. If animals raised for food are treated humanely, have no foreknowledge of death, and are killed painlessly, and if the demand for meat results in a huge population of such animals, then eating meat may well increase rather than reduce overall utility, even when the utility of the animals raised for food is taken into account. Even *animal* utility might be reduced by banning the eating of meat, especially if animal species that are maintained primarily as sources of human food became extinct.

Singer, a strong proponent of vegetarianism, acknowledges that "as a matter of strict logic, perhaps, there is no contradiction in taking an interest in animals on both compassionate and gastronomic grounds....One could consistently eat animals who had lived free of all suffering and been instantly, painlessly slaughtered." But, he adds weakly, "Practically and psychologically it is impossible to be consistent in one's concern for nonhuman animals while continuing to dine on them."

It can be argued that Darwinism shows that there is nothing special about human beings; we are an accident of nature's blind processes just like all other animals and so it is arbitrary for us to put ourselves on a higher plane than the other animals. (This is the negative implication of Darwinism; the positive implication, which seems to me dubious, or at least arbitrary, is that Darwinism establishes our kinship with animals, and we should be kind to our kin.) This may well be true, but it ignores the potential social value of a rhetoric of human specialty—think only of how the Nazis used Darwinian rhetoric to justify a law-of-the-jungle conception of the relations between human groups. What is more, if natural law is understood naturalistically, not as Christianity or any other religion that asserts a deep and wide gulf between animal and human nature but as the law of the jungle, then as denizens of the jungle we have no greater duties to the other animals than the lion, say, has to the gazelle. But all that these points show is that there is no normative significance to our having descended from apes.

Yet are not pragmatists Darwinists? Don't they believe that human beings are just clever animals rather than demiangels? If Christianity, by teaching that people are demiangels, ensouled by and created in the image of God, and that animals are not demiangels, opened up a huge moral gulf between man and the animals (*not* "and the *other* animals"), does not Darwinism, and hence pragmatism, close it? Should not pragmatists therefore be animal liberationists?

There are three misunderstandings here. The first is the conflation of philosophical and everyday pragmatism. The proposition that people are clever animals is part of the philosophical side of pragmatism; it is related to the distinctive pragmatic conception of inquiry and the associated pragmatic rejection of metaphysical realism. Second, it is arbitrary to draw a normative inference from a biological fact (or theory). Why should the percentage of genes that I have in common with other creatures determine how much consideration I owe them? And third, a pragmatist need not be committed to a particular vocabulary, realistic or otherwise, such as "man as animal." A vocabulary of human specialness may have social value despite its descriptive inaccuracy. To call human life "sacred" or to distinguish human beings from animals may be descriptively, which is to say scientifically, inaccurate yet serve a constructive function in political discourse, perhaps nudging people to behave "better" in a sense with which most everyday pragmatists would agree.

The philosophical discourse on animal rights is inherently inconclusive because there is no metric that enables utilitarianism, Romanticism, normative Darwinism, and other possible philosophical groundings of animal rights to be commensurated and conflicts among them resolved. Let me nonetheless press on, examining Singer's approach in greater detail because he is the most influential, and also and relatedly the most accessible, philosophical proponent of what I am calling animal rights but that he prefers to call "animal liberation" (utilitarians are not comfortable with "rights"). In his book of that title he makes several points with which I agree, such as that human beings are not infinitely superior to nor infinitely more valuable than other animals; indeed, I am prepared to drop "infinitely." I agree that we are animals and not ensouled demiangels, that gratuitous cruelty to and neglect of animals are wrong, and that some costs should be incurred to reduce the suffering of animals raised for food or other human purposes or subjected to medical or other testing and experimentation.

But I do not agree with any of these things under the compulsion of philosophical argument. And I disagree that we have a duty to (the other) animals that arises from their being the equal members of a community composed of all those creatures in the universe that can feel pain, and that it is merely "prejudice" in a disreputable sense akin to racial prejudice or sexism that makes us discriminate in favor of our own species. Singer assumes the existence of the universe-wide community of pain and demands reasons that the boundary of our concern should be drawn any more narrowly: "If a being suffers there can be no moral justification for refusing to take that suffering into consideration." That is sheer assertion, and particularly dubious is his further claim that (the title of the first chapter of his book) "all animals are equal," a point that he defends by arguing that the case for treating women and blacks equally with white males does not depend on the existence of *factual* equality among these groups. But the history of racial and sexual equality is the history of a growing belief that the factual inequalities among these groups are

either a consequence of discrimination or have been exaggerated.

Singer wants to seize the commanding heights in the debate over animal rights by using his premises about the moral claims of suffering and the equality of all animals to shift the burden of proof to his opponents. That is just an argumentative gambit and cannot be shown to be superior to proceeding from the bottom up, with the brute fact that we, like other animals, prefer our own—our own family, the "pack" that we happen to run with (because we are a social animal), and the larger sodalities constructed on the model of the smaller ones, of which the largest for most of us is our nation. Americans have less feeling for the pains and pleasures of foreigners than of other Americans and even less for most of the nonhuman animals with which we share the world.

Singer will doubtless reply that these are just facts about human nature, that they have no normative significance. Yet I doubt that he actually believes that in his heart of hearts. Suppose a dog menaced a human infant and the only way to prevent the dog from biting the infant was to inflict severe pain on the dog—more pain, in fact, than the bite would inflict on the infant. Singer would have to say, let the dog bite, for Singer's position is that if an animal feels pain, the pain matters as much as it does when a human being feels pain, provided the pain is as great; and it matters more if it is greater. But any normal person (and not merely the infant's parents), including a philosopher when he is not self-consciously engaged in philosophizing, would say it would be monstrous to spare the dog, even though to do so would minimize the sum of pain in the world.

I feel no obligation to defend this reaction, any more than I do to prove that my legs remain attached to my body when I am asleep, or for that matter when I am awake. My certitude about my bodily integrity is deeper than any proof that could be offered of it to refute a skeptic. Likewise the superior claim of the human infant than of the dog on our consideration is a moral intuition deeper than any reason that could be given for it and impervious to any reason that anyone could give against it. Membership in the human species is not a morally irrelevant fact, as the race and gender of human beings have come to seem. If the moral irrelevance of humanity is what philosophy teaches, so that we have to choose between philosophy and the intuition that says that membership in the human species *is* morally relevant, philosophy will have to go.

Moral intuitions can change. The difference between science and morality is that while it has never been true, whatever people believed, that the sun revolves around the earth, morality, which as a practical matter is simply a department of public opinion, changes unpredictably; there are no unchanging facts to anchor it. Someday we may think animals as worthy of our solicitude as human beings, or even more worthy. But that will mean that we have a new morality, not that philosophers have shown that we were making an erroneous distinction between animals and humans all along.

I am sure that Singer would react the same way as I do to the dog-child example. He might consider it a weakness in himself if he were unable to act upon his philosophical beliefs. But he would be wrong; it would not be a weakness; it would be a sign of sanity. Just as philosophers who have embraced skepticism about the existence of the external world, or hold that science is just a "narrative" with no defensible claim to yield objective truth, do not put their money where their mouth is by refusing to jump out of the way of a truck bearing down on them, so

philosophers who embrace weird ethical theories do not act on those theories even when they could do so without being punished. There are exceptions, but we call them insane.

Singer distinguishes between pain and death and acknowledges that the mental abilities of human beings may make their lives more valuable than those of animals. This is the pleasure side (in a broad sense of the world *pleasure*) of the utilitarian pleasure-pain calculus. People make plans, have intimate relations with other people, who may grieve for their deaths, and for these and other reasons the painless death of a human being causes on average a greater loss of utility than the painless death of a mouse. But even this rather appealing argument turns out to be at war with our deepest intuitions when we consider what it implies. It implies that the life of a chimpanzee is more valuable than the life of a human being who, because he is profoundly retarded (though not comatose), has less ability to make plans or foresee future events than the chimpanzee does. There are undoubtedly such cases. Indeed, there are people in the last stages of Alzheimer's disease who, though conscious, have less mentation than a normal dog. But killing such a person would be murder, while it is no crime at all to have a veterinarian kill one's pet dog because it has become incontinent with age. The logic of Singer's position would require that the law treat these killings alike. (I assume he would think both permissible.) And if, for example, we could agree that although a normal human being's life is more valuable than a normal chimpanzee's life, it is only a hundred times more valuable, Singer would have to concede that if we had to choose between killing one human being and 101 chimpanzees, we should kill the human being. Against the deep revulsion that such results engender, the concept of a trans-human community of sufferers beats its tinsel wings ineffectually.

For Singer, the ability to see oneself as existing over time, with a past and a future, is an important part of what makes killing some living beings more seriously wrong than killing others. And there is scientific evidence that nonhuman primates have some of that ability. One way to interpret my numerical example is asserting that this ability might be as much as 1 percent of the ability of a *normal* human being—and then it follows from the logic of Singer's position that it is indeed worse to kill 101 of these primates than to kill a single normal human being, let alone a single retarded human being whose ability to see himself as existing over time, with a past and a future, may be little superior to that of the average chimpanzee.

A HUMANCENTRIC APPROACH

What is needed to persuade people to alter their treatment of animals is not philosophy, let alone an atheistic philosophy (for one of the premises of Singer's argument is that we have no souls) in a religious nation. It is to learn to feel animals' pains as our pains and to learn that (if it is a fact, which I do not know) we can alleviate those pains without substantially reducing our standard of living and that of the rest of the world and without sacrificing medical and other scientific progress. Most of us, especially perhaps those of us who have lived with animals, have sufficient empathy for animal suffering to support the laws that forbid cruelty and neglect. We might go further if we knew more about animal feelings and about the existence of low-cost alternatives to pain-inflicting uses of animals. It follows that to expand and invigorate the laws that protect animals will require not philosophical arguments for reducing human beings to the level of the other animals but facts that will stimu-

late a greater empathic response to animal suffering and alleviate concern about the human costs of further measures to reduce animal suffering. If enough people come to feel the sufferings of these animals as their own, public opinion and consumer preference will induce the business firms and other organizations that inflict such suffering to change their methods. In just the same way, the more altruistic that American people become toward foreigners (for example, the impoverished populations of the Third World), the greater the costs that they will be willing to incur for the benefit of foreigners.

But it does not follow that *ethical* argument either can or should affect how we feel about animals (or foreigners). Indeed I believe that ethical argument is and should be powerless against tenacious moral instincts. Such instincts may, it is true, be based on erroneous factual premises. But then what is needed is to point out the mistakes. The belief behind making it a capital offense for a human being to have sexual intercourse with an animal—that such intercourse could produce a monster—was unsound, and showing that it was unsound undermined the case for punishment. To the extent that lack of consideration for animal suffering is rooted in factual errors, pointing out those errors can change our intuitions concerning the consideration that we owe animals. Descartes believed that animals felt no pain, that the outward expressions which we took to reveal pain were deceptive. People who believe this would have no truck with laws forbidding cruelty to animals; they would not think it possible to *be* cruel to an animal, any more than to a stone. We now have good reason to believe that Descartes was mistaken. We likewise have good reason to believe that the Aztecs were mistaken about the efficacy of human sacrifice and that Nazi ideology, like other racist ideologies, rested on misconceptions about evolutionary and racial biology. To accept Cartesian, or Aztec, or Nazi premises and argue merely against the inferences from them would be futile.

The information that Singer's book *Animal Liberation* conveys, partly by means of photographs, about the suffering of animals is a valuable corrective to ignorant thinking. But arguments that do not identify factual errors that underlie or buttress our moral instincts do nothing to undermine those instincts, nor should they. I have said that it is wrong to give as much weight to a dog's pain as to an infant's pain, and wrong to kill one person to save 101 chimpanzees even if a human life is only a hundred times as valuable as a chimpanzee's life. I rest these judgments on intuition. Against this intuition there is no factual reply, as there would be if my intuition were founded on a belief that dogs feel no pain and that chimpanzees have no mentation.

I do not claim that our preferring human beings to other animals is "justified" in some rational sense—only that it is a fact deeply rooted in our current thinking and feeling, a fact based on beliefs that can change but not a fact that can be shaken by philosophy. I particularly do not claim that we are rationally justified in giving preference to the suffering of humans just because it is humans who are suffering. It is because *we* are humans that we put humans first. If we were cats, we would put cats first, regardless of what philosophers might tell us. Reason doesn't enter.

There are more than a few people who would like to be able to sign a contract to be killed if they become demented. Such a contract would be unenforceable, and the physician who honored it by killing the Alzheimer's patient would be a murderer. The moral intuition that powers this result may be vulnerable to factual challenge

as we learn more about Alzheimer's, as more people suffer from it, and as people come to accept more than they do today the role of physicians as "angels of mercy." What the moral intuition is not vulnerable to is an ethical argument that makes the issue contingent on a comparison of human and canine mental abilities.

Singer claims that readers of *Animal Liberation* have been persuaded by the ethical arguments in the book and not just by the facts and the pictures. If so, it is probably so only because these readers do not realize the radicalism of the ethical vision that powers Singer's views, an ethical vision that finds greater value in a healthy pig than in a profoundly retarded child, that commands inflicting a lesser pain on a human being to avert a greater pain to a dog, and that implies that, provided only that a chimpanzee has 1 percent of the mental ability of a normal human being, it is right to sacrifice the human being to save the chimpanzees. Had *Animal Liberation* emphasized these implications of Singer's utilitarian philosophy, it would have persuaded many fewer readers—and likewise if it had sought merely to persuade our rational faculty, and not to stir our empathic regard for animals.

Our moral norms regarding race, homosexuality, nonmarital sex, contraception, and suicide have changed in recent times, but not as a result of ethical arguments. Philosophers have not been prominent in any of the movements. (Singer, a philosopher, has been influential in the animal rights movement, but that is a tribute to his rhetorical skills rather than to the cogency of his philosophical reasoning.) Thurgood Marshall, Earl Warren, and Martin Luther King, Jr., had a lot more to do with the development of an antidiscrimination norm than any academic philosopher. The most influential feminists, such as Betty Friedan and

Catharine MacKinnon, have not been philosophers either. As far as our changing attitudes toward sex are concerned, the motive forces have again not been philosophical or, even, at root, ideological. They have been material. As the economy shifted from manufacturing (heavy, dirty work) to services (lighter, cleaner), as contraception became safer and more reliable, as desire for large families diminished (the substitution of quality for quantity of children), and as the decline in infant mortality allowed women to reduce the number of their pregnancies yet still hit their target rate of reproduction, both the demand for and the supply of women in the labor market rose. With women working more and having as a consequence greater economic independence, they demanded and obtained greater sexual independence as well. Nonmarital, nonprocreative sex, including therefore homosexual sex, began to seem less "unnatural" than it had. At the same time, myths about homosexual recruitment were exploded; homosexuality was discovered to be genetic or in any event innate rather than a consequence of a "lifestyle" choice; and so hostility to homosexuals diminished. So it is wrong to think that a vow of abstinence from philosophical argument would disempower us to condemn racism and homophobia. It was the lessons of history, and not the thought of Plato or Aristotle or Kant or Heidegger, that caused most philosophers, along with nonphilosophers, eventually to turn against racism and homophobia. Philosophy follows moral change; it does not cause it, or even lead it.

Thrasymachus in Plato's *Republic* teaches that might makes right. Socrates, while rejecting Thrasymachus's definition of justice, advocates censorship, the destruction of the family, and totalitarian rule by—philosophers. So moral philosophy has its hard side (consider also Aristo-

tle's defense of slavery, and Kant's of capital punishment), and it is Singer, the philosopher, who is the tough guy, and I the softy, the sentimentalist, willing to base animal rights on empathy, unwilling to follow the utilitarian logic to the harsh conclusions sketched above.

I am not a moral skeptic in the sense of believing that moral beliefs have no effect on human behavior. I am merely skeptical that such beliefs can be changed by philosophical arguments as distinct from being changed by experience, by changes in material circumstances, by the demonstrated success or failure of particular moral principles as means of coping with the problems of life, and by personal example, charismatic authority, and appeals to emotion.

And although the efficacy and the soundness of moral arguments are *analytically* distinct issues, they are related. One reason that moral arguments are ineffective in changing behavior is their lack of cogency—their radical inconclusiveness—in a morally diverse society such as ours, where people can and do argue from incompatible premises. But there is something deeper. Moral argument often appears plausible when it is not well reasoned or logically complete, but it is almost always implausible when it is carried to its logical extreme. An illogical utilitarian (a "soft" utilitarian, we might call him) is content to say that pain is bad, that animals experience pain, so that, other things being equal, we should try to alleviate animal suffering if we can do so at a modest cost. Singer, a powerfully logical utilitarian, a "hard" utilitarian, is not content with such pabulum. He wants to pursue to its logical extreme the proposition that pain is bad for whoever or whatever experiences it. He does not flinch from the logical implication of his philosophy that if a stuck pig experiences more pain than a stuck human, the pig has the superior claim to our solicitude, or that a chimpanzee is entitled to more consideration than a profoundly retarded human being. (He does not flinch from these implications, but, as I said, in his popular writing, and in particular in *Animal Liberation*, he soft-pedals them so as not to lose his audience.)

The soft-utilitarian position on animal rights is a moral intuition of many Americans. We realize that animals feel pain, and we think that to inflict pain without a reason is bad. Nothing of practical value is added by dressing up this intuition in the language of philosophy; much is lost when the intuition is made a stage in a logical argument. When kindness toward animals is levered into a duty of weighting the pains of animals and of people equally, bizarre vistas of social engineering are opened up. Singer acknowledges that it would be odd for a democratic government to prohibit the eating of meat if the majority of its citizens were strongly and consistently in favor of meat eating, but he does not say that it would be *wrong* to force vegetarianism on the majority (not all democratic legislation is majoritarian). Nor does he indicate any reservations about legislation that would force vegetarianism on a minority of the population that was strongly and consistently in favor of meat eating. If 49 percent of the population very much wanted to eat meat, he apparently would think it right to forbid them to do so, merely because they were a minority in a democratic system.

The approach that I am urging, the humancentric, takes account of such things as worry about leveling down people to animals, people's love of nature and of particular animal species, and people's empathic concern with suffering animals (feeling their pain as our pain). The approach assigns no *intrinsic* value to animal welfare. It seeks reasons strictly of human welfare for according or denying rights to animals, and focuses on the consequences *for us* of recognizing animal rights. Those consequences are both good (benefits) and bad (costs—a word I am using broadly without limitation to pecuniary costs) and can be either direct or indirect. A direct human-centric benefit of giving animals rights would be the increase in human happiness brought about by knowledge that the animals we like are being protected. There is nothing surprising about human altruism toward animals. Remember what I said earlier about the dependence of early man on animals. The relationship with animals which that dependence established was not primarily one of kindness, but one of use. As our dependence on animals declined, however, our empathy with animals could stand free from any felt need to kill. If the current regard for animals on the part of members of the animal rights movement seems sentimental, we should remind ourselves that the sentiments are in all likelihood the expression of an adaptive preference that we acquired in the ancestral environment.

No doubt the most aggressive implementations of animal rights thinking would benefit animals more than commodification and a more determined program of enforcing existing laws against cruelty to animals. But those implementations are unlikely, and so the modest alternatives are worth serious consideration. We may overlook this simple point if, however much we love animals, we listen too raptly to the siren song of animal rights.

There Are Strong Moral Arguments for Animal Rights

Peter Singer

EQUAL CONSIDERATION FOR ANIMALS

Most people draw a sharp moral line between humans and other animals. Humans, they say, are infinitely more valuable than any "lower creatures." If our interests conflict with those of animals, it is always their interests which should be sacrificed. But why should this be so? To say that everyone believes this is not enough to justify it. Until very recently it was the common view that a woman should obey her father, until she is married, and then her husband (and in some countries, this is still the prevailing view). Or, not quite so recently, but still not all that long ago, it was widely held that people of African descent could properly be enslaved. As these examples show, the fact that a view is widespread does not make it right. It may be an indefensible prejudice that survives primarily because it suits the interests of the dominant group.

How should we decide whether a widely held view is justifiable, or a prejudice based on the interests of the dominant group? The obvious answer is that we should consider what reasons are offered for the view. Putting aside religious grounds that would force us to examine the foundations of the particular religions of which they are a consequence, the reason given usually refers to some kind of human superiority over animals. After all, are not human beings more rational, more self-aware, more capable of a sense of justice, and so on, than any nonhuman animals? But while this claim may be true if limited to normal mature human beings, it does not help us to defend the place where we now draw the moral line, which is between *all* members of our species and *all* nonhuman animals. For there are many humans who are not rational, or self-aware, and who have no sense of justice—all humans under one month of age, for a start. And even if infants are excluded on the grounds that they have the potential to become rational, self-aware, and have a sense of justice, not all humans have this potential. Sadly, some are born with brain damage so severe that they will never be rational or self-aware, or capable of a sense of justice. In fact, some of these humans will never possess any intellectual or emotional capacities that are not also possessed by any normal, non-infant chimpanzee, dog, cat, pig, cow, or even laboratory rat.

Hence it seems that no adequate reason can be given for taking species membership, in itself, as the ground for putting some beings inside the boundary of moral protection and others either totally or very largely outside it. That doesn't mean that all animals have the same rights as humans. It would be absurd to give animals the right to vote, but then it would be no less absurd to give that right to infants or to severely retarded human beings. Yet we still give equal consideration to the interests of those humans incapable of voting. We don't raise them for food, nor test cosmetics in their eyes. Nor should we. But we do these things to nonhuman animals who show greater rationality, self-awareness, and a sense of justice than they do.

Once we understand that in respect of any valuable characteristic we can think of, there is no gap between humans and animals, but rather an overlap in the possession of that characteristic by individuals of different species, it is easy to see the belief that all humans are somehow infinitely more valuable than any animal is a prejudice. It is in some respects akin to the prejudice that racists have in favor of their own race, and sexists have in favor of their own gender (although there are also differences, as with any complex social phenomena). Speciesism is logically parallel to racism and sexism, in the sense that speciesists, racists, and sexists all say: The boundary of my own group is also the boundary of my concern. Never mind what you are like, if you are a member of my group, you are superior to all those who are not members of my group. The speciesist favors a larger group than the racist, and so has a larger circle of concern, but all of these prejudices use an arbitrary and morally irrelevant fact—membership in a race, gender, or species—as if it were morally crucial.

The only acceptable limit to our moral concern is the point at which there is no awareness of pain or pleasure and no conscious preferences of any kind. That is why pigs are objects of moral concern, but lettuces are not. Pigs can feel pain and pleasure, they can enjoy their lives, or want to escape from distressing conditions. To the best of our knowledge, lettuces can't. We should give the same weight to the pain and distress of pigs as we would give to a similar amount of pain and distress suffered by a human being. Of course, pigs and humans may have different interests, and there are some human interests that a pig is probably incapable of having—like, for example, our interest in living to see our grandchildren. There may, therefore, sometimes be grounds for giving preference to the human over the pig—but if so, it can only be because in the particular circumstances the human has greater interests at stake, and not simply because the human is a member of our own species.

MORAL AND OTHER INSTINCTS

The argument I have just sketched leads to the conclusion that we should change the moral status of animals in order to give greater consideration to the interests of the animals. We should do this, obviously, for the sake of the animals. In contrast, Posner tells us that he prefers a "pragmatic" to a "philosophical" approach to the question of changing the moral status of animals, and we should do so only insofar as this fits with a "humancentric" perspective. I shall argue that this position is indefensible.

The foundation of Posner's position is summed up in this quoted sentence: "I believe that ethical argument is and should be powerless against tenacious moral instincts."

The meaning of the sentence is not as clear as it first appears. What are "moral instincts"? If the word *moral* is doing any work here, Posner must have a way of distinguishing moral instincts from nonmoral instincts. Drawing lines between what is moral and what is nonmoral is a much-debated issue in moral philosophy. I am willing to save Posner the work of investigating it by offering him a criterion for drawing the distinction. Here it is:

> We can distinguish the moral from the nonmoral by appeal to the idea that when we think, judge, or act within the realm of the moral, we do so in a manner that we are prepared to apply to all others who are similarly placed.

Thus, if I am making moral judgments about thefts of loaves of bread from a bakery, I may make different judgments in cases in which the thief was well-fed from cases in which the thief was starving, but I may not do so in cases in which I am the thief and other cases in which I am the baker. "It makes *me* better off" is not an acceptable ground for differentiating two otherwise relevantly similar moral situations. Thus to make a moral judgment is to accept constraints on the extent to which you can give preference to your own interests or to those of your own group.

If the criterion I offer lacks originality, at least it comes with the endorsement of a long line of philosophers going back through Kant to Stoics like Marcus Aurelius. Following R. M. Hare, I shall use the term *universalizable* to refer to this distinguishing feature of moral judgments. Universalizability does not mean that it is never justifiable to give preference to one's own family, or nation. Giving preference to one's own group may itself be justifiable from a universal point of view, for example, in accordance with the principle "all parents should put the welfare of their own children above the welfare of other children." But this principle must itself be justifiable from a universal point of view.

Suppose that Posner accepts this solution to the problem of distinguishing the moral from the nonmoral, and uses it to explain his claim that ethical argument is and should be powerless against tenacious moral instincts. He would then be saying that ethical argument is and should be powerless against those instincts which are both tenacious and universalizable. But note that this way of distinguishing moral instincts from nonmoral instincts already provides scope for a certain amount of ethical argument. Whenever Posner claims that an instinct is a moral one, we can inquire whether those who act on this instinct, or make judgments based on it, are acting or judging in a way that they are prepared to apply universalizably. Hence

the sentence I quoted must be rewritten as: "I believe that ethical argument is and should be powerless against those tenacious instincts that survive the universalizability test." But now the sentence has become much less significant than it first appeared, because the whole issue will come down to: Which instincts survive the test of universalizability? One cannot know whether one is prepared to hold a judgment universalizably unless one is prepared to put oneself in the position of all those affected by it. That requires both information—about what it is like to be one of those affected by the act being judged—and sincerity in taking on, and not discounting, the perspectives of others affected.

I would argue that many of our instincts regarding animals *cannot* survive the test of universalizability. We humans instinctively do things to animals that are for our benefit, without in any way putting ourselves in their situation. The humancentric view that Posner endorses is prima facie based on just such an instinct and will not, without more argument, survive the universalizability test.

By this time the reader will have realized that in offering Posner a solution to his problem of distinguishing moral and nonmoral instincts, I was not being entirely altruistic. But if Posner rejects my offer, what else might do the job of distinguishing moral and nonmoral interests?

Since the word *instincts* suggests something fairly deeply rooted in human nature, and Posner accepts that human nature is best understood as the outcome of Darwinian evolution (on this, we are in agreement) the most obvious candidate is that by "moral instincts" we mean those instincts that evolved in the social mammals to make it easier for them to survive together in the small groups in which we and our ancestors lived for most of our evolutionary history. This is very vague, however, and fails to provide any clear line between moral instincts and other instincts. Presumably a sense of reciprocity counts as a moral instinct, since it helps primates to bond with unrelated members of the group and can be seen as the basis for ethical precepts that are universal, or virtually so, among humans, such as the precept of gratitude, or doing good to those who do good to us, and the precept of retribution, or doing harm to those who harm us. Some sense of group loyalty, leading us to respond more favorably to members of our own group than we do to strangers, might be another moral instinct. But what else?

Consider two more examples of instincts that are very typical of humans and other primates: parent-child bonds and competition for leadership among males. Is care for one's own children, in preference to the children of others, a moral instinct? Is the male drive to get to the top a moral instinct? Both offer some benefit to the wider group—without the former, the group would have no future, and the latter serves to ensure that the group is led by aggressive males—but both also benefit the parent and the successful males and can lead to conflict within the group, sometimes with fatal results. Without a criterion like universalizability by which to screen such instincts, the decision to include or reject them within the sphere of moral instincts seems arbitrary.

Nevertheless, suppose that Posner were to agree, as many people might, that to care for one's own children is a moral instinct, whereas ambition to get to the top is a nonmoral instinct. Then the sentence under discussion would mean that ethical argument is and should be powerless against the instinct to care for one's own children in preference to those of others but is not, or should not be, powerless against the instinct to get to the top. In factual terms, ethical argument seems as effective (or not) against the latter as it is against the former. Can Posner defend the conclusion that it *should* be powerless against the former, but not against the latter? It is hard to see how Posner could produce an argument for this conclusion that would not violate his own (sound) warning that we should not "draw a normative inference arbitrarily from a biological fact." An evolutionary account of the formation of some of our instincts does not allow us to deduce what ought to be the case.

Even at a commonsense level, Posner's position is implausible. Whatever the moral instincts may turn out to be, why exempt just those ones from the power of ethical argument? Our instincts, moral and nonmoral, developed during the eons of time in which we and our ancestors lived in circumstances very different from those in which we live today. For most of our evolutionary history, we lived in small groups in which everyone knew everyone else in the group, and interactions with members of our species who were not also members of our group were rare. The planet was sparsely populated, which was just as well, since we had no way of consciously regulating our reproductive capacities. There were ample uncleared forests, no ill effects from our emissions of greenhouse gases, and our weapons killed one at a time, and only in close proximity. Isn't it highly probable that moral instincts formed under those circumstances *should* be changed by ethical argument based on our current, very different circumstances?

The only way in which Posner is prepared to allow argument to have an impact on our moral instincts is by demonstrating a factual error in the assumptions on which our instincts are based. (For example, correcting factual errors about the capacities of animals to suffer, or that sexual intercourse with an animal leads to the birth of a monster, is in his view an acceptable way of arguing against an instinct.) Sometimes, however, we need to change moral instincts that do not rest on factual errors. Although it is always controversial what is really an instinct, and what is acquired by culture and education, we can take, as an example, preference for my "own kind" over someone who talks, looks, or smells differently. This preference, which is plausibly instinctive, does not require any false factual beliefs. Rather, people add factual beliefs about the negative characteristics of the outsiders in order to strengthen the hold of the instinct that they already have.

So far I have been arguing that Posner's inclusion of the word *moral* in the sentence we are discussing creates a dilemma for him. Either he uses something like the universalizability criterion to separate the moral instincts from the nonmoral ones, in which case he has to admit that there is scope for ethical argument, or he is left with a distinction between different kinds of instincts that is irrelevant to which of them should, and which should not, be immune from the power of ethical argument. Faced with this dilemma, Posner might contemplate dropping the word *moral* from the sentence. But Posner would still have to explain why he thinks ethical argument (based, for example, on the requirement that we hold our judgments universalizably) not only is, but *should be* powerless to change *any* tenacious instinct, no matter how aggressive, murderous, or xenophobic that instinct may be.

IS ETHICAL ARGUMENT POWERLESS AGAINST INSTINCTS?

Perhaps, in seeking to understand why Posner might want to defend this view, we should return to his original sentence. I have focused on the claim that ethical ar-

gument *should be* powerless against instincts, and so far have not considered the claim that ethical argument *is* powerless against instincts. Logically, these are separate claims, and Posner himself phrased the question he wished to pursue, in the second half of his essay, as an inquiry into "reasons for changing the law to entitle animals." What actually leads people to change their votes about laws relating to animals or to change their diets or other aspects of their behavior toward animals is one thing; what reasons there are for changing the law about animals is another thing. It would be perfectly possible to hold that ethical argument *is* powerless against instincts, but that it *should not* be. Nevertheless, the way in which Posner amalgamates the two claims in the sentence we are examining suggests that he may believe that the two claims go together. This much can, at least, be said for that amalgamation: If the factual claim were true, the normative claim would become much less interesting. If ethical argument simply cannot have any power over tenacious instincts, then there isn't a lot of point in discussing whether it ought to have such power. Hence it is worth examining the truth of the factual claim.

Is ethical argument powerless against tenacious instincts? If so, it would be hard to explain the moral progress that has been made in areas in which, previously, some of our most tenacious moral instincts have held sway. Consider areas like race relations, crimes of genocide and crimes against humanity, gender issues, attitudes to homosexuality, and the area here under discussion, the treatment of animals. In discussing such changes, Posner provides us with a textbook example of *ignoratio elenchi*, or the fallacy of the irrelevant conclusion:

> Our moral norms regarding race, homosexuality, nonmarital sex, con-

traception, and suicide have changed in recent times, but not as a result of ethical arguments. Philosophers have not been prominent in any of the movements....Thurgood Marshall, Earl Warren, and Martin Luther King, Jr., had a lot more to do with the development of an antidiscrimination norm than any academic philosopher.

Note how the initial claim that "ethical arguments" did not bring about these changes is suddenly turned into the entirely separate claim that "philosophers" were not prominent in these movements, and then at the end, this becomes a claim about "academic philosopher[s]." But that is not what was to be shown. Can anyone read the judgments of Thurgood Marshall or Earl Warren, or the speeches of Martin Luther King, Jr., and not believe that they were putting forward ethical arguments?

How is it possible that ethical argument can be effective given that, as Posner and many others have pointed out, there is great difficulty in establishing the first premises of any ethical position? The answer is that ethical argument does not always proceed from first premises. It may, for example, show that a widely held view is inconsistent, or leads to conflicts with other views that its supporters hold. (Look again at the ethical argument about the moral status of animals with which this essay opened, and you will see that it takes this form.) Ethical argument can also show that particular views have been held unreflectively. Once they are subjected to critique, and applied to a wider range of situations than had previously been considered, the view may become less attractive. Though ethical argument would be easier if we could establish first premises, it is a mistake to assume that without it, it must be ineffective.

Universalizability also plays a role, as we have already seen. We are reasoning beings, capable of seeking broader justifica-

tions. There may be some who are ruthless enough to say that they care only for their own interests or for the interests of those in their own group, and if anyone else gets in the way, too bad for them; but many of us seek to justify our conduct in broader, more widely acceptable terms. That is how ethical argument gets going, and why it can examine, criticize, and, in the long run, overturn tenacious moral instincts.

THE USEFULNESS OF AVOIDING PRAGMATISM IN ETHICS

Shorn of the pretension of being something other than a philosophical position and of its belief in the total inefficacy of ethical reasoning, Posner's pragmatism turns out to be an undefended and indefensible form of selective moral conservatism. It is also, ironically, a potentially dangerous position, which makes it self-refuting, or at least self-effacing (i.e., those who hold it will, if they follow their own principles, pretend that they don't). Consider the way in which Posner takes the "brute fact that we, like other animals, prefer our own" as a starting point for moral argument. If this supports our current treatment of animals, why should it not also be used to support other preferences for "our own," which appear to be just as much a brute fact about human beings as a preference for our own species? Here is one example: "We must be honest, decent, loyal, and friendly to members of our blood and to no one else. What happens to the Russians, what happens to the Czechs, is a matter of utter indifference to me." The speaker is Heinrich Himmler. He goes on to say, "Whether the other races live in comfort or perish of hunger interests me only insofar as we need them as slaves for our culture; apart from that it does not interest me."

I am, of course, far from suggesting that Posner would support such sentiments.

But how, consistently with what he says about one instinctive preference, can he reject the other? Posner's difficulty is made totally intractable by his refusal to defend his preference for humans over animals: "I do not claim that our preferring human beings to other animals is 'justified' in some rational sense—only that it is a fact deeply rooted in our current thinking and feeling." Why should Himmler not say the same, with the substitution of "Germans" for "human beings" and "human beings" for "animals"? The Nazis were, in fact, strong defenders of moral "feeling," elevating "the healthy sensibility of the people" (*gesundes Volksempfinden*) to a supreme legal precept and using it as the basis for outlawing homosexuality. Moreover, looking coolly at human history, an instinctive preference for "our own" in a racial or ethnic sense seems scarcely less firm and enduring than the preference for our own species. So Himmler could have been quite at home with a Posner-style, pragmatic defense of his position.

Posner comments on the possible application of his argument for a preference for "our own" to race and gender, but what he says raises more questions than it answers: "Membership in the human species is not a morally irrelevant fact, as the race and gender of human beings have come to seem." Note the curious choice of the words "have come to seem," in respect of the relevance of race and gender. This suggests that, for Posner, there is no fact of the matter here. If race and gender had not "come to seem" morally irrelevant, they would not be morally irrelevant. Posner has to say that, given what he has said about ethical argument. For the rest of us, however, it is precisely because there is and should be such a thing as ethical argument that we do not have to accept racism and sexism, whether they *seem* morally relevant to people or not.

Posner seems to be a kind person, and significantly kinder than his philosophy requires. He writes: "I agree that...gratuitous cruelty to and neglect of animals are wrong, and that some costs should be incurred to reduce the suffering of animals raised for food or other human purposes or subjected to medical or other testing and experimentation." But one has to wonder why, on his own terms, he believes this. He favors a humancentric approach, which "assigns no *intrinsic* value to animal welfare" and "seeks reasons strictly of human welfare for according or denying rights to animals." Why then should humans incur any costs in order to reduce the suffering of farm animals? If we are unhappy knowing that animals are suffering in factory farms, we have a choice between changing the conditions that cause this suffering, or instigating a campaign of public education to persuade people not to worry about animal suffering. If we opt for the latter, perhaps we could combine with the public education an offer of free psychotherapy for those who are still unable to get rid of their unhappiness about animal suffering. If there is no intrinsic value to animal welfare, the "pragmatic" approach to this choice would be to work out which option will most benefit us. That will depend on the costs of public education and psychotherapy, as compared with the costs of changing our ways of raising farm animals. Is that really the basis on which Posner thinks we should make such a choice? I do him the honor of believing that if he had the power to make such a decision, he would not be consistent with his own pragmatist philosophy.

Posner believes that animals may be better off as property than they would be if they had "human-type 'rights.'" There are 10 billion animals raised for food in the United States each year. The overwhelming majority of those animals endure miserable factory-farm conditions and are slaughtered by workers trying to kill the largest possible number of animals per hour, conditions that allow them to give little or no care or attention to the welfare of the individual animals. All of those animals are fully "commodities," and their property status is indisputable. It does them no good at all. We need to look elsewhere for an ethic that will provide a basis for improving their position. That ethic is the principle of equal consideration of interests, which was the outcome of the ethical argument that I defended at the beginning of this essay. Posner has not refuted this argument. Nor has he given any sound reasons for believing that it should not prevail over whatever "tenacious moral instincts" to the contrary that we may have.

THE CONTINUING DEBATE:
Do Animals Have Rights?

What Is New?

Much of the current controversy concerning animal rights is occurring in the court-house, as well as in arguments among leading legal writers such as Cass Sunstein, Richard Posner, Steven Wise, Mariann Sullivan, and David Wolfson. One issue cur-rently debated is whether animals can be considered *property*, and dealt with as sim-ply one branch of property law. Current legal standards seem to be ambivalent: if I rustle your cattle, then I am guilty of stealing your property. But on the other hand, you can generally do as you wish with your property: you can smash your desk into tiny pieces if you wish. You cannot do that with your dog or your horse, because of laws against cruelty to animals. Some argue that at least some nonhuman animals should be recognized as having some level of practical autonomy, and their own rec-ognized rights. The Great Ape Project has been a strong voice for recognizing the legal rights of such close human kin as chimpanzees.

Where to Find More

For an interesting debate on animal rights, see *The Animal Rights Debate*, by Carl Cohen and Tom Regan (Lanham, Md.: Rowman & Littlefield, 2001). Cass R. Sunstein and Martha C. Nussbaum, Editors, *Animal Rights* (New York: Oxford University Press, 2004), is an excellent collection of contemporary articles, including the two by Posner and Singer that were excerpted for this debate; the introduction by Sunstein is especially helpful, and there are very good articles on the contemporary legal debates surrounding animal treatment and animal rights. *Animal Rights and Human Obligations*, edited by Tom Regan and Peter Singer, 2nd ed. (Englewood Cliffs, N.J.: Prentice-Hall, 1989), is a good collection of essays, both pro and con, ranging from the ancient to contemporary. Another good collection of pro and con articles, covering a wide range of subjects in the area of animal rights and the treat-ment of animals, is by Andrew Harnack, *Animal Rights: Opposing Viewpoints* (San Diego, Cal.: Greenhaven Press, 1996). Harlan B. Miller and William H. Williams, eds., *Ethics and Animals* (Clifton, N.J.: Humana Press, 1983), contains a very good collection of philosophical articles by leading philosophers. *The Animal Rights Reader*, edited by Susan J. Armstrong and Richard G. Botzler (London: Routledge, 2003), is a broad ranging collection of excellent essays from a variety of perspectives.

Peter Singer's *Animal Liberation* first appeared in 1976, and is now in a second edition (New York: Avon Books, 1990); it is probably the most famous book in the campaign for animal rights. Tom Regan's *The Case for Animal Rights* (Berkeley: The University of California Press, 1983) is another modern classic; his more recent essays are collected in *Defending Animal Rights* (Urbana: University of Illinois Press, 2001). Paola Cavalieri's *The Animal Question: Why Nonhuman Animals Deserve Human Rights*, trans. Catherine Woollard (Oxford: Oxford University Press, 2001) is a brief but creative and well-argued case for animal rights. Another excellent defense of ani-mal rights is Bernard E. Rollin, *Animal Rights and Human Morality*, revised edition (Buffalo, N.Y.: Prometheus Books, 1992). Stephen R. L. Clark, in *The Moral Status of Animals* (Oxford: Clarendon Press, 1977), offers a detailed, powerful, and philosophically complex argument for a radical revision of our view of animals (as well as ourselves). See also Clark's fascinating book, *The Nature of the Beast: Are Animals Moral?* (Oxford: Oxford University Press, 1982), for his argument that the study of animal behavior can enhance our understanding of ethics. Two very good books, whose authors emphasize the close biological links between humans and other animals, are Mary Midgley, *Animals and Why They Matter* (Athens, Georgia: University of Georgia Press, 1983); and James Rachels, *Created From Animals: The Moral Implications of Darwinism* (Oxford: Oxford University Press, 1991). Steven M. Wise argues the case for animal rights using both scientific and legal resources; see his *Drawing the Line: Science and the Case for Animal Rights* (Cambridge, Mass.: Perseus Books, 2002), and *Rattling the Cage: Toward Legal Rights for Animals* (Cambridge, Mass.: Perseus Books, 2000). A remarkable and very readable book, that examines both recent research on teaching chimpanzees American Sign Language and recent attempts to stop the mistreatment of chimpanzees in research settings, is Roger Fouts, *Next of Kin: What Chimpanzees Have Taught Me About Who We Are* (New York: William Morrow, 1997); Fouts also has an interesting website at http://www.cwu.edu/~cwuchi/.

Books opposing animal rights arguments, written from a variety of perspectives, are R. G. Frey, *Interests and Rights: The Case Against Animals* (Oxford: Clarendon Press, 1980); Michael P. T. Leahy, *Against Liberation: Putting Animals in Perspective* (London and New York: Routledge, 1991); and Peter Carruthers, *The Animals Issue* (Cambridge: Cambridge University Press, 1992).

On a subject in which the debate has raged for decades, even centuries, it is difficult to find a new perspective; but novelist J. M. Coetzee manages it brilliantly, in *The Lives of Animals* (Princeton, N.J., 1999).

The Great Ape Project, an organization dedicated to securing basic moral and legal protection for nonhuman great apes, has a website that is well worth a visit, at http://www.greatapeproject.org. Lawrence Hinman's Ethics Updates Website has a superb collection of material on the moral status of animals, including many links to other sites; go to http://ethics.sandiego.edu/Applied/Animals.

14   SHOULD OUR COUNTRY PROMOTE A SPECIFIC MORAL CODE?

The State Should Promote a Set of Basic Values

ADVOCATE: Michael J. Sandel, Anne T. and Robert M. Bass Professor of Government at Harvard University, and author of *Democracy's Discontent: America in Search of a Public Philosophy* (Cambridge, Mass.: Harvard University Press, 1996) and *Liberalism and the Limits of Justice*, 2nd ed. (Cambridge and New York: Cambridge University Press, 1998).

SOURCE: "Morality and the Liberal Ideal," *The New Republic* (May 7, 1984); reprinted in *Public Philosophy: Essays on Morality in Politics* (Cambridge, Mass.: Harvard University Press, 2005).

The State Should Maintain Neutrality Toward Basic Value Issues

ADVOCATE: Thomas Nagel, University Professor at New York University; author of many books, including *The View from Nowhere* (New York: Oxford University Press, 1986) and *The Last Word* (New York: Oxford University Press, 1997).

SOURCE: "Progressive but Not Liberal," *The New York Review of Books*, volume 53, number 9 (May 25, 2006): 45–48.

Should pornographic literature be banned, as a violation of our values concerning sexuality and the treatment of women? Should hate speech—against ethnic groups, or gays, or women—be forbidden by law? Should the government provide funds to promote sexual values (such as celibacy for unmarried persons)? This is an old but obviously still vigorous controversy. On the one side are those who insist that a flourishing society or nation must share a substantial system of values: Not just the basic political values concerning a system of government—for example, the value of democracy over dictatorship—but a wider set of values, such as those espoused by specific religious groups. Without such a broad value system the society lacks stability and is likely to fragment into warring factions. On the other side are those who believe that a democratic society should protect the values of free speech and free thought, and the value of civic harmony, and obviously protect all citizens from being harmed by others; but beyond that the government should leave each individual free to make his or her own value choices without governmental or societal pressure. Lord Patrick Devlin, a British judge and writer of the mid-twentieth century, champions the view that government should promote and even coerce certain values and ways of life (including such laws as the criminalization of homosexual relations) as a necessary element of social cohesiveness and harmony:

> It is generally accepted that some shared morality, that is, some common agreement about what is right and wrong, is an essential element in the consti-

tution of any society. Without it there would be no cohesion. *The Enforcement of Morals* (London: Oxford University Press, 1965), p. 114.

In opposition to Devlin, John Stuart Mill's *On Liberty* is the classic and still inspiring source for the view that freedom of opinion and freedom of action are vital goods, both for a society and for its members:

> As it is useful that while mankind are imperfect there should be different opinions, so is it that there should be different experiments of living; that free scope should be given to varieties of character, short of injury to others; and that the worth of different modes of life should be proved practically, when any one thinks fit to try them. It is desirable, in short, that in things which do not primarily concern others, individuality should assert itself. Where, not the person's own character, but the traditions or customs of other people are the rule of conduct, there is wanting one of the principal ingredients of human happiness, and quite the chief ingredient of individual and social progress. *On Liberty,* Chapter III (1859)

This controversy continues on many fronts, as conservatives (such as Devlin) strive to condemn and penalize the "homosexual lifestyle," prohibit the private use of marijuana, outlaw physician-assisted suicide, and promote the governmental endorsement of religious displays (such as the Biblical Ten Commandments), and liberals (in the tradition of Mill) promote individual freedom of choice.

"Liberal" is a confusing term, carrying two quite different meanings. In the current political usage, "liberal" signifies a loose collection of views, roughly including belief in universal health care, abortion rights, civil rights, a strong social safety net, freedom of speech, labor rights, and environmental protection. Of course this is not a list of necessary conditions for being a liberal: some liberals oppose abortion rights, and some conservatives are strong supporters of gay rights (Barry Goldwater was a leading conservative who was also a firm advocate of gay rights). But there is a second sense of "liberal" that is different. "Liberal" in this second sense refers to the political philosophy that emphasizes *liberty* as the most basic political value; that is, for liberals (in this second sense) government must protect individual liberty, and any *limitation* of individual liberty requires strong justification. Obviously we want some restrictions on liberty: we do not want our citizens to have the liberty to murder, steal, and dump deadly chemicals into our drinking water. But such restrictions require special justification, with the presumption always being in favor of liberty for the individual.

That leaves many open questions. What sort of justification is required for a legitimate restriction on individual liberty? Another is the question of exactly what individual liberty *is*. Is it merely the freedom to be left alone, and not coerced? Is it freedom from any threat or possibility of coercion? Or is freedom something more positive? Must liberty involve freedom to develop and exercise my abilities? (If I am merely left alone, and not given the opportunity to gain an education or pursue a career or earn a decent living, then my exercise of liberty will be severely stunted.)

However one fills in the details of liberal political theory, the emphasis remains on the freedom of the individual to make his or her own choices. But some critics of liberalism maintain that the emphasis on individual liberty leads to distortions. One group of critics—generally known as communitarians, though they do not always embrace that title—claim that the liberal focus on individual liberty neglects the essential role of the *community* in shaping and sustaining both community values and virtuous citizens, and thus neglects the importance of a shared positive value framework. Thus Michael Sandel, a "communitarian," maintains that a good community must promote specific and substantive values. Thomas Nagel—defending the liberal perspective—holds that such a view can lead to oppressive social systems, and that we are better off emphasizing the individual right to make our own value decisions; and when larger political values must be addressed, the community should focus on fair procedures for settling such issues, rather than on a set of basic values which all community members should share.

POINTS TO PONDER

➤ Sandel suggests that "communitarians would be more likely than liberals to allow a town to ban pornographic bookstores." *Could* liberals (in the second political philosophy sense of "liberal") favor the banning of pornographic bookstores? What grounds might they give for such a ban? Is there some other specific social issue where you think liberals and communitarians are more likely to disagree?

➤ Nagel claims that on the liberal view he shares with Rawls, "the state is supposed to be neutral not about all contested moral questions, but only about those that do not have to be decided politically." How is that distinction to be drawn? Can you think of an issue that one person might think *must* be decided politically, while another believes the issue does not require a political resolution? Is the question of abortion such an issue?

➤ Suppose I believe my own religion to be the only true religion, and firmly believe that all who favor other religions are fundamentally misguided. Could I *also* embrace the view that all members of my society should be free to practice whatever religion they favor?

➤ Both Sandel and Nagel want to promote the value of religious tolerance, but they differ about the best way of accomplishing that goal. Sandel believes that we should promote religious tolerance as a positive value, and argue that it is *better* than religious dogmatism. Nagel holds that it is better to remain neutral on whether tolerance or dogmatism is morally superior, and instead focus on the individual right to hold whatever religious doctrines (tolerant or dogmatic) one favors; that is, it is alright to maintain that one's own religion is the only true religion, so long as one allows that others may hold opposing views. Purely as a question of *political strategy*, which strategy is more likely to succeed in promoting and protecting religious tolerance?

The State Should Promote a Set of Basic Values

Michael J. Sandel

Liberals often take pride in defending what they oppose—pornography, for example, or unpopular views. They say the state should not impose on its citizens a preferred way of life, but should leave them as free as possible to choose their own values and ends, consistent with a similar liberty for others. This commitment to freedom of choice requires liberals constantly to distinguish between permission and praise, between allowing a practice and endorsing it. It is one thing to allow pornography, they argue, something else to affirm it.

Conservatives sometimes exploit this distinction by ignoring it. They charge that those who would allow abortions favor abortion, that opponents of school prayer oppose prayer, that those who defend the rights of Communists sympathize with their cause. And in a pattern of argument familiar in our politics, liberals reply by invoking higher principles; it is not that they dislike pornography less, but rather that they value toleration, or freedom of choice, or fair procedures more.

But in contemporary debate, the liberal rejoinder seems increasingly fragile, its moral basis increasingly unclear. Why should toleration and freedom of choice prevail when other important values are also at stake? Too often the answer implies some version of moral relativism, the idea that it is wrong to "legislate morality" because all morality is merely subjective. "Who is to say what is literature and what is filth? That is a value judgment, and whose values should decide?"

Relativism usually appears less as a claim than as a question. "Who is to judge?" But it is a question that can also be asked of the values that liberals defend. Toleration and freedom and fairness are values too, and they can hardly be defended by the claim that no values can be defended. So it is a mistake to affirm liberal values by arguing that all values are merely subjective. The relativist defense of liberalism is no defense at all.

What, then, can be the moral basis of the higher principles the liberal invokes? Recent political philosophy has offered two main alternatives—one utilitarian, the other Kantian. The utilitarian view, following John Stuart Mill, defends liberal principles in the name of maximizing the general welfare. The state should not impose on its citizens a preferred way of life, even for their own good, because doing so will reduce the sum of human happiness, at least in the long run; better that people choose for themselves, even if, on occasion, they get it wrong. "The only freedom which deserves the name," writes Mill in *On Liberty*, "is that of pursuing our own good in our own way, so long as we do not attempt to deprive others of theirs, or impede their efforts to obtain it." He adds that his argument does not depend on any notion of abstract right, only on the principle of the greatest good for the greatest number. "I regard utility as the ultimate appeal on all ethical questions; but it must be utility in the largest sense, grounded on the permanent interests of man as a progressive being."

Many objections have been raised against utilitarianism as a general doctrine of moral philosophy. Some have questioned the concept of utility, and the assumption that all human goods are in principle commensurable. Others have objected that by reducing all values to preferences and desires, utilitarians are unable to admit qualitative distinctions of worth, unable to distinguish noble desires from base ones. But most recent debate has focused on whether utilitarianism offers a convincing basis for liberal principles, including respect for individual rights.

In one respect, utilitarianism would seem well suited to liberal purposes. Seeking to maximize overall happiness does not require judging people's values, only aggregating them. And the willingness to aggregate preferences without judging them suggests a tolerant spirit, even a democratic one. When people go to the polls we count their votes, whatever they are.

But the utilitarian calculus is not always as liberal as it first appears. If enough cheering Romans pack the Colosseum to watch the lion devour the Christian, the collective pleasure of the Romans will surely outweigh the pain of the Christian, intense though it be. Or if a big majority abhors a small religion and wants it banned, the balance of preferences will favor suppression, not toleration. Utilitarians sometimes defend individual rights on the grounds that respecting them now will serve utility in the long run. But this calculation is precarious and contingent. It hardly secures the liberal promise not to impose on some the values of others. As the majority will is an inadequate instrument of liberal politics—by itself it fails to secure individual rights—so the utilitarian philosophy is an inadequate foundation for liberal principles.

The case against utilitarianism was made most powerfully by Immanuel Kant.

He argued that empirical principles, such as utility, were unfit to serve as basis for the moral law. A wholly instrumental defense of freedom and rights not only leaves rights vulnerable, but fails to respect the inherent dignity of persons. The utilitarian calculus treats people as means to the happiness of others, not as ends in themselves, worthy of respect.

Contemporary liberals extend Kant's argument with the claim that utilitarianism fails to take seriously the distinction between persons. In seeking above all to maximize the general welfare, the utilitarian treats society as a whole as if it were a single person; it conflates our many, diverse desires into a single system of desires. It is indifferent to the distribution of satisfactions among persons, except insofar as this may affect the overall sum. But this fails to respect our plurality and distinctness. It uses some as means to the happiness of all, and so fails to respect each as an end in himself.

In the view of modern-day Kantians, certain rights are so fundamental that even the general welfare cannot override them. As John Rawls writes in his important work, *A Theory of Justice*, "Each person possesses an inviolability founded on justice that even the welfare of society as a whole cannot override....The rights secured by justice are not subject to political bargaining or to the calculus of social interests."

So Kantian liberals need an account of rights that does not depend on utilitarian considerations. More than this, they need an account that does not depend on any particular conception of the good, that does not presuppose the superiority of one way of life over others. Only a justification neutral about ends could preserve the liberal resolve not to favor any particular ends, or to impose on its citizens a preferred way of life. But what sort of justification could this be? How is it possible to affirm certain liberties and rights as fundamental without embracing some vision of the good life, without endorsing some ends over others? It would seem we are back to the relativist predicament—to affirm liberal principles without embracing any particular ends.

The solution proposed by Kantian liberals is to draw a distinction between the "right" and the "good"—between a framework of basic rights and liberties, and the conceptions of the good that people may choose to pursue within the framework. It is one thing for the state to support a fair framework, they argue, something else to affirm some particular ends. For example, it is one thing to defend the right to free speech so that people may be free to form their own opinions and choose their own ends, but something else to support it on the grounds that a life of political discussion is inherently worthier than a life unconcerned with public affairs, or on the grounds that free speech will increase the general welfare. Only the first defense is available in the Kantian view, resting as it does on the ideal of a neutral framework.

Now, the commitment to a framework neutral with respect to ends can be seen as a kind of value—in this sense the Kantian liberal is no relativist—but its value consists precisely in its refusal to affirm a preferred way of life or conception of the good. For Kantian liberals, then, the right is prior to the good, and in two senses. First, individual rights cannot be sacrificed for the sake of the general good; and second, the principles of justice that specify these rights cannot be premised on any particular vision of the good life. What justifies the rights is not that they maximize the general welfare or otherwise promote the good, but rather that they comprise a fair framework within which individuals and groups can choose their own values and ends, consistent with a similar liberty for others.

Of course, proponents of the rights-based ethic notoriously disagree about what rights are fundamental, and about what political arrangements the ideal of the neutral framework requires. Egalitarian liberals support the welfare state, and favor a scheme of civil liberties together with certain social and economic rights—rights to welfare, education, health care, and so on. Libertarian liberals defend the market economy, and claim that redistributive policies violate peoples' rights; they favor a scheme of civil liberties combined with a strict regime of private property rights. But whether egalitarian or libertarian, rights-based liberalism begins with the claim that we are separate, individual persons, each with our own aims, interests, and conceptions of the good; it seeks a framework of rights that will enable us to realize our capacity as free moral agents, consistent with a similar liberty for others.

Within academic philosophy, the last decade or so has seen the ascendance of the rights-based ethic over the utilitarian one, due in large part to the influence of Rawls's *A Theory of Justice*. The legal philosopher H. L. A. Hart recently described the shift from "the old faith that some form of utilitarianism must capture the essence of political morality" to the new faith that "the truth must lie with a doctrine of basic human rights, protecting specific basic liberties and interests of individuals....Whereas not so long ago great energy and much ingenuity of many philosophers were devoted to making some form of utilitarianism work, latterly such energies and ingenuity have been devoted to the articulation of theories of basic rights."

But in philosophy as in life, the new faith becomes the old orthodoxy before long. Even as it has come to prevail over its utilitarian rival, the rights-based ethic has recently faced a growing challenge from a different direction, from a view that gives fuller expression to the claims of citizenship and community than the liberal vision allows. The communitarian critics, unlike modern liberals, make the case for a politics of the common good. Recalling the arguments of Hegel against Kant, they question the liberal claim for the priority of the right over the good, and the picture of the freely choosing individual it embodies. Following Aristotle, they argue that we cannot justify political arrangements without reference to common purposes and ends, and that we cannot conceive of ourselves without reference to our role as citizens, as participants in a common life.

This debate reflects two contrasting pictures of the self. The rights-based ethic, and the conception of the person it embodies, were shaped in large part in the encounter with utilitarianism. Where utilitarians conflate our many desires into a single system of desire, Kantians insist on the separateness of persons. Where the utilitarian self is simply defined as the sum of its desires, the Kantian self is a choosing self, independent of the desires and ends it may have at any moment. As Rawls writes, "The self is prior to the ends which are affirmed by it; even a dominant end must be chosen from among numerous possibilities."

The priority of the self over its ends means I am never defined by my aims and attachments, but always capable of standing back to survey and assess and possibly to revise them. This is what it means to be a free and independent self, capable of choice. And this is the vision of the self that finds expression in the ideal of the state as a neutral framework. On the rights-based ethic, it is precisely because we are essentially separate, independent selves that we need a neutral framework, a framework of rights that refuses to choose among competing purposes and ends. If

the self is prior to its ends, then the right must be prior to the good.

Communitarian critics of rights-based liberalism say we cannot conceive ourselves as independent in this way, as bearers of selves wholly detached from our aims and attachments. They say that certain of our roles are partly constitutive of the persons we are—as citizens of a country, or members of a movement, or partisans of a cause. But if we are partly defined by the communities we inhabit, then we must also be implicated in the purposes and ends characteristic of those communities. As Alasdair MacIntyre writes in his book, *After Virtue*, "What is good for me has to be the good for one who inhabits these roles." Open-ended though it be, the story of my life is always embedded in the story of those communities from which I derive my identity—whether family or city, tribe or nation, party or cause. In the communitarian view, these stories make a moral difference, not only a psychological one. They situate us in the world and give our lives their moral particularity.

What is at stake for politics in the debate between unencumbered selves and situated ones? What are the practical differences between a politics of rights and a politics of the common good? On some issues, the two theories may produce different arguments for similar policies. For example, the civil rights movement of the 1960s might be justified by liberals in the name of human dignity and respect for persons, and by communitarians in the name of recognizing the full membership of fellow citizens wrongly excluded from the common life of the nation. And where liberals might support public education in hopes of equipping students to become autonomous individuals, capable of choosing their own ends and pursuing them effectively, communitarians might support public education in hopes of equipping students to become good citizens, capable of contributing meaningfully to public deliberations and pursuits.

On other issues, the two ethics might lead to different policies. Communitarians would be more likely than liberals to allow a town to ban pornographic bookstores, on the grounds that pornography offends its way of life and the values that sustain it. But a politics of civic virtue does not always part company with liberalism in favor of conservative policies. For example, communitarians would be more willing than some rights-oriented liberals to see states enact laws regulating plant closings, to protect their communities from the disruptive effects of capital mobility and sudden industrial change. More generally, where the liberal regards the expansion of individual rights and entitlements as unqualified moral and political progress, the communitarian is troubled by the tendency of liberal programs to displace politics from smaller forms of association to more comprehensive ones. Where libertarian liberals defend the private economy and egalitarian liberals defend the welfare state, communitarians worry about the concentration of power in both the corporate economy and the bureaucratic state, and the erosion of those intermediate forms of community that have at times sustained a more vital public life.

Liberals often argue that a politics of the common good, drawing as it must on particular loyalties, obligations, and traditions, opens the way to prejudice and intolerance. The modern nation-state is not the Athenian polis, they point out; the scale and diversity of modern life have rendered the Aristotelian political ethic nostalgic at best and dangerous at worst. Any attempt to govern by a vision of the good is likely to lead to a slippery slope of totalitarian temptations.

Communitarians reply, rightly in my view, that intolerance flourishes most where forms of life are dislocated, roots unsettled, traditions undone. In our day, the totalitarian impulse has sprung less from the convictions of confidently situated selves than from the confusions of atomized, dislocated, frustrated selves, at sea in a world where common meanings have lost their force. As Hannah Arendt has written, "What makes mass society so difficult to bear is not the number of people involved, or at least not primarily, but the fact that the world between them has lost its power to gather them together, to relate and to separate them." Insofar as our public life has withered, our sense of common involvement diminished, we lie vulnerable to the mass politics of totalitarian solutions. So responds the party of the common good to the party of rights. If the party of the common good is right, our most pressing moral and political project is to revitalize those civic republican possibilities implicit in our tradition but fading in our time.

The State Should Maintain Neutrality Toward Basic Value Issues

Thomas Nagel

1.

The political system of the United States manages to contain, under conditions of peace if not civility, a remarkable range of moral, ideological, and religious conflicts. The conflicts are not so severe as those that led to the Civil War, but they are greater than those that divide most European countries—where public opinion occupies a narrower political range, and religion is not an important element. Because of its size and regional differences, and the historical shadow of slavery and the Civil War, the United States is radically divided over issues of war, taxes, welfare, race, religion, abortion, and sex.

These conflicts are not just about the best means to pursue generally accepted ends. They are about ultimate values. Yet they do not threaten the stability and legitimacy of the system. Except for a small lunatic fringe, citizens of the United States are prepared to accept the results of the political and legal process even when those results contravene some of their most fundamental convictions. Americans vilify one another as bigoted religious fanatics or morally depraved atheists, racist reactionaries or crypto-totalitarian socialists, but they know they will not be put up against the wall if their party loses an election. That Americans can share a common political system with people whose views they despise, and try to fight out their disagreements legally through the pursuit of power under that system, shows that the cohesion of American society is stronger than its divisions.

This cohesion is possible only because of a general commitment to the principles of limited government embodied in the Constitution. Individuals and groups can be confident that they will be protected by the rule of law from the arbitrary exercise of governmental power, and that the way they conduct their lives will be largely on majority preferences. The precise definition of the limits on governmental power is controversial, but no one doubts that they exist.

Their importance has been brought home to us again by the current administration's contempt for the rule of law and its attempts to evade the limits on executive power, under the color of a war on terror. The worst of these abuses, like torture and indefinite detention, have been mostly inflicted on foreigners, but surveillance increasingly threatens domestic rights of privacy. I am optimistic enough to believe that our society's attachment to constitutional limits will prevent the domestic abuses from going very far; but in the treatment of non-Americans, there is reason to expect the worst, precisely because of their weak or nonexistent legal protection.

Still, Americans continue to be embroiled in virulent conflicts, largely between conservatives and progressives. They disagree about what, if anything, the state should do about economic, racial, and sexual inequality; about the separation of church and state; about sexual and reproductive freedom; and about what limits, if any, to put on the freedom of expression. Conservatives are more interested in enforcing moral standards on the community and protecting private property, and less interested in protecting personal liberty and reducing inequality; with progressives, it is the reverse.

Within the progressive camp there is a further question about how some of these conflicts should be pursued. Should the argument be about "first-order principles"—fundamental beliefs about religion, abortion, and homosexuality, for example—or should it be about "second-order principles" concerning what kinds of first-order principles may be used to justify the exercise of political and legal power? The liberal strand of progressive thought, shaped by such thinkers as John Rawls, holds, for example, that to defend a woman's right to terminate her pregnancy it is not necessary to prove that the Catholic position that the fetus is a person from the moment of conception is false. It is sufficient to show that under our system of rights, the first-order principles embodied in Catholic doctrine cannot legitimately be used to constrain private choice. This argument could be accepted as a political principle of limited government even by those who hold that abortion is always morally impermissible. The same issue arises about gay rights. In the liberal view, their defense need not depend on the argument that there is nothing wrong with homosexuality; it can be based instead on the narrower political principle that private sexual conduct should not fall under government control.

But another school of thought, which can be described as progressive but not liberal, holds that those who oppose conservative positions on such issues as abortion and homosexuality should engage directly with conservatives on the first-order moral and religious questions. Proponents of this view argue that in defending rights to abortion and to sexual freedom it is a political and philosophical mistake to rely on limits to the legitimate scope and grounds of collective control over the individual. Instead, they maintain, defenders of these rights should argue frankly that conservative religious views on sexual morality and abortion are false. Since that is what most liberals believe anyway, the claim not to be relying on it looks phony. Progressives should not devote their energies to defending individual rights against majority opinion. They should concentrate instead on changing majority opinion.

Michael Sandel, a professor of government at Harvard University, is a prominent contributor to this debate. He is a progressive who is opposed to contemporary liberalism. He believes that liberal appeals to individual rights and to the broad values of fairness and equality make a poor case for the progressive cause, both as a matter of strategy and as a matter of principle. The country and the Democratic Party would be better off, he thinks, if progressives made more of an effort to inspire the majority to adopt their vision of the common good and make it the democratic ground for public policy and law. In the introduction to his new book, *Public Philosophy: Essays on Morality in Politics*, Sandel writes:

> Fairness isn't everything. It does not answer the hunger for a public life of larger meaning, because it does not connect the project of self-government with people's desire to participate in a common good greater than themselves.

He goes on to argue:

> Liberals often worry that inviting moral and religious argument into the public square runs the risk of intolerance and coercion. The essays in this volume respond to that worry by showing that substantive moral discourse is not at odds with progressive public purposes, and that a

pluralist society need not shrink from engaging the moral and religious convictions its citizens bring to public life.

In place of liberalism, Sandel endorses a "republican" tradition of self-government that he identifies with the earlier history of the United States. In contrast to the individualism that he claims is at the heart of liberal theory, republicanism, as he understands it, gives primacy to the communal aim of shared self-government, and what he calls "soulcraft," the cultivation of virtue in the citizenry by the design of political, social, and economic institutions. It gives personal morality a larger part in political life than liberalism does, and in this respect tries to meet the moralism of the right on its own ground:

> The problems in the theory of procedural liberalism show up in the practice it inspires. A politics that brackets [i.e., that excludes from discussion] morality and religion too completely soon generates its own disenchantment. Where political discourse lacks moral resonance, the yearning for a public life of larger meaning finds undesirable expression. The Christian Coalition and similar groups seek to clothe the naked public square with narrow, intolerant moralisms. Fundamentalists rush in where liberals fear to tread.

Anyone concerned over the political success of conservatism in recent years must be interested in this critical analysis.

2.

Sandel's views on substantive issues of social welfare and personal liberty are not very different from those of most liberals. He supports affirmative action, gay rights, abortion rights, and stem cell research, opposes state lotteries and advertising in the classroom, and is doubtful about assisted suicide. In economic policy, he is a sentimentalist who thinks small is beautiful:

> Where the liberal regards the expansion of individual rights and entitlements as unqualified moral and political progress, the communitarian [a name for Sandel's position which he will eventually reject; see below] is troubled by the tendency of liberal programs to displace politics from smaller forms of association to more comphrehensive ones. Where libertarian liberals defend the private economy and egalitarian liberals defend the welfare state, communitarians worry about the concentration of power in both the corporate economy and the bureaucratic state, and the erosion of those intermediate forms of community that have at times sustained a more vital public life.

Such nostalgic rhetoric may suggest that Sandel is uneasy about Social Security and Medicare, and would oppose a single payer health system as an extension of the faceless bureaucratic state. But so far as I know, he does not draw such conclusions.

His theoretical differences with liberalism are more significant, and he has used this disagreement to define himself as a thinker. Unfortunately his understanding of liberal political theory is defective, and his description of the principles and arguments of those he wants to criticize is persistently inaccurate—for example, his claim that a liberal couldn't have opposed slavery before the Civil War because it was too controversial. Caricaturing the opposition can be a polemical strategy, but in Sandel's case I believe it is due primarily to philosophical weakness exacerbated by the difficulty of understanding a view that he thinks is wrong. This leads him to interpret it in a way that makes it incomprehensible how anyone else could believe it. To evaluate Sandel's disagreement with the principles of contemporary liberalism, we have first to disentangle it from his faulty account of what those principles are.

The term "liberalism" applies to a wide range of political positions, from the libertarianism of economic laissez-faire to the democratic egalitarianism of the welfare state. In its European usage the term suggests the former rather than the latter; in American usage it is the reverse. But all liberal theories have this in common: they hold that the sovereign power of the state over the individual is bounded by a requirement that individuals remain inviolable in certain respects, and that they must be treated equally. The state is a human creation, and it is subject to moral constraints that limit the subordination of the individual to the collective will and the collective interest. Those constraints have to be embodied in political institutions. They include not only the familiar freedoms of religion, expression, associations, and privacy, but also equality of political status, equality before the law, and, in the welfare state version, equality of opportunity and fairness in the social and economic structure of the society.

Liberal constraints on the exercise of collective power are therefore both negative and positive. The purely negative liberalism of Friedrich Hayek and Robert Nozick is unusual; most American liberals favor not just the protection of individual rights but a form of distributive justice that combats poverty and large inequalities perpetuated by inheritance and class. It is this form of egalitarian liberalism, particularly as represented by its leading theorist, John Rawls, that Sandel has spent his career opposing.

Sandel's point of attack is Rawls's central claim that individual rights and principles of social justice should take prece-

dence over the broad advancement of human welfare according to some standard of what constitutes the good life. Rawls's argument makes precise the familiar moral intuition that the end does not always justify the means, that there are principles of right—principles that govern how individuals should be treated by the state— that may not be violated on grounds of expediency. As Sandel writes:

> For Rawls, as for Kant, the right is prior to the good in two respects, and it is important to distinguish them. First, the right is prior to the good in the sense that certain individual rights "trump," or outweigh, considerations of the common good. Second, the right is prior to the good in that the principles of justice that specify your rights do not depend for their justification on any particular conception of the good life.

The distinction between these two kinds of priority is important because some liberals accept the priority of rights in practice (the first kind) but not in justification (the second kind). John Stuart Mill, for example, was a great defender of individual rights to freedom of expression and to other forms of liberty as a bar to the tyranny of the majority. But in contrast to Rawls, Mill justified those rights on the ground that protecting them strictly was the best way to serve the cause of general human happiness. As a utilitarian, Mill believed that the only way to justify a moral or political principle is to show that it will promote good lives, which to him meant happy lives.

While acknowledging the achievements of utilitarianism, Rawls argues that this derivation of rights and justice from a particular conception of the general welfare is morally mistaken. His main criticism of utilitarianism is that while the promotion of good overall outcomes is important, there is another type of moral requirement that underlies rights and social justice. This is the requirement that a society should treat its members as equals, and it explains directly why there are limits on the degree to which individuals can be subordinated to the collective interest, the general welfare, or the preferences of the majority. Equal treatment means protecting the equal rights of all members of a society, even if they belong to an unpopular minority, and refusing to allow any members to be excluded from social or economic opportunities or to fall below some decent minimum standard of living. Furthermore, since "the right," so understood, has a different moral foundation from the promotion of good overall outcomes, its principles can be identified without settling some of the major disagreements about the ultimate ends of life that divide the citizens of a typically pluralistic modern society.

Utilitarians have not been persuaded, and neither has Sandel. Sandel is not a utilitarian, since he believes in goods other than the sum of happiness, such as communal solidarity, strong family ties, and the search for higher meaning in our lives. But he agrees with utilitarians, in opposition to Rawls, that individual rights and principles of distributive justice are subordinate to the collective good, and have to be justified by reference to it: "Principles of justice depend for their justification on the moral worth or intrinsic good of the ends they serve."

The protection of religious or sexual freedom, or freedom of expression, depends, he believes, on whether those freedoms serve valuable ends. So he says protection should be extended to demonstrators against racism and segregation, but not to Nazi demonstrators. On that principle, those who regard homosexuality as sinful should be opposed to allowing a parade for gay rights. Sandel acknowledges that "on any theory of rights, certain general rules and doctrines are desirable to spare judges the need to recur to first principles in every case that comes before them." In other words, he might accept a fairly strict rule protecting political speech because it would be too time-consuming to decide in every case whether it was on balance beneficial or harmful. But he seems to think that if there are limits on censorship, they have no more fundamental justification than that.

As for freedom of religion, Sandel holds that it depends on the assumption "that religious belief, as characteristically practiced in a particular society, produces ways of being and acting that are worthy of honor and appreciation—either because they are admirable in themselves or because they foster qualities of character that make good citizens." So if someone believes that this is not true of most religions other than his own, or of atheism, he has no reason, according to Sandel's theory of rights, to support their toleration. He may in fact have an overwhelming reason to suppress heresy, since it puts other members of the society in spiritual danger. Sandel would presumably regard such a person's religious beliefs as mistaken, and he may even hold that the value of a religion doesn't depend on its truth. But he could not fault the opponent of religious liberty for failing to conform to Sandel's theory of rights or justice.

3.

As these examples show, there is something paradoxical about liberalism, for it asks us on moral grounds to refrain from using the power of the state to enforce on others some of our most deeply held moral convictions about how people should conduct themselves—religiously, sexually, or expressively. This liberal restraint comes from our special moral relation to fellow members of our society—a collectivity that can coerce each of its members, but only if it claims to act in the name of all of them. Sandel's response, that there are no legitimate rights which cannot be derived from the good, and therefore no limits, in principle, on the use of political power to pursue the good as the majority sees it, is much simpler and easier to understand. It belongs to the enduring tradition of teleological theories, according to which all moral principles are just means to an end, whether it be happiness, salvation, or human perfection.

This disagreement runs through the history of moral philosophy, and will continue to do so. But when Sandel attempts to argue for his position, the result is deeply confused: Sandel finds Rawls's nonteleological liberalism so incomprehensible that he misinterprets it as a teleological theory with a very special conception of the good, based on a peculiar conception of the self, one that calls to mind Sartre's existentialism. This is the notion of "the unencumbered self, a self understood as prior to and independent of its purposes and ends."

> The unencumbered self describes first of all the way we stand toward the things we have, or want, or seek. It means there is always a distinction between the values I *have* and the person I *am*. To identify any characteristics as *my* aims, ambitions, desires, and so on, is always to imply some subject "me" standing behind them, at a certain distance, and the shape of this "me" must be given prior to any of the aims or attributes I bear....It rules out the possibility of what we might call *constitutive* ends. No role or commitment could define me so completely that I could not understand myself without it. No project could be so essential that

turning away from it would call into question the person I am....

> Only if the self is prior to its ends can the right be prior to the good. Only if my identity is never tied to the aims and interests I may have at any moment can I think of myself as a free and independent agent, capable of choice.

In Sandel's view, then, liberalism depends on the absurd assumption that no end is valuable unless it is freely chosen by a completely featureless self, without ties, obligations, values, or commitments. From this he draws the political consequence that the liberal state must be a neutral system of rights that refuses to choose among competing purposes and ends, leaving each individual free to pursue those ends on which his choice has conferred the only value it can have. Liberalism is therefore unable to make sense of the idea of the common good. Instead it favors "a procedural republic, concerned less with cultivating virtue than with enabling persons to choose their own values."

To this caricature of Rawls and other liberals Sandel offers the following counterargument:

> Certain moral and political obligations that we commonly recognize—such as obligations of solidarity, for example, or religious duties—may claim us for reasons unrelated to a choice. Such obligations are difficult to dismiss as merely confused, and yet difficult to account for if we understand ourselves as free and independent selves, unbound by moral ties we have not chosen.

I know of no liberal theorist who subscribes to the extreme freedom from moral ties that Sandel describes. It is preposterous to attribute such a view to Rawls, whose argument in *A Theory of Justice* is explicitly based on the importance of religious commitments and family ties, and who regards communal solidarity and concern for a just version of the common good as fundamental requirements of justice.

For Rawls, the requirement of limited political neutrality among religions or comparably ambitious secular ideals such as hedonism is based on the overwhelming importance and self-defining character of commitments and values that different members of a society may not share. It is precisely because we care so deeply, in ways we cannot change, about very different things that it is so important to protect individual liberty and avoid the wholesale imposition of ultimate values. Evangelical Christians, atheistic libertines, and Buddhist monks do not have a common vision of the good life. Rawls sees the task of liberalism as that of upholding a form of solidarity and a conception of the common good that respects these differences. If we are going to treat as equals in a collective social enterprise those whose religious convictions we reject, we have to define the common good and the legitimate aims and applications of political control in a way that does not exclude them from the outset.

The alternative would be to allow the majority to use state power to promote the good of everyone as defined by their religion. But if I were part of such a majority, I would then be treating the minority in a way that I could not accept as politically legitimate if I were subjected to it myself—if, that is, my own unconditional religious commitments put me in the minority instead. My sense of justice and equal respect should therefore inhibit the blanket enforcement of my own view in ways that are not essential to the public pursuit of the common good. Taxes, military spending, and environmental policies

have to be decided collectively. Religious observance doesn't—though it took a long time to realize this.

4.

Sandel's misunderstanding becomes particularly clear in his comments on abortion. Liberals propose to "bracket," or set aside, the question whether abortion is morally wrong, and to defend the legal right to abortion on the ground that women's liberty in a personal matter of this kind may not be overruled simply because of the religious convictions of the majority. Sandel's reply is that we can "bracket" the moral question only if we first determine that the Catholic position is false. He argues:

> The more confident we are that fetuses are, in the relevant moral sense, different from babies, the more confident we can be in affirming a political conception of justice that sets aside the controversy about the moral status of fetuses.

This is not a counterargument but a mere begging of the question: to use as a premise the falsity of the Catholic position on abortion is not to "bracket" the question but to answer it, so it cannot be a condition for setting it aside. Sandel has again interpreted the priority of right as being intelligible only if it serves the good.

Sandel's obtuseness reaches its peak in the longest essay in *Public Philosophy*, a review of Rawls's second book, *Political Liberalism*. There Sandel ridicules Rawls's aim of trying to set aside conflicts among conceptions of the good life in determining principles of justice by claiming that such a principle of neutrality would have favored Stephen Douglas's position in the debates with Lincoln over slavery. Because the free and slave states were so divided on the matter, Douglas advocated leaving the choice concerning the authorization of slavery to the individual states and territories, and avoiding a national decision. Sandel sees this as an example of the sort of liberal neutrality with respect to deeply contested moral issues that Rawls favors.

But the state is supposed to be neutral not about all contested moral questions, but only about those that do not have to be decided politically. Slavery, unlike religion or private sexual relations, was a public institution, part of the legal system of property. It carried profound implications for political representation and equality (according to the Three-Fifths Compromise of 1787, each slave counted as three fifths of a person in both the distribution of taxes and the apportionment of seats in Congress). Slavery was part of the basic structure of American society, and had been a central issue of justice since the Revolution.

Insofar as Rawls favors state neutrality and limits to the enforcement of the majority's values, he does so only in regard to those questions concerning values that can be left to private choice, and that do not have to be answered collectively in order to reach important political decisions. This boundary is itself contested, but slavery was never regarded, either by its defenders or by its opponents, merely as a question of private, personal morality. The idea makes no sense, and Sandel's invocation of it shows how deeply he misunderstands the liberal position.

He points out, as if it were an objection to liberalism, that moral disagreements about justice and rights are just as deep as disagreements about religion and sexual morality. But liberals have always known this. They claim only that there are some disagreements about the good life and ultimate values that we don't have to settle in order to decide collectively how we will pursue justice and the common good.

This leaves plenty of disagreements that we do have to battle over, and that demand all our resources of solidarity and trust to settle peacefully.

5.

Notwithstanding his many misinterpretations of Rawls, Sandel's disagreement with liberalism is real and important. He denies that the right is prior to the good, and he opposes even the limited state neutrality about nonpolitical values that liberals favor.

In the flood of response that followed the publication of Rawls's *A Theory of Justice* in 1971, Sandel was grouped with Michael Walzer and Alasdair MacIntyre as a defender of "communitarianism," as opposed to individual rights, and their argument was called the communitarian critique of liberalism. Sandel doesn't like the term, and in this book he explains why it doesn't accurately describe his position:

> The term "communitarian" is misleading...insofar as it implies that rights should rest on the values or preferences that prevail in any given community at any given time. Few, if any, of those who have challenged the priority of the right are communitarians in this sense. The question is not whether rights should be respected, but whether rights can be identified and justified in a way that does not presuppose any particular conception of the good.

Sandel rejects majoritarianism or the authority of community values:

> The mere fact that certain practices are sanctioned by the traditions of a particular community is not enough to make them just. To make justice the creature of convention is to deprive it of its critical character, even if allowance is made for com-

peting interpretations of what the relevant tradition requires.

Instead, Sandel thinks justice and rights depend on what is actually good, and what rules or institutions serve those ends; he is not a relativist. So there is for him no substitute for moral argument and moral reasoning about what is truly valuable in determining the character of a just society.

He applies this principle most effectively in the essay "Moral Argument and Liberal Toleration: Abortion and Homosexuality." There he distinguishes between two styles of argument,

> the "naive" and the "sophisticated." The naive view holds that the justice of laws depends on the moral worth of the conduct they prohibit or protect. The sophisticated view holds that the justice of such laws depends not on a substantive moral judgment about the conduct at stake, but instead on a more general theory about the respective claims of majority rule and individual rights, of democracy on the one hand, and liberty on the other.

He prefers the naive view and it is hard not to sympathize with him. He believes he can show that abortion is not wrong and that homosexuality is just as good as heterosexuality, and he is willing to stake the legal issue on those claims. As I have said, there is something paradoxical about the sophisticated, liberal alternative. Why should anyone, except for strategic reasons, want to defend the legal right to abortion and toleration for homosexuals in a way that someone who regards both practices as sinful can accept?

The answer depends on a certain understanding of the complexity of moral theory. This is a deep issue: Do all moral standards derive from a single principle, or are there different basic principles for different kinds of entities? Rawls, for example, believed that the moral standards for social and political institutions were not derived from the standards for personal life, or from a common principle that yielded them both. Rather, he thought that justice, which is the special virtue of social institutions like the state, depended on the distinctive moral character of the state itself, as an immensely powerful form of collective agency.

As citizens, we are subject to the will of the majority, coercively enforced. The extent of that control, and the grounds on which it is exercised, are what is at issue. Rawls believed that constitutional limitations and requirements should reflect the democratic ideal that each member ought to be able to regard the system as acting on his authority, even when he may disagree with particular decisions or policies. He believed that this required not only political equality and civil liberties, but also strong measures to combat racial, sexual, and socioeconomic inequality. This is the fairness that Sandel derides.

Sandel's alternative, the untrammeled pursuit of the good, means that the state is not governed by special moral standards because of its collective power. He thinks we should join together to decide on the true ends of life, and then use the power of the state to create virtue and give everyone's life a meaning as part of something larger than themselves. This will lead to liberal toleration if we accept Mill's conception of human good. Or if we accept what seems to be Sandel's ideal, it will lead to an unmaterialistic culture of closely knit communities and strong family ties. But it will lead to theocracy, fascism, or communism for those who accept alternative conceptions of the human good.

The question, finally, is whether there is a special moral requirement that applies to political institutions and that has enough force to inhibit the coercive enactment of more comprehensive ideals. Sandel is convinced that we cannot justifiably subordinate our deepest personal convictions about the ultimate good for humanity to a system of respect for individual rights. Rawls and other Kantian liberals think that respect for our fellow citizens provides the moral resource needed to justify the protection of rights, and that it defines the restricted political terrain on which we ought to argue about our common institutions.

Liberalism may be a minority conviction in the world at large. To most people values are values, and political power should be used to implement them: What else is it for? But Sandel's ideal republic of comprehensive virtue would abandon a form of civic respect that has been of inestimable value, and threaten one of the indispensable grounds of political stability in our free, stormy, magnificently diverse nation. To use a phrase of Jürgen Habermas, constitutional patriotism should be enough to satisfy what Sandel calls our "hunger for a public life of larger meaning." A hunger that demands more from the state will lead us where history has shown we should not want to go.

THE CONTINUING DEBATE:
Should Our Country Promote a Specific Moral Code?

What Is New

One very interesting practical development of communitarian ideas (noted by the communitarian philosopher Daniel Bell, and one which many liberals would applaud) is the "New Urbanist" movement of architects and urban planners. Concerned about increasing isolation and anonymity—a trend that is exemplified by "gated communities" that deny access to anyone without a pass, and in which residents live in large isolated houses that are not connected by sidewalks—the New Urbanists have sought to design cities and communities in ways that promote interconnection and communication among residents: common areas where people meet, sidewalks to encourage walking in the community, shared shopping and work and residential areas that promote walking rather than sitting isolated in a car, effective public transport. As an alternative to conventional suburban development (with its massive sprawl and heavy dependence on cars for practically every aspect of life), New Urbanism emphasizes the power of traditional neighborhoods to restore strong and enduring communities.

Where to Find More

The work of John Rawls had an enormous influence on the development of contemporary political liberalism, and it is often the focus of communitarian critics. His *A Theory of Justice* (Cambridge, Mass.: Harvard University Press, 1971) was the most influential book in political philosophy during the second half of the 20th Century; see also his *Political Liberalism* (New York: Columbia University Press, 1993). Another very important liberal thinker is Ronald Dworkin; see his *Sovereign Virtue: The Theory and Practice of Equality* (Cambridge, Mass.: Harvard University Press, 2000). Other important writers in this tradition include Brian Barry, *Justice as Impartiality* (Oxford: Clarendon Press, 1995), and Will Kymlicka, *Liberalism, Community and Culture* (Oxford: Clarendon Press, 1989).

In addition to Michael Sandel, major proponents of communitarian theory include Alasdair MacIntrye, *After Virtue*, 2nd ed. (Notre Dame: University of Notre Dame Press, 1984) and *Whose Justice? Which Rationality?* (Notre Dame: University of Notre Dame Press, 1988); Michael Walzer, *Spheres of Justice* (Oxford: Blackwell, 1983); Amitai Etzioni, *Rights and the Common Good: The Communitarian Perspective* (New York: St. Martins Press, 1995); and Charles Taylor, *Sources of the Self: The Making of the Modern Identity* (Cambridge: Cambridge University Press, 1989).

Several important articles in the liberal-communitarian debate can be found in Derek Matravers and Jon Pike, *Debates in Contemporary Political Philosophy* (New York: Routledge, 2003). Amitai Etzioni, *The Essential Communitarian Reader* (Lanham, Md.: Rowman & Littlefield, 1998), is a good collection of communitarian writings. Alan Ryan has a helpful review article on liberalism in Robert E. Goodin and Philip Pettit, eds., *A Companion to Contemporary Political Philosophy* (Oxford: Blackwell, 1993). Daniel Bell, *Communitarianism and its Critics* (Oxford: Clarendon Press, 1993), is a very helpful survey of the communitarian landscape.

The online *Stanford Encyclopedia of Philosophy*, at http://plato.stanford.edu, contains two excellent articles on this subject: "Communitarianism," by Daniel Bell; and "Liberalism," by Gerald Gaus and Shane D. Courtland.

The New Urbanist movement is described and discussed in Peter Katz, *The New Urbanism: Toward an Architecture of Community* (New York: McGraw-Hill, 1994); a clear introduction to New Urbanism can be found in an essay by Robert Steuteville, the editor of *New Urban News*: "The New Urbanism: An Alternative to Modern, Automobile-Oriented Planning and Development," available online at http://www.newurbannews.com/AboutNewUrbanism.html.

15   IS PATRIOTISM A VIRTUE?

We Should Promote Patriotism

ADVOCATE: David Miller, Official Fellow in Social and Political Theory at Nuffield College, Oxford; author of *On Nationality* (Oxford University Press, 1995).

SOURCE: "In Defence of Nationality," *Journal of Applied Philosophy*, volume 10, number 1 (1993).

We Should Favor a Broader Cosmopolitan View

ADVOCATE: Martha C. Nussbaum, Professor of law and ethics at the University of Chicago, author of *Love's Knowledge* and *Poetic Justice*.

SOURCE: "Patriotism and Cosmopolitanism," *Boston Review* (October/November 1994).

Patriotism is one of the most enthusiastically celebrated virtues. (Very few virtues are celebrated with fireworks and parades.) The great Roman poet, Horace, long ago insisted that "it is sweet and honorable to die for one's country." But few "virtues" lend themselves so readily to exploitation and abuse: patriotic fervor seems to flame as easily for wars of aggression and conquest as for noble causes, and patriotic slogans are a favorite form of political manipulation. While there is surely something noble about making sacrifices for the good of one's fellow citizens, there is also something curious about supposing that the accident of one's birth in a particular country should carry any weight when one is deciding questions of justice and right. During the U.S. war against Mexico, several Americans soldiers who were recent immigrants from Europe began to question the justice of the U.S. invasion of Mexico, and deserted the U.S. forces to join the Mexicans in their defense of Mexico City. When the U.S. forces overran the city, those soldiers were hanged as traitors; but had they instead immigrated to Mexico, they would have been lauded as patriots.

For many years patriotism was little discussed, particularly by philosophers. Of course it was often invoked in stirring speeches and political campaigns and military recruiting posters. But little discussed, and even less debated. The absence of debate and discussion was not due to widespread agreement concerning patriotism, but instead because those who disagreed concerning the value of patriotism held such different views that they rarely talked with one another: shouted at each other occasionally, but rarely talked together.

The slogans invoked by the different sides mark the depth of the conflict: On one side, "My country, right or wrong"; on the other, "Patriotism is the last refuge of a scoundrel." Or "Our Country—whether bounded by the St. John's and the Sabine, or however otherwise bounded or described, and be the measurements more or less— still our Country, to be cherished in all our hearts, to be defended by all our hands," as opposed to "Love of country is what an ass feels for its stall." It is not surprising that one should feel affection for the place of one's birth, as one feels affection for one's home town or even one's family. Nor it is surprising that countries celebrate their heroes and strive to instill devotion in their citizens. But the question of whether patriotism is actually a virtue cannot be answered by such facts.

POINTS TO PONDER

➤ Suppose that at Washington High School there are two teachers who teach United States history, and one teacher agrees with Nussbaum, the other with Miller. How would the courses they teach differ?

➤ Martha Nussbaum favors a cosmopolitan view over the patriotic, but she still maintains that we can and should have special concern for our own special sphere of country, community, and family. How does she attempt to reconcile the two, and does her reconciliation attempt succeed?

➤ David Miller claims that there are five elements that distinguish nationality: "A community constituted by mutual belief, extended in history, active in character, connected to a particular territory, and thought to be marked off from other communities by its members' distinct traits"; and then he adds a 6th: a nation requires a sustaining myth of its history. Do you agree that all six of these elements are essential for constituting a genuine nation? Is there any other essential characteristic that Miller has omitted? Could one of the six characteristics be dropped?

➤ One of the characteristics Miller claims is essential for nationality is that the members of their nation are "marked off from other communities by its members' distinct traits." Shortly thereafter, however, Miller asserts that: "Nationality…is associated with no particular social programme: the flexible content of national identity allows parties of different colours to present their programmes as the true continuation of the national tradition and the true reflection of national character." But is there a tension between these claims? The first seems to suggest essential enduring traits that mark the national identity, while the second leaves everything open to change. If (for example) a distinctive trait of U.S. nationality is belief in "rugged individualism," could (in Miller's model) reformers who wish to promote a stronger commitment for the less fortunate (such as Franklin Roosevelt or Lyndon Johnson) be accused of "destroying the national identity"? Miller claims that does not follow; is he correct?

➤ Obviously Nussbaum and Miller have different views about the value of patriotism, and the simple way to express that might be to say that Nussbaum thinks it is bad while Miller thinks it is good. But more specifically, what is the key point of difference that leads them to their different conclusions concerning the value of patriotism?

We Should Promote Patriotism

DAVID MILLER

My story begins on the river bank of Kenneth Grahame's imagination.

> "And beyond the Wild Wood again?" [asked the Mole]: "Where it's all blue and dim, and one sees what may be hills or perhaps they mayn't, and something like the smoke of towns, or is it only cloud drift?"

> "Beyond the Wild Wood comes the Wide World," [said the Rat]. "And that's something that doesn't matter, either to you or me. I've never been there, and I'm never going, nor you either, if you've got any sense at all. Don't ever refer to it again, please."

The Rat, so very sound in his opinions about most things, boats especially, seems in this moment to reveal exactly what so many people find distasteful about national loyalties and identities. He displays no overt hostility to foreign lands and their ways. But the combination of wilful ignorance about places beyond the Wild Wood, and complete indifference to what is going on there, seems particularly provoking. Aggressive nationalism of the "my country right or wrong" variety is something we might at least argue with. But the narrowing of horizons, the contraction of the universe of experience to the river bank itself, seems to amount to the triumph of sentiment over reasoned argument.

Philosophers, especially, will have great difficulty in coming to grips with the kind of national attachments for which I am using the Rat's riverbankism as an emblem. Philosophers are committed to forms of reasoning, to concepts and arguments, that are universal in form. "What's so special about this river bank?" a philosophical Mole might have asked in reply. "Why is this river bank a better place than other river banks beyond the Wood?" To which the Rat could only have said, "This is *my* place; I like it here; I have no need to ask such questions."

The Rat, clearly, is no philosopher. Yet in contemplating his frame of mind we might be led to recall the words of one who was [David Hume]:

> ...there are in *England*, in particular, many honest gentlemen, who being always employ'd in their domestic affairs, or amusing themselves in common recreations, have carried their thoughts little beyond those objects, which are every day expos'd to their senses. And indeed, of such as these I pretend not to make philosophers...They do well to keep themselves in their present situation; and instead of refining them into philosophers, I wish we cou'd communicate to our founders of systems, a share of this gross earthy mixture, as an ingredient, which they commonly stand much in need of, and which wou'd serve to temper those fiery particles, of which they are composed.

Plainly the Rat is well supplied with gross earthy mixture, literally and metaphorically, and the question is whether any philosophical system can make use of what he has to offer. The sort that can is the Humean sort. By this I mean a philosophy which, rather than dismissing ordinary beliefs and sentiments out of hand unless they can be shown to have a rational foundation, leaves them in place until strong arguments are produced for rejecting them. The Rat's beliefs cannot be deduced from some universally accepted premise; but that is no reason for rejecting them unless the arguments for doing so seem better founded than the beliefs themselves. In moral and political philosophy, in particular, we build upon existing sentiments and judgments, correcting them only when they are inconsistent or plainly flawed in some other way. We don't aspire to some universal and rational foundation such as Kant tried to provide with the categorical imperative.

It is from this sort of stance (which I shall not try to justify) that it makes sense to mount a philosophical defense of nationality. There can be no question of trying to give rationally compelling reasons for people to have national attachments and allegiances. What we can do is to start from the premise that people generally do exhibit such attachments and allegiances, and then try to build a political philosophy which incorporates them. In particular we can do two things: we can examine the critical arguments directed against nationality—arguments trying to undermine the validity of national loyalties—and show that they are flawed; and we can try to assuage the tension between the ethical particularism implied by such commitments and ethical universalism, by showing why it may be advantageous, from a universal point of view, that people have national loyalties.

Philosophers may protest that it is a caricature of their position to suggest that the only reasons for belief or action that they will permit to count are those that derive from an entirely impersonal and universal stand-point. It is common now to distinguish between agent-neutral and agent-relative reasons and to give each some weight in practical reasoning. But what motivates this concession is mainly a concern for individuals' private goals and for their integrity: people must be given the moral space, as it were, to pursue their own projects, to honor their commitments, to live up to their personal ideals. National allegiances, and the obligations that spring from them, are harder to fit into this picture, because they appear to represent, not a different segment of moral life, but a competing way of understanding the concepts and principles that make up the impartial or agent-neutral stand-point (consider, for example, the different conceptions of distributive justice that emerge depending on whether you begin from a national or a universal starting-point). That is why such loyalties appear to pose a head-on challenge to a view of morality that is dominant in our culture, as Alasdair MacIntyre has argued.

It is a curious paradox of our time that while nationalism is politically on the advance, its would-be defenders (in the West at least) find themselves on the defensive. I have just given one reason for this: the view that national allegiances cannot withstand critical scrutiny, so a rational person cannot be a nationalist. There is also a more mundane reason: nationality is widely felt to be a backward-looking, reactionary notion; it is felt to stand in the way of progress. In the European context, for instance, we are invited to look forward to a "Europe of the regions" in which Catalonia, Brittany, Bavaria, Scotland and the rest co-exist harmoniously under a common administrative umbrella, free from the national rivalries which have plunged us into two world wars. Progress means the overcoming of nationality. In the Oxford branch of the Body Shop (and doubtless in the branches in Paris, Tokyo, and elsewhere) you can buy a lapel badge that quotes H. G. Wells: "Our true nationality is mankind." H. G. Wells and the Body Shop in tandem epitomize the modern idea of progress, whose disciples were described by George Orwell in such a wonderfully acid way: "all that dreary tribe of high-minded women and sandal-wearers and bearded fruit-juice drinkers who come flocking towards the smell of 'progress' like bluebottles to a dead cat." If you are one of those bluebottles, and most of us are to some degree, then you will think that ordinary national loyalties amount to reactionary nostalgia and queue up to sport the H. G. Wells slogan.

So the would-be nationalist has two challenges to meet: the philosophical challenge and the progressive challenge. And now it is time to spell out more precisely the notion of nationality that I want to defend. Nationality as I shall understand it comprises three interconnected propositions. The first concerns personal identity, and claims that it may properly be part of someone's identity that they belong to this or that national grouping; in other words that if a person is invited to specify those elements that are essential to his identity, that make him the person that he is, it is in order to refer to nationality. A person who in answer to the question "Who are you?" says "I am Swedish" or "I am Italian" (and doubtless much more besides) is not saying something that is irrelevant or bizarre in the same way as, say, someone who claims without good evidence that he is the illegitimate grandchild of Tsar Nicholas II. Note that the claim is a permissive one: national identity may, but need not, be a constitutive part of personal identity.

The second proposition is ethical, and claims that nations are ethical communi-

ties. They are contour lines in the ethical landscape. The duties we owe to our fellow-nationals are different from, and more extensive than, the duties we owe to human beings as such. This is not to say that we owe *no* duties to humans as such; nor is it to deny that there may be other, perhaps smaller and more intense, communities to whose members we owe duties that are more stringent still than those we owe to Britons, Swedes, etc., at large. But it is to claim that a proper account of ethics should give weight to national boundaries, and that in particular there is no objection in principle to institutional schemes that are designed to deliver benefits exclusively to those who fall within the same boundaries as ourselves.

The third proposition is political, and states that people who form a national community in a particular territory have a good claim to political self-determination; there ought to be put in place an institutional structure that enables them to decide collectively matters that concern primarily their own community. Notice that I have phrased this cautiously, and have not asserted that the institution must be that of a sovereign state. Historically the sovereign state has been the main vehicle through which claims to national self-determination have been realized, and this is not just an accident. Nevertheless national self-determination *can* be realized in other ways, and as we shall see there are cases where it must be realized other than through a sovereign state, precisely to meet the equally good claims of other nationalities.

I want to stress that the three propositions I have outlined—about personal identity, about bounded duties and about political self-determination—are linked together in such a way that it is difficult to feel the force of any one of them without acknowledging the others. It is not hard to see how a common identity can support both the idea of the nation as an ethical community and the claim to self-determination, but what is more subtle—and I shall try to bring this out as I go along—is the way in which the political claim can reinforce both the claim about identity and the ethical claim. The fact that the community in question is either actually or potentially self-determining strengthens its claims on us both as a source of identity and as a source of obligation. This interlinking of propositions may at times seem circular; and the fact that the nationalist case cannot be spelt out in neat linear form may confirm philosophical suspicions about it. But I believe that if we are to understand the power of nationality as an idea in the modern world—the appeal of national identity to the modern self—we must try to understand its inner logic.

So let me now begin to look more closely at national identities themselves, and in particular ask what differentiates them from other identities—individual or communal—that people may have. What does it mean to think of oneself as belonging to a national community?

The first point to note, and it has been noted by most of those who have thought seriously about the subject, is that national communities are constituted by belief: a nationality exists when its members believe that it does. It is not a question of a group of people sharing some common attribute such as race or language. These features do not of themselves make nations, and only become important in so far as a particular nationality takes as one of its defining features that its members speak French or have black skins. This becomes clear as soon as one looks at the candidates that have been put forward as objective criteria of nationhood, as Ernest Renan did in his famous lecture on the subject: to every criterion that has been proposed there are clear empirical counter-examples. The

conclusion one quickly reaches is that a nation is in Renan's memorable phrase "a daily plebiscite"; its existence depends on a shared belief that its members belong together, and a shared wish to continue their life in common. So in asserting a national identity, I assume that my beliefs and commitments are mirrored by those who I take to share that identity, and of course I might be wrong about this. In itself this does not distinguish nationality from other kinds of human relationship that depend on reciprocal belief.

The second feature of nationality is that it is an identity that embodies historical continuity. Nations stretch backwards into the past, and indeed in most cases their origins are conveniently lost in the mists of time. In the course of this history various significant events have occurred, and we can identify with the actual people who acted at those moments, reappropriating their deeds as our own. Often these events involve military victories and defeats: we imagine ourselves filling the breach at Harfleur or reading the signal hoisted at Trafalgar. Renan thinks that historical tragedies matter more than historical glories. I am inclined to see in this an understandable French bias, but the point he connects to it is a good one: "sorrows have greater value than victories; for they impose duties and demand common effort." The historic national community is a community of obligation. Because our forebears have toiled and spilt their blood to build and defend the nation, we who are born into it inherit an obligation to continue their work, which we discharge partly towards our contemporaries and partly towards our descendants. The historical community stretches forward into the future too. This then means that when we speak of the nation as an ethical community, we have in mind not merely the kind of community that exists between a group of contemporaries who practice mutual aid among themselves and which would dissolve at the point at which that practice ceased; but a community which, because it stretches back and forward across the generations, is not one that the present generation can renounce. Here we begin to see something of the depth of national communities which may not be shared by other more immediate forms of association.

The third distinguishing aspect of national identity is that it is an active identity. Nations are communities that do things together, take decisions, achieve results, and so forth. Of course this cannot be literally so: we rely on proxies who are seen as embodying the national will: statesmen, soldiers, sportsmen, etc. But this means that the link between past and future that I noted a moment ago is not merely a causal link. The nation becomes what it does by the decisions that it takes—some of which we may now regard as thoroughly bad, a cause of national shame. Whether this active identity is a valuable aspect of nationality, or whether as some critics would allege merely a damaging fantasy, it clearly does mark out nations from other kinds of grouping, for instance churches or religious sects whose identity is essentially a passive one in so far as the church is seen as responding to the promptings of God. The group's purpose is not to do or decide things, but to interpret as best it can the messages and commands of an external source.

The fourth aspect of a national identity is that it connects a group of people to a particular geographical place, and here again there is a clear contrast with most other group identities that people affirm, such as ethnic or religious identities. These often have sacred sites or places of origin, but it is not an essential part of having the identity that you should permanently occupy that place. If you are a good Muslim you should make a pilgrimage to Mecca at least once, but you need not set up house there. A nation, in contrast, must have a homeland. This may of course be a source of great difficulties, a point I shall return to when considering objections to the idea of nationality, but it also helps to explain why a national community must be (in aspiration if not yet in fact) a political community. We have seen already that nations are groups that act; we see now that their actions must include that of controlling a chunk of the earth's surface. It is this territorial element that makes nations uniquely suited to serve as the basis of states, since a state by definition must exercise its authority over a geographical area.

Finally it is essential to national identity that the people who compose the nation are believed to share certain traits that mark them off from other peoples. It is incompatible with nationality to think of the members of the nation as people who merely happen to have been thrown together in one place and forced to share a common fate, in the way that the occupants of a lifeboat, say, have been accidentally thrown together. National divisions must be natural ones; they must correspond to real differences between peoples. This need not, fortunately, imply racism or the idea that the group is constituted by biological descent. The common traits can be cultural in character: they can consist in shared values, shared tastes or sensibilities. So immigration need not pose problems, provided only that the immigrants take on the essential elements of national character. Indeed it has proved possible in some instances to regard immigration as itself a formative experience, calling forth qualities of resourcefulness and mutual aid that then define the national character—I am thinking of the settler cultures of the

New World such as the American and the Australian. As everyone knows, there is nothing more illustrious for an Australian today than to have an ancestor who was carried over in chains by the First Fleet.

When I say that national differences must be natural ones, I mean that the people who compose a nation must believe that there is something distinctive about themselves that marks them off from other nations, over and above the fact of sharing common institutions. This need not be one specific trait or quality, but a range of characteristics which are generally shared by the members of nation A and serve to differentiate them from outsiders. In popular belief these differences may be exaggerated. Hume remarked that the vulgar think that everyone who belongs to a nation displays its distinctive traits, whereas "men of sense" allow for exceptions; nevertheless aggregate differences undoubtedly exist. This is surely correct. It is also worth noting that people may be hard pressed to say explicitly what the national character of their people consists in, and yet have an intuitive sense when confronted with foreigners of where the differences lie. National identities can remain unarticulated, and yet still exercise a pervasive influence on people's behavior.

These five elements together—a community constituted by mutual belief, extended in history, active in character, connected to a particular territory, and thought to be marked off from other communities by its members' distinct traits— serve to distinguish nationality from other collective sources of personal identity. I shall come in a moment to some reasons why such identities may be thought to be particularly valuable, worth protecting and fostering, but first I should emphasize what has so far merely been implicit, namely the mythical aspects of national identity. Nations almost unavoidably depend on beliefs about themselves that do not stand up well to impartial scrutiny. Renan once again hit the nail on the head when he said that "to forget and—I will venture to say—to get one's history wrong, are essential factors in the making of a nation." One main reason for this is that the contingencies of power politics have always played a large part in the formation of national units. States have been created by force, and, over time, their subject peoples have come to think of themselves as co-nationals. But no one wants to think of himself as roped together to a set of people merely because the territorial ambitions of some dynastic lord in the thirteenth century ran thus far and no further. Nor indeed is this the right way to think about the matter, because the effect of the ruler's conquests may have been, over time, to have produced a people with real cultural unity. But because of the historical dimension of the nation, together with the idea that each nation has its own distinct character, it is uncomfortable to be reminded of the forced nature of one's national genesis. Hence various stories have been concocted about the primeval tribe from which the modern nation sprang.

The real question, however, is not whether national identities embody elements of myth, but whether they perform such valuable functions that our attitude, as philosophers, should be one of acquiescence if not positive endorsement. And here I want to argue that nationality answers one of the most pressing needs of the modern world, namely how to maintain solidarity among the populations of states that are large and anonymous, such that their citizens cannot possibly enjoy the kind of community that relies on kinship or face-to-face interaction. That we need such solidarity is something that I intend to take for granted here. I assume that in societies in which economic markets play a central role, there is a strong tendency towards social atomization, where each person looks out for the interests of herself and her immediate social network. As a result it is potentially difficult to mobilize people to provide collective goods, it is difficult to get them to agree to practices of redistribution from which they are not likely personally to benefit, and so forth. These problems can be avoided only where there exists large-scale solidarity, such that people feel themselves to be members of an overarching community, and to have social duties to act for the common good of that community, to help out other members when they are in need, etc.

Nationality is *de facto* the main source of such solidarity. In view of the broadly Humean approach that I am adopting, where our moral and political philosophy bends to accommodate pre-existing sentiments, this in itself would be enough to commend it. But I should like to say something more positive about nationality before coming to the difficulties. It is precisely because of the mythical or imaginary elements in national identity that it can be reshaped to meet new challenges and new needs. We have seen that the story a nation tells itself about its past is a selective one. Depending on the character of contemporary politics, the story may gradually alter, and with it our understanding of the substance of national identity. This need not take the crude form of rewriting of history as practiced in the late Soviet Union and elsewhere (airbrushing pictures of Trotsky out of the Bolshevik central committee and so on). It may instead be a matter of looking at established facts in a new way. Consider, as just one example, the very different interpretation of British imperialism now current from that which prevailed at the time of my father's birth in Edwardian Britain. The tone has changed from one of triumphalism to one of equivocation or

even mild apology. And this goes naturally along with a new interpretation of British identity in which it is no longer part of that identity to shoulder the white man's burden and carry enlightenment to the heathen.

From a political stand-point, this imaginary aspect of nationality may be a source of strength. It allows people of different political persuasions to share a political loyalty, defining themselves against a common background whose outlines are not precise, and which therefore lends itself to competing interpretations. It also shows us why nationality is not a conservative idea. A moment's glance at the historical record shows that nationalist ideas have as often been associated with liberal and socialist programs as with programs of the right. In their first appearance, they were often associated with liberal demands for representative government put forward in opposition to established ruling elites. Linda Colley's studies of the emergence of British nationalism in the late 18th and early 19th centuries show that nationalist ideas were developed by middle class and popular movements seeking to win a place in the public realm, and resisted by the state and the landowning class that supported it. This picture was repeated in its essentials throughout Europe. It is easy to see why a conservative may resist nationalism. Nationality invokes the activist idea of a people collectively determining its own destiny, and this is anathema to the conservative view of politics as a limited activity best left in the hands of an elite who have been educated to rule.

Nationality, then, is associated with no particular social program: the flexible content of national identity allows parties of different colors to present their programs as the true continuation of the national tradition and the true reflection of national character. At the same time it binds these parties together and makes space for the idea of loyal opposition, an individual or faction who resist prevailing policy but who can legitimately claim to speak for the same community as the government of the day.

I have referred to the liberal origins of the idea of nationality, but the first objection that I want to consider amounts essentially to a liberal critique of nationality. This holds that nationality is detrimental to the cultural pluralism that liberals hold dear; it is incompatible with the idea of a society in which different cultural traditions are accorded equal respect, and whose vitality springs from competition and exchange between these traditions. The classic statement of this critique can be found in Lord Acton's essay on "Nationality" in which he argues in favor of a multi-national state in which no one nation holds a dominant place. Such a state, he claims, provides the best guarantee of liberties, "the fullest security for the preservation of local customs" and the best incentive to intellectual progress.

This argument derives from the assumption that national identities are exclusive in their nature; that where a state embodies a single nationality, the culture that makes up that nationality must drive out everything else. There is no reason to hold this assumption. Nationality is not of its nature an all-embracing identity. It need not extend to all the cultural attributes that a person might display. So one can avow a national identity and also have attachments to several more specific cultural groups: to ethnic groups, religious groups, work-based associations and so on and so forth. A line can be drawn between the beliefs and qualities that make up nationality, and those that fall outside its scope. The place where the line is drawn will be specific to a particular nationality at a particular time, and it will be a subject for debate whether its present position is appropriate or not. For instance one may argue in a liberal direction that a person's religion, say, should be irrelevant to their membership of this nation, or argue in a nationalist direction that language is not irrelevant, that each member should at least be fluent in the national tongue. The Acton argument supposes that no such line can be drawn. It supposes, contrary to all evidence, that one cannot have a pluralist society in which many ethnic, religious, etc. groups co-exist but with an overarching national identity in common.

Indeed one can turn Acton's argument around, as J. S. Mill did by anticipation in his chapter on Nationality in *Representative Government*. Unless the several groups that compose a society have the mutual sympathy and trust that stems from a common nationality, it will be virtually impossible to have free institutions. There will, for instance, be no common interest in stemming the excesses of government; politics becomes a zero-sum game in which each group can hope to gain by the exploitation of the others.

Philosophers may find it restricting that they have to conduct their arrangements about justice with reference to national identities at all. My claim is that unless they do they will lose contact entirely with the beliefs of the people they seek to address; they must try to incorporate some of Hume's gross earthy mixture, the unreflective beliefs of everyday life. Nonetheless there is a tension here. We should return to Kenneth Grahame's Rat who on his first appearance seems to stand for unlimited acquiescence in the everyday world of the river bank. As the story draws towards its conclusion, however, a more troubled Rat emerges. Disturbed first by the departure of the swallows to Southern climes, he then encounters a seafaring Rat who regales him with tales of the colorful and vibrant world beyond the river bank.

The Rat is mesmerized. His eyes, normally "clear and dark and brown" turn to "a streaked and shifting grey." He is about to set out for the South with stick and satchel in hand, and has to be physically restrained by the Mole, who gradually leads his thoughts back to the everyday world, and finally leaves him writing poetry as a kind of sublimation of his wandering instincts.

The Rat's earlier refusal to contemplate the Wide World, it emerges, was a wilful repression of a part of himself that it was dangerous to acknowledge. Something of the same dilemma confronts the philosophical nationalist. He feels the pull of national loyalties, and he senses that without these loyalties we would be cast adrift in a region of great moral uncertainty. Yet he is also alive to the limitations and absurdities of his and other national identities. He recognizes that we owe something to other human beings merely as such, and so he strains towards a more rationally defensible foundation for ethics and politics. There is no solution here but to strive for some kind of equilibrium between the everyday and the philosophical, between common belief and rational belief, between the river bank and the Wide World. But, as the cases of both the Rat and of David Hume in their different ways demonstrate, this is far easier said than done.

We Should Favor a Broader Cosmopolitan View

Martha C. Nussbaum

I

In Rabindranath Tagore's novel *The Home and the World*, the young wife Bimala, entranced by the patriotic rhetoric of her husband's friend Sandip, becomes an eager devotee of the *Swadeshi* movement, which has organized a boycott of foreign goods. The slogan of the movement is *Bande Mataraam* (Hail Motherland). Bimala complains that her husband, the cosmopolitan Hindu landlord Nikhil, is cool in his devotion to the cause:

> And yet it was not that my husband refused to support *Swadeshi*, or was in any way against the Cause. Only he had not been able wholeheartedly to accept the spirit of *Bande Mataram*.

> "I am willing," he said, "to serve my country; but my worship I reserve for Right which is far greater than my country. To worship my country as a god is to bring a curse upon it."

Americans have frequently supported the principle of *Bande Mataram*, giving the fact of being American a special salience in moral and political deliberation, and pride in a specifically American identity and a specifically American citizenship a special power among the motivations to political action. I believe, as do Tagore and his character Nikhil, that this emphasis on patriotic pride is both morally dangerous and, ultimately, subversive of some of the worthy goals patriotism sets out to serve—for example, the goal of national unity in devotion to worthy moral ideals of justice and equality. These goals, I shall argue, would be better served by an ideal that is in any case more adequate to our situation in the contemporary world, namely the very old ideal of the cosmopolitan, the person whose allegiance is to the worldwide community of human beings.

My articulation of these issues is motivated, in part, by my experience working on international quality-of-life issues in an institute for development economics connected with the United Nations. It is also motivated by the renewal of appeals to the nation, and national pride, in some recent discussions of American character and American education. In a well-known op-ed piece in the *New York Times* (13 February 1994), philosopher Richard Rorty urges Americans, especially the American left, not to disdain patriotism as a value, and indeed to give central importance to "the emotion of national pride" and "a sense of shared national identity." Rorty argues that we cannot even criticize ourselves well unless we also "rejoice" in our American identity and redefine ourselves fundamentally in terms of that identity. Rorty seems to hold that the primary alternative to a politics based on patriotism and national identity is what he calls a "politics of difference," one based on internal divisions among America's ethnic, racial, religious, and other subgroups. He nowhere considers the possibility of a more international basis for political emotion and concern.

This is no isolated case. Rorty's piece responds to and defends Sheldon Hackney's recent call for a "national conversation" to discuss American identity. As a participant in its early phase, I was made vividly aware that the project, as initially conceived, proposed an inward-looking task, bounded by the borders of the nation, rather than considering ties of obligation and commitment that join America to the rest of the world. As with Rorty's piece, the primary contrast drawn in the project was between a politics based on ethnic and racial and religious difference and a politics based on a shared national identity. What we share as both rational and mutually dependent human beings was simply not on the agenda.

One might wonder, however, how far the politics of nationalism really is from the politics of difference. *The Home and the World* (better known, perhaps, in Satyajit Ray's haunting film of the same title) is a tragic story of the defeat of a reasonable and principled cosmopolitanism by the forces of nationalism and ethnocentrism. I believe that Tagore sees deeply when he observes that, at bottom, nationalism and ethnocentric particularism are not alien to one another, but akin—that to give support to nationalist sentiments subverts, ultimately, even the values that hold a nation together, because it substitutes a colorful idol for the substantive universal values of justice and right. Once someone has said, I am an Indian first, a citizen of the world second, once he or she has made that morally questionable move of self-definition by a morally irrelevant characteristic, then what, indeed, will stop that person from saying, as Tagore's characters so quickly learn to say, I am a Hindu first, and an Indian second, or I am an upper-caste landlord first, and a Hindu second? Only the cosmopolitan stance of the landlord Nikhil—so boringly flat in the eyes of his young wife Bimala and his passionate nationalist friend Sandip—has the promise of transcending these divisions, because only this stance asks us to give our first allegiance to what is morally good—and that which, being good, I can commend as such to all human beings.

Proponents of nationalism in politics and in education frequently make a weak concession to cosmopolitanism. They may argue, for example, that although nations should in general base education and political deliberation on shared national values, a commitment to basic human rights should be part of any national education system, and that this commitment will in a sense hold many nations together. This seems to be a fair comment on practical reality; and the emphasis on human rights is certainly necessary for a world in which nations interact all the time on terms (let us hope) of justice and mutual respect.

But is it sufficient? As students here grow up, is it sufficient for them to learn that they are above all citizens of the United States but that they ought to respect the basic human rights of citizens of India, Bolivia, Nigeria, and Norway? Or should they—as I think—in addition to giving special attention to the history and current situation of their own nation, learn a good deal more than they frequently do about the rest of the world in which they live, about India and Bolivia and Nigeria and Norway and their histories, problems, and comparative successes? Should they learn only that citizens of India have equal basic rights, or should they also learn about the problems of hunger and pollution in India, and the implications of these problems for the larger issues of global hunger and global ecology? Most important, should they be taught that they are, above all, citizens of the United States, or should they instead be taught that they are, above all, citizens of a world of human beings, and that, while they happen to be situated in the United States, they have to share this world with the citizens of other countries? I suggest four arguments for the second concept of education, which I call *cosmopolitan education*. But first I introduce a historical digression, which traces cosmopolitanism to its origins, and in the process recover some excellent arguments that have traditionally supported it.

II

When Diogenes the Cynic replied, "I am a citizen of the world," he meant, apparently, that he refused to be defined by his local origins and group memberships, so central to the self-image of the conventional Greek male; instead, he defined himself in terms of more universal aspirations and concerns. The Stoics, who followed his lead, further developed his image of the *kosmou politês* (world citizen) arguing that each of us dwells, in effect, in two communities—the local community of our birth, and the community of human argument and aspiration that "is truly great and truly common, in which we look neither to this corner nor to that, but measure the boundaries of our nation by the sun" (Seneca, *De Otio*). It is this community that is, fundamentally, the source of our moral obligations. With respect to the most basic moral values, such as justice, "We should regard all human beings as our fellow citizens and neighbors" (Plutarch, *On the Fortunes of Alexander*). We should regard our deliberations as, first and foremost, deliberations about human problems of people in particular concrete situations, not problems growing out of a national identity that is altogether unlike that of others. Diogenes knew that the invitation to think as a world citizen was, in a sense, an invitation to be an exile from the comfort of patriotism and its easy sentiments, to see our own ways of life from the point of view of justice and

the good. The accident of where one is born is just that, an accident; any human being might have been born in any nation. Recognizing this, his Stoic successors held, we should not allow differences of nationality or class or ethnic membership or even gender to erect barriers between us and our fellow human beings. We should recognize humanity wherever it occurs, and give its fundamental ingredients, reason and moral capacity, our first allegiance and respect.

This clearly did not mean that the Stoics were proposing the abolition of local and national forms of political organization and the creation of a world state. Their point was even more radical: that we should give our first allegiance to no mere from of government, no temporal power, but to the moral community made up by the humanity of all human beings. The idea of the world citizen is in this way the ancestor and the source of Kant's idea of the "kingdom of ends," and has a similar function in inspiring and regulating moral and political conduct. One should always behave so as to treat with equal respect the dignity of reason and moral choice in every human being. It is this concept that also inspires Tagore's novel, as the cosmopolitan landlord struggles to stem the tide of nationalism and factionalism by appeals to universal moral norms. Many of the speeches of the character Nikhil were drawn from Tagore's own cosmopolitan political writings.

Stoics who hold that good civic education is education for world citizenship recommend this attitude on three grounds. First, they hold that the study of humanity as it is realized in the whole world is valuable for self-knowledge: we see ourselves more clearly when we see our ways in relation to those of other reasonable people.

Second, they argue, as does Tagore, that we will be better able to solve our problems if we face them in this way. No theme is deeper in Stoicism than the damage done by faction and local allegiances to the political life of a group. Political deliberation, they argue, is sabotaged again and again by partisan loyalties, whether to one's team at the Circus or to one's nation. Only by making our fundamental allegiance to the world community of justice and reason do we avoid these dangers.

Finally, they insist that the stance of the *kosmou politês* is intrinsically valuable, for it recognizes in people what is especially fundamental about them, most worthy of respect and acknowledgment: their aspirations to justice and goodness and their capacities for reasoning in this connection. These qualities may be less colorful than local or national traditions and identities—it is on this basis that the young wife in Tagore's novel spurns them in favor of qualities in the nationalist orator Sandip that she later comes to see as superficial—but they are, the Stoics argue, both lasting and deep.

The Stoics stress that to be a citizen of the world one does not need to give up local identifications, which can be a source of great richness in life. They suggest that we think of ourselves not as devoid of local affiliations, but as surrounded by a series of concentric circles. The first one encircles the self, the next takes in the immediate family, then follows the extended family, then, in order, neighbors or local groups, fellow city-dwellers, and fellow countrymen—and we can easily add to this list groupings based on ethnic, linguistic, historical, professional, gender, or sexual identities. Outside all these circles is the largest one, humanity as a whole. Our task as citizens of the world will be to "draw the circles somehow toward the center" (Stoic philosopher Hierocles, 1st–2nd CE), making all human beings more like our fellow city-dwellers, and so on. We need not give up our special affections

and identifications, whether ethnic or gender-based or religious. We need not think of them as superficial, and we may think of our identity as constituted partly by them. We may and should devote special attention to them in education. But we should also work to make all human beings part of our community of dialogue and concern, base our political deliberations on that interlocking commonality, and give the circle that defines our humanity special attention and respect.

In educational terms, this means that students in the United States, for example, may continue to regard themselves as defined partly by their particular loves—their families, their religious, ethnic, or racial communities, or even their country. But they must also, and centrally, learn to recognize humanity wherever they encounter it, undeterred by traits that are strange to them, and be eager to understand humanity in all its strange guises. They must learn enough about the different to recognize the common aims, aspirations, and values, and enough about these common ends to see how variously they are instantiated in the many cultures and their histories. Stoic writers insist that the vivid imagining of the different is an essential task of education, and that it requires, in turn, a mastery of many facts about the different. Marcus Aurelius gives himself the following advice, which might be called the basis for cosmopolitan education: "Accustom yourself not to be inattentive to what another person says, and as far as possible enter into that person's mind" (VI. 53). "Generally," he adds, "one must first learn many things before one can judge another's action with understanding."

A favored exercise in this process of world thinking is to conceive of the entire world of human beings as a single body, its many people as so many limbs. Referring to the fact that it takes only changing a single letter in Greek to convert the word "limb" (*melos*) into the word "part" (*meros*), Marcus says, "If, changing the word, you call yourself merely a [detached] part rather than a limb, you do not yet love your fellow men from the heart, nor derive complete joy from doing good; you will do it merely as a duty, not as doing good to yourself" (VII. 13). It is important to recall that, as emperor, he gave himself that advice in connection with daily duties that required coming to grips with the cultures of remote and, initially, strange civilizations, such as Parthia and Sarmatia.

I would like to see education adopt this cosmopolitan Stoic stance. The organic model could, of course, be abused—if, for example, it was taken to deny the fundamental importance of the separateness of people and of fundamental personal liberties. Stoics were not always sufficiently attentive to these values and to their political salience; in that sense, their thought is not always a good basis for a scheme of democratic deliberation and education. But as the image is primarily intended—as a reminder of the interdependence of all human beings and communities—it has fundamental significance. There is clearly a huge amount to be said about how such ideas might be realized in curricula at many levels. Instead of beginning that more concrete task, however, I focus on the present day and offer four arguments for making world citizenship, rather than democratic or national citizenship, the focus for civic education.

III

1. Through cosmopolitan education, we learn more about ourselves.

One of the greatest barriers to rational deliberation in politics is the unexamined feeling that one's own preferences and ways are neutral and natural. An education that takes national boundaries as morally salient too often reinforces this kind of irrationality, by lending to what is an accident of history a false air of moral weight and glory. By looking at ourselves through the lens of the other, we come to see what in our practices is local and nonessential, what is more broadly or deeply shared. Our nation is appallingly ignorant of most of the rest of the world. I think this means that it is also, in many crucial ways, ignorant of itself.

To give just one example of this: If we want to understand our own history and our choices about child-rearing and the structure of the family, we are helped immeasurably by looking around the world to see in what configurations families exist, and through what strategies children are in fact being cared for. (This would include a study of the history of the family, both in our own and other traditions.) Such a study can show us, for example, that the two-parent nuclear family, in which the mother is the primary homemaker and the father the primary breadwinner, is by no means a pervasive style of child-rearing in today's world. The extended family, clusters of families, the village, women's associations—all these groups, and others, in various places in the world have major child-rearing responsibilities. Seeing this, we can begin to ask questions—for example, about how much child abuse there is in a family that involves grandparents and other relatives in child-rearing, as compared with the relatively isolated Western-style nuclear family; or about how the different structures of child care support women's work. If we do not undertake this kind of educational project, we risk assuming that the options familiar to us are the only ones there are, and that they are somehow "normal" and "natural" for all humans. Much the same can be said about conceptions of gender and sexuality, about conceptions of work and its division, about schemes of property holding, or about the treatment of children and the aged.

2. We make headway solving problems that require international cooperation.

The air does not obey national boundaries. This simple fact can be, for children, the beginning of the recognition that, like it or not, we live in a world in which the destinies of nations are closely intertwined with respect to basic goods and survival itself. The pollution of third-world nations that are attempting to attain our high standard of living will, in some cases, end up in our air. No matter what account of these matters we will finally adopt, any intelligent deliberation about ecology—as, also, about the food supply and population—requires global planning, global knowledge, and the recognition of a shared future.

To conduct this sort of global dialogue, we need knowledge not only of the geography and ecology of other nations—something that would already entail much revision in our curricula—but also a great deal about their people, so that in talking with them we may be capable of respecting their traditions and commitments. Cosmopolitan education would supply the background necessary for this type of deliberation.

3. We recognize moral obligations to the rest of the world that are real and that otherwise would go unrecognized.

What are Americans to make of the fact that the high living standard we enjoy is one that very likely cannot be universalized, at least given the present costs of pollution controls and the present economic situation of developing nations, without ecological disaster? If we take Kantian morality at

all seriously, as we should, we need to educate our children to be troubled by this fact. Otherwise we are educating a nation of moral hypocrites who talk the language of universalizability but whose universe has a self-serving, narrow scope.

This point may appear to presuppose universalism, rather than being an argument in its favor. But here one may note that the values on which Americans may mostly justly pride themselves are, in a deep sense, Stoic values: respect for human dignity and the opportunity for each person to pursue happiness. If we really do believe that all human beings are created equal and endowed with certain inalienable rights, we are morally required to think about what that conception requires us to do with and for the rest of the world.

Once again, that does not mean that one may not permissibly give one's own sphere a special degree of concern. Politics, like child care, will be poorly done if each thinks herself equally responsible for all, rather than giving the immediate surroundings special attention and care. To give one's own sphere special care is justifiable in universalist terms, and I think this is its most compelling justification. To take one example, we do not really think our own children are morally more important than other people's children, even though almost all of us who have children would give our own children far more love and care than we give others'. It is good for children, on the whole, that things work this way, and that is why our special care is good, rather than selfish. Education may and should reflect those special concerns—for example, in a given nation, spending more time on that nation's history and politics. But my argument does entail the idea that we should not confine our thinking to our own sphere, that in making choices in both political and economic matters we should most seriously consider the right of other human beings to life, liberty, and the pursuit of happiness, and that we should work to acquire the knowledge that will enable us to deliberate well about those rights. I believe this sort of thinking will have large-scale economic and political consequences.

4. We make a consistent and coherent argument based on distinctions we are prepared to defend.

In Richard Rorty's and Sheldon Hackney's eloquent appeals to shared values, there is something that makes me very uneasy. They seem to argue effectively when they insist on the centrality to democratic deliberation of certain values that bind all citizens together. But why should these values, which instruct us to join hands across boundaries of ethnicity, class, gender, and race, lose steam when they get to the borders of the nation? By conceding that a morally arbitrary boundary such as the boundary of the nation has a deep and formative role in our deliberations, we seem to deprive ourselves of any principled way of persuading citizens they should in fact join hands across these other barriers.

For one thing, the very same groups exist both outside and inside. Why should we think of people from China as our fellows the minute they dwell in a certain place, namely the United States, but not when they dwell in a certain other place, namely China? What is it about the national boundary that magically converts people toward whom we are both incurious and indifferent into people to whom we have duties of mutual respect? I think, in short, that we undercut the very case for multicultural respect within a nation by failing to make central to education a broader world respect. Richard Rorty's patriotism may be a way of bringing all Americans together; but patriotism is very

close to jingoism, and I'm afraid I don't see in Rorty's argument any proposal for coping with this very obvious danger.

Furthermore, the defense of shared national values in both Rorty and Hackney, as I understand it, requires appealing to certain basic features of human personhood that obviously also transcend national boundaries. So if we fail to educate children to cross those boundaries in their minds and imaginations, we are tacitly giving them the message that we don't really mean what we say. We say that respect should be accorded to humanity as such, but we really mean that Americans as such are worthy of special respect. And that, I think, is a story that Americans have told for far too long.

IV

Becoming a citizen of the world is often a lonely business. It is, as Diogenes said, a kind of exile—from the comfort of local truths, from the warm, nestling feeling of patriotism, from the absorbing drama of pride in oneself and one's own. In the writings of Marcus Aurelius (as in those of his American followers Emerson and Thoreau), a reader can sometimes sense a boundless loneliness, as if the removal of the props of habit and local boundaries had left life bereft of any warmth or security. If one begins life as a child who loves and trusts his or her parents, it is tempting to want to reconstruct citizenship along the same lines, finding in an idealized image of a nation a surrogate parent who will do one's thinking for one. Cosmopolitanism offers no such refuge; it offers only reason and the love of humanity, which may seem at times less colorful than other sources of belonging.

In Tagore's novel, the appeal to world citizenship fails. It fails because patriotism is full of color and intensity and passion, whereas cosmopolitanism seems to have a hard time gripping the imagination. And yet in its very failure, Tagore shows, it succeeds. For the novel is a story of education for world citizenship, since the entire tragic story is told by the widowed Bimala, who understands, if too late, that Nikhil's morality was vastly superior to Sandip's empty symbol-mongering, that what looked like passion in Sandip was egocentric self-exaltation, and that what looked like lack of passion in Nikhil contained a truly loving perception of her as a person. If one goes today to Santiniketan, a town several hours by train from Calcutta where Tagore founded his cosmopolitan university, Vishvabharati (which means "all the world")—one feels the tragedy once more. For all-the-world university has not achieved the anticipated influence or distinction within India, and the ideals of the cosmopolitan community of Santiniketan are increasingly under siege from militant forces of ethnocentric particularism and Hindu-fundamentalist nationalism. And yet, in the very decline of Tagore's ideal, which now threatens the very existence of the secular and tolerant Indian state, the observer sees its worth. To worship one's country as if it were a god is indeed to bring a curse upon it. Recent electoral reactions against Hindu nationalism give some grounds for optimism that this recognition of worth is widespread and may prove efficacious, averting a tragic ending of the sort that Tagore describes.

I am in fact optimistic that Tagore's ideal can be successfully realized in schools and universities in democracies around the world, and in the formation of public policy.

The life of the cosmopolitan, who puts right before country and universal reason before the symbols of national belonging, need not be boring, flat, or lacking in love.

THE CONTINUING DEBATE:
Is Patriotism a Virtue?

What Is New?

One place where the issue of patriotism often becomes contentious is in the choice of elementary and secondary school history textbooks by state textbook selection commissions; and nowhere is that more evident than in the state of Texas, where history textbooks are expected to tell a very positive story of American history, with emphasis on heroic deeds and noble purposes. In fact, the Texas State Board of Education explicitly requires that textbooks adopted in Texas should promote patriotism and the free enterprise system. Racism and slavery, which do not inspire patriotic pride, are understated. Recently a history textbook that noted widespread prostitution in 19th Century cattle towns was rejected. Since Texas is a huge market (it spends better than $300 million annually on history and social sciences texts), textbook publishers often tailor their books to make them acceptable to Texas standards, and so books used throughout the country are influenced by the rules adopted by Texas.

A similar issue has caused great controversy in Japan, where there have been calls from the ruling party for greater emphasis on patriotism and a reduction of "excessive descriptions" of Japanese war crimes (such as the atrocities committed in Nanking and the sexual slavery of women in occupied countries for Japanese soldiers). In some contemporary textbooks, modern wars launched by Japan (including against China) are characterized as wars of liberation.

Where to Find More

An outstanding collection of articles is edited by Igor Primoratz, *Patriotism* (Amherst, N.Y.: Humanity Books, 2002), including important articles by Alasdair MacIntyre and Igor Primoratz. Another excellent anthology is by N. Miscevic, *Nationalism and Ethnic Conflict: Philosophical Perspectives* (Chicago and LaSalle, Ill.: Open Court, 2000); and Robert McKim and Jeff McMahan, editors, *The Morality of Nationalism* (Oxford: Oxford University Press, 1997), contains a number of worthwhile essays.

An interesting defense of "moderate patriotism" is offered in a very readable book by Stephen Nathanson, *Patriotism, Morality, and Peace* (Lanham, Md.: Rowman & Littlefield, 1993). Yael Tamir's *Liberal Nationalism* (Princeton, N.J.: Princeton University Press, 1993) is an intriguing effort to reconcile nationalism with liberalism.

Joshua Cohen is the editor of *For Love of Country: Debating the Limits of Patriotism* (Boston: Beacon Press, 1996). The book starts with an essay by Martha C. Nussbaum in which she argues for replacing our limited national and patriotic loyalties with a broader and more cosmopolitan perspective that emphasizes allegiance to principle rather than country. Following Nussbaum's essay are responses by sixteen distinguished writers, and finally by Nussbaum's reply.

Nationalism is an issue that obviously has close connections with questions concerning patriotism. For a contemporary defense of nationalism, see David Miller, *On Nationality* (Oxford: Oxford University Press, 1995).

An issue that often arises in connection with questions of patriotism is whether our schools should strive to instill patriotism in our children; in particular, should we teach the history of our country with special emphasis on the positive elements of its history and the noble principles it espouses, or should we include all the blemishes and shortcomings? Should we remember the Alamo, and forget the imperialist attack on Mexico to expand the American empire? Should we note that in our Declaration of Independence we championed the principle that all men are created equal, and ignore the fact that the United States continued to hold slaves long after most other countries had abolished slavery? Should we teach about the Boston Massacre, but ignore the massacre at Wounded Knee? The controversy over what should be included—and omitted from—our history textbooks often makes it into the popular press; it is also debated in the journals. An excellent collection of articles on this question is edited by Robert K. Fullinwider, *Public Education in a Multicultural Society: Policy, Theory, Critique* (Cambridge: Cambridge University Press, 1996). Recent interesting essays on the issue are David Archard, "Should We Teach Patriotism?" *Studies in Philosophy and Education*, volume 18 (1999): 157–173, which argues against teaching patriotism, and John White supporting teaching for patriotism in "Patriotism Without Obligation," *Journal of Philosophy of Education*, volume 35, number 1 (2001): 141–151. An excellent study of the long struggle over what should be included in American history textbooks is John Moreau, *School Book Nation: Conflicts Over American History Textbooks from the Civil War to the Present* (Ann Arbor: The University of Michigan Press, 2003). An excellent and very readable book exploring the heated contemporary debate over how history should be taught to elementary and high school students is Gary B. Nash, Charlotte Crabtree, and Ross E. Dunn, *History on Trial: Culture Wars and the Teaching of the Past* (New York: Random House, 1997).

SHOULD FELLOW CITIZENS
GET SPECIAL TREATMENT?

Partiality Toward Fellow Citizens Should Be Very Limited

ADVOCATE: Jeff McMahan, Professor of Philosophy, Rutgers University; author of *The Ethics of Killing: Problems at the Margins of Life* (New York: Oxford University Press, 2002).

SOURCE: "The Limits of National Partiality," in *The Morality of Nationalism*, edited by Robert McKim and Jeff McMahan (New York: Oxford University Press, 1997): 1107–138.

Significant Partiality Toward Fellow Citizens Is Justified

ADVOCATE: Thomas Hurka, Jackman Distinguished Professor of Philosophical Studies, University of Toronto; author of *Virtue, Vice, and Value* (New York: Oxford University Press, 2001) and *Perfectionism* (New York: Oxford University Press, 1993).

SOURCE: "The Justification of National Partiality," in *The Morality of Nationalism*, edited by Robert McKim and Jeff McMahan (New York: Oxford University Press, 1997): 139–157.

You are an American citizen, and you are able to donate $100 to disaster relief. Should you send the money to aid hurricane victims in Florida, or earthquake victims in Pakistan? If both groups are equally in need, and your donation would provide equal assistance in either place, is there any special obligation to aid your fellow citizens first? Suppose that the victims in Pakistan are in much greater need: their situation is life-threatening, while the circumstances in Florida are not so dire. Would it be morally *permissible* to give the money to the Florida victims, even though the Pakistan citizens are in greater need?

Ethical theories rarely make mention of national affiliation. When utilitarians state that the right act is the act that produces the greatest balance of pleasure over suffering for everyone, there is no national border restricting whose pain or pleasure counts. Kant pronounced a basic categorical imperative that applies equally to all rational agents, without regard to their nationality. Indeed, membership in a nation or group is more often mentioned in order to deny its relevance. Jesus of Nazareth taught that you should "love your neighbor as yourself," and in answer to the query of who counts as my neighbor, he told his famous parable of the Good Samaritan who provided care for an unfortunate robbery victim, with no regard for the man's nationality or ethnic group.

If there is an ethical obligation to count all persons equally when making our ethical judgments, without halting our deliberations at national boundaries or demanding a citizenship card, then clearly that ethical obligation is honored more by the breach than by the observance. The wealthy Western developed nations control the lion's share of the world's wealth, and they share but a tiny fraction with those in poverty. In Western developed nations excellent health care is provided for all citizens, housing is guaranteed for every citizen, education is offered to all children, and at least a sustenance level of food is provided for all citizens (the United States is the exception to this rule, but even the U.S. provides universal education for its children and minimal health care, housing, and food for a significant number of its impoverished citizens); but there is no aid at anything approaching that level for those hungry, sick, and impoverished persons of other countries and continents.

It is very common to suppose that we owe special treatment to our compatriots (or "conationals"), while having much less obligation to those who happen to live beyond our borders; yet it is difficult to reconcile this strong partiality—based on accident of birth—with our reflective ethical views. Is there a basis for this special partiality toward those within our national borders, or is this merely a traditional belief that cannot withstand scrutiny?

The basic contrast is between *cosmopolitan* and *nationalist* views of distributive justice. The cosmopolitan contends that principles of just distribution apply globally; while the nationalist limits distributive justice concerns within the nation (the nationalist may believe that it is generous and good to aid those in other countries, but does not believe that justice *requires* it—or if there does exist some distributive justice obligation to those of other nations, the obligation is significantly weaker than the obligation to conationals). The nationalist position is sometimes identified with a communitarian perspective; but the communitarian approach to ethics, with its emphasis on the importance of nurturing and sustaining special social community relationships, is usually focused on smaller communities than nation-states (if we speak of nations like the United States or Mexico or China or Italy as communities, that is more metaphorical than literal). Furthermore, many of the key arguments for nationalism are quite distinct from the communitarian position, and so the cosmopolitan/nationalist characterization is probably more helpful.

Jeff McMahan acknowledges the ethical demands of impartiality, but he also accepts the "common sense" belief that special obligations may hold toward those with whom we have special relations. His goal is to find a way to reconcile those distinct models of obligation, and his main tool in this reconciliation project is his concept of "complex identification." Thomas Hurka focuses on partiality toward conationals, and argues that the justification of such partiality requires a shared history of producing significant benefits; and that given such a genuine history, significant partiality toward conationals may be morally legitimate.

POINTS TO PONDER

➤ Nationalists compare relations among conationals with relations among family members, and seek to confer the blessings of the latter upon the former; cosmopolitans compare preferential treatment of conationals to racism, and thus cast nationalism in a much uglier light. Do these analogies elucidate or obfuscate the issue?

➤ If we pursue the "complex identification" that McMahan recommends, is it likely to evolve into a purely cosmopolitan outlook, with little room for nationalism?

➤ On Hurka's account of justified partiality toward conationals, would the degree of justified partiality among conationals vary widely with the nature and quality

309

of the nation? For example, if scientists in Venezuela discovered a plentiful and renewable and environmentally friendly source of energy that proved of great worldwide benefit, would citizens of Venezuela now be justified in showing a higher degree of partiality toward their fellow citizens?

Partiality Toward Fellow Citizens Should be Very Limited

Jeff McMahan

PARTIALITY AND IMPARTIALITY

Nations and Nationalism

"Nationalism" refers to a cluster of beliefs about the normative significance of nations and nationality....Nationalists typically hold...that the continued existence and flourishing of their own nation is a fundamental good, that the members of the nation ought to control their own collective affairs, and that membership in the nation makes it not only permissible but in many instances morally required to manifest loyalty and partiality to fellow members.

The defining characteristic of nationalism that will be the focus of this inquiry is its insistence that members of the same nation—*conationals*—are in many contexts permitted or even required to be partial to one another—that is, that they generally may and often must give some degree of priority to one another's interests over those of foreigners or nonmembers. This commitment to partiality within the nation appears to render nationalism incompatible with the guiding principle of liberalism that all persons are of equal worth and as such are entitled to equal concern and respect. It is, indeed, an axiom of modern moral thought that "no one is more important than anyone else....[E]veryone counts the same. For a

given quantity of whatever it is that's good or bad—suffering or happiness or fulfillment or frustration—its intrinsic impersonal value doesn't depend on whose it is." But to give priority to conationals is to show greater concern and respect for them than for others; it is to count one's conationals more than others.

The conflict here is not quite as stark as it may initially seem. The claim that partiality may be permitted or required among conationals does not necessarily deny that people have equal worth; it may instead deny that an individual's worth is the sole determinant of how he or she ought to be treated. It is possible to acknowledge that all persons have equal worth, and thus matter equally sub specie aeternitatis, while also holding that a person's moral status vis-à-vis a particular moral agent may depend not just on the intrinsic properties that determine this person's objective moral worth but also on the ways in which he or she is related to the agent. What the nationalist claims is that we are not all morally equidistant from one another—that a special relation between two people may give each a special moral reason to favor the other that neither has with respect to others outside the relation. These reasons are "agent-relative," specific to those who share a certain relation rather than universal. They do not imply that anyone is owed partiality by virtue of an objectively superior moral worth.

Still, nationalism does insist that conationals should have greater concern for one another than for others and should, other things being equal, give priority to one another's interests over the interests of others. And this is at least prima facie incompatible with the idea that all persons are entitled to equal concern and respect or that no one's interests count more than the equivalent interests of another.

Here, I believe that common sense should not be lightly dismissed. What most of us in fact believe is that there are at least two distinct sources of moral reasons, neither reducible to the other. First, an impartial core to morality imposes duties on all of us to respect the worth of others irrespective of whether or how we are related to them. But, second, the basic duties that we owe to one another may be supplemented by special moral reasons that arise from our relations with one another. The reasons deriving from these different sources compete for our attention, time, and resources. It is therefore one of the central tasks of moral and political philosophy to seek a coherent, determinate, and stable reconciliation of the competing demands that issue from these divergent sources. It is important to determine, in particular, what sorts of relation are capable of legitimizing partiality as well as how extensive the justified departures from strict impartiality are.

The Spectrum of Special Relations

The sentiment of partiality toward particular individuals is elicited by a variety of relations that one may bear to those individuals. One may be partial to members of one's family, friends, acquaintances, coworkers, coreligionists, members of one's local community, citizens of one's state, members of one's race, or even the members of one's species. In some instances—for example, friendship—the sentiment of partiality is partly constitutive of the nature of the relation. But manifestations of these various forms of partiality are not all equally defensible. Partiality within the family is almost universally recognized as paradigmatically legitimate. Parents are not only permitted to give a certain priority to the interests of their own children but also morally required to do so in a wide variety of circumstances. At the other end of the spectrum, partiality toward members of one's own race is widely condemned as a paradigmatically arbitrary, illegitimate, and pernicious form of discrimination.

Where does partiality within the nation lie along the spectrum from familial to racial partiality? Is conationality a legitimate or illegitimate basis for partiality? Intuitively, nationalism is an intermediate case. It is a phenomenon about which many are profoundly ambivalent. We tend to judge it by its effects, which are mixed. On the positive side, nationalism summons forth many virtues: loyalty, commitment, and self-sacrifice. Those who share the bonds of nationality enjoy the security of belonging as well as the self-esteem that is the paradoxical concomitant of self-transcendence; and when the nationalist ideal of self-determination is achieved, members of the nation typically find a measure of dignity and autonomy that they are denied by even the most benign paternalism that fails fully to share and therefore to understand or respect their culture. But to understand the moral ambiguity of nationalism one must also note its darker side, and each positive feature casts a deep shadow. The nationalist virtues are inherently truncated: it is betrayal to exercise them equally on behalf of outsiders. The comfortable sense of identity and belonging is obtained at the expense of those who are necessarily excluded. And even national pride and self-esteem may depend on a judgment, implicit or explicit, of the lesser worth of outsiders. Viewed thus, the pursuit of national self-determination may seem less an assertion of human dignity than a meretricious expression of atavistic tribal impulses that threaten endless political fragmentation and conflict. We therefore find it heartening when barriers between nations give way to recognition, cooperation, and integration—as seemed, until recently, to be happening in much of Europe. For, in general, it is better that people concentrate their attention on what they have in common than on what divides them. While it is true, of course, that nationalism, also, encourages the members of a nation to focus on their commonalities rather than their differences, nationalism seeks a heightened unity within the nation by stressing the otherness of those without. It unites some by dividing them from others.

THE JUSTIFICATION OF PARTIALITY

The Personal Point of View

One defense of partiality appeals to our nature as persons. We are not disinterested and impartial spectators; each of us has a distinct identity, is variously related to some individuals and not to others, and views the world from a unique perspective that naturally generates a pattern of concern and valuation that is inherently partial. Since morality must respect and reflect our nature as persons, it must acknowledge that each person has reasons for action that are generated by or within his or her own personal point of view. The personal point of view is thus an autonomous and authoritative source of moral reasons, though most theorists concede that it is not the only such source. According to one prominent theory, while our fundamental moral reasons are independent of the personal point of view, morality nevertheless accommodates the personal point of view by permitting each person to give somewhat greater weight to those things that specially matter from his or her own point of view than they would be assigned from an impartial point of view.

This is an important view. But there are reasons for skepticism about its ability to justify national partiality. It seems, for example, to make the permissibility of partiality toward a person depend upon subjective factors, such as whether one specially cares or is concerned about that person. But while this may be the principal basis for partiality in the case of certain comparatively rare personal relations, it is at most an ancillary factor in the case of most special relations. It is, for example, not because a mother specially cares about her son that she is justified in giving him priority over others; rather, it is the objective nature of the relation she bears to him that both warrants her special concern and grounds the special reasons she has to favor him. If merely caring more about some person were a sufficient reason for giving that person priority, then racist and other pernicious forms of partiality could be readily defended.

To assess whether it is legitimate for one person to show partiality to another, it is more important to understand the objective moral significance of the relations that obtain between them than to know what the one person's perceptions, sentiments, or interests are.

Instrumental Considerations

Special relations may be morally significant in various ways. Many special relations are, for example, instrumental to or even partially constitutive of human well-being. This is most obvious in the case of relations involving love. A life devoid of either the bestowal or the receipt of love would be incalculably impoverished. But love is discriminating or selective and involves a powerful disposition to favor those who are its objects; it is therefore necessarily partial. This form of partiality must be permitted, since it is an ineliminable concomitant of a relation that is necessary for human flourishing.

Against this, some have claimed that one should love impartially by loving everyone equally. But this is a psychological and perhaps conceptual impossibility. The empathetic bond established by love imposes a limit to one's capacity to endure the emotional strains of loving. No one could bear for long the death of a loved one each day. More important, a set of dispositions that could be evoked by anyone, whatever his or her personal characteristics, would have to be wholly undiscriminating and largely unchanged by emotion. But nothing that anemic could be so critical to individual well-being. We need not only to love selectively but also to be loved with a degree of exclusivity, in a way that distinguishes us as special. We need more than to be fairly illuminated by the diffuse light of a universal affection or to be ministered to by the cold hand of impartial benevolence. Thus even those who now suffer most from lack of love would surely prefer a world in which each person is specially loved by a few to a world in which each is cared about equally and impartially by everyone else. George Orwell was right when he observed that "love means nothing if it does not mean loving some people more than others"—and, one might add, loving some not at all.

Moral theories that insist on impartiality must take into account that many relations, like those based on love, have instrumental significance. Unless these theories treat impartiality as an end in itself, they must accept that it is often best, from the impartial point of view, to encourage participation in special relations that require partiality.

Dispositions that it is overall and impartially best for one to have will sometimes cause one to do what, in the circumstances, is worse from an impartial point of view—for example, succoring one's ailing spouse rather than working overtime in order to make a larger contribution to Oxfam. Some impartial theories imply that being guided by one's disposition in these circumstances is wrong, though this is an acceptable price to pay for having the disposition. In this respect, these theories clearly diverge from commonsense morality. But this is also true, though to a lesser degree, of those impartial theories that accept that it cannot be wrong to be compelled to act by dispositions that it is overall and impartially best for one to have. For given the vast inequalities between rich and poor in the contemporary world, the dispositions that it would be best in impartial terms for those in affluent countries to have are not those that are presently approved by commonsense morality. It would clearly be better, from the impartial point of view, for those in affluent societies to be less strongly disposed to care for family and friends and correspondingly more strongly disposed to make sacrifices to benefit the poor in other countries. Doubtless this would significantly impoverish our lives, but our losses would be amply counterbalanced by the gains to the poor.

Even if the rules or dispositions enjoined by the variants of Indirect Consequentialism were to coincide with those approved by commonsense morality, the convergence would be contingent and the theories would require the right acts for the wrong reasons. The suggestion that parents ought to cultivate strong dispositions to favor their own children because this arrangement is more conducive to the general happiness than the alternatives is a grotesque caricature of the sources of parental obligation.

The same objections apply to another common argument for the view that it is best in impartial terms for people to form strong personal attachments and to devote special care and concern to those to whom they are closely related. According to this argument, the most efficient way to ensure that people receive the care they need is to assign each person special responsibility for those to whom he or she is specially related. Although it has been repeatedly echoed in the recent literature, the classic statement of this argument appears in William Paley's *Principles of Moral and Political Philosophy*, which contends that "the good order and happiness of the world are better upholden whilst each man applies himself to his own concerns and the care of his own family...than if every man, from an excess of mistaken generosity, should leave his own business, to undertake his neighbour's, which he must always manage with less knowledge, conveniency, and success."

It is of course true that, in general, one is better situated than most others to promote the well-being of those to whom one is specially related, for typically one has a superior understanding of the nature of their interests, one is naturally motivated by ties of affection to enhance their well-being, and one's physical proximity gives one the capacity to assist in ways that those who live elsewhere cannot. But the affluent in the contemporary world are again an exception. The affluent are in a better position to care for the needs of millions of impoverished people in other countries than are those people's families, friends, or conationals. They know that what the impoverished most need is food and medicine, and they have the ability to fulfill these needs via such organizations as Oxfam. At least in the case of the affluent, therefore, the impartial perspective requires a distribution of responsibility that is radically different from that demanded by commonsense morality; they must divide their care and concern, and more particularly their resources, more evenly between those to whom they are specially related and those who are utter strangers.

One could dispute the details. But again the more important point is that this account fails altogether to capture our understanding of the moral significance of special relations. Could any parents really suppose that it is simply a matter of administrative efficiency that they have special responsibilities to their own children and that they would be relieved of those responsibilities were there an alternative distribution of duties that would be better for children generally, even if it would be worse for their own?

To deny that instrumental considerations are the essence of the morality of special relations is not to say that they have no moral significance. In many instances it may be part of the moral case for permitting partiality within special relations that these relations are important in various ways to human flourishing. In some instances this may indeed be the sole reason. But in general instrumental considerations are only a small, though conspicuous, part of the story.

The Intrinsic Significance of Special Relations

I have acknowledged that many special relations have a profound instrumental significance. Nothing could be more obvious than that our relations with one another, and particularly our close personal relations, are vital and indispensable elements of our happiness and well-being. In many cases, however, the moral significance of special relations is not exhausted by the valuable contributions they make to our lives. It seems, rather, that the territory marked out by certain relations between people constitutes an autonomous area within the domain of morality, so that the existence of these relations and the forms of behavior that are appropriate within them do not require justification in terms of anything else. It is part of the meaning or significance of these relations that they legitimize certain forms of partiality. The relations themselves are fundamental or foundational sources of moral reasons, including permissions and requirements. These reasons coexist and in some instances compete with reasons that arise in response to people's intrinsic or nonrelational properties.

The radical particularist gives one account of the reasons stemming from special relations: a morality just *is* a set of norms that evolve within and govern the various fundamental human relations. But many relations, I believe, have a universal moral significance, though of course they may take somewhat different forms in different settings, with each variant absorbing some of its moral flavor from the surrounding culture. Mutual love, for example, demands partiality wherever it occurs—which is to say, virtually everywhere. A relation that did not, given opportunities, both call forth and require partial behavior on at least some occasions would not be love at all. And while loving relations are among the essential ingredients of a good human life, the primary justification for love and its associated partiality is not instrumental. Morality urges us to foster loving relations and to care specially for those we love not just because this is good for both us and them, making all our lives richer and deeper, but because this is the *right* way to live. Loving relations are not just essential to the good life but are also partly constitutive of the *moral* life. Within

certain constraints that morality also imposes, expressions of love and special caring represent fundamental virtues whose justifiability does not depend on the contribution they make to any other good.

The relation that a parent bears to his or her child is similarly of intrinsic moral significance. This is not to say, however, that parental duties are morally primitive or unanalyzable. There seem, rather, to be multiple sources of parental duties: for example, the genetic or biological connection between parent and child, the voluntary assumption of responsibility (as in the case of adoption), responsibility for the child's need for aid arising from the act of having caused the child to exist, and so on. None of these possible bases for parental duties is instrumental to character. Purely instrumental considerations— for example, that the natural affection of parents for their children tends to make parents more competent caregivers for their own children than others—cannot, as we have noted, provide an adequate account of the grounds of parental duties.

We should recall, however, the multiplicity of human relations, some of which appear to legitimize partiality while others do not. Can we identify the features that tend to give certain relations their intrinsic significance? Are there any features that the various significant relations have in common? I will begin to explore these questions below, focusing particularly on the question whether conationality is a relation that has intrinsic moral significance. Before that, however, I will consider some arguments for nationalism that appeal to the instrumental significance of conationality. Even if there is much more to certain relations than their positive instrumental significance, the contribution they may make to certain goods, such as individual well-being, may alone be sufficient to justify our engaging in them and practicing the forms of partiality they require. This might be true of nationalism, independently of whether conationality itself has intrinsic moral significance.

THE INSTRUMENTAL CASE FOR NATIONALISM

The literature is replete with claims about the importance that membership in a national community and participation in its culture have in the lives of individuals. It is argued, for example, that particular cultures provide "horizons of significance," background standards of value by reference to which individuals are able to assess their options and choices. National identification and solidarity are also held to be necessary in large and otherwise impersonal modern societies in order to motivate the forms of cooperation and self-sacrifice that are needed to ensure a decent material standard of living. Finally, and most important, various claims have been made about the psychological significance of national affiliation. We all seek some measure of self-transcendence, an enlargement of the self beyond its narrow boundaries, an escape from the isolation and insignificance of singularity. Group membership offers an accessible mode of self-transcendence, and the nation, for reasons that remain somewhat obscure, offers a particularly compelling focus for collective identification. In the modern world, the nation has superseded the family and the religious community as the primary locus of collective self-identification and has become a fecund source of self-esteem. By investing our egos in it, we ensure that its triumphs become our own; by making its goals our own, we partake in its greater permanence; it becomes a continuer of the self, bestowing vicarious survival. It provides a sense of belonging, security, strength, and stability.

These and other claims about the value that national affiliation has within the lives of individuals form the basis of an argument that parallels that given above for the partiality that goes with love. The second step in this argument is to note that, like love, participation in national life necessarily involves partiality. Social psychologists have long known that people naturally tend to favor fellow members of any groups to which they belong, however arbitrarily those groups may be distinguished from others. And the impulse to partiality is that much stronger in national communities, whose members tend to share certain values and to be engaged in the pursuit of common goals. Therefore, we may conclude that national partiality must be accepted as an unavoidable aspect of arrangements that are necessary for the good human life.

Matters are, however, more complicated than this. We may grant that national affiliation and partiality contribute much of value to the lives of individuals. But their darker side—the exclusivity, chauvinism, and hostility to outsiders—must also be taken into account. And even if the good features do outweigh the bad, that alone is insufficient to establish an instrumental justification for nationalism if there are alternative forms of collective identification that would fulfill the same needs that national membership does but without some of nationalism's more disturbing features. (If, moreover, it is assumed that conationality has no intrinsic moral significance, so that the instrumental argument must stand on its own, then the net benefit that people derive from national attachments must be sufficiently great to override the objection that it is unjust to discriminate among people on the basis of relations that lack intrinsic significance.)

Some, of course, have argued that the cosmopolitan ideal of identification with humanity as a whole—of being, as Diogenes put it, "a citizen of the world"—can offer much the same range of benefits that identification with one's nation provides. But this is improbable. Given that people have always tended to bond together in bounded communities, there are doubtless evolutionary mechanisms that make an eradication of particularist identities unfeasible. Moreover, the sense of identity and belonging that accompanies membership in a nation may crucially depend on the contrast between one's own nation and others. Without others to serve as foils, there would be nothing distinctive about one's own nation and thus no basis for identification. Similarly, the enhanced self-esteem that accompanies the enlargement of one's ego through identification with the nation may require an implied comparison with other nations, a sense that one's own nation is superior, at least in certain respects, to others.

But nationalism and cosmopolitanism are not exhaustive of the possibilities. There is no necessity to choose between, for example, being simply a Serb and being a citizen of the world. While it is impossible to avoid being to some extent a child of one's culture, it is also the mark of a drone to accept with docility or without reflection a ready-made, mass-manufactured, one-dimensional conception of oneself as a Serb, Hutu, Chechen, or whatever. This is the stuff of which impoverished lives are made. Thus Schopenhauer noted that "the cheapest form of pride is national pride; for the man affected therewith betrays a want of *individual* qualities of which he might be proud, since he would not otherwise resort to that which he shares with so many millions." To acquiesce in a vision of oneself in which nationality overshadows the other variegated dimensions of one's life, character, and relations with others is to suffer a miserable reduction of the richness of one's identity. Other elements of

one's actual identity, as well as further possibilities for self-creation, get crowded out of one's self-conception and may, from inattention and neglect, eventually fade from one's identity altogether.

It is not only the distinctive individual qualities of which Schopenhauer wrote that may be displaced from one's conception of oneself by a hypertrophied, metastasizing national identity; other forms of group identification may be withered as well. In most cases, there are numerous social and political dimensions to a person's identity; we are all mongrel to a greater or lesser degree. One may be, for example, a pacifist, a philosopher, a socialist, a southerner, a vegetarian, a ruralist, a belletrist, a squash player, or all of these at once. Membership in and identification with a range of groups may enrich one's life, extend one's sympathies and bonds with others, and thereby lessen the potential for incomprehension of and conflict with others. Both prudence and an impartial concern with consequences therefore suggest that it is desirable for people to cultivate complex, multilayered group identifications.

Let us call this model of self-identification "complex identification" and contrast it with "national identification," in which nationality has a commanding role in shaping a person's identity. Complex identification does not, of course, exclude nationality as an element of individual identity; it merely denies nationality the preeminent importance assigned to it by the nationalist. The possibility of complex identification suggests that national identification is not necessary for the goods that it often provides: a cultural context, the security of belonging, self-esteem, social solidarity, and so on. These goods seem compatible with complex identification. Culture, for example, need not be monolithic. One may participate in and draw sustenance from a variety of overlapping cultures. And nations are only one source of culture. Many subnational cultures can exist within a single nation, whose unity may be more political or religious than cultural, and there can also be a union of nations whose historical cultures coexist within and contribute to a larger, encompassing culture based in part on respect for diversity. Who can say, in advance of experience, where the limits to what is possible lie? Collectivities other than the nation can, moreover, provide a sense of belonging, security, self-esteem, and so on. A robust sense of connectedness with others can be achieved through identifying oneself with a variety of collectivities.

In addition to offering richer, more distinctive individual identities, complex identification has the advantage of recognizing and fostering diverse attachments that cross national boundaries, thereby broadening people's understanding of and sympathy with others and reducing the propensity for conflict characteristic of more exclusive national identities. While complex identification preserves the disposition to loyalty and partiality, it generates a more complex pattern of differentiation and commonality in one's relations with others and thus gives partiality a more diffuse focus than the national identification allows.

Complex identification also calls for different political and institutional structures from those that are appropriate to national identification. Complex identification is naturally expressed not by molding political life to fit the national unit but by separating the two. Political units should be built around explicitly political rather than national or cultural identities. Thus solidarity in political life should to the maximum extent be based on shared political ideals and commitments, not on inherited national or ethnic ties. Correlatively, national life should be relegated, in-sofar as possible, to the private sphere, with national self-determination expressed more in cultural than in political terms.

THE INTRINSIC SIGNIFICANCE OF CONATIONALITY

The idea that we should seek to diminish the role national identification plays in our lives loses force if conationality is a relation that has deep intrinsic moral significance. In this section, we will consider whether conationality is indeed a source of moral reasons that are underived from anything other than the nature of the relation itself.

Commonalities

Conationality is not a simple relation but is compounded out of the various relations mentioned earlier that unite people into nations—relations involving commonalities of language, ethnicity, religion, culture, custom, and so on. Conationality consists in these *relations of commonality* and typically does not involve *personal* relations at all, for most of a person's conationals are strangers to him or her. It is the various ways in which one's conationals are *like oneself* that primarily distinguish them from others. Are these various commonalities of intrinsic or foundational moral significance and thus capable of generating special moral reasons for those who share them to favor one another in certain contexts?

Which commonalities, if any, do have intrinsic moral significance? *Commonalities of virtue*—that is, shared values, ideals, commitments, or even interests (in the sense of *being* interested in the same thing rather than *having* an interest in the same thing)—seem more likely to be morally significant than commonalities that do not involve any congruence of values. Of course, obvious restrictions apply. Shared values that are perverse or evil do not legitimize partiality. Nor, it seems, do shared values that are utterly trivial. Assuming that commonalities of value can be intrinsically significant, the degree to which they are significant depends on the worthiness or importance of the relevant values. It also depends on how large a role the values have in people's lives.

Is it a reason for being partial to conationals that they share one's values or share with oneself certain features or characteristics that one values or admires? Certainly commonalities of value and valued commonalities constitute a basis for harmony, compatibility of character, and mutual understanding, sympathy, and esteem—things that draw people together and make them comfortable with one another. These commonalities are therefore elements in the psychological basis for partiality within nations. But as we have seen, the fact that a relation elicits partiality is no guarantee that it is a legitimate basis for partiality.

Even if we can detect certain broad and general commonalities of value or valued commonalities among the members of a nation, a significant number of members will not share the relevant values or manifest the national character and many nonmembers will. Suppose, however, that certain commonalities of value or valued commonalities are intrinsically significant, and suppose that some of these were to bind all and only the members of a particular nation together. How much would this pair of assumptions yield? It seems that commonalities of these sorts could at most make it *permissible* for those who share them to show a limited degree of partiality to one another. These commonalities could not support special *obligations*. Suppose that two philosophers both value rational argument and that both excel at it. Between them there is both a commonality of value and a valued commonality. While this might make it per-

missible for them to be partial to one another in certain contexts, it clearly does not *require* them to, even if the value they share is a worthy one. Special obligations cannot, it seems, be contingent on something as changeable as an individual's personal values. If there really were special obligations between the two philosophers, neither could be released simply by converting to mysticism.

In sum, what seem to be the most intrinsically significant commonalities within nations cannot provide the justification for the forms of partiality essential to nationalism. For the relevant commonalities are not universal within the nation and are, in fact, shared by many outside the nation. And even if they were possessed by all and only the members of the nation, they would be incapable of grounding special obligations rather than mere permissions. And nationalism certainly holds that loyalty to and partiality within the nation are duties rather than mere options.

Reciprocity, Gratitude, and Devotion

The relations of commonality that obtain between conationals, as individuals, do not seem intrinsically sufficiently significant to ground duties of mutual partiality. However, other aspects of their relations do seem capable of generating special duties among them that are not merely instrumentally justified. I will suggest that there are two distinct sources of special duties among conationals, one found in their relations with one another, the other in each individual's relation to the nation as a whole.

One source of special duties among conationals is familiar from the theory of political obligation. One who engages in voluntary cooperative endeavors with others normally benefits from the contributions that others make to these endeavors and thereby acquires duties of fair play to reciprocate. Conationals are typically engaged with one another in multifarious, continuing cooperative activities. Salient among these are the normal political, economic, and social forms of cooperation necessary among citizens of the same state, for conationals are usually, though obviously not invariably, citizens of the same state. To this extent, the account of permitted and required partiality among conationals overlaps with the theory of political obligation. But conationals also engage in various common projects and activities that are nonpolitical or unconnected with citizenship. For insofar as they together constitute a nation, which is an active association spanning many generations, they are necessarily involved in sustaining and continuously re-creating their culture and way of life as well as transmitting the cultural heritage to their descendants. These various activities that make up the life of a nation are a further source of duties of reciprocity.

The second source of special duties among conationals is related to the first. As we just noted, a nation is, among other things, a grand collective project spanning many generations that furnishes countless profound and indispensable benefits to its members. However much one may repudiate certain elements of it, one is nevertheless deeply indebted to one's nation and its culture. They have provided the language in which one thinks and speaks, the intellectual and artistic heritage that informs one's sensibility and one's understanding of both oneself and the world, many of the values that give purpose to one's life and structure one's relations with others, numerous elements of the material and social infrastructures that make a decent life possible, and so on, almost indefinitely. In short, the nation itself, as a transhistorical entity, is one's benefactor, and there are duties that one owes to it in consequence.

DOMESTICATING NATIONALISM

In the previous two sections, I have advanced two claims. First, I suggested that it would be better, where considerations of consequences are concerned, if we were to foster more complex individual identities, with the present intensive focus on national identification yielding to a richer, more varied pattern of collective identifications. This would result in people's having more diversified group affinities and loyalties and thus a diminished inclination to national partiality. Second, I claimed that people are bound by duties of gratitude to endeavor to preserve and to promote the flourishing of their nations and that the fulfillment of these duties often requires people to favor their conationals over others. It may be doubted, however, whether these claims are compatible. For it may seem that to fulfill one's duties of gratitude to one's nation one must manifest a degree of loyalty and partiality to its members that would exceed what the proposal for complex identification regards as desirable.

These are not matters that can be readily quantified. But it is reasonable to suppose that the diminution of national identification and partiality required by complex identification is compatible with the fulfillment of one's duties of gratitude to one's nation. The central goals of complex identification are to diminish national chauvinism and exclusivity and to facilitate and encourage mutual understanding and recognition, cooperation, and mutual aid among nations. And what these goals require is mainly that people's individual identities should accord appropriate recognition to the numerous profound commonalities that span divisions between nations and that national life and culture should be confined to a greater degree to the private rather than the political sphere. To see that this is compatible with extensive loyalty to the nation and partiality to its members, consider the case of the family.

There have been times when families were more like nations are now. Clans, family dynasties, and landed aristocratic families have at times had many of the characteristic features of modern nations: they have been important sources of individual identity, boasted of mythical bloodlines traceable back to ancient heroes, endowed their members with an invincible conviction of their superiority to others, and even been territorially based and often expansionist. But the family as a social unit and locus of partiality has now, with some exceptions in certain countries, been tamed. In contemporary Western societies, families are neither competitive nor antagonistic, are not a basis for political organization, do not compete with one another for power, and are considerably less important as sources of individual identity than they once were (for example, it is now rare for one to identify oneself as "one of the Shropshire Smiths" or "the Virginia Jone-

ses"). Yet the family retains a vital role in people's lives, and family members remain intensely loyal and partial to one another. This shows, I think, that people may care intensely about one another, share a way of life together, and recognize an array of special duties to one another without regarding other groupings of the same sort as "outgroups" that are appropriately despised as alien and inferior.

What we should seek through complex identification is a transformation of the nation that parallels, in relevant respects, that which the family has gradually undergone. The nation must be tamed and domesticated. This requires action at the individual and institutional levels. Individuals must be encouraged to see themselves as more than drones in the national hive, and institutions must be arranged, both within and between states, to enable nations to coexist harmoniously while at the same time retaining their autonomy and cultural integrity.

Significant Partiality Toward Fellow Citizens Is Justified

Thomas Hurka

The moral issues about nationalism arise from the character of nationalism as a form of partiality. Nationalists care more about their own nation and its members than about other nations and their members; in that way nationalists are partial to their own national group. The question, then, is whether this national partiality is morally justified or, on the contrary, whether everyone ought to care impartially about all members of all nations. As Jeff McMahan emphasizes, a philosophical examination of this question must consider the specific features of nationalism as one form of partiality among others. Some partiality—for example, toward one's spouse and children—seems morally acceptable and even a duty. According to commonsense moral thinking, one not only may but also should care more about one's family members than about strangers. But other instances of partiality, most notably racial partiality, are in most circumstances widely condemned. Is national partiality more like familial partiality or more like racial partiality? To answer this question, we must know what in general justifies attitudes of partiality. Caring more about certain people is appropriate when one stands in certain special relations to those people. But what are these relations, and to what degree do they hold among members of the same nation? Assuming they are present within families and not within races, to what degree are they present within nations?

NATIONALISM AND IMPERSONAL GOODS

Many writers speak simply of being partial to one's nation without explaining further what that means. Some speak, more specifically, of being partial toward one's conationals—that is, of giving more weight to the interests of individuals in one's nation than to those of other individuals. This is certainly one aspect of nationalism, but I believe there is often another aspect.

In a number of writings Charles Taylor has emphasized the importance of cultural survival as a good and value for minority groups. In *Multiculturalism and "The Politics of Religion,"* for example, he writes: "It is axiomatic for Quebec governments that the survival and flourishing of French culture in Quebec is a good." Noting the importance of this insight, McMahan says it shows how for participants in a culture its survival has "impersonal value." I agree that in one important sense the survival of a culture is an "impersonal" value or good, but in another sense, which seems to be the one McMahan has in mind, it is not, or is not most importantly, impersonal.

The survival of a culture is an impersonal good in the sense that it is not reducible to the goods of individual persons, or to goods located in individual persons' lives. Consider francophone Quebeckers who care deeply that there be a French culture in Quebec three generations from now. Do they believe that the survival of

French culture is a good because better human lives will be lived if French culture survives than if it does not? Do they believe, more specifically, that their great-grandchildren will lead better lives if they are born and raised in a French culture than if, that culture having disappeared, those great-grandchildren are born and raised as full members of an English culture? I do not believe these Quebeckers need or even should, if they wish to avoid chauvinism, believe this. They should grant that after enough time the disappearance of French culture would not be worse for persons in the sense of making the lives lived by persons worse. If, despite this, they continue to view the survival of their culture as a good, they must view it as an impersonal good in the following sense: it would be better if French culture survived even if this would not make the lives persons live more valuable.

Valuing cultural survival in this way does not require the metaphysical view that cultures or nations exist separately from, or over and above, their individual members. It is fully compatible with the reductionist view that facts about nations consist entirely in facts about individuals and the relations between them. According to this reductionist view, for French culture to survive in Quebec is only and entirely for individuals in Quebec to live and interact in certain ways. But while holding that the *existence* of a culture is reducible to facts about individuals, a nationalist can deny that the *good* of the culture's existing is reducible to the *goods* of individuals. The fact that people interact in certain ways can have a value that is separate from the values present in their individual lives.

Cultural survival, then, is an impersonal good in the sense that it does not consist in the goods of individual persons. But the word "impersonal" is often used in another sense, one equivalent to "impartial." In this sense, an impersonal good is one it is appropriate for all agents to desire and pursue and to weigh impartially against other similar goods. This seems to be the sense McMahan has in mind when he calls cultural survival an "impersonal value." He introduces the topic of survival while discussing the instrumental arguments that can be given, from an impartialist standpoint, for endorsing some degree of national partiality, and he considers it alongside a value that cannot but be impersonal in this second sense—namely, that of the overall cultural diversity of the world. But it seems to me that cultural survival is valued by nationalists, and is thought by them appropriately valued, in a highly partial way. Who is it who cares about the survival of French culture in Quebec? It is surely, above all, francophone Quebeckers. And they do not care about their culture's survival only in an impartial way, or merely as contributing to a universal good such as overall cultural diversity. If they did, they would gladly accept the disappearance of French culture in Quebec if that somehow allowed the survival of two other cultures elsewhere in the world. This is not their attitude; they care specially about the survival of *their own* culture. In the same way, it seems to me, people outside a culture do not have nearly as much reason to care about its survival as a good. McMahan writes that people outside a culture "are capable of appreciating its intrinsic value" and of "perceiving in a particular alien culture a variety of merits that may not be replicated in any other culture." But these remarks, though true, do not suffice to establish the appropriateness of impartial concern for another culture. I can appreciate that the well-being of someone else's children is a good while believing that I ought to care much more about my own children's wellbeing. And in my view commonsense nationalism does not give people outside a culture much moral duty to care directly about the culture's survival. This is obscured in many actual situations by the fact that the members of the culture do desire its survival. Thus if francophone Quebeckers care deeply about their culture's survival, this gives other people, and especially anglophone Canadians, a reason of a more familiar kind to support measures that will ensure the culture's survival—namely, that Quebeckers desire it. But what if a majority of Quebeckers ceased to care about their culture's survival and instead preferred assimilating into English culture? In this situation I believe Quebeckers in the minority would still feel a strong duty to fight for their culture and to try to persuade the majority to change their minds. But non-Quebeckers would surely not feel any such strong duty, nor would they be failing in not feeling it. They might appropriately feel some mild regret about the loss of a distinctive culture and the loss of some overall diversity in the world, but they would not feel strongly bound to prevent the assimilation, for example, by offering subsidies to Quebeckers who retain their French culture. When it is considered in itself and apart from the desires it gives rise to in members, the survival of a culture does not seem to be something that, according to commonsense nationalism, nonmembers have a strong reason to care about or pursue.

I have suggested that cultural survival, though an impersonal good in the sense that it is not reducible to the goods of individuals, is the object of highly partial attitudes. The same can be true of other impersonal goals associated with a culture. For example, nationalists can care that their cultures not only survive but also achieve the full flowering or self-expression that comes through sovereignty and independent statehood. In this case the importance of the impersonal good may be harder to see because there can also be personal goods at stake in sovereignty. Thus nationalists may believe that the individuals in their culture will engage in more valuable political activity or live under more culturally sensitive institutions if their government is entirely their own. But if it is possible to value the survival of one's culture apart from any benefits to individuals, it is surely possible to value sovereignty and statehood in the same way, and I think those active in independence movements do commonly have this impersonal desire. They value their nation's sovereignty and statehood in the same way, and I think those active in independence movements do commonly have this impersonal desire. They value their nation's sovereignty, as they value their culture's survival, as something good partly in itself. Thus a central force in the Quebec sovereignty movement has been the desire that francophone Quebeckers affirm their status as *un peuple* by establishing their own nation-state. In fact, nationalists can have many impersonal goals that they value in a partial way: that their culture flourish in the arts and sciences, that it be economically vigorous, that it produce athletes who win medals at the Olympics. Beyond this, nationalists can have impersonal political goals that they value partially: that their nation occupy a large territory, that it be militarily powerful, that it dominate its neighbors and even dictate to the world.

In this list of impersonal goals, there is a large moral difference between the innocuous first goal, cultural survival, and the politically threatening ones that come later, such as military power and world domination. But this is nothing new in the study of nationalism, which is often described as Janus-faced, attractive in some forms and terrifying in others. And our responses to the list may be guided by the view, which many writers on this subject endorse, that any acceptable form of national partiality must be constrained by respect for the basic rights of all individuals, no less in other countries than in one's own. One may pursue one's own nation's good and do so in preference to other nations' good but only in ways that respect fundamental rights. As it happens, the more acceptable impersonal goals, such as cultural survival, can usually be pursued successfully without violating anyone's rights, whereas it is hard to see territorial expansion or world domination achieved without violating rights. The different impersonal goals may differ morally not so much in themselves, therefore, as in the means likely to be necessary for their achievement.

I do not claim that every form of nationalism involves concern for impersonal goods; some nationalists may favor only the interests of their individual conationals. But it seems to me that the two forms of partiality often go together, and I will therefore define *full-blooded nationalism* as combining a greater concern for the impersonal goods of one's own culture, such as its survival and flourishing, with a greater concern for the interests of one's conationals. In a phrase I have used above, full-blooded nationalism involves partiality both toward one's nation, seen as having certain impersonal goods, and toward one's conationals. If this characterization is correct, it has an important implication for the morality of nationalism.

If full-blooded nationalism involves two components, a successful moral justification of it must address both. It must show the appropriateness of partiality toward one's conationals and also toward one's nation's impersonal good. Here the difficulties facing the two justifications seem interestingly different.

Consider, first, partiality toward one's conationals. There is no doubt that one ought morally to care about one's conationals; they are people, and one ought in general to care about people. The difficulty is to show why one should care more about these people than about others who are not members of one's nation, or why partiality toward this particular group is appropriate. In the situation where partiality seems most clearly justified, that of the family, it rests on a special relationship between people that is both rich and intense. The members of a family care deeply about each other, have lived together for many years, and have to a significant degree shaped each other's characters. Their interactions have been as close as people's typically ever are. But the relations among conationals are nothing like this. I have never met the vast majority of my fellow Canadians and do not know who they are; the causal links between our lives are tenuous at best. Especially worrisome is the fact that these links do not seem closer than my links with many non-Canadians—for example, with Americans living just across the Alberta-Montana border. In fact, with respect to closeness, the relations among conationals seem comparable to those among members of a race, who likewise mostly have not met. If the relations between conationals hold only to a limited degree, and not much more than between non-nationals, how can they justify any substantial degree of partiality?

The justification of the second form of partiality, toward one's nation's impersonal good, faces the opposite difficulty. Here there does not seem to be a large problem about justifying the attitude's partiality. Only one culture or nation in the world is mine; all the others are not mine. This is not just a small difference in degree but a large difference, perhaps a difference in kind. So if the justification of strong partiality requires a large difference in linkage or connectedness, we have that here. The problem, rather, is to show that impersonal goods are morally appropriate objects of any concern in the first place. What can be called "individualist" theories of the good deny this. Individualist theories hold that the only goods there are, and thus the only objects of rational concern, are personal goods, or the goods of individuals. According to individualism, nationalists who value the survival or flourishing of their culture apart from any effects on individuals are being irrational and fetishistic. Their attitude is objectionable not because of its partiality but because of its object, which is not a genuine good because it is not a feature of individuals' lives. Nor is it only individualism in the strict sense that counts against the second form of partiality. A more moderate view allows that there can be impersonal goods and rational concern for them but insists that these goods are always relatively minor and the concern they call for always of less weight than the concern required for individuals. According to this moderate view, a partial attitude toward one's nation's impersonal good is allowed but not in a strength that often allows promoting that good at the expense of benefits to individuals.

To summarize: If there are two forms of national partiality, they need two justifications, and the difficulties facing these justifications are different. That one should care somehow about one's conationals is not in doubt; the question is whether it is right to care more about them than about non-nationals. As for a nation's impersonal good, if some concern for it is appropriate, it seems plausible that this is a highly partial concern. The difficult question here is

whether that initial concern is appropriate: whether impersonal goods are worth caring about or whether the only, or only important, goods are those of individuals.

PARTIALITY AND HISTORY

Having suggested the importance to nationalism of impersonal goods, I will now set them aside and consider the more commonly recognized aspect of nationalism: partiality toward one's conationals. This partiality has many more specific manifestations. Nationalists typically care much more about relieving economic hardship within the nation than outside it; compare what nations spend on domestic welfare programs with what they spend on foreign aid. Nationalists also want immigration policy decided primarily by considering the effects on people already within the nation rather than on those who want to join. These various positions may receive some support from concern for impersonal goals like the nation's flourishing as a collective, but they are primarily directed at individuals. Setting aside the impersonal component of nationalism, therefore, I will consider the moral justification of partiality toward one's individual conationals. When partiality toward certain individuals is justified, it is because certain special relations hold between oneself and them. To what degree do these relations hold between members of a nation?

Because the arena in which partiality seems most clearly justified is the family, defenders of nationalism often try to assimilate the relations among conationals to those among family members. As we have seen, however, this assimilation is problematic; especially in the degree of interaction they involve, nations are not like large families. To many writers, therefore, it has seemed that the degree of national partiality that is justified is even in the most favorable circumstances much less than most nationalists desire.

In this section I will sketch a reply to this widespread skepticism about national partiality. This reply concedes that along one important dimension the relations between conationals have much less of the character that justifies partiality than do familial relations, but it claims that along another dimension, which most writers ignore, they have roughly as much.

First, however, I must state a presupposition of my argument: that the basis of partiality among conationals must be an objective rather than a subjective relation and, in particular, cannot be just the fact that conationals care more about each other than about non-nationals. It may be, as is sometimes argued, that certain subjective facts—that is, certain attitudes on the part of individuals—are necessary for a nation to exist. For example, it may be that individuals must view membership in a group as an important part of their identity before the group constitutes a nation. But questions about when a nation exists are different from questions about when its members should be partial toward each other, and the latter questions cannot turn on mere facts about caring. There are two decisive arguments for this conclusion. One is that a purely subjective basis could not rule out the racial partiality that most of us find morally offensive. The fact that racists care more about people with their own skin color would by itself make it right for them to do so. The second argument is that a subjective basis cannot justify what nationalists typically affirm—namely, a duty to favor one's conationals that is binding even on those who do not now care about their conationals. I will assume, then, that the basis of national partiality must be some objective relation—that is, some relation that

holds independently of people's attitudes. To determine which relation this is, we must look more closely at the objective side of personal or familial relations.

Consider my relation to my wife. If I love her specially, it is partly for certain qualities that she has. Some of these qualities I am attracted to without judging them to be intrinsically good, such as her appearance and the sound of her voice. Others I do judge to be good, such as her trustworthiness, her intelligence, and her concern for other people. Especially with these latter qualities it is important that my beliefs about them be true, that she, in fact, have the qualities, and that they truly be good. But even if all my relevant beliefs are true, my wife's having these qualities does not explain all my emotional attachment to her. If it did, I would abandon my wife the moment someone else came along with the same properties to a higher degree. Or if, just before dying, my wife had a clone of herself made to stay with me, I would think myself no worse off for the exchange. But of course I would not trade in my wife in this way. Though I love her partly for her qualities, I do not do so in a way that would accept substitution. I also love her, in the common phrase, "as an individual," or for herself.

What does it mean to love a person "as an individual"? In my view, it does not mean loving a person apart from any qualities at all but rather loving the person for certain historical qualities, ones deriving from his or her participation with one in a shared history. Thus I love my wife not only as trustworthy, intelligent, and so on but also as the person who nursed me through that illness, with whom I spent that wonderful first summer, and with whom I discovered that hotel on Kootenay Lake. These historical qualities focus my love on my wife as an individual, since no substitute, not even a clone, can be the very person who did those things with me.

A highly romantic view of love and friendship holds that once these historical qualities are established they entirely determine the relationship, which should therefore never end and always imposes duties of partiality. This is the view expressed in Shakespeare's line: "Love is not love / Which alters when it alteration finds." But I think most of us believe that historical qualities, though part of the basis for love and friendship, are, again, not the entire basis. If my wife changes radically, losing the general or shareable qualities I admire and taking on ones I find despicable, I will no longer feel attached to her or bound by duties of partial concern. My love, in other words, has a dual basis. My wife's role in a shared history with me explains why I love her more than other people with similar general qualities, but her general qualities matter, too. If those qualities changed enough, our history would not be a sufficient basis to maintain my love or to continue to demand partiality toward her.

We can see the same dual basis in nationalists' attachment to their nation and conationals. Nationalists are, first, attracted to their culture and the activities that define it, thinking them to a considerable degree good. They need not believe that their culture is superior in the sense of being the single best in the world. That chauvinist belief would not be credible and, in any case, would justify not universalist nationalism but the belief that everyone in the world should promote the one best culture. Instead, nationalists need only believe that their culture is one of perhaps many in the world that are good. What attaches them specially to this culture and its members are historical facts: that this is the culture *they* grew up in, that their conationals share *with them* a

history of being shaped by, participating in, and sustaining this culture. The favorable evaluation of their conationals' cultural activities is a necessary basis for this nationalist attachment, but it is not sufficient. There is also, and distinguishing their conationals from other people whose culture is equally good, the crucial fact of a shared cultural history.

This dual basis can lead to conflicts about national attachment. As Yael Tamir writes, "Citizens of a state involved in an unjust war may be torn between the feeling that they have an associative obligation to serve in the army together with their enlisted fellows, and their commitment to a moral code dictating they should refuse." In the situation Tamir describes, the citizens' state is not now good; it has at least some general qualities that are evil. But the citizens are still historically connected to this state as the one they grew up under. How they resolve this conflict depends on which of the two bases of national attachment they find more important, which in many particular cases will depend on how evil their state currently is. If it is not irredeemably evil, the citizens may continue to feel special duties toward it and work harder to reform it than to reform other equally evil states elsewhere. But if their state degenerates too far, their historical connection to it may be outweighed and their feelings of national attachment, like love for an individual whose character has changed utterly, may end.

If national attachment rests partly on the belief that one's culture is good, it is important that that belief be true, which requires the culture to be, in fact, good. This is one point where evaluative considerations bear on the justification of national partiality, but there is another point as well. Considerations about good and evil also help determine when a shared history is of the right kind to justify partial concern and, when it is, what degree of partiality is justified.

Consider again a personal relationship like that between spouses. Here the shared history is predominantly one of mutual benefit or beneficence; two people have helped each other through difficult times and also shared good times, giving and taking pleasure in each other's company. And I think a history of reciprocal benefit or, alternatively, one where people have jointly benefited others, such as the students in a school where these people taught, can be a legitimate basis of partiality. The same is true of a history of shared suffering; people who lived in the same barracks in a Nazi labor camp and suffered the same evils there can appropriately feel on the basis of their shared history some greater concern for each other's well-being. But I do not think a shared history justifies partiality when it is a history of doing evil, as for former members of an SS unit that ran and terrorized a labor camp. Many of us find something obscene in the idea of nostalgic reunions, even at this late date, of former SS colleagues, and there is a similar obscenity in the idea of partiality toward former SS colleagues. If an SS veteran receives a letter from one of his former colleagues claiming financial hardship and requesting a loan of $1,000, should he feel a special duty to honor the request or to help his former colleague before helping others who are equally in need? It seems to me that he should not, even if his former colleague is now morally reformed. If anything, given the evil of the history they share, he should feel a duty not to associate with his former colleague and should contribute first to others who did not participate in that aspect of his past. Whereas a shared history of doing good or suffering evil can justify duties of partiality, a shared history of doing evil cannot.

These points suggest a general account of the basis of duties of partiality. Some activities and states of people, most notably their doing good or suffering evil, call for a positive, caring, or associative response. Others, such as their doing evil, call for a negative or dissociative response. Partiality between people is appropriate when they have shared in the past in the first kind of activity or state. For example, if two people have a shared history of doing good, either reciprocally or to others, partiality between them in the present is a way of honoring that good fact about their past. (This is why partiality among former SS colleagues is troubling; it seems to honor a past that properly calls for dishonor.) One should, in general, care more about people who have shared with one in activities and states that call for a caring response. This account does not claim to justify partiality of concern as a general moral phenomenon; on the contrary, it assumes it. It assumes that one has a special duty to honor past doings of good or sufferings of evil *that involved oneself.* But it does give particular duties of partiality a more abstract basis. In the many realms where partiality is appropriate—the family, private clubs, perhaps the nation—it is an appropriate response to a history that joins oneself and other people in activities or states that are good or that call for association.

This general account can explain our attitudes to racial partiality. As McMahan notes, while we condemn racial discrimination by members of a dominant racial group, we often think it appropriate for minority races to celebrate their distinctness and even to implement discriminatory policies that benefit their members at the expense of others. In current conditions, black and aboriginal solidarity movements have a different moral status than white supremacy movements. The explanation, I would argue, is that minority racial groups have a shared history of the kind that makes partiality morally appropriate—namely, a shared history of suffering evil because of one's racial membership. But the history of dominant racial groups, which is largely one of oppressing the minority, is not the kind that justifies partiality. Among members of the minority, there is a shared history that morally warrants partiality toward other members; among members of the majority, there is one that positively precludes it.

More important, the account suggests a defense of national partiality against the skeptical argument mentioned above. If certain people have a shared history of doing good, what determines the degree of partiality that is justified between them? Two factors suggest themselves: the degree to which the people's history is shared or involves interaction between them, and the amount of good their interaction produced. Other things being equal, people whose history involves closer relations or more intimate contact have stronger duties of partiality. Also, other things being equal, people whose interactions produced more good, for themselves or for others, have stronger duties of partiality.

The history of family members scores extremely high on the first of these dimensions—namely, closeness of contact. Family members interact intimately on a daily basis, with large effects on each other's lives. Family history also scores high on the dimension of good done, given the large benefits given by parents to their children, spouses to each other, and even children to their parents. Surely family members benefit each other as much as they do any individuals.

A nation's history, by contrast, scores very low on the first dimension. As I have said, I have not met the majority of my fellow Canadians and do not know who they are. But a nation's history does much

better on the second dimension. Consider another example from my history. In the 1960s Canadians created a national health care system that continues to provide high-quality medical care to all citizens regardless of their ability to pay. The benefit this medicare system provides any one citizen is probably less than that provided by his or her family, but it is still substantial, and it is one Canadians have provided together. Canadians derive equally substantial benefits from many other aspects of their political activity. When these benefits are added together, they constitute a significant counterweight to the weakness of national relations on the first dimension, that of closeness of contact. The critique of national partiality considers only this first dimension, of closeness. But if we believe that a necessary basis for justified partiality is a shared history, that this history must be good rather than evil, and that the degree of partiality a history justifies depends partly on the quantity of goodness it produces or embodies, we have some response to the critique. On the one dimension, a national history does indeed have much less of the character that justifies partiality than a family history. But on another dimension, the national history has roughly as much.

This account of the basis of national partiality fits most obviously those many nationalisms that point to glorious deeds in the nation's past, such as saving Europe for Christendom or inventing representative democracy. But the account should not be too closely tied to these nationalisms, for two reasons. First, if the basis of national partiality is objective rather than subjective, it must depend on the nation's actual history rather than on beliefs about that history that are all too often false. A national mythology with no basis in fact cannot justify nationalist policies today. Second, the benefits produced in a nation's history need not be specially grand; on the contrary, they can be perfectly ordinary. Consider again familial partiality. The benefits my wife and I have given each other, such as companionship and love, are also given to each other by countless other couples. What ties my wife and me specially together is not that we have produced unique goods but that we have produced familiar goods jointly, in interactions with each other. The goods in a nation's history can likewise be familiar. Before enacting medicare, Canadians together maintained political institutions and through them the rule of law in Canada, which ensured liberty and security for all Canadian citizens. The same liberty and security were produced in other nations, but only my fellow Canadians produced them with me, and it is that historical fact that is decisive. According to the account I am proposing, it is important that a nation's history have produced significant benefits, but these benefits need not be the grand ones of national mythologies or even at all different from those produced in other nations' histories.

Nations as defined by political institutions are not the only large groups that can have this kind of history. Consider a linguistic and cultural group. Its members have together sustained a language and through it the possibility of beneficial communication for all its speakers. Other groups have also sustained languages, but this group has done it here. They have also, as writers and readers, sustained a literature and an artistic tradition that provide further benefits. When political and cultural groups coincide, these two grounds of partiality reinforce each other. The nation's members have two separate reasons for being partial to the same individuals. But when political and cultural boundaries do not coincide, there can be conflicts about partiality. Consider fran-

cophone Quebeckers. They share a political history with all Canadians and a cultural history with a smaller number of francophone Canadians. Which group they feel more partial to will depend on how good they think the groups' present qualities are and how beneficial they think the groups' histories have been. Those who think of Canada as a successful country with an admirable political history will be strongly attached to the larger group; those who see present failure and a past of suppressing minorities will not.

Whether a nation is defined politically or culturally, its history differs from a family's in involving many more people, both as recipients of its benefits and as participants in producing them. If only the first of these differences, in the number of beneficiaries, mattered morally, the nation's history would score much higher on the dimension of good done than the family's, since its benefits are much more widely dispersed. The total good resulting from Canadian medicare, for example, is vastly greater than any produced in a family. But it is more plausible to count both differences about numbers, so that what matters for this dimension is not the total benefit produced in a history but something closer to the average benefit per participant, which in the national case roughly equals the average benefit per recipient. Even when we take this view, however, the good produced in a national history is comparable to that in a family history. If we consider the benefits each Canadian receives from living under the rule of law and with social programs such as medicare, they are surely of similar size to those that person receives from his or her family. If this is so, a national history scores roughly as well on the dimension of good done as a family history. Since the national history scores less well on the dimension of interaction, the result on balance is that less partiality is justified toward one's conationals than toward one's family members. This is an intuitively plausible result. Not even the most ardent nationalist claims that one should care as much about one's conationals, as conationals, as about one's spouse or child. And the degree of concern that is justified toward conationals is considerably greater than toward non-nationals, since one's history with the latter scores very poorly on both dimensions. One not only has had no close interactions with non-nationals but also has produced no significant goods with them. The political and cultural institutions of a nation enable its members to cooperate, however indirectly, in producing significant benefits. But there are no comparable institutions joining non-nationals, even ones living just across a national border, and therefore no comparable goods they can be said jointly to have produced.

I wish I could say more precisely what degree of national partiality this historical account justifies. Unfortunately, that would require weighing against each other more precisely the two dimensions of closeness of contact and good done in a history, which I cannot now do. Nor do I see that more precise weightings of these dimensions follow from the general ideas I

have advanced. So I will content myself with two more modest conclusions. The first is that, whatever degree of national partiality is intrinsically justified, it is more than the limited degree that the comparison with families initially suggested. Though a national history scores less well on one dimension than a family history, it scores comparably well on another and therefore justifies at least a moderate degree of partiality. It may be that any morally acceptable national partiality must be constrained by respect for the basic rights of all persons, both within one's nation and outside it. But familial partiality is likewise constrained by respect for rights, and it still has considerable room to express itself. The second conclusion is that it is no surprise that nations and cultures are prime objects of partial attitudes. According to the historical account, partiality is justified when the members of a group have worked together in the past to produce significant benefits. But nations and cultures embody just the institutions that make such beneficial interactions possible. My nation is an appropriate object of partial attitudes because it more than other similarly sized groups has allowed me to act with others to produce significant human goods.

THE CONTINUING DEBATE:
Should Fellow Citizens Get Special Treatment?

What Is New

The question of partiality toward conationals has a long history, but current interest in the issue is intensified by the vast and growing disparity between the wealthy and impoverished areas of the world. In 2001, Charles Derber noted that 450 billionaires hold more wealth than half of all humanity; and the gap between the haves and the have nots continues to widen. Even if one believes that some partiality among conationals is justified, the enormous differences in living standards between the fortunate persons living in wealthy nations and the impoverished, undernourished, and disease-ravaged persons in poor nations prompts important ethical questions concerning conational partiality and our obligations to fellow humans who are not conationals.

For those who believe that obligations to promote the welfare of others extends beyond our obligations to conationals, there are important questions of what such aid would be and how it would be raised and distributed. The economist Amartya Sen pays close attention to the specifics of economic systems (and their effects on overall well-being); and Nobel laureate economist James Tobin has proposed a tax on international currency markets to provide the resources for alleviating poverty (a proposal supported by Thomas Pogge, who has offered interesting proposals of his own).

Where to Find More

The Morality of Nationalism, edited by Robert McKim and Jeff McMahan (New York: Oxford University Press, 1997) contains a particularly good collection of articles (including the essays reprinted for this debate). Another good anthology is Jocelyn Couture, Kai Nielsen, and Michel Seymour, editors, *Rethinking Nationalism* (Calgary: University of Calgary Press, 1996). Ian Shapiro and Lea Brilmayer, editors, *Global Justice* (New York: New York University Press, 1999) is a small collection of very interesting and well-argued essays, with many of the writers giving special attention to the issue of partiality toward conationals. Ronald Beiner, editor, *Theorizing Nationalism* (Albany: State University of New York Press, 1999), is a good collection of essays on nationalism, though it contains less on the specific issue of partiality.

Yael Tamir, in *Liberal Nationalism* (Princeton, N.J.: Princeton University Press, 1993), seeks a combination of national and cosmopolitan (or "liberal") values, though she pursues a path to that goal that is somewhat different from that taken by Jeff McMahan. David Miller, *On Nationality* (Oxford: Clarendon Press, 1995), offers a contemporary defense of nationalism; and Miller expands on those ideas in *Citizenship and National Identity* (Cambridge: Polity Press, 2000). Defenses of various versions of cosmopolitanism can be found in David Held, *Democracy and the Global Order: From the Modern State to Cosmopolitan Governance* (Cambridge: Polity Press, 1995); Brian Barry, "International Society from a Cosmopolitan Perspective," in D. Mapel and T. Nardin, editors, *International Society: Diverse Ethical Perspectives* (Princeton, N.J.: Princeton University Press, 1998): 144–163; and Charles Jones, *Global Justice: Defending Cosmopolitanism* (Oxford: Oxford University Press, 1999).

Simon Caney, "International Distributive Justice," *Political Studies*, volume 49 (2001): 974–997, offers an excellent overview of the issues involved and the major positions taken.

Charles Derber, "Change the World!" in *Boston Research Center for the 21st Century, Newsletter*, number 16 (Winter 2001): 1–17, includes interesting but disturbing data on the vast differences in wealth distribution around the world; Derber's paper is cited in a thoughtful essay by Fred R. Dallmayr, "Globalization and Inequality," *International Studies Review*, volume 4, number 2 (2002):137–156. James Tobin's proposal for alleviating poverty through a tax on international currency markets can be found in "A Proposal for International Monetary Reform," in *Essays in Economics: Theory and Policy* (Cambridge, Mass.: MIT Press, 1982): 488–494. Amartya Sen's work is beautifully written and rich in both ethical analysis and economic detail; see *Inequality Reexamined* (Cambridge, Mass.: Harvard University Pres, 1992); *Development as Freedom* (New York: Anchor Books, 1999); and "Human Rights and Economic Achievement," in J. Bauer and D. Bell, editors, *The East Asian Challenge for Human Rights* (Cambridge: Cambridge University Press, 1999). Thomas Pogge's work includes "A Global Resources Dividend," in D. Crocker and T. Linden, editors, *Ethics of Consumption: The Good Life, Justice, and Global Stewardship* (Lanham, Md.: Rowman and Littlefield, 1998): 501–536; and "Priorities of Global Justice," *Metaphilosophy*, volume 32, numbers 1 and 2 (January 2001): 6–24.

CREDITS

Baier, Annette. From "What Do Women Want in a Moral Theory?" in *Moral Prejudices: Essays on Ethics*, 1994.

Brueckner, Anthony. "The Elusive Virtues of Contextualism" from *Philosophical Studies*, 2004, Vol. 118: pp. 401–405.

Churchland, Paul M. "Betty Crocker's Theory of Consciousness: A Review of John Searle's *The Rediscovery of the Mind*" from *London Review of Books*, 1994. Reprinted by permission of Dr. Paul M. Churchland.

Cohen, Stewart. "Contextualism, Skepticism and the Structure of Reasons" from *Philosophical Perspectives*, 1999, Vol. 13: pp. 57–69. Reprinted by permission of Blackwell Publishing Ltd.

Dawkins, Richard. "You Can't Have It Both Ways: Irreconcilable Differences?" from *Quarterly Review of Biology*, 1997, Vol. 72: pp. 397–399. Reprinted by permission of the University of Chicago Press.

Dennett, Daniel C. "The Future of Human Freedom" from *Freedom Evolves*. Copyright © 2003 Daniel C. Dennett. Used by permission of Viking Penguin, a division of Penguin Group (USA) Inc.

Doris, John M. From *Lack of Character: Personality and Moral Behavior*, 2002.

Elgin, Catherine Z. From "Non-foundationalist Epistemology: Holism, Coherence, and Tenability" in *Contemporary Debates in Epistemology*, edited by Matthias Steup and Ernest Sosa, 2005. Reprinted by permission of Blackwell Publishing Ltd.

Fischer, John Martin. From "Responsibility, History and Manipulation," *The Journal of Ethics*, 2000, Vol. 4: pp. 385–391.

Friedman, Marilyn. "Beyond Caring: The De-Moralization of Gender" from *Science, Morality, and Feminist Theory*, edited by Marsha Hanen and Kai Nielsen. Copyright © 1987 Marilyn Friedman. Reprinted by permission of Marilyn Friedman.

Gauthier, David. From "Why Contractarianism" in *Contractarianism and Rational Choice: Essays on David Gauthier's Morals by Agreement*, edited by Peter Vallentyne, 1991.

Gould, Stephen Jay. From *Leonardo's Mountain of Clams and the Diet of Worms*, copyright © 1998 Turbo, Inc. Used by permission of Harmony Books, a division of Random House Inc.

Hampton, Jean. From "Two Faces of Contractarian Thought" in *Contractarianism and Rational Choice: Essays on David Gauthier's Morals by Agreement*, edited by Peter Vallentyne, 1991.

Hurka, Thomas. From "The Justification of National Partiality" in *The Morality of Nationalism*, edited by Robert McKim and Jeff McMahan, 1997.

Kane, Robert. "Free Will and Responsibility: Ancient Dispute, New Themes" from *Journal of Ethics*, 2000, Vol. 4: pp. 315–322.

Korsgaard, Christine M. "Personal Identity and the Unity of Agency: A Kantian Response to Parfit" from *Philosophy & Public Affairs*, Spring 1989, Vol. 18, No. 2, pp. 101–132. Reprinted by permission of Blackwell Publishing Ltd.

McMahan, Jeff. From "The Limits of National Partiality" in *The Morality of Nationalism*, edited by Robert McKim and Jeff McMahan, 1997.

Miller, David. From "In Defence of Nationality" in *Journal of Applied Philosophy*, Nov. 1, 1993, Vol. 10. Reprinted by permission of Blackwell Publishing Ltd.

Nagel, Thomas. From "Ethics" in *The Last Word*, 1997.

Nagel, Thomas. "Progressive but Not Liberal" from *The New York Review of Books*, May 25, 1006, Vol. 53, No. 9. Reprinted with permission from *The New York Review of Books*. Copyright © 2006 NYREV, Inc.

Nelkin, Dana. From "Freedom, Responsibility and the Challenge of Situationism" in *Midwest Studies in Philosophy*, Sept. 2005, Vol. 29, Issue 1. Reprinted by permission of Blackwell Publishing Ltd. and Dana Nelkin.

Nussbaum, Martha C. "Patriotism and Cosmopolitanism" from *For Love of Country* by Martha C. Nussbaum and Joshua Cohen. Copyright © 1996 by Martha C. Nussbaum and Joshua Cohen. Reprinted by permission of Beacon Press, Boston, MA.

Parfit, Derek. From "Why Our Identity Is Not What Matters" in *Reasons and Persons*, 1986.

Posner, Richard A. From "Animal Rights: Legal, Philosophical and Pragmatic Perspectives" in *Animal Rights*, edited by Cass R. Sunstein and Martha C. Nussbaum, 2004.

Sandel, Michael J. "Morality and the Liberal Ideal." Originally published in *The New Republic*, May 7, 1984. Reprinted by permission of the author.

Searle, John R. "Reductionism and the Irreducibility of Consciousness" from *The Rediscovery of the Mind*, 1992. Reprinted by permission of MIT Press.

Singer, Peter. From "Ethics Beyond Species and Beyond Instincts" in *Animal Rights*, edited by Cass R. Sunstein and Martha C. Nussbaum, 2004.

Smilansky, Saul. "Compatibilism: The Argument from Shallowness" from *Philosophical Studies*, 2003, Vol. 115: pp. 257–273.

van Cleve, James. From "Why Coherence Is Not Enough: A Defense of Moderate Foundationalism" in *Contemporary Debates in Epistemology*, edited by Matthias Steup and Ernest Sosa, 2005. Reprinted by permission of Blackwell Publishing Ltd.

Wallace, Stan W. "The Craig-Flew Debate" from *Does God Exist?*, 2003, originally presented at the University of Wisconsin, Feb. 18, 1998. Reprinted with permission of Ashgate Publishing Ltd.

Williams, Bernard. From "Foundations: Practical Reason" in *Ethics and the Limits of Philosophy*, 1985.

NOTES